Chinese Indonesians in Post-Suharto Indonesia

Chinese Indonesians in Post-Suharto Indonesia

Democratisation and Ethnic Minorities

Wu-Ling Chong

Hong Kong University Press
The University of Hong Kong
Pokfulam Road
Hong Kong
www.hkupress.hku.hk

© 2018 Hong Kong University Press

ISBN 978-988-8455-99-7 (*Hardback*)

All rights reserved. No portion of this publication may be reproduced or transmitted in any form or by any means, electronic or mechanical, including photocopying, recording, or any information storage or retrieval system, without prior permission in writing from the publisher.

British Library Cataloguing-in-Publication Data
A catalogue record for this book is available from the British Library.

Cover photo courtesy of Franciscus Nanang Triana.

10 9 8 7 6 5 4 3 2 1

Printed and bound by Paramount Printing Co. Ltd., Hong Kong, China

Contents

Preface	vii
1. Contemplating the Role of the Ethnic Chinese: Ethnic Politics, Criminality, and Civil Society in Post-Suharto Indonesia	1
Part One: 'Pariah' Ethnic Minorities and Democratisation	23
2. A Short History of the Ethnic Chinese in Indonesia: Creating a 'Pariah' Class	25
3. Democratisation and Ethnic Minorities: A Look at Indonesia's Democratisation and the Ethnic Chinese	40
Part Two: Civil Society, Business, and Politics: The Ambivalent Position of the Chinese in Post-Suharto Indonesia	61
4. Opening Up the Chinese Socio-cultural Sphere: The Ambivalence of Increasing Visibility	63
5. Local Ethnic Chinese Business	97
6. Electoral Politics and the Chinese in Post-Suharto Indonesia	120
7. Conclusion	168
Appendix I: List of Informants	171
Appendix II: Major Ethnic Chinese Organisations in Post-Suharto Medan and Surabaya	175
Appendix III: Chinese-Language Newspapers in Post-Suharto Medan and Surabaya	177
Appendix IV: Occupational Backgrounds of the Leaders of Local Major Chinese Organisations in Medan and Surabaya, 2010–2011	178

Appendix V: Numbers of Protégés of Sultan Iskandar Muda Educational Foundation, 1990/1991–2011/2012	180
Appendix VI: Original Text of Letter in *Koran Tempo* (May 15, 2012)	181
Appendix VII: List of Chinese Indonesian Candidates Running for Legislative Elections in Medan and Surabaya, 1999–2014	182
Abbreviations and Glossary	190
Glossary of Personal Names	196
References	199
Index	232

Preface

This book offers a way of understanding the complex situation of ethnic Chinese Indonesians in post-Suharto Indonesia. It focuses on Chinese in two of the largest Indonesian cities, Medan and Surabaya. This book is based on my PhD dissertation presented to the Department of Sociology at the National University of Singapore (NUS) in 2014.

The fall of Suharto in May 1998 led to the opening up of a democratic and liberal space that included a diversity of political actors and ideals in the political process. However, due to the absence of an effective, genuinely reformist party or political coalition, predatory politico-business interests nurtured under the New Order managed to capture the new political and economic regimes. As a result, corruption and internal mismanagement continue to plague the bureaucracy in the country. The indigenous Indonesian population generally still perceives the Chinese as an alien minority who are wealthy, selfish, exclusive, and opportunistic; this is partially due to the role some Chinese have played in perpetuating corrupt business practices. As targets of extortion and corruption by bureaucratic officials and youth/crime organisations, the Chinese are not merely passive bystanders of the democratisation process in Indonesia nor powerless victims of corrupt practices. By focusing on the important, interconnected aspects of the role Chinese play in post-Suharto Indonesia, via business, politics, and civil society, I argue, through a combination of Anthony Giddens's structure-agency theory as well as Pierre Bourdieu's notion of habitus and field, that although the Chinese are constrained by various conditions, they also have played an active role in shaping these conditions. They have thus played an active role in shaping the democratisation process in Indonesia and perpetuating their increasingly ambivalent position.

This book is the first major analysis of the situation of Chinese Indonesians in post-Suharto Medan and Surabaya. It will be of interest to scholars and students of ethnic studies and political sociology as well as to a general readership in Asia that is concerned with the role and situation of Chinese minority communities throughout the region.

In the preparation of this book and the PhD dissertation upon which it is based, I am grateful to a number of people who assisted me throughout the period of research. First and foremost, I would like to thank my supervisor, Associate Professor Maribeth Erb, whose guidance and assistance were critical in seeing me through my research. I have benefited enormously from her advice, criticisms, and suggestions. I would also like to express my appreciation to Professor Vedi R. Hadiz, my former supervisor, for his earlier guidance, and Associate Professor Douglas Kammen, my thesis committee member, for his input on my thesis, which was later turned into this book. My sincere gratitude goes as well to the Faculty of Arts and Social Sciences at NUS, which provided funding for my research.

I would also like to thank two anonymous reviewers for their valuable comments and suggestions on the earlier draft of my manuscript.

Sections of this book have earlier appeared elsewhere. Part of Chapter 2 was first published in *Sejarah*, a journal of the Department of History at the University of Malaya (UM). See Chong Wu Ling, 2016, 'Rethinking the Position of Ethnic Chinese Indonesians', *Sejarah* 25(2): 96–108. Part of Chapter 5 is found in Chong Wu-Ling, 2015, 'Local Politics and Chinese Indonesian Business in Post-Suharto Era', *Southeast Asian Studies* 4(3): 487–532. *Southeast Asian Studies* is a journal of Kyoto University's Center for Southeast Asian Studies (CSEAS). I thank Associate Professor Sivachandralingam Sundara Raja, the editor-in-chief of *Sejarah*, and Ms. Narumi Shitara, the managing editor of *Southeast Asian Studies*, for granting me permission to use these materials here.

I am particularly grateful to Ms. Maria Ling and Dr. Tsai Yen-Ling for introducing me to a few friends in Medan who later assisted me in looking for informants in the city. My gratitude also goes to Dr. Christian Chua, Dr. Manuel Victor J. Sapitula, and Dr. Thomas Barker for their advice on conducting fieldwork.

I am thankful to Dr. Linda Darmajanti and Dr. Rochman Achwan, both from the Department of Sociology at the University of Indonesia, for their sponsorship of my fieldwork research in Indonesia.

I wish to express my appreciation to a number of individuals in Indonesia who provided me invaluable help during my fieldwork: Mr. Elfenda Ananda, Ms. Suci Al-Falah, Mr. Edward Sinaga (deceased), Mr. J. Anto, Mr. Johan Tjongiran, Dr. Sofyan Tan, a.k.a. Tan Kim Yang (mayoral candidate in 2010 Medan's mayoral election), Mr. Hasyim, a.k.a. Oei Kien Lim (Medan city councillor from the Indonesian Democratic Party of Struggle, 2009–present), Mr. Law Kek Ping, Dr. Indra Wahidin, Ms. Yustiana Khosasih and her husband Mr. Yeoh, Mr. Daud Kosasih, Mr. Johnny Halim, Dr. Dédé Oetomo, a.k.a. Oen Tiong Hauw, Mr. Anton Prijatno, Mr. Aditya Nugraha, Madam Elisa Christiana, Mr. Hendi Prayogo, Mr. William Rahardja, Mr. Samas H.

Widjaja, Mr. Oei Hiem Hwie, Professor Kacung Marijan, Professor Hotman Siahaan, Ms. Evi Sutrisno, Dr. Setefanus Suprajitno, Ms. Vanda Augustine and her aunt Ms. Winnie, Dr. Mely G. Tan, Mr. Christianto Wibisono, and Ms. Titi Kusumandari. I also owe a debt of gratitude to all my informants, who were very generous in sharing their views and stories with me over the period of fieldwork in Indonesia.

My sincere gratitude also goes to the staff of the various institutions who have assisted me in various ways throughout the research: in Singapore, the library of NUS, the library of the Institute of Southeast Asian Studies (ISEAS), and the National Library; in Jakarta, the National Library of Indonesia, the library of the Central Statistics Agency (BPS, or Badan Pusat Statistik), and the library of KITLV-Jakarta; in Medan, the North Sumatra Provincial Library, the library of the University of North Sumatra, and the library of the Central Statistics Agency of North Sumatra (BPS Sumatera Utara); in Surabaya, the library of the Petra Christian University, the library of the Airlangga University, the library of the Central Statistics Agency of East Java (BPS Jawa Timur), and the Medayu Agung Library; in Taipei City, the Joint Library of Humanities and Social Sciences at the Academia Sinica; and in Kuala Lumpur, the library of the University of Malaya (UM). I am also grateful to the staff of *Subei Ribao*, a Chinese-language newspaper in Medan, for allowing me to access their newspaper archives during my fieldwork.

I would also like to thank my colleagues at the Department of Southeast Asian Studies, University of Malaya, for their encouragement of my efforts to complete this book.

Many thanks to Dr. Stefani Haning Swarati, Dr. Kim Jiyoon, Ms. Phoon Yuen Ming, Dr. Hoon Chang Yau, Dr. Wong Chin Huat, Mr. Teng Kok Liang, Professor Bridget Welsh, Associate Professor Sivachandralingam Sundara Raja, and Associate Professor Chia Oai Peng for their moral support and encouragement throughout my PhD journey. And for their constant prayer and continuous encouragement, I am blessed to have friends like the Lim family, Ms. See Shen Leng, Ms. Chrissy Christa Craats, Ms. Phoon Yen Mei, Dr. Emelyn Tan, Ms. Carrie Chia, Ms. Peggy Koh, Pastor Pauline Ong, and the late Reverend Yap Kim Hao.

I reserve my final thanks for my family in Malaysia for their sacrifices and support in allowing me to pursue this aspiration for postgraduate studies.

Wu-Ling Chong (鍾武凌)

1
Contemplating the Role of the Ethnic Chinese

Ethnic Politics, Criminality, and Civil Society in Post-Suharto Indonesia*

In 2010, Sofyan Tan, a.k.a. Tan Kim Yang (陳金揚), a Chinese Indonesian social activist who had previously been a physician, made history in the city of Medan by becoming the first ethnic Chinese to run for mayor. Not a stranger to politics (having lost in the race for a seat in the North Sumatra regional representatives council [DPD, Dewan Perwakilan Daerah] in 2004), Tan was initially chosen by the incumbent mayor as his candidate for deputy mayor. Later, when the incumbent decided to choose someone else to be his running mate, Tan was nominated by the Indonesian Democratic Party of Struggle (PDI-P, Partai Demokrasi Indonesia Perjuangan, a powerful party in Indonesia) and the Prosperous Peace Party (PDS, Partai Damai Sejahtera, a party led by Christians). He was paired with a Muslim woman, in the hopes that this cross-ethnic, cross-religious pairing would attract many voters. The race was an interesting one for what it shows us about the politics of ethnicity, money, criminality, and civil society associations as they affect the Chinese in post-Suharto Indonesia. Tan insisted that he would run an honest government if elected, making no promises of political favours to anyone who backed him. One of the main Chinese Indonesian civil society organisations, the Chinese Indonesian Social Association (PSMTI, Paguyuban Sosial Marga Tionghoa Indonesia), backed Tan, but the other, the Chinese Indonesian Association (INTI, Perhimpunan Indonesia Tionghoa), turned away from him, possibly due to his refusal to promise business contracts for their support. In fact, in the first round of the election, INTI openly supported a candidate (not the incumbent) who had been the regional leader of an influential youth/crime organisation in North Sumatra and who had many criminal ties, important for business in Medan city. Tan and his running mate unexpectedly defeated eight other candidate pairs in

---

* The names of informants in this chapter are pseudonyms except for the following public figure: Dédé Oetomo.

the first round by gaining the second-highest number of votes and thus ran against the incumbent in the second round. Afraid of Tan's popularity with the poor, to whom he had given much support, the incumbent conducted a major smear campaign against him. Rumours were spread that Tan would turn Medan into a 'Chinatown' and build many Chinese temples instead of mosques. In addition, many Chinese voters were intimidated by rumours and mobile phone text messages that warned that, if Tan won the election, there would be riots against the Chinese. Consequently, it appeared that voters were scared off. Tan and his running mate lost in the second round of the race.

Tan's story implies a paradox of Indonesia's new democracy as well as of the position of ethnic Chinese Indonesians since the collapse of Suharto's authoritarian regime. Although in Indonesia's new democracy there has been an opening up of a more democratic and liberal political space, which has led to the emergence of competitive electoral politics in Indonesia, at the same time this democratic space has been marred by money politics and electoral smear campaigns. In this democratic space, the Chinese are free to participate in electoral politics and run for public office, but very few of them have been elected because the Chinese are still perceived as an alien minority by the *pribumi* (indigenous Indonesians). It is ironic that although Tan has made significant contributions to the indigenous population, he is still regarded as a Chinese by the indigenous majority. This reflects the ambivalent feelings of the *pribumi* towards the Chinese in Indonesia. But it is even more ironic that some businesspeople in INTI, who shared Tan's ethnicity and who themselves are often deemed a target of bureaucratic extortion, preferred not to support Tan, who was relatively clean and was committed to end all sorts of corruption and bureaucratic abuse. Instead, they channelled their support to another candidate who could promise them business favours. In so doing, these Chinese perpetuated their ambivalent position in Indonesian society and to a certain extent helped shape the predatory characteristics of Indonesia's new democracy.

This study looks at how the new political, business, and socio-cultural environment in post-Suharto Indonesia influences the actions of the Chinese minority, while examining how the Chinese display agency in reacting to and shaping this environment, which constrains and facilitates their actions. In this way, the Chinese contribute to the shaping of their continuing ambivalent position. In business, Chinese often resort to semi-legal and illegal means to safeguard their business and personal interests. Very few Chinese businesspeople refuse to become targets of extortion by power-holders and gangsters or choose to get themselves organised and protest against this extortion. From a socio-cultural perspective, Chinese Indonesians have established several ethnic-based voluntary associations that focus on promoting Chinese culture and socialisation activities among the Chinese. These organisations have assisted local governments in establishing cultural and business connections with China, as well as promoting philanthropy. These organisations, although involved in many positive activities, contribute to the view that the Chinese are very insular and exclusive. There are Chinese community leaders and social activists who have reached out to the wider society by establishing non-ethnic-based socio-cultural organisations that focus on promoting cross-ethnic understanding and solidarity; however, such leaders and activists are rare. In electoral politics, some Chinese Indonesians have run for public office with the aim of bringing positive change for the people, but some have participated in electoral politics in order to safeguard their business and personal interests. In addition, some Chinese businesspeople have supported reform-minded electoral candidates without expecting any benefits in return, but some have sponsored politicians associated with predatory forces in order to get political favours for their businesses. Therefore, there are Chinese Indonesians who have acted as both agents of change and reform, while others have been involved in maintaining the status quo inherited from Suharto's New Order regime. It is not surprising that the ambivalence of their position in post–New Order Indonesia has increased.

This study further argues that, under a democratic society where there is a lack of good governance promoting the rule of law, accountability, and transparency, the economically privileged ethnic minority deemed as an 'outsider' group as well as a target of extortion, and has not been fully accepted by the majority indigenous population, tends actively to resort to illegal and semi-legal means as well as opportunistic tactics to gain business and personal interests, and to make use of intra-ethnic linkages to safeguard their ethnic identity and culture.

This study adopts a combination of Anthony Giddens's structure-agency theory as well as Pierre Bourdieu's notion of habitus and field as a framework for examining the strategies and tactics that Chinese Indonesians adopt to safeguard their business and personal interests as well as their ethnic and cultural identities in the post-Suharto era. Both Giddens and Bourdieu perceive social actors as agents that actively respond to and shape their social structures. Giddens (1984) argues that our social reality is shaped by both social forces and active human agency. All people are knowledgeable about the conditions and consequences of their actions in their daily lives. Although people are not entirely free to choose their own actions—in other words, people do not have complete free will—they have agency. Therefore, Giddens sees social structures as both the medium and the outcome of actors' actions.

> As human beings, we do make choices, and we do not simply respond passively to events around us. The way forward in bridging the gap between

'structural' and 'action' approaches is to recognize that we *actively make and remake* social structure during the course of our everyday activities. (Giddens 1989, 705, emphasis in the original)

Habitus, according to Bourdieu (1990a, 131), is a system of acquired dispositions through which people deal with the social world. Bourdieu (1990b) also notes that 'as an acquired system of generative schemes, the habitus makes possible the free production of all the thoughts, perceptions and actions inherent in the condition of production' (55). In other words, habitus is an orientation to individual action. The concept of field complements the idea of habitus. A field is a relatively autonomous arena within which people act strategically, depending on their habitus, to enhance their capital. Examples of fields include politics, religion, and philosophy (Bourdieu 1993, 72–74). Bourdieu considers the habitus the union of structures and agency: 'habitus operates as a structuring structure able to selectively perceive and to transform the objective structure [field] according to its own structure while, at the same time, being re-structured, transformed in its makeup by the pressure of the objective structure' (Bourdieu 2005, 46–47). In other words, habitus shapes the objective structure (field) but at the same time it is also shaped by the objective structure. This concept is parallel to Giddens's structure-agency theory. One of the significant strengths of Bourdieu's notion of habitus lies in its consideration of actors' social positions in the study of habitus; this is never discussed in Giddens's theory. Bourdieu (1984, 114; 1998, 6–8) argues that a person's habitus is structured by his or her position within a social space, which is determined by his or her sociological characteristics in the form of volume and kinds of economic, cultural, and social capital possessed. Economic capital refers to material resources that can be turned into money or property rights. Cultural capital refers to non-material goods such as types of knowledge, skills and expertise, educational credentials, and aesthetic preferences acquired through upbringing and education that can be converted into economic capital. Social capital refers to networks of contacts that can be used to maintain or advance one's social position (Bourdieu 1986).

According to Bourdieu (1993, 73), actors who are well endowed with capital and therefore enjoy privileged positions in a particular field tend to defend the status quo of the field in order to safeguard their capital, whereas those least endowed with capital and therefore occupy less advantaged positions within the field are inclined to challenge the status quo of the field via subversion strategies in order to enhance their capital and improve their social positions. This argument offers a valid explanation of why some Chinese businesspeople in the opening story of this chapter chose to support the mayoral candidate who could promise them business favours if elected and not Tan, who was committed to end all sorts of corruption and bureaucratic abuse. However, Bourdieu's argument cannot explain why, on the other hand, some actors who possess a lot of capital within a field choose to challenge the status quo through certain subversion strategies. For instance, in the 2010 mayoral election in Medan, there were also some wealthy Chinese businesspeople who decided to support Tan, even though he made no promises of political favours to anyone who supported him (I will elaborate more on this in Chapter 6). I argue that Giddens's emphasis on actors' free will within the constraints imposed by social structures is useful in explaining such actions:

> Although . . . [social structures] might constrain what we do, they do not determine what we do. I could choose to live without using money, should I be firmly resolved to do so, even if it might prove very difficult to eke out an existence from day to day . . . The fact that I use the monetary system contributes in a minor, yet necessary, way to the very existence of that system. If everyone, or even the majority of people, at some point decided to avoid using money, the monetary system would dissolve. (Giddens 1989, 705)

Although the example used in Giddens's quotes is extreme and unimaginable in the present day, it clearly shows that Giddens sees social structures as being both constraining and enabling to human actions. Social structures may constrain human actions but at the same time they also enable social actors to challenge the status quo. In other words, social actors have a choice to defend or challenge the status quo.

Hence, this is the theoretical framework for this study: social structures constrain and enable the actors' actions. The actors' actions are always oriented by their habitus, which is dependent on the volume and kinds of capital possessed. Those who are well endowed with capital in a social structure tend to defend the status quo of the structure in order to safeguard their capital and positions, whereas those least endowed with capital within the structure are inclined to challenge it via subversion strategies. However, the actors' actions are also dependent on their free will within the constraints imposed by the social structure. They have a choice to defend or challenge the status quo of the social structure.

The Chinese Indonesians are an ethnic minority who play a crucial role in the Indonesian economy, but at the same time are still perceived by the indigenous majority as 'outsiders'. While anti-Chinese sentiments among non-Chinese and the corrupt bureaucracy in the post–New Order era have constrained the Chinese from enjoying full civil rights and equality, these factors do not determine the Chinese people's reactions. Chinese Indonesians have reacted to such circumstances in different ways. In the opening story of this chapter, for instance, Sofyan Tan chose to initiate and engage in endeavours that sought to alter indigenous Indonesians' perceptions of the Chinese. He also ran for the mayorship and was committed to eliminating corruption and bureaucratic abuse. On the other hand, many wealthy Chinese businesspeople in Medan decided to support another candidate who could promise them business favours should he get elected. I argue that the position of Chinese Indonesians as a whole is increasingly ambivalent and more complex in the post–New Order era because Chinese Indonesians like Sofyan Tan who have been relentlessly working to rectify the racial stereotypes of Chinese among *pribumi* are fewer than those who continue to reinforce such stereotypes. It can be said that Chinese Indonesians like Tan are 'a minority within a minority'. Thus following Giddens's structure-agency theory and Bourdieu's notion of habitus and field, this study considers Chinese Indonesians as social actors who, by taking actions within the constraints imposed by social structures on the one hand perpetuate their ambivalent position, but on the other hand may attempt to rectify it.

1.1 Rethinking the Position of Ethnic Chinese Indonesians

According to Benedict Anderson (1998), who studied ethnicity in Southeast Asia from the perspective of constructivism, the 'separateness' of the Chinese from the indigenous majority in Indonesia is actually a result of Dutch colonial rule. In order to prevent the Chinese and indigenous people from combining forces to challenge them, the Dutch implemented a divide-and-rule policy that separated the Chinese from the indigenous population in the aspects of 'legal status, required costuming and barbering, residence, possibility of travel, and so on' (321). Furthermore, very few Chinese in Indonesia believe in Islam, which is the religious belief of most indigenous people (Ong 2008). Consequently, the Chinese became increasingly detached from the indigenous population.

In contrast with the Dutch, Spanish and American colonial authorities in the pre-independence Philippines and kings in Thailand encouraged the assimilation and intermarriage of the Chinese into indigenous societies. In addition, the Chinese minorities and the majority of indigenous populations in the Philippines and Thailand shared the same religious beliefs.[1] Thus, the Chinese in both countries have generally been well assimilated into indigenous populations and play an essential role not only in the economic development of their countries, but also in politics (Sidel 2008, 131; Skinner 1957; 1996; Akira 2008; Wickberg 1965; Carino 2004). There have been politicians with some Chinese ancestry who became members of parliament or prime ministers in Thailand or presidents in the Philippines (McCargo and Pathmanand 2005, 4; Suryadinata 1993a, 298–300; Hau 2014).

---

1. Most of the Chinese in Thailand and the Philippines are respectively Buddhists and Roman Catholics.

In British Malaya (present-day Peninsular Malaysia), the colonial regime also introduced a divide-and-rule policy by encouraging the Malays, who formed the largest indigenous group, to remain in rural areas as peasants or to join the civil service, while the other two significant ethnic minority groups, i.e., the Chinese and Indians, were encouraged to work on tin mines and the plantation sector respectively (Dhillon 2009, 66–67; Liew 2003, 88). Moreover, just like their counterparts in Indonesia, very few Chinese in Malaya believe in Islam, which is the religious belief of the Malays (Tan 2000). Therefore, the Chinese in Malaya and later Malaysia are also generally perceived as an alien minority group by the indigenous majority and have been encountering various entry barriers into the civil service and public universities as well as in business activities, especially after the implementation in 1970 of the New Economic Policy (NEP), an affirmative action programme in favour of the indigenous majority (Thock 2005; Lee and Heng 2000, 208–9).[2]

However, the proportion of ethnic Chinese in Malaysia has always been much larger than that of their counterparts in Indonesia.[3] Moreover, massive anti-Chinese violence has been fairly minimal in Malaysia and post-independence governments have never implemented assimilation policies to curtail Chinese culture, as happened during the New Order regime in Indonesia.[4] Therefore, most Chinese in Malaysia still maintain Chinese languages and many Chinese customs. In addition, the Chinese in Malaysia have always been actively involved in politics. Since independence, there have been several Chinese members of parliament and a few cabinet ministers, deputy ministers, and state chief ministers (*ketua menteri negeri*) (Suryadinata 1993a, 300–303; Lee and Heng 2000; Cao 2005).[5]

Hence, it can be said that in comparison with ethnic Chinese in other Southeast Asian countries such as Thailand, the Philippines, and Malaysia, the social and political positions of ethnic Chinese in Indonesia are relatively vulnerable. It is therefore not surprising that research on ethnic Chinese in

---

2. The NEP was formulated after the breakout of interethnic riots between Chinese and Malays (the largest indigenous ethnic group in Malaysia) on May 13, 1969. For the background and factors behind the riots, see Kua (2007) and Comber (2009a).

3. When Malaya first achieved independence in 1957, the Chinese constituted 37.17% of the total population (Phang 2000, 96, Table 4.1). In 1970 (seven years after the formation of Malaysia, which comprised Malaya, Sabah, and Sarawak), their share of the total population had declined to 35.51% (Phang 2000, 96, Table 4.1). Due to the slow-down in the population growth rate of the Chinese, their proportion further declined to 24.6% in 2010 (Department of Statistics Malaysia 2010). In Indonesia, the Chinese constituted about 2.03% of the total population in 1930 and their proportion declined to 1.2% in both 2000 and 2010 (Ananta, Arifin, and Bakhtiar 2008, 20, 23, Table 2.1; Ananta et al. 2013, 14, Table 2).

4. The inter-ethnic riots between Chinese and Malays on May 13, 1969 represent the only incident of mass violence against the Chinese in Malaysia since independence.

5. However, to date, no Chinese Malaysian has ever become prime minister or deputy prime minister of Malaysia.

Indonesia over the last few decades has generally been sympathetic; academics tend to focus on their marginalised position, their experiences of being discriminated against as a minority, and their experiences as victims of ethnic violence.

However, I suggest that leading scholarly works in this field of study portray Chinese Indonesians as passive and powerless actors, as victims of prejudice and discrimination, unable to take independent action. The long history of anti-Chinese sentiments in Indonesia and the long-standing discriminatory policies of Suharto's authoritarian regime against the Chinese are key reasons for this tendency in the field of study. For examples, Leo Suryadinata's (1992) and Charles A. Coppel's (1983) studies focus on how the discriminatory policies of the pre–New Order and New Order regimes marginalised the Chinese minority politically, socially, and economically. They attribute the reasons behind such policies to the jealousy of *pribumi* against the Chinese, who play a dominant role in the Indonesian economy, and the perceptions that the Indonesian nation includes only indigenous Indonesian people. The Chinese minority is perceived as an alien minority; other minorities considered external to the Indonesian nation, such as Arabs and Indians, do not encounter as much suspicion or hostility from indigenous Indonesians because their numbers are relatively small compared to the Chinese.[6] Hence, they are considered too few to cause political and social instability. In addition, unlike the Arabs, who are almost exclusively Muslim, very few Chinese are Muslim.[7] Therefore, the Chinese do not tend to be associated with Islam; this tends to give them a double-minority status in the world's largest Muslim-majority nation.[8]

---

6. In 2000, it was estimated that Chinese Indonesians constituted about 1.2% of the total Indonesian population (Ananta, Arifin, and Bakhtiar 2008, 23, Table 2.1). At the same time, Arabs and Indians formed 0.043% and 0.017% respectively of the total Indonesian population (Ananta, Arifin, and Bakhtiar 2008, 29). The figures, which are the latest data on the percentage of ethnic Chinese, Arabs, and Indians in the total Indonesian population, were calculated directly from the raw data of the 2000 population census, as the census includes only quantitative information on these ethnic minorities in some provinces. See also Ananta, Arifin, and Bakhtiar (2008, 21).

7. In 2000, 98.27% of Arab Indonesians were Muslim. Conversely, only 5.41% of Chinese Indonesians were Muslim (Ananta, Arifin, and Bakhtiar 2008, 30, Table 2.3).

8. In 2000, Muslims constituted 88.22% of the population in Indonesia, while Christians and Buddhists were 8.92% and 0.84% respectively (Suryadinata, Arifin, and Ananta 2003, 104, Table 4.1.1). Of the Chinese population, 35.09% were Christians and 53.82% Buddhists (Ananta, Arifin, and Bakhtiar 2008, 30, Table 2.3). In 2010, the percentages of Muslims and Buddhists had slightly decreased to 87.54 and 0.71 respectively, while Christians had increased to 9.87%. Of the Chinese, 42.80% were Christians and 49.06% Buddhists (Ananta et al. 2013, 21, Table 3). The figures for 2010 are the latest official figures on the religious composition of Indonesia and of Chinese Indonesians. However, to date, the official figures on Arab and Indian Indonesian populations as well as the religious composition of both ethnic groups in 2010 are not available.

Mona Lohanda (2002), in her study of the Chinese in colonial Java, argues that despite having lived in Java for generations the Chinese minority was still perceived as an outsider group that had ties with an external power, that is, the land of their ancestors. They were consequently marginalised politically by Dutch colonial rulers and excluded by indigenous Indonesian nationalists from the Indonesian nationalist movement. A recent study by Nobuto Yamamoto (2011) points out that, although *peranakan* Chinese[9] journalists of Sino-Malay newspapers had played a pivotal role in the development of the Indonesian nationalist movement during the 1920s and 1930s, they were excluded from formal indigenous politics. No Indonesian political parties (with the exception of the Indonesian Communist Party, PKI) accepted ethnic Chinese as members. Consequently, *peranakan* Chinese journalists were left out from accounts of Indonesian national history. In a similar way, Helen Pausacker (2005) examines the historical and contemporary involvement of the *peranakan* Chinese in Javanese *wayang* (shadow puppetry). The contributions of the Chinese politically and culturally, according to both authors, have been lost from the collective memory due to political factors and racism.

J. A. C. Mackie (1976) and Jemma Purdey (2005; 2006) look into events of violence against the ethnic Chinese and argue that the Chinese are always made scapegoats during economic crisis and political turbulence because of anti-Chinese sentiments among *pribumi*. In his study on the identity of ethnic Chinese in post-Suharto Jakarta, Hoon Chang-Yau (2008) points out that, although the relatively open and liberal environment after the overthrow of the New Order regime has allowed the Chinese openly to express their identity and organise themselves, they continue to occupy a vulnerable position in Indonesian society, as anti-Chinese sentiments are still alive among the *pribumi*. The Chinese have yet to be fully accepted by their *pribumi* counterparts, since many *pribumi* still have stereotypes of the Chinese based on essentialist assumptions of race, origin, and class. Chinese Indonesians are perceived as foreign descendants because they still practise Chinese culture that is different from indigenous cultures in the country. Moreover, they are still perceived by many *pribumi* as economically strong but exclusive and selfish (125–45). Thung Ju Lan (2009), in her article on the direct participation of Chinese Indonesians in electoral politics, makes a similar argument that not many Chinese electoral candidates have been elected into local, regional, or national parliaments because indigenous Indonesians have generally not yet been willing to accept Chinese Indonesians' role in formal politics.

---

9. *Peranakan* Chinese are acculturated Chinese who have little or no command of Chinese languages or dialects and practise culture and customs that are neither purely Chinese nor purely indigenous Indonesian. I will elaborate more on the origins of *peranakan* Chinese in Section 1.2 and Chapter 2.

The connection between violence and the unacceptability of the Chinese in formal politics is made explicit in Hui Yew-Foong's (2011) ethno-historical study of the Chinese communities in West Kalimantan and their plight as political orphans. Hui reveals that the Chinese were seen as 'signifiers of wealth' (277) by the indigenous population and that they experienced harassment and extortion from local indigenous gangsters from time to time (275–76). During the 1999 anti-Madurese violence perpetrated by the indigenous Malays and Dayaks in Sambas District, West Kalimantan, the Chinese, although not targeted, nevertheless closed their shops; some placed food, drinks, and other supplies outside their doors for the Malays and Dayaks in order to safeguard their property from being looted (274–77).

According to Hui, the position of the Chinese in the province remains ambivalent even after the opening up of political space in the post–New Order era. The political freedom and political achievement of the Chinese in post–New Order West Kalimantan have been met with a backlash from local indigenous communities. In November 2007, a Chinese, Christiandy Sanjaya (黃漢山), paired with a Dayak, was elected as deputy governor of West Kalimantan during the gubernatorial election of November 2007. The Malays, another major indigenous group in West Kalimantan, were upset as 'they had been denied representation in the highest offices of the province' (299). In early December 2007, a dispute between a Chinese and a Malay over a purported accident in Pontianak turned violent; rioters attacked and vandalised properties owned by ethnic Chinese. Hui suggests that the riots may be traced back to the gubernatorial election that saw the victory of a Chinese candidate. Some Malays 'are willing to resort to violence to express their displeasure with the Chinese for gaining political ascendance at their expense' (Hui 2011, 303). Later, nine Chinese community leaders in Pontianak issued a public apology in local newspapers to the Malay community. Hui saw the issuance of the public apology as an act to 'appease the injured Malay community' (302), which had experienced electoral defeat.

Although these works have documented important events and attitudes towards the Chinese in Indonesian history, they still ascribe a largely passive and powerless role to Chinese Indonesians. They scarcely touch on the active human agency of Chinese Indonesians in creating, deploying, or shaping their position in Indonesian society. Mary F. Somers's PhD thesis (1965) on *peranakan* Chinese politics in the 1950s and Leo Suryadinata's work (1981) on *peranakan* Chinese politics from the 1910s to the early 1940s are two of the few scholarly works that focus on the active role of Chinese Indonesians in shaping their political fortunes. To my knowledge, Marleen Dieleman and colleagues' edited volume (2011) is the first scholarly work that claims to adopt Giddens's structure-agency theory in examining how Chinese Indonesians have demonstrated active agency in shaping their destinies and crucial social trends in the country during periods of crisis and regime change. The work covers the role of Chinese Indonesians in dealing with issues of assimilation, identity, and civil rights. The contributors have made a compelling case that Chinese Indonesians have not merely been passive and powerless bystanders and victims in Indonesian history, but also active agents of change during periods of crisis. The paper by Patricia Tjiook-Liem, for example, examines the experience in early twentieth-century Batavia (present-day Jakarta) of a simple Chinese shopkeeper, Loe Joe Djin, who was found guilty of being an accessory to theft. During the Dutch colonial era, Europeans in the Indies were subject to a different legal system from that governing indigenous people and other Asians. The sentences inflicted on Asians were often arbitrary and harsher than those imposed upon Europeans; at the same time, appeal was impossible. Insisting he was innocent and that the sentence was unjust, Loe upon his release complained by telegram to the Chinese minister of foreign affairs in Beijing and to the Chinese ambassador in The Hague. His appeal prompted the Chinese government to pressure the Dutch to treat the Chinese as equals of the Europeans in the criminal administration of justice under Dutch law. Subsequently the system was changed; in minor criminal cases, Europeans and Asians were equated without distinction.[10] Tjiook-Liem's work demonstrates that Loe was not a passive and powerless victim of injustice. He displayed active agency in fighting against the unjust legal system and his action triggered a legal reform in the Indies.

There are some political economists who portray wealthy Chinese businesspeople as active agents of capitalism in New Order Indonesia. Richard Robison (1986; 1992) and Jamie Mackie (2003) depict how the highly patrimonial New Order regime co-opted a few ethnic Chinese capitalists into networks of patronage in which *pribumi* politico-bureaucrats had dominant power. Although the Chinese capitalists were economically powerful, their marginalised ethnicity made them politically impotent and rendered them what Christian Chua (2008, following Riggs 1964, 189–93; 1966, 249–54) refers to as a 'pariah business class'. Riggs created the concept of 'pariah entrepreneurship' to refer to Chinese businesspeople in his research in Thailand; these businesspeople were politically vulnerable and had to depend on politico-bureaucrats for patronage and privileged access to facilities. In return, the businesspeople contributed unofficial funds to the personal income of their protectors and patrons. Chua suggests that, in Suharto's New Order, the Chinese played a similar game; in order to gain patronage and privileged access to licenses, contracts, and state bank credit, they established patron-client relations with politico-bureaucrats. This shows that Chinese capitalists

---

10. However, for serious criminal cases, Europeans and indigenous people as well as other Asians were still subject to different legal systems until the end of the Dutch colonial period (Fasseur 1994, 42–43).

played a significant role in forming the political-business oligarchy in New Order Indonesia.

In his work, Chua explores in detail the active role played by Chinese Indonesian big business in shaping its position and reinforcing stereotypes about the Chinese in the post–New Order era. His works (2005; 2008; 2009) examine the impact of political democratisation in post-Suharto Indonesia on Chinese Indonesian conglomerates and how these conglomerates managed to resist, influence, and even mould political reforms. All his works point out that, although the collapse of the New Order regime put an end to the highly centralised, predatory patronage networks that secured the dominance of Chinese conglomerates in the private sector, Chinese conglomerates were able to react and adapt to the post-authoritarian environment in six ways. First, in the process of bank restructuring carried out by the new government, Chinese tycoons tried to buy back their assets on sale through third parties or offshore companies. They did not encounter much competition since external investors were not enthusiastic about taking over the assets, due to the inscrutability of the actual composition of the companies and to the generally muddy business environment in Indonesia. Second, some Chinese business elites tried to infiltrate the new regulatory institutions by bringing in and supporting close or bribable people in order to influence the composition, orientation, and arbitration of the institutions. Third, Chinese tycoons established political connections with new and potential power-holders such as opposition leaders by contributing money to their political activities. Fourth, Chinese conglomerates resorted to financial coercion to keep the media favourable to them. Their tactics included bribes, lawsuits, intimidation of journalists, threats to withdraw advertising, and takeovers of media that were critical to Chinese big business. Fifth, Chinese tycoons bribed the new politico-bureaucrats to expedite the facilitation of business opportunities. Sixth, some Chinese big businesspeople hired thugs in the provinces outside Jakarta to intimidate local populations and politicians and subordinated them to private interests. Chua's works show that Chinese conglomerates were able to survive in democratised Indonesia by resorting to various extra-legal tactics, because political democratisation in the post-Suharto era has yet to lead to the emergence of good governance emphasising transparency and the rule of law, although there is an increasing effort to enforce the rule of law. By actively adopting these corrupt tactics, Chinese tycoons played a crucial role in shaping and perpetuating the new corrupt, predatory political-business system. At the same time, the ongoing wealth accumulation, exploitation, and corruption by Chinese tycoons has reinforced stereotypes of the Chinese as corrupt and opportunistic. As Jemma Purdey (2009) in her review of Chua's work (2008) rightly puts it,

Contemplating the Role of the Ethnic Chinese

Chua's Chinese conglomerates play a very large and largely detrimental part (as they did during the New Order) in rendering futile any efforts to remove [the boundaries between ethnic Chinese and *pribumi* Indonesians] and alter the nation's perceptions of the "ethnic Chinese". (113)

Tsai Yen-Ling's work (2008; 2011) on Chinese exclusivity and the asymmetrical relationship between ethnic Chinese and *pribumi* is another body of scholarly work that focuses on the active role of Chinese Indonesians in reproducing and perpetuating their ambivalent position in post-Suharto Indonesia. Based on her field research in Medan and Jakarta, Tsai notes that, after the anti-Chinese violence in May 1998, many Chinese thought that they could no longer depend on the state's security apparatus. Thus, they chose to live in gated communities which were significantly more expensive than non-gated communities.[11] Security guards, mostly *pribumi*, are employed to ensure the safety of the communities. Tsai points out that the more the Chinese choose to protect themselves by living in gated communities, the more they reinforce the *pribumi* perception of the Chinese as an exclusive ethnic minority. In addition, the more the Chinese rely on *pribumi* security guards for safety and protection, the more they reproduce the stereotypes of Chinese as wealthy and as the perfect target of extortion.

Scholarly works on ethnic Chinese Indonesians show that the historical development of ethnic relations and various policies of the different governments in Indonesia have constrained what Chinese have been able to do, but at the same time it is possible to see that the Chinese themselves have contributed to creating and reproducing their ambivalent position. This will be further explored in the chapters to come. At the same time, the changing political climate has both opened up possibilities and made the situation more complex for the ethnic Chinese. As will be explored further in the next chapters, I suggest that the Indonesian case can contribute to a more general understanding of the relationship between democratisation and ethnic minorities.

1.2 Scope of Research

What is the relationship between democratisation and ethnic minorities? It is hoped that this study will open up further questions about what the democratisation process means to minority populations, particularly when those minorities have the ambivalent position of being marginalised at the same time as having economic power—as stated above, a 'pariah class'. This study looks into the increasingly ambivalent position of Chinese Indonesians in

---

11. It should be noted that gated communities are not entirely new—they already existed before May 1998—but class-based residential patterns have certainly intensified after the May 1998 riots.

post-Suharto Medan and Surabaya by looking at the interconnectedness of business, electoral politics, and the revitalisation of the socio-cultural life of the Chinese in the post-Suharto era. Medan and Surabaya were selected as field sites for this study as both cities are economically and politically significant but also have some interesting contrasts in regard to their Chinese populations. These cities are the capitals of North Sumatra and East Java respectively, 'the sites of vibrant urban and industrial centers' (Hadiz 2004, 623). Medan is a historically important centre of plantation, manufacturing, and trade, while Surabaya is a vital port city which functions as a gateway to eastern Indonesia (Buiskool 2004, 1; Hadiz 2004, 623). According to *City Population*, an online atlas, Medan and Surabaya were the fifth- and second-largest cities in the country respectively in 2010 (2012).[12] Both cities have a significant Chinese Indonesian population; according to the Indonesian Population Census of 2010, the concentration of the Chinese Indonesian population was 9.7% in Medan and 5.3% in Surabaya (cited in Fossati [2016, 8, Table 2]), figures which are much higher than the percentage (1.2%) of Chinese Indonesians in the total population of Indonesia (Ananta, Arifin and Bakhtiar 2008, 27, Table 2.2).

Medan and Surabaya are also, however, quite different in terms of their ethnic Chinese communities. It is widely observed that ethnic Chinese in Medan are less indigenised (at least in terms of their daily language use)— in other words, they are more *totok* compared to their counterparts in Java, where Surabaya is situated (Mabbett and Mabbett 1972, 9). The term 'totok' originally meant pure-blood Chinese who migrated to Indonesia more recently than the *peranakan*, i.e., acculturated Chinese who have little or no command of Chinese languages or dialects and who practise culture and customs that are neither purely Chinese nor purely indigenous Indonesian. Some *peranakan* Chinese are descendants of intermarriage between Chinese male immigrants and local indigenous women before mass Chinese immigration to Indonesia occurred in the second half of the nineteenth century. The *totok-peranakan* distinction began to emerge after mass Chinese immigration to Indonesia took place at the second half of the nineteenth century. In the 1950s and 1960s, the term 'totok' was used to refer to Chinese Indonesians who had a China-oriented upbringing and who had command of some Chinese languages or dialects (Suryadinata 1992, 2; Hoon 2008, 4–5, 190–91).[13] Edward Aspinall and colleagues (2011) highlight that the Chinese population in Medan 'is recognized as having a distinctive culture that largely survived the ban on public expressions of Chinese language and culture under the New Order government' (32). They also point out that

---

12. The data in *City Population* is based on the Indonesian Population Census of 2010, which is the most recent census of Indonesia.

13. I will elaborate more on the origins of *totok* and *peranakan* Chinese in Chapter 2.

most Chinese Indonesians in the city are Buddhists and they speak in their daily life Hokkien, a Chinese dialect originating from the southern part of Fujian Province in southern China (Aspinall, Dettman, and Warburton 2011, 32). According to surveys conducted by M. Rajab Lubis and Peter D. Weldon on languages usually spoken at home by ethnic Chinese in Medan and Surabaya respectively, 73% of ethnic Chinese respondents in Medan spoke a Chinese language at home, but only 22% of their counterparts in Surabaya use a Chinese language at home (Lubis 1995, 76; Weldon 1978, 270, Table 11). According to another survey conducted by RM. H. Subanindyo Hadiluwih on languages usually spoken by Chinese Indonesians in Medan, 51.92% of Chinese Indonesians in the city spoke a Chinese dialect (read Hokkien) in their workplace, 57.69% spoke a Chinese dialect with friends, and up to 90.38% spoke Hokkien or another Chinese language at home (Hadiluwih 1994, 97–98).

During my fieldwork in Medan, I also observed that most Chinese in Medan, including those who are very young, spoke Hokkien. There are also some Chinese who can speak Mandarin as well. This marks a sharp contrast to their Chinese counterparts in several places in Java such as Jakarta and Surabaya. I visited the Chinatowns in Jakarta (Glodok) and Surabaya (Kembang Jepun); the common language of communication in both places was Indonesian instead of Mandarin or any other Chinese language. The cultural differences between Chinese in Medan and Surabaya are probably due to two factors. The first factor has much to do with the inter-ethnic relationships between Chinese and indigenous Indonesians in these two cities. According to Judith Nagata (2003, 275), Medan has a long history of tensions between local Chinese and indigenous groups. The use of Chinese languages among Chinese in Medan creates a gulf between them and the indigenous Indonesians. The Chinese are also considered wealthier and often encounter opposition and antagonism from indigenous Indonesians, as in the words of an ethnic Chinese stuffed-toy distributor in Medan:

> Many *pribumi* still think that ethnic Chinese are rich because they have stolen much wealth from *pribumi*. Some *pribumi* children even throw stones at any Chinese who pass in front of their houses because they are taught by their parents that the Chinese are bad. Many local Muslim *pribumi* often target ethnic Chinese as their scapegoat. If all Chinese have disappeared, I believe those Muslims would target local Batak Christians because of their different religious background. . . . I believe the stereotype of ethnic Chinese among *pribumi* will only disappear considerably after the older and middle generations of *pribumi* have passed away. (Interview with Susanto in Mandarin, August 4, 2010)

In fact, Medan was the site of the first violence against Chinese in May 1998 (Purdey 2006, 114). The situation is quite different in Surabaya;

according to an article in *Gatra* magazine (Trihusodo and Herawati 1998) and also mentioned in an interview with Dédé Oetomo (溫忠孝) (interview in English, December 24, 2010), an ethnic Chinese social activist in Surabaya, the Chinese in Surabaya generally maintain good relationships with indigenous Indonesians and did not encounter massive riots in May 1998. It was also alleged that the local ethnic Chinese business community in Surabaya was able to guarantee relative peace in the city by paying generously for local military protection, in contrast to many other major cities in Java such as Jakarta and Solo, where troops mysteriously disappeared when the anti-Chinese riots broke out (Dick 2003, 475). According to one informant in Surabaya, although initially violence against the Chinese did occur in the far north of the city where Chinatown is situated, it was immediately suppressed by the local armed forces and did not spread to other parts of the city (interview with Susana, in Mandarin, January 14, 2011).[14]

The second factor is that Medan is very near to Malaysia (particularly Penang and Kedah) and Singapore, two neighbouring countries with ethnic Chinese communities that still maintain Chinese languages and many Chinese customs. Many Chinese in Medan have relatives or close friends in Malaysia and Singapore. The interaction between Chinese in Medan and those of Malaysia and Singapore exposes the former to cultural influence from the latter. As Cao Yunhua (2010) notes,

> Medan is near to Singapore, Penang, and Kuala Lumpur. It is separated only by the Straits of Melaka from these cities. It only takes 40 to 50 minutes to travel from Medan to these cities by flight. Such convenience in transportation has enabled the Chinese in Medan to have frequent interaction and to establish close relationships with the Chinese in Singapore, Penang and Kuala Lumpur. . . . In recent years, the Chinese in Medan like to send their children to these three cities to study. After graduation, many of them stay and work in these cities. (77, my translation from Chinese original)

1.3 Methods of Research

The original objective of my research was to analyse the political economy of ethnic Chinese businesses in Medan and Surabaya since the advent of democratisation and decentralisation in Indonesia. I intended to explore how ethnic Chinese businesspeople had adapted to the democratic environment that had emerged since 1998. Specifically, I intended to discover the issues involved in interactions between businesspeople and local government and political parties, and how these might have evolved in the decade since the

---

14. For a detailed analysis of the different magnitudes of violence experienced by local Chinese communities in Medan, Surabaya, Solo, and Yogyakarta and the reasons behind the difference, see Panggabean and Smith (2011).

implementation of decentralisation as part of the democratisation process. I found this specific focus to be difficult for several reasons.

The first reason was due to problems in obtaining data that were essential for that specific research. The information on patrimonial relationships between Chinese businesspeople and power-holders was very essential; however, during my fieldwork in Indonesia, most of the businesspeople I interviewed were reluctant to talk about these relationships. Additionally, some Chinese businesspeople who were close to power-holders were unwilling to be interviewed and such information was generally not covered in the media. Therefore, to get such information I had to rely on other informants who knew those businesspeople or had some knowledge of patrimonial relationships involving Chinese businesspeople. In addition, I could not obtain more concrete information on local regulations concerning business activities, also essential to my research, due to problems of accessing the local bureaucracy. The local regulations are also not entirely available on the Internet. Therefore, I needed to rely on the media and individual interviews to get more information on local regulations. The data on patrimonial relationships involving Chinese businesspeople and local regulations concerning business activities that I received from individual interviews and the media were not sufficient in and of themselves for a book.

On the other hand, there has been a lack of in-depth research on Chinese Indonesian civil society groups and the participation of Chinese Indonesians in electoral politics in post-Suharto Medan and Surabaya. According to my review of literature on ethnic Chinese Indonesians, there was (and still is) no scholarly work that has discussed the role of Chinese Indonesians in both of these aspects in detail. However, I believe that it is essential to understand the role of Chinese Indonesians with regard to politics and civil society in order to get a better picture of their position in the post-Suharto era. As it turns out, my informants in Medan and Surabaya were willing to share more information on these issues than they were about my original research topic. In addition, as I mentioned earlier, most scholarly works on Chinese Indonesians have ascribed a largely passive and powerless role to this minority in Indonesian history. These works do not give due credit to the active agency of Chinese Indonesians in creating, deploying, or shaping their position in Indonesian society. Therefore, I decided to focus on the active agency of Chinese Indonesians in responding to democratisation and shaping the democratisation process as well as their position in Indonesian society since the end of the Suharto regime, and to focus on the aspects of business, civil society, and politics since they are clearly interconnected in terms of the role Chinese Indonesians have been playing in the post-Suharto era.

The methods used in this research are library research, in-depth, semi-structured individual interviews, as well as participant observation. The fieldwork was conducted in Jakarta (June 2010 and May 2011), Medan (July 2010 to December 2010), and Surabaya (December 2010 to May 2011). Library research was conducted by consulting both primary and secondary sources. The primary sources include statistical reports published by the Central Statistics Agency (BPS, Badan Pusat Statistik), news magazines published in Indonesia, and newspapers, both at national and local levels. The secondary sources include books, journals, and academic writings regarding the background of Chinese Indonesian communities in Medan and Surabaya; the changing political landscape in post-Suharto Indonesia; decentralisation policies; the associational life and the participation of Chinese Indonesians in formal politics in post-Suharto Medan and Surabaya; Chinese-language newspapers established in Medan and Surabaya since the end of the New Order; and local Chinese business in Medan and Surabaya since the advent of democratisation and regional decentralisation. I also interviewed in both cities Chinese Indonesian businesspeople, leaders of local major ethnic Chinese organisations, persons in charge or staff of local Chinese-language newspapers, journalists, politicians, academics, and NGO activists (see Appendix I for a complete list of informants).[15] The interviews were conducted in Mandarin, Hokkien, Indonesian, or English. All names of informants used in this study, except for public figures, are pseudonyms. In addition, I conducted participant observation to look into the 'Chineseness' of ethnic Chinese in Medan and Surabaya during my interactions with Chinese families in Medan and Surabaya.

1.4 Outline for the Book

I have divided the book into two parts. In the first part, I examine the construction of the Chinese minority in Indonesia as a type of 'pariah class' and query what effect democratisation has had on this construction. I do this through two chapters: Chapter 2, which explores the origins of the ambivalent position of ethnic Chinese in Indonesia, and Chapter 3, which looks at the marginalised position of ethnic minority 'pariah classes' and their role in democratisation processes. In this part, I suggest that the ambivalent position of the Chinese is not due only to the policies of colonial and post-colonial regimes and to prejudice among indigenous Indonesians, but also to the actions of the Chinese themselves. At the same time, I question the concepts of democracy, the democratisation process in post-Suharto Indonesia, its

---

15. I also conducted online follow-up interviews with one of my informants after my fieldwork in order to gather further relevant information.

impact on the state and society, and the role of Chinese Indonesians in the democratisation process.

The second part, which consists of Chapters 4, 5, and 6, showcases how the ambivalence of democratisation in post-Suharto Indonesia and the response of Chinese Indonesians to such ambivalence have created an even more paradoxical position for the Chinese.

The freedom for cultural expression opened up in the *reformasi* era has led to the emergence of two different Chinese ethnic and cultural identities. One emphasises the revival of Chinese culture and the bolstering of Chinese ethnic identity, another focuses on the integration of Chinese Indonesians into the wider Indonesian society. In Chapter 4, I look into the sociological factors behind the emergence of these two different Chinese ethnic and cultural identities, and examine how these two identities are manifested in two different approaches towards opening up the Chinese socio-cultural sphere in post-Suharto Medan and Surabaya. Chinese Indonesians who strongly support Chinese ethnic and cultural identities have made use of the more liberal environment to establish Chinese-based organisations and Chinese-language newspapers. In general, these organisations and newspapers have made use of intra-ethnic linkages to safeguard Chinese ethnic and cultural identities, thus contributing to multiculturalism in post-Suharto Indonesia. The rise of China as an economic power has also prompted leaders of some Chinese organisations to utilise their intra-ethnic linkages and social networks in China to assist local governments in establishing cultural and business connections with China. Many indigenous Indonesians, however, perceive that the active role of Chinese organisations in promoting Chinese culture indicates an insistence upon separateness—this is one thing that has made the Chinese targets of dislike. At the same time, there are Chinese Indonesians who favour the integration of the Chinese into the wider Indonesian society and who have established non-ethnic-based socio-cultural organisations to promote cross-ethnic understanding and solidarity. On the whole, however, the socio-cultural activities and endeavours of Chinese organisations and Chinese-language newspapers have reproduced and perpetuated stereotypes of the Chinese as insular, exclusive, opportunistic, and oriented towards China instead of Indonesia. I suggest that the education system of Indonesia could promote more people, including Chinese Indonesians, to become actively involved in cross-ethnic endeavours if schools introduce programmes and activities that promote inter-ethnic understanding and solidarity.

The corrupt and muddy business environment of the post–New Order era has influenced the ways Chinese Indonesian businesspeople in Medan and Surabaya gain and safeguard their business interests, as well as deal with illegal practices by government officials, police, and *preman* (gangsters/

thugs). In Chapter 5, I examine, against the background of these structural conditions, how Chinese Indonesian businesspeople tend to resort to various illegal or semi-legal means, such as giving in to the illegal requests of government officials, police, and *preman*; establishing collusion with local power-holders, heads of security forces, and youth/crime organisations; as well as exerting financial coercion on critical media to gain and protect their business and personal interests. These business practices in turn perpetuate and reproduce the corrupt and muddy business environment, as well as the predatory political-business system. They also reproduce and reinforce stereotypes of the Chinese as wealthy, corrupt, and opportunistic, the perfect targets of extortion. Although there are also Chinese businesspeople who refuse to be victims of extortion and choose to fight against these illegal practices, such businesspeople are rare. If one wishes to see more Chinese Indonesian businesspeople who refuse to be extorted and do not get involved in illegal and semi-legal practices, a better-enforced rule of law must be in place.

Chapter 6 focuses on the involvement of Chinese Indonesians in electoral politics in post-Suharto Medan and Surabaya and how this intersects with their stereotypical position as businesspeople. On the one hand, the opening up of a democratic environment in post-Suharto Indonesia has prompted many Chinese Indonesians to get involved in electoral politics. Some of them become electoral candidates in order to push for reform and positive changes in Indonesia and reject approaches of support for their campaigns in return for political and business favours. On the other hand, there are those who become actively involved in politics with the aim of gaining political protection for their business instead of fighting for the interests of the general public. Ironically, they often have a higher chance of getting elected, because of the increased cost of campaigning in direct elections introduced during the democratisation process. Their own wealth, or the willingness to accept support from corrupt businesspeople, often Chinese, ensures enough funds to obtain party support and to bribe voters. In this way, Chinese businesspeople continue to establish corrupt and patrimonial relationships with aspiring politicians in exchange for political favours for their business. In addition, some Chinese who strongly support the re-emergence of cultural expression and Chinese ethnic identity are reluctant to support some reform-minded Chinese politicians, whom they deem as not 'Chinese' enough and not close to the Chinese community. This has led to the marginalisation of genuinely reform-minded politicians such as Sofyan Tan. It has also perpetuated the predatory characteristics of Indonesia's new democracy and reinforced stereotypes of the Chinese as corrupt and opportunistic.

The seventh chapter provides an analysis and summary of the active role of ethnic Chinese in reproducing and perpetuating their ambivalent position as well as in shaping Indonesia's political, business, and socio-cultural environment in the post-Suharto era. I also suggest that studying the Chinese in Indonesia may direct us to rethink the effect of democratisation on ethnic minorities and the role that those minorities may have in how transformative democratisation can be both for their situation and the betterment of the wider society. I conclude that effective enforcement of the rule of law as well as an education system that promotes inter-ethnic understanding and solidarity could promote more open- and reform-minded people, including those from resented, economically dominant minorities, such as the Chinese in Indonesia.

Part One

'Pariah' Ethnic Minorities and Democratisation

Part One deals with the construction of the Chinese minority in Indonesia as a 'pariah class' and the effect democratisation has had on this construction. The ambivalent position of the Chinese minority has been shaped by historical and structural factors, but it is also necessary to recognise the agency of the Chinese themselves. Historically, the Chinese have their ancestral roots in China and do not have particular regions in Indonesia to identify with. During the Dutch period, the colonial regime's divide-and-rule policy, the granting of economic privileges to the Chinese, and subsequently the emergence of nationalist sentiments oriented towards China in early twentieth-century Dutch East Indies effectively prevented the Chinese from integrating into the wider indigenous population. The Chinese therefore began to be perceived as an alien minority associated with various negative attributes, occupying an ambivalent position in Indonesian society. During the New Order, the Chinese were excluded from politics and were given opportunities only to get involved in economic activities. Some Chinese business elites who were politically vulnerable established patron-client relations with politico-bureaucrats to gain patronage and privileged access to facilities. Thus, the New Order era saw the construction of Chinese Indonesians as a 'pariah class'.

2
A Short History of the Ethnic Chinese in Indonesia

Creating a 'Pariah' Class*

The ethnic Chinese have always been a small minority in Indonesia. In 1930, they represented an estimated 2.03% of the total population (Ananta, Arifin, and Bakhtiar 2008, 20). It was estimated that Chinese Indonesians formed about 1.2% of the total Indonesian population in both 2000 and 2010 (Ananta, Arifin, and Bakhtiar 2008, 23, Table 2.1; Ananta et al., 2013, 14, Table 2).[1] Despite their small proportion in the country, it has been widely acknowledged that ethnic Chinese Indonesians have played an important and vital role in the economic development of Indonesia. The economically privileged position of Chinese Indonesians is largely due to historical factors. The Chinese were already residents in Java and coastal communities of the Maluku Islands, Sulawesi, Sumatra, and Kalimantan before the arrival of the Dutch. The Chinese settled in the Indonesian archipelago for trading purposes (Reid 1993; Sidel 2006, 19). Many local regents (also known as *bupati* or district heads) appointed Chinese merchants as intermediary traders between themselves, the indigenous population, and external markets. These local regents preferred the Chinese to indigenous people to fill this occupational niche in order to prevent the rise of an indigenous merchant class that might challenge their position (Reid 1992, 497). In precolonial times, the Chinese in Java and other parts of Southeast Asia could assimilate into the indigenous population, because increasingly numbers of those who travelled to Southeast Asia for trade were themselves Muslim (Wertheim 1965, 46–47; Chua 2008, 31; Skinner 1996, 55; Anderson 1998, 321; Lembong 2008, 48).

---

*   Part of this chapter was earlier published in Chong (2016). The names of informants in this chapter are pseudonyms except for the following public figure: Anton Prijatno.
1.   This figure was calculated directly from the raw data of the 2000 and 2010 population censuses. The figure, which is significantly smaller than that in 1930, is based on self-identification. Only those who identified themselves as Chinese were recorded as ethnic Chinese.

As mentioned earlier in Chapter 1, Anderson (1998) points out that the 'separateness' of the Chinese from the indigenous majority in Indonesia began to emerge after the Dutch colonised the Indonesian archipelago. Under Dutch colonial rule, which began in the seventeenth century, the Chinese could no longer be completely assimilated into the indigenous society. According to Mona Lohanda (1996, 1), in the days of the Dutch East India Company (VOC) during the seventeenth and eighteenth centuries, people in the Indonesian archipelago were classified into Christians and non-Christians and, on a racial basis, Westerners (Europeans) and non-Westerners (non-Europeans). Each non-Western ethnic group was ruled by local headmen appointed by the VOC. All Chinese from different speech groups (e.g., Hokkien, Hakka, and Hainanese) were classified as Chinese. The headman of the Chinese community in each locality was known as *Kapitan Cina* (Chinese captain) (Lohanda 1996). Like the local regents before them, the VOC used the Chinese as middlemen between the Dutch and the indigenous population (Suryadinata 1988, 262; Chua 2008, 31; Hoadley 1988). After the collapse of the VOC in 1800, its territories were taken over by the Dutch colonial government. In 1854, the colonial government divided the population of the Dutch East Indies into three groups (Govaars 2005, 20). The first group was European; they formed the upper level. The middle level comprised Foreign Orientals, which included Chinese, Arabs, Indians, and Japanese who had been born in the Dutch East Indies or had resided there for 10 years or above. The bottom level was the indigenous population (Suryadinata 1993b, 83; Shiraishi and Shiraishi 1993, 8). According to The Siauw Giap (1967, 91), it was this stratification which made Islam less attractive to the Chinese, because Muslims were considered indigenous people with a status inferior to that of the Chinese.

Under Dutch rule, Chinese businesspeople became indispensable to the colonial economy. The colonial government granted the Chinese licenses to engage in 'the selling of opium, the operation of gambling establishments, ferries, pawnshops, and abattoirs, and the gathering of birds' nests for export to the gourmets of China' (Williams 1960, 24). Such a monopoly concession system was known as revenue or tax farming; the license holder was known as a revenue farmer (Govaars 2005, 27; Williams 1960, 25). Among all monopoly concessions the opium concession was the most lucrative (Govaars 2005, 28).[2] The monopoly concession system produced many wealthy Chinese revenue farmers.

In order to prevent the Chinese and the indigenous people from combining forces to challenge them, the Dutch introduced zoning and pass systems in 1835 and 1863, respectively, that required the Chinese to reside in restricted

---

2. For the history of the opium revenue farming system in the Dutch East Indies, especially in Java, see Rush (2007).

areas and prevented them from travelling out of these areas unless they had passes (Suryadinata 1993b, 81–82). These systems effectively prevented the Chinese from living among the indigenous population and restricted interaction between the Chinese and other ethnic groups. Moreover, according to Leo Suryadinata, the zoning system 'had a far-reaching impact on the "separateness" of the Chinese' (Suryadinata 1993b, 82). The Chinese therefore began to occupy an ambivalent position in Indonesian society during Dutch rule. On the one hand, they played a crucial role in the colony's economic development. On the other hand, the Chinese began to be perceived as the 'Other' because of this and were increasingly regarded with suspicion and prejudice by the indigenous majority.

In the 1890s Dutch humanitarians pressured the Dutch colonial government to abolish the revenue farming system, since they saw it as detrimental to the welfare of the indigenous population (Williams 1960, 25–27). This move broke part of the Chinese economic power. The Chinese in Indonesia were also further angered when, in 1899, after the defeat of China in the First Sino-Japanese War (1894–1895), the Dutch government acceded to the Japanese government's request to classify Japanese in the Dutch East Indies as Europeans (Fasseur 1994, 37). Although the Chinese also demanded equal status with Europeans, the Dutch rejected this demand as the colonial government was concerned that the concession would exert a considerable impact on the growing nationalist forces among indigenous Indonesians.[3] As Mona Lohanda (1996) notes:

> Considering the turbulent political circumstances of the colony, particularly from the first decade of the twentieth century, the Dutch were very cautious in their handling of Chinese affairs. Yielding to the Chinese request for equal status would provoke anti-Chinese feeling among the Indonesians, which in turn might endanger the Dutch themselves. (151)

At the same time, political events in China stimulated the nationalist sentiments of the Chinese in the Dutch East Indies. China had been invaded by foreign powers in the nineteenth century, losing in the Opium War (1840–1842) to the British and suffering an immense defeat in the First Sino-Japanese War (1894–1895). After the Boxer Uprising in 1900, Beijing was invaded and plundered by the allied armies, an alliance of the armies of Austria-Hungary, France, Germany, Italy, Japan, Russia, the United Kingdom (UK), and the United States (US) (Govaars 2005, 49).[4] As Ming Govaars (2005) remarks, 'The division of China into foreign concessions and spheres of influence

---

3. For the origins of the nationalist movement among indigenous Indonesians in the early twentieth century and its relationship with the Chinese in the Dutch East Indies, see Lohanda (2002, 171–205) and Shiraishi (1997).
4. The Boxer Uprising was an anti-foreigner movement that took place in China in 1900. For the origins and background of the uprising, see Esherick (1987).

threatened to make it "a kind of international colony"' (49). Two prominent Chinese political leaders, Kang Youwei (康有為) and Sun Yat-sen (孫逸仙／孫中山), sought to rescue China 'while living in exile among the overseas Chinese' (Govaars 2005, 49). Kang was a reformist while Sun was a revolutionary. The Chinese in the Dutch East Indies, who had suffered great loss of prestige, could identify with the difficulties of China and offered financial support to both Kang and Sun, hoping to 'contribute to the future greatness of their ancient homeland' (Govaars 2005, 49). In addition, the lifting of the prohibition on Chinese emigration by the Manchu government (Qing dynasty) in 1894 and the issuance of the Chinese law of nationality in 1909, which was based on *jus sanguinis* and claimed that every legal or extra-legal child of a Chinese father or mother would be considered a Chinese citizen, regardless of birthplace, further strengthened the nationalist sentiments of the Chinese in the Indonesian archipelago (Govaars 2005, 50; Willmott 1961, 14).[5]

These various factors contributed to the Pan-Chinese Movement in the Dutch East Indies, which revolted against the restrictions placed on the Chinese, particularly the zoning and pass systems. 'Pan-Chinese Movement' is a term used by scholars such as Lea E. Williams (1960), Leo Suryadinata (1981), and Ming Govaars (2005) to refer to the emergence of nationalist sentiments oriented toward China and the revival of Chinese culture among the *peranakan* Chinese in early twentieth-century Dutch East Indies. The *peranakan* Chinese tried to preserve their Chinese identity and safeguard their business as well as political interests by forming various Chinese organisations. These included the Tiong Hoa Hwe Koan (THHK), a Chinese organisation which promoted Chinese nationalism based on the teachings of Confucius through the Chinese-medium schools set up by the organisation in the Indies; the Siang Hwee (Chinese Chamber of Commerce), which championed the interests of Chinese business and community; and the Soe Po Sia (Chinese reading club), which disseminated modern political ideas through the distribution of reading materials (Williams 1960, 54–113; Kwee 1969, 1–21; Govaars 2005, 58–61; Suryadinata 1981, 5–6). The *peranakan* Chinese also established newspapers in Bahasa Melajoe Tionghoa (Sino-Malay language) such as *Li Po, Chabar Perniagaan/Perniagaan, Pewarta Soerabaia, Djawa Tengah*, and *Sin Po* to promote Chinese nationalism and Chinese culture (Suryadinata 1981, 5–6, 21).[6] In order to curb Chinese nationalism and placate the Pan-Chinese Movement, the colonial government passed a nationality law in 1910 based

---

5. Previously, the Manchu government prohibited the emigration of Chinese and those returning to China from abroad were subjected to death penalty. For more details on this policy, see Lim (1967, 63) and Chong (1983/84, 3).

6. *Sin Po* later published its Chinese-language edition, known as *Xin Bao*, in 1921 (Suryadinata 1997, 254).

on *jus soli*, which declared that all persons born in the Indies of parents residing there were Dutch subjects even if not Dutch citizens (Willmott 1961, 15). Thus, the Indies-born Chinese were both Chinese citizens and Dutch subjects.[7] Later in 1917 and 1918, the Dutch abolished the hated zoning and pass systems (Suryadinata 1981, 10–11).

Takashi Shiraishi (1997, 187–207), however, argues that these systems restricting Chinese movement and residence were abolished because the Dutch saw that anti-Sinicism was already firmly in place among indigenous Indonesians in the early 1910s as a result of the rise of a new nationalist politics that emphasised racial distinctions. Hence, it was no longer necessary to require Chinese and indigenous people to reside in different quarters. In fact, the abolition of both systems in the late 1910s did not bring significant improvement in relations between the Chinese and the indigenous population. Many *pribumi* perceived the Chinese as foreigners who were culturally different from them.[8] They also believed that the Chinese were economically strong but exclusive and selfish (Suryadinata 1993b, 78; Coppel 1983, 5). The loyalty of the Chinese to the Indies was also doubted by many *pribumi*. Before independence, the Chinese were often suspected of allying with the Dutch and China (Dawis 2009, 2). Such stereotypes and prejudice manifested in anti-Chinese violence that broke out in Tangerang, Jakarta, Bandung, Pontianak, Palembang, Bagan Siapi-Api, and Medan during the early phase of the revolution (1945–1946) (Somers 1965, 110–19; Heidhues 1974, 101–2, 109; Cribb 1991, 53; 111). Many Chinese traders were attacked because they were deemed rivals of indigenous small businesses. Some Chinese were caught in the riots because they were suspected of being in league with the Dutch (Heidhues 1974, 109; Hoon 2008, 33). The violence prompted the Chinese in some areas of the Dutch East Indies to form self-defense corps, known as *Pao An Tui* (or *Poh An Tui*), to protect the Chinese and their property from attacks by Indonesian army irregulars (Setiono 2003, 624–25; Coppel 1983, 25–26; Tsai 2011, 145). The Dutch sanctioned the formation of the *Pao An Tui* and armed the corps (Purcell 1965, 479; Setiono 2003, 625–26). As Benny G. Setiono (2003, 627) notes, the formation of the corps in East Java and North Sumatra turned out to be a disaster, leading to several violent conflicts between ethnic Chinese residents and pro-independence

---

7. This foreshadowed the emergence of the Chinese dual citizenship status as a political issue in post-colonial Indonesia.

8. It should be noted that the indigenous population were not homogeneous in terms of ethnicity and religious background. Apart from Javanese, the largest indigenous ethnic group in Indonesia, there are other groups such as the Sundanese, Madurese, Bugis, etc. Although the majority of the indigenous population are Muslims, there are also indigenous Indonesians who are non-Muslims. For instance, most of the indigenous people in North Sulawesi are Protestant Christians. In Bali, the indigenous people are predominantly Hindu.

troops in both provinces.[9] Abdul Baqir Zein (2000, 10) also points out that the *Pao An Tui* of Medan, North Sumatra, was involved in the invasion of Bagan Siapi-Api and the terrorisation of the residents.[10] This gave the impression to many pro-independence Indonesians that the *Pao An Tui* was formed to support the Dutch in fighting against the pro-independence revolutionaries (Coppel 1983, 26). The *Pao An Tui* was disbanded at the end of the revolution in 1949 (Zein 2000, 11).

After independence, some indigenous leaders assumed that the Chinese were oriented to China instead of Indonesia (Dawis 2009, 2). Many Chinese in Indonesia, especially those who were recent immigrants, had a strong sense of pride in China (Coppel 1983, 26). The victory of the communists in China in 1949 triggered Chinese nationalism among Chinese Indonesians and prompted some to return to China to receive further Chinese-language education and to build their ancestral land (Godley 1989; Hui 2011, 98–99). In the eyes of some indigenous Indonesian leaders, the Chinese minority was oriented toward China. They perceived the Chinese minority as a potential 'fifth column' for China (Suryadinata 1992, 167).[11] They were therefore uncomfortable with the dual citizenship of the Chinese, which emerged again out of the relatively liberal Citizenship Act of 1946 and the Round Table Agreement on Citizenship in 1949 between Indonesia and the Netherlands. Under these provisions, those Chinese who had been Dutch subjects and did not reject Indonesian citizenship were considered citizens of both Indonesia and China (Hoon 2008, 33). For many indigenous nationalists, as Hoon Chang-Yau (2008) puts it, 'dual nationality meant that the political loyalty of the Chinese must be divided between Indonesia and China' (34). Moreover, during the 1955 Bandung Asian-African Conference, China abandoned its traditional claim that all ethnic Chinese were Chinese citizens (Suryadinata 1992, 171). Both President Sukarno and the Chinese prime minister, Zhou Enlai (周恩來), agreed that ethnic Chinese should choose only one citizenship (Liu 2011, 177–79). Hence, in 1958, a new and less liberal citizenship act known as 'Act No. 62 of the year 1958 Concerning Republic of Indonesia Citizenship' was passed (Willmott 1961, 118). Under the new act, Chinese in Indonesia would lose their citizenship if they did not submit an official

---

9. There were also Chinese militias that fought for the Republic. In Pemalang, Central Java, the Chinese formed their own struggle group known as the Chinese Youth Irregulars (LPT, Laskar Pemuda Tionghoa) in 1945 to fight for the independence of Indonesia. The LPT played a prominent role in overthrowing the Japanese administration in Pemalang and exhorting (often violently) the Chinese community to fly the Indonesian flag after Japan's surrender (Lucas 1991, 86–87).
10. Zein, however, does not explain why the *Pao An Tui* of Medan invaded Bagan Siapi-Api.
11. According to *Encyclopaedia Britannica* (2013), the expression 'fifth column' refers to a 'clandestine group or faction of subversive agents who attempt to undermine a nation's solidarity by any means at their disposal'.

statement abjuring Chinese citizenship (Willmott 1961, 120; Hoon 2008, 34). However, the act was only fully implemented in 1960, leaving the citizenship of most Chinese in an ambiguous state between 1958 and 1960 (Hoon 2008, 35). In November 1959, as part of the steps towards reducing the economic role of ethnic Chinese, the government issued the Presidential Decree No. 10, which banned 'alien' (i.e., Chinese) retail trade in rural areas and required all aliens to transfer their business to Indonesian citizens by January 1, 1960 (Badan Koordinasi Masalah Cina—BAKIN, 1979, 301–5). Although the decree was officially directed only at Chinese without Indonesian citizenship, in reality, those with Indonesian citizenship encountered similar distress as the distinction between citizens and aliens was still unclear (Hoon 2008, 35). In West Java alone, 9,927 Chinese were forced to move from rural areas to urban places (Huang 2000, 19). There were also Chinese who were sent back to China. According to Thee Kian Wie (2006, 88), around 119,000 Chinese citizens were repatriated to China during 1960–1961. Some chose to leave for China because they thought that the presidential decree had threatened their livelihood (Mackie 1976, 95).

Under Dutch rule and during the Sukarno years (1949–1965), ethnic Chinese in Indonesia were allowed to form ethnic-based organisations (ranging from cultural associations to clan groups to business chambers), establish Chinese-language newspapers, open Chinese-medium schools, and be involved in politics (Heidhues 2006, 77–83; 1974, 74–86; Huang 2000, 75–100, 158–72, 101–57; Pandiangan 2003, 409–13; Suryadinata 1981, 74–86; 1992, 149–53; 1993, 80–81, 86–88; 1997, 253–59). In fact, in the new parliament elected in the 1955 election, which was the first national election held in Indonesia after independence, nine appointed seats were reserved for ethnic Chinese (Heidhues 1974, 77). During the Sukarno era (both the parliamentary democracy [1950–1957] and Guided Democracy [1957–1965] periods), there were even a few cabinet ministers of Chinese origin (Suryadinata 1992, 14n10, 14n11; 1993b, 88).

It is important to note that the ethnic Chinese in Indonesia are by no means culturally homogenous. Conventionally, scholars have divided them into *peranakan* and *totok*. The *peranakan*s were local-born and acculturated Chinese. Some of them were products of intermarriage between Chinese male immigrants and local indigenous women. They had been residing in Indonesia for centuries. Although the *peranakan*s still identified themselves as Chinese, they had adopted many elements of the majority Indonesian indigenous culture; some of them could not speak Chinese (Skinner 1958, 2; Somers 1964, 4; Hoon 2008, 4–5). The *totok*, on the other hand, were pure-blooded Chinese who were born in China and migrated to the Indies. They spoke Chinese and maintained most Chinese customs and cultural traditions. In addition, they were generally more politically oriented to China. According to Leo Suryadinata (1992, 90), the *peranakan*s also used the Hokkien term *singkeh*, meaning 'new guests', to refer to the *totok*. Mass Chinese immigration to the Indies took place in the second half of the nineteenth century. The mass immigration was a result of the Taiping Rebellion, a civil war against the Manchu imperial government which began in Guangxi in 1850 and later spread to other provinces.[12] The immigrants included a significant number of women; it became possible for Chinese men to marry China-born women rather than indigenous or *peranakan* women.[13] Many more Chinese women immigrated to Indonesia after 1900 as a result of the Boxer Uprising, mentioned earlier in this chapter. Descendants of these new immigrants usually remained culturally Chinese and formed the distinct and separate *totok* community (Somers 1964, 4; Hoon 2008, 5).

In post-colonial Indonesia during the 1950s and 1960s, the Chinese *peranakan* community was divided into two competing streams. The 'integrationist' group led by the Consultative Body for Indonesian Citizenship (BAPERKI, Badan Permusjawaratan Kewarganegaraan Indonesia) fought

---

12. For the origins and background of the Taiping Rebellion, see Jen (1973).
13. Prior to the second half of the nineteenth century, there was no female emigration from China to Southeast Asia. This was due to a few factors. First, although the Manchu imperial government officially prohibited the emigration of Chinese, in reality, the regulation was often strictly enforced with respect to women but not men. This was because officials knew that the male emigrants often returned with their savings or had to send money to their families in China, thus allowing the officials to extort money from them. Second, women were accorded very low social status in traditional Chinese society. The main duty of women was to remain at home to look after their children and parents-in-law. Therefore, they were forced to remain in China. In fact, this special role of Chinese women was manifested in the custom of foot-binding, which forced women to stay indoors. Third, most of the male emigrants were too poor to bring their families overseas (Lim 1967, 63–64; Chong 1983/84, 3–4). Chinese female immigration to Southeast Asia began only from the latter half of the nineteenth century as some of the hindrances that had earlier prevented them from leaving the country were removed. The immediate factor that prompted Chinese female emigration was the economic and political upheavals in China brought about by the Taiping Rebellion. The chaotic situation in China forced many Chinese women to migrate overseas. Besides that, the contact the Chinese had with the West as a consequence of the Opium and Arrow Wars in nineteenth-century China played an essential role in eliminating the traditional prejudice the Chinese had against female emigration (for the origins and background of the Opium and Arrow Wars, see Elleman [2001, 3–56]). The opening of the 'treaty-ports' in Guangdong and Fujian brought an increase in the interaction of the Chinese in these two provinces with Europeans. This interaction resulted in the establishment of several girls' schools by European Christian missionaries. Both Christian and non-Christian female students attended these schools. Apart from their educational work, the Christian missionaries also joined certain Chinese women in fighting against the foot-binding custom that discriminated against women. Such efforts contributed to educational and social advancement of Chinese women, thus removing the traditional prejudice among Chinese against female emigration. Furthermore, in 1860, the Manchu government officially allowed Chinese women to emigrate as wives and dependents of the male emigrants. These factors prompted female emigration from China in the second half of the nineteenth century (Lim 1967, 72–75; Chong 1983/84, 5–6).

for citizenship rights for ethnic Chinese and advocated for recognition of a separate Chinese ethnic identity yet one remaining part of the Indonesian nation. This group believed Chinese Indonesians did not need to give up their cultural heritage to participate fully in national politics (Suryadinata 1992, 33; Aizawa 2011, 49–50; Hoon 2008, 35). BAPERKI was founded in March 1954 with the aim of promoting the understanding of Indonesian citizenship and the elimination of discrimination against ethnic Chinese who were Indonesian citizens (Coppel 1976, 45–46; Somers 1964, 11; Hoon 2008, 35). On the other hand, the 'assimilationists' group formed by a number of Chinese *peranakan*s who were Christians or right-wing elements associated with the military, advocated the complete assimilation of the Chinese into the indigenous Indonesian population (Suryadinata 1992, 70; Hoon 2008, 35–36). According to Suryadinata (1992, 70–72), these assimilationist Chinese *peranakans* included Junus Jahja, a.k.a. Lauw Chuan Tho (劉全道), an economist; Ong Hok Ham, a.k.a. Onghokham (王福涵), a university student; and K. Sindhunatha (王宗海), a navy captain. The assimilationists were of the opinion that the Chinese needed to 'abandon their cultural background and exclusionary lifestyle – that is, living separately from other Indonesian ethnic groups' in order to eliminate discrimination against them (Aizawa 2011, 49). Junus Jahja, one of the assimilationists, later converted to Islam in 1979 and advocated Chinese conversion to Islam as a means for the Chinese to be fully assimilated into the indigenous population (Suryadinata 1997, 190–91; Setyautama 2008, 159). His open advocation for the assimilation of the Chinese upset some Chinese Indonesians, especially those with a strong ethnic identity. As interviewed in *Kompas,* Jahja revealed that he had been accused outright of being a 'traitor' (*pengkhianat*) by other Chinese Indonesians for abandoning his cultural roots (Setianingsih 2009, my translation from the Indonesian original).

The anti-Communist violence instigated by the Suharto-led military after the military takeover on October 1, 1965 took a strong anti-Chinese turn at times from 1965 to 1968 (Mackie 1976; Davidson 2009b, 47–84; Hui 2011, 115–46; Tsai and Kammen 2012).[14] Many Chinese in Indonesia were accused of being Communist sympathisers; at least 2,000 were killed from 1965 to 1966 (Coppel 1983, 58). The last and worst major anti-Chinese violence broke out in late 1967 and early 1968 in West Kalimantan. The military provoked Dayaks to murder Chinese who were accused of supporting the communist party (Mackie 1976, 126–28; Davidson 2009b, 47–84; Hui 2011, 115–46). Between 2,000 and 5,000 Chinese were killed and nearly 100,000 were

---

14. For a comprehensive discussion on the background of the military takeover and the subsequent mass violence against the Indonesian Communist Party (PKI, Partai Komunis Indonesia) and the Left, see Kammen and McGregor (2012).

relocated to coastal cities and towns such as Pontianak and Singkawang (Davidson 2009b, 68, 74–77).[15]

Later, Suharto's government began to enforce assimilation policies to curtail Chinese culture and control the ethnic Chinese. Public displays of Chinese characters were forbidden. Ethnic Chinese were not allowed openly to celebrate Chinese holidays or festivals. Ethnic Chinese organisations were banned except those dealing with health, religion, burial services, sports, and recreation.[16] Schools that offered all instruction in Chinese were closed down. Chinese-language newspapers were prohibited, except for one produced by the government. Furthermore, ethnic Chinese were urged to adopt indigenous-sounding names (Coppel 1983, 165; 2002, 22–23; Suryadinata 1992, 153–64; Chua 2008, 39–40).

It is worth noting that although many Chinese in Indonesia became more 'peranakanised', if not 'Indonesianised', under Suharto's policy of forced assimilation, in some places like Medan, Pontianak, Singkawang, Bangka, and Belitung, the local Chinese can still generally speak Mandarin and certain Chinese dialects. Many older Chinese can read and write Chinese as they had studied in pre–New Order Chinese-medium schools. The younger generation generally cannot read and write Chinese but they can still speak Mandarin and certain Chinese dialects. Moreover, many Chinese in those places still practise most Chinese customs as well as cultural traditions.[17]

During the New Order period, Suharto's regime also issued regulations and decrees that marginalised and stigmatised the Chinese. For instance, a particular code was attached to the national identity cards and passports of Indonesians of Chinese origin (Tan 1991, 123; Aizawa 2011, 60–61). This coding system stigmatised the Chinese and 'constantly exposed them to discrimination and exploitation by the bureaucracy, police and military' (Hoon 2008, 39). Chinese Indonesians also had to produce a Citizenship Letter

---

15. It should be noted that the anti-Communist violence was never anti-Chinese in general, although the massacres that broke out in West Kalimantan in 1967 and 1968 were targeted exclusively at Chinese (see Davidson [2009b, 47–84] for more details on massacres of Chinese in West Kalimantan). There were about half a million people killed in 1965–1966 and the victims were mostly indigenous Indonesians who were members and associates of the Indonesian Communist Party (PKI). Relatively few Chinese were murdered in this period (Cribb and Coppel 2009, 447–65; Tsai and Kammen 2012, 131–55). Prior to its collapse in 1965, the PKI was relatively tolerant of the Chinese minority due to the 'anti-racist character of Marxist ideology' (McVey 1968, 359). The party leaders often stood up against racial attacks on the Chinese minority (Mackie 1976, 79).

16. Some Chinese organisations therefore converted into charitable foundations (yayasan) that focused on health, religion, burial services, sports, or recreation in order to continue to operate.

17. In fact, a lecturer at the University of Indonesia once told me that many people in Jakarta deemed Chinese Indonesians from 'PBBM' (Pontianak, Bangka, Belitung, and Medan) as less assimilated and exclusive (personal communication with Timothy, in Indonesian, January 31, 2011).

(SBKRI, Surat Bukti Kewarganegaraan Republik Indonesia) to obtain documents such as birth certificates, passports, or marriage certificates (Aizawa 2011, 61). In addition, unwritten barriers restricted the Chinese from politics, public service, the military, and entrance to public universities. During the New Order era, there were very few ethnic Chinese members of parliament.[18] These were Chinese *peranakans* from the 'assimilationists' group.[19] As Benedict R. O'G. Anderson (1990) notes, 'In another sort of regime, men of their abilities [i.e., the very few ethnic Chinese members of parliament in New Order Indonesia] would probably long since have achieved cabinet rank' (115n52). In general, the Chinese were only given the right to participate in economic activities (Chua 2008, 42). As a result, as Hoon Chang-Yau (2006b) notes, 'This continuous and intentional official discrimination against the Chinese placed them in a vulnerable position of ethnic and class hostility' (153).

So why did Suharto's New Order issue regulations and decrees that contradicted the assimilation policies? In his study of the background of the assimilation policies, Nobuhiro Aizawa (2011) suggests a possible reason. According to Aizawa (2011, 60), the Ministry of Home Affairs (DEPDAGRI, Departemen Dalam Negeri), which drafted and issued the assimilation policies, considered assimilation as a way 'to prevent possible sources of political opposition and, thus, pave the way for the president's re-election'. Therefore, the Chinese, who continued to be perceived as a potential 'fifth column' of China, needed to be depoliticised to ensure that the government took better control of any political threat or opposition (Aizawa 2011, 60–61).[20] Chua makes a similar argument that such contradictions were meant

---

18. A few months before the collapse of the New Order regime, Suharto appointed as minister of trade and industry Bob Hasan, a.k.a. The Kian Seng (鄭建盛), his long-time crony and golf partner, who was of Chinese descent (Setyautama 2008, 410). But Hasan had been adopted by an indigenous Muslim military officer as a child and was highly assimilated into indigenous society. Hence, as Li Zhuohui (李卓輝) (2007, 153), chief editor of Indonesian Chinese-language newspaper *Guoji Ribao* (國際日報) points out, the Chinese community did not perceive Hasan as an 'ethnic Chinese businessperson' and did not think he represented the Chinese community.

19. They included Sofyan Wanandi, a.k.a. Liem Bian Khoen (林綿坤) (representing the university student group); Jusuf Wanandi, a.k.a. Liem Bien Kie (林綿基) (Golkar); L. B. G. Surjadinata, a.k.a. Lie Beng Giok (Indonesian Protestant Party); Lo S. H. Ginting (Catholic Party); Harry Tjan Silalahi, a.k.a. Tjan Tjoen Hok (曾春福) (Catholic Party); Budi Dipojuwono, a.k.a. Lie Po Yoe (李保佑) (Indonesian Nationalist Party); Djoko Sudjatmiko, a.k.a. Lie Giok Houw (李玉虎) (Golkar); and Anton Prijatno (王炳金) (Golkar) (Suryadinata 1992, 14n12; Suryadinata 1993, 88; Setyautama 2008, 170, 182, 193, 433, 434; interview with Anton Prijatno, in Indonesian, February 24, 2011).

20. To further control possible sources of political opposition, Suharto's regime even reduced the number of political parties to three in 1973, i.e., Golkar, which was set up by the Suharto group, United Development Parties (PPP, Partai Persatuan Pembangunan) and the Indonesian Democratic Party (PDI, Partai Demokrasi Indonesia) (Suryadinata 2002a, 30–31).

to ensure that the Chinese, who were economically significant, remained politically weak. Under such circumstances, the Chinese would not be able to challenge the position of the power-holders. This would then secure the social and financial base of the politico-bureaucratic rulers' power (Chua 2008, 37–38, 41–43). In other words, the assimilation policies were aimed to secure the power of Suharto's regime and were never meant to integrate the Chinese into the general Indonesian population.

The New Order policy, therefore, deliberately excluded the ethnic Chinese from politics, and thus many Chinese, as had been the case over the centuries, chose to get involved in economic activities. The New Order also saw the emergence of a substantial number of *cukongs*, Chinese Indonesian capitalists who collaborated with members of the Indonesian power elite, usually from the military and the Suharto family, both of these being dominant political forces during the Suharto era. These *cukongs* included Liem Sioe Liong, a.k.a. Sudono Salim (林紹良); Tjia Kian Liong, a.k.a. William Soerjadjaja (謝建隆); and Lie Mo Tie, a.k.a. Mochtar Riady (李文正). They were all owners of conglomerates. The Suharto regime provided protection and various facilities such as privileged access to licenses, contracts, and state bank credit to these *cukongs*. In return, the power elite and their families became the Chinese capitalists' business partners (Robison 1986, 271–322; Suryadinata 1997, 33–34). Many *cukongs* channelled part of their profits to their political patrons' foundations (*yayasan*) in the form of 'donations' (Chua 2008, 49). However, as Suryadinata has maintained, the number of such *cukongs* was small and did not represent Chinese Indonesians in general (Suryadinata 2002b, 15). Most of the Chinese in Indonesia were, and still are, professionals or owner-managers of small- and medium-scale enterprises. Nevertheless, the corrupt relationships between a handful of Chinese Indonesian tycoons and power elites greatly influenced indigenous Indonesians' perception of the Chinese. As a result, Chinese Indonesians were (and are) generally perceived to be wealthier than indigenous Indonesians, corrupt, and opportunistic. I argue that Chinese Indonesian tycoons during the New Order played a crucial role in reinforcing the negative stereotypes against ethnic Chinese.

It is ironic that some ethnic Chinese Indonesians preferred to cooperate with and even be part of Suharto's autocratic regime, even though they were aware that the regime systematically discriminated against, marginalised, and stigmatised the Chinese minority. For instance, Jusuf Wanandi, a Chinese *peranakan* member of parliament affiliated with Golkar during the New Order period, notes in his memoir that

> We [the Chinese minority] remained discriminated against in many fields, from education to employment. We were never really well assimilated.

This, I think was in large part because of the attitude from the top. Soeharto, A. H. Nasution and other top brass of the military never recognised the contribution of the ethnic Chinese. Soeharto made use of us. He used Chinese businessmen like Liem Sioe Liong to get money. He asked the cronies to help his family with business. He asked for our support on political issues. But he would never recognise us.

If the Chinese were attacked he never said anything . . . Never once did he give us a decent place within the New Order because he wanted to keep things – including the credit for what his government achieved – for himself. It was sadly fitting that the New Order should later collapse amid the rubble of anti-Chinese riots. We were treated as minor wives, enjoyed but not recognised. (Wanandi 2012, 126–27)

The text implies that Wanandi was well aware that Suharto used Chinese capitalists only for his own benefit. But it is telling that Wanandi still chose to stay in Golkar and continued to be part of the New Order regime. I argue that, in the process of safeguarding their political interests, ethnic Chinese politicians such as Wanandi also contributed to perpetuating the Chinese minority's marginalised and vulnerable position in New Order Indonesia.

By confining the Chinese to the economic sector and forming an alliance with a handful of well-connected Chinese tycoons, the New Order regime managed to fortify the perception of the Chinese as economically powerful and responsible for social and economic inequalities in the country. The Chinese had no means to rectify this impression since they were socially and politically weak. Christian Chua (2008) has noted that

[the Chinese] were at the regime's mercy and had to put up with these kinds of stigmatisation that were meant to instrumentalise them as scapegoats in several ways. . . . They were blamed for the misery of the *pribumi*. The discontent of the powerless masses and the anger about their economic situation could be diverted from the rulers towards the Chinese minority. (44)

Consequently, the Chinese were exposed to periodic anti-Chinese riots during economic crises (e.g., in 1997–1998) and workers' strikes (e.g., in Medan in 1994) (Purdey 2006, 77–141; Yang 2006, 2007; Chua 2008, 44).[21] Even minor incidents such as traffic accidents, street fights, and employer-worker disputes involving Chinese and *pribumi* could turn into anti-Chinese riots (Dahana 2004, 48–49). In addition, as John T. Sidel (2006) observes, the anxiety of Muslims about the ambiguous political position of Islam in New Order Indonesia also led to attacks on the Chinese. The ambiguous political position of Islam had its origins in the colonial period, when the Dutch colonial government prioritised Indonesian Christians from missionary schools in the recruitment of civil servants, teachers, and army officers, besides granting economic privileges to the Chinese minority. As a result,

---

21. For the background of the workers' strike in Medan, see Yang (2006, 241–42).

Muslims became subordinate in Indonesia. These conditions persisted even after independence. Although Muslims were the majority in Indonesia, they were unable to hold a dominant position in the political arena. Sidel points out that in post-colonial Indonesia, key posts in the bureaucracy and the military were held by those who had been educated in secular and Christian schools, not those with Islamic educational backgrounds. Moreover, there was no organisation that could be considered to represent the voice of all Muslims in the country. Muslim organisations like the All-Indonesian Association of Islamic Intellectuals (ICMI, Ikatan Cendekiawan Muslim Se-Indonesia), which was founded by Suharto's close associate B. J. Habibie in the early 1990s, spoke only for middle-class Muslim professionals, while Nahdlatul Ulama (NU) was an organisation that represented only rural Muslims. Moreover, while the New Order era saw the rise of Chinese conglomerates, local indigenous small business communities were at the same time undermined and marginalised due to the lack of access to capital and technology, as well as the lack in established connections with the state. The anxiety and feelings of inferiority among Muslims prompted them to spread violence against the mostly non-Muslim Chinese across the country.[22] As Jemma Purdey (2005) puts it, 'incidents of violence against the Chinese took place frequently and signified a disturbing trend' (14).[23]

In summary, it can be said that the Chinese in the Dutch East Indies and in the Republic of Indonesia after independence were treated as a 'pariah class' (Riggs 1964; 1966; Chua 2008), powerful in business but hated for their wealth. They came to be perceived as the 'Other' by the indigenous Indonesians. To borrow Fredrik Barth's term (1969, 15), the Chinese and the *pribumi* came to be separated by an *ethnic boundary*, that is, a social boundary that emerges if an ethnic group maintains its identity when its members interact with outsiders (Barth 1969, 15). Even though the cultural characteristics within an ethnic group may change and transform, as long as the dichotomisation between members and outsiders persists, the ethnic group will continue to exist (Barth 1969, 14). It can be said that although the Chinese and the *pribumi* generally became culturally more similar under Suharto's forced assimilation, the boundary that separated them was strengthened at the same time. As a result, the Chinese continued to occupy an ambiguous, outsider position in Indonesian society. As Hui Yew-Foong (2011) explains, 'The Chinese are strangers in Indonesian society' (15). According to Simmel (1950), the 'stranger' is a person 'who comes today and stays tomorrow'

---

22. It should be noted that these attacks were fundamentally religious and not ethnic in nature.
23. However, it should be pointed out that during the New Order period, the real upswing of anti-Chinese violence only took place between 1995 and 1998. Violence against the Chinese was fairly minimal prior to that. For an account of violence against the Chinese during the New Order era, see Coppel (1983); Mackie (1976, 111–38); Purdey (2006); Yang (2006; 2007).

(402). He or she is not an 'owner of soil' since he or she is deemed as a stranger by the other (Simmel 1950, 403).

Hence, it can be concluded that the divide-and-rule policy during the Dutch colonial period and the stigmatisation of the Chinese minority as an economically dominant minority group by post-independence regimes, especially during Suharto's presidency, resulted in the 'separateness' of the Chinese from the indigenous majority, although many of them became more 'Indonesianised' under Suharto's policy of forced assimilation.

3
Democratisation and Ethnic Minorities

A Look at Indonesia's Democratisation and the Ethnic Chinese*

In this chapter, I will examine the marginalised position of the ethnic minority and their role in democratisation processes. This discussion will allow me to question concepts of democracy and the democratisation process in post-Suharto Indonesia. This chapter first discusses the major theoretical approaches to democratisation and how this relates to ethnic minorities. It questions the democratisation process in post-Suharto Indonesia and its impact on the state and society. This chapter also discusses specifically what the role has been of Chinese Indonesians in the democratisation process in Indonesia.

3.1 Democratisation and Ethnic Minorities

Conceptualising democracy is not easy; scholars have yet to reach a consensus on its definition. In general, there are two broad theoretical approaches to democracy. Some scholars adopt a minimalist, one-dimensional procedural conception that focuses on elections, where democracy is '[an] institutional arrangement in which all adult individuals have the power to vote, through free and fair competitive elections, for their chief executive and national legislature' (Lipset and Lakin 2004, 19). A further elaboration of this adds an element of uncertainty; a regime is considered democratic '[o]nly if the opposition is allowed to compete, win, and assume office' (Przeworski et al. 1996, 50). Other scholars such as Larry Diamond (1999) and Jeff Haynes (2001) see this as merely as a limited type of democracy, an 'electoral democracy', whereas 'liberal' (Diamond 1999) or 'full' (Haynes 2001) democracy extends the idea of democracy beyond electoral procedures to include substantial individual freedoms and citizens' rights to participate in the

---

* The names of informants in this chapter are pseudonyms except for the following public figure: Dédé Oetomo.

political process. According to Diamond (1999, 10–12) and Haynes (2001, 10), in addition to the core elements of electoral democracy, liberal or full democracies have the following components:

— The armed forces are subordinated to civilian rule.
— Executive power is constrained by the rule of law and independent government institutions, thereby guaranteeing horizontal accountability of public officials.
— Beyond periodic elections, citizens have multiple channels through which to express their interests via elected political representatives as well as independent organisations and movements.
— Traditionally marginalised groups such as ethnic minorities and the poor have the opportunity to participate in the political process.

In thinking about democracy in this book, it is important to explore the role that ethnic minorities play in the democratisation process, and what democracy means for them. Many authors have reservations about considering democracy as a political system that will necessarily guarantee minority rights. A volume on ethnicity and democratisation in Europe edited by Karl Cordell (1999) argues that the interests of minority groups in new democracies are safeguarded only if governments have the political will, political capital, or economic capital to implement minority rights legislation. Nalini Rajan (2002) maintains that democracy tends to promote majoritarian rule that is inimical to minority rights. She argues that minority rights can flourish only in a democratised state which promotes equal consideration of individual autonomy and 'opt[s] for consensus rather than simple majority decision-making' (68). Daniel A. Bell (2004) points out that democratisation in East and Southeast Asia tends to emerge with nation-building projects that centre on the culture of the majority ethnic group. Therefore, he asserts that democratisation in these regions may marginalise or even eliminate expressions of minority culture as well as languages and consequently worsen the situation of vulnerable ethno-cultural minority groups.

In her works on democratisation and market-dominant minorities, i.e., economically privileged minorities, in newly democratised countries, Amy Chua (2003a; 2003b) argues that democratisation tends to bring a backlash against minorities. Citing cases such as the genocides of economically dominant minorities in the former Yugoslavia (the Croats) and Rwanda (the Tutsis), as well as the nationalisation in post-Suharto Indonesia of industrial assets formerly owned by ethnic Chinese capitalists, Chua argues that the simultaneous introduction of democratisation and free markets in developing countries with a deeply resented market-dominant minority often results in backlash against the minority through expulsion, atrocities, or economic restrictions. She explains such outcomes by suggesting that with democratisation 'politicians will have powerful incentives to scapegoat the resented economically dominant minority and foment ethnic hatred to their advantage' (Chua 2003a, 154). As a result, the aroused ethnic majority may demand policies that will end the resented market-dominant minority's economic dominance. To resolve ethnic tensions and conflict, Chua proposes that multi-ethnic developing countries should be ruled by authoritarian regimes until equality in wealth distribution among all ethnic groups is achieved. She also recommends the introduction of economic policies that positively discriminate against ethnic minorities and benefit the poor indigenous majorities.

Chua's controversial argument has been criticised by several scholars. For instance, Tom Ginsburg (2004) points out that Chua's conception of democracy is too narrow because she defines democracy as rule by majority, including any violence perpetuated by a majority group against a minority group. Due to such a narrow conception of democracy, Chua attributes many things to democracy that may not actually have much to do with it. For instance, she attests that the massive genocide of the Tutsis perpetrated by the Hutus in Rwanda in 1994 was a result of political liberalisation in the early 1990s. The Tutsis were the ethnic minority that played a dominant role in Rwanda's economy while the Hutus were the ethnic majority in the country. Ginsburg (2004) rightly refutes such a view by arguing that 'the fact that a majority of a population commits an atrocity, or is complicit with it, hardly renders that action a result of democracy' (317).

Edmund Terence Gomez (2008) and Emile Kok-Kheng Yeoh (2008) also criticise Chua for homogenising communities of the economically privileged minorities and over-emphasising obscenely wealthy tycoons from minority groups. Yeoh argues that the structure of the economically privileged minority communities is actually more complicated than Chua's readers are led to understand from her works. He points out that in Southeast Asian countries, apart from a few wealthy business tycoons, there are also large labouring masses within Chua's 'market-dominant minorities'. I agree with their views since throughout Chua's works there is little mention of those who do not belong to the wealthy trading class (such as Sofyan Tan) within the so-called economically privileged minorities.

Gomez (2008) also argues that the affirmative action proposed by Chua to target disadvantaged groups along ethnic lines could reinforce racial identities and, in the long term, hinder ethnic cohesion. He maintains that, under truly democratic rule, ethnic harmony is promoted and discrimination against minorities will be curbed. To resolve ethnic conflict due to economic inequality, Gomez (2008, 13) strongly recommends the introduction of 'an electoral system that encourages moderation as well as accommodates difference, a government led by a coalition of parties representing different interest groups that promotes dialogue and encourages politicians to seek compromises that eventually help benefit all communities'.

In my view, these authors (including those who criticise Chua's perspective) have made significant contributions in opening up discussion and debate on the relationship between democratisation and minority rights. But I also wish to point out that they have largely ascribed a passive and powerless role to the minorities. The locus of power is assumed to be within the ruling classes while the minorities are perceived as passive and powerless outsiders. This literature does not touch on the active and dynamic role of the minorities in shaping their destinies as well as that of their countries, and in dealing with the democratisation process.

3.2 Democratisation in Post–New Order Indonesia

Suharto's authoritarian rule ended in 1998 amid the Asian financial crisis (Suryadinata 2001, 506). Social unrest in Indonesia, aggravated by the financial crisis, escalated and peaked in mid-May in Jakarta and other parts of the country. Chinese shops and properties were looted and burned down; it was alleged that many Chinese women were brutally tortured, raped, and murdered (Mackie 1999, 189).[1] According to the Joint Fact-Finding Team (Joint Team) appointed by the Habibie government to investigate the riots, the violence was probably instigated by someone 'at the country's "highest levels" of decision-making' to create a critical upheaval so that martial law could be imposed (The Joint Fact-Finding Team [TGPF], 2013). Leo Suryadinata (2001, 507) suggests another possible scenario, that the violence was an outcome of internal conflict within the military.[2] It has also been argued that the violence was instigated by the military to deflect public anger from the Suharto regime and towards the Chinese minority (Heryanto 1999, 327). However, to date there is still no concrete evidence available and therefore it is difficult to prove such involvement conclusively.

The fall of Suharto in May 1998 led to a process of democratisation in Indonesia, with the implementation of a few significant institutional reforms. During the New Order, political activities were highly restricted. The populace was thought of as a 'floating mass' which had no role to play in politics except during the period of the national elections every five years.

---

1. However, as Hoon (2008) stated in his published dissertation, the rapes are still 'a contested issue as there has been no consensus on the number of rape victims' and 'there is still a general denial of the rapes in Indonesia's official discourse' (46).
2. Suryadinata (2001, 507) points to the power struggle between General Prabowo Subianto, Suharto's son-in-law, and General Wiranto, Suharto appointee. According to this analysis, Prabowo instigated the violence to discredit Wiranto, who was the then commander of the armed forces, so that he could seize power from the latter.

These elections, referred to as 'festivals of democracy', allowed the country to look like a functioning 'democracy' even though the outcomes of the elections were fixed through various means (Shiraishi 1994, 75–99; Clear 2005, 142). The number of political parties had been confined to three—i.e., Golkar (Golongan Karya, controlled by President Suharto), the Development Unity Party (PPP), and the Indonesian Democratic Party (PDI)—and had to be approved by the government (Lindsay 2007, 58; Suryadinata 2002a, 74).[3] Anyone involved in PPP and PDI would find themselves potentially excluded from the patronage links of power that ran through Golkar (Vickers 2005, 175).

After succeeding to the presidency on May 21, 1998, B. J. Habibie attempted to distance himself from the previous highly centralised authoritarian regime and to gain legitimacy for his *reformasi* government. On January 28, 1999, the Habibie government passed a new law on political parties (Law No. 2/1999) which permitted the formation of parties based on any principle and aspiration that did not conflict with the *Pancasila*, the official philosophical foundation of the Indonesian state (King 2000, 90; Abdulbaki 2008, 158).[4] However, communist and separatist parties were and are still prohibited. The new law removed restrictions on forming political parties, thus allowing people to organise themselves. The first free and open elections since 1955 were held in June 1999 (Suryadinata 2002a, vii; Hadiz and Robison 2005, 231; Wessel 2005, 12). In 2004 Indonesians were also given their first opportunity to elect the president and vice-president directly (Suryadinata 2005). There have been four rounds of legislative elections and numerous local direct elections since the end of Suharto's autocracy. In general, there are many different political parties competing in these elections, which have on the whole been carried out democratically and peacefully.[5] Post–New Order elections saw the rise of a few new major political parties. These included

---

3. Golkar was originally founded as 'Joint Secretariat of Functional Groups' (Sekber Golkar, Sekretariat Bersama Golongan Karya) by Indonesian military leaders in 1964. The objective of the organisation was to counterbalance the increasing influence of the Indonesian Communist Party (PKI). After Suharto came to power, he turned the organisation into 'the electoral vehicle of the New Order regime' (Tomsa 2008, 36).

4. *Pancasila* comprises five principles: 'Belief in the one and only God', 'Just and civilized humanity', 'The unity of Indonesia', 'Democracy guided by the inner wisdom in the unanimity arising out of deliberations amongst representatives' and 'Social justice for the whole of the people of Indonesia' (Embassy of The Republic of Indonesia, Washington D.C. 2008).

5. However, it should be noted that small-scale violence had occurred during direct elections for local government heads in some locations. These incidents of violence included 'destroying political parties' campaign materials, . . . persecution, destructive demonstrations and clashes between supporters of rival candidates' ('Local Elections are a Violent Business' 2013). Large-scale violence that resulted in deaths broke out in conflict areas such as Aceh and Papua. In the face of these incidents of violence, Home Minister Gamawan Fauzi stated that he would recommend the government to switch back to the former indirect election system whereby local government heads were elected by local assembly members

the Indonesian Democratic Party of Struggle (PDI-P),[6] led by Sukarno's daughter, Megawati Sukarnoputri; the National Awakening Party (PKB, Partai Kebangkitan Bangsa), led by Abdurrahman Wahid, the leader of Nahdlatul Ulama, the largest mass-based Muslim organisation in Indonesia; the National Mandate Party (PAN, Partai Amanat Nasional), led by Amien Rais, the leader of Muhammadiyah, the second-largest mass-based Muslim organisation in Indonesia; the Prosperous Justice Party (PKS, Partai Keadilan Sejahtera), an Islamic party which adopts Islam as its ideological basis; and the Democratic Party (PD, Partai Demokrat), the political vehicle of retired general Susilo Bambang Yudhoyono (Suryadinata 2002a; Ananta, Arifin, and Suryadinata 2005; Tomsa 2010). The 2009 election also saw the emergence of two new parties founded and led by controversial retired generals, i.e., the Great Indonesian Movement Party (Gerindra, Partai Gerakan Indonesia Raya), founded and led by Prabowo Subianto, and the People's Conscience Party (Hanura, Partai Hati Nurani Rakyat), founded and led by Wiranto (Tomsa 2010). However, it should be noted that Golkar, an integral part of the New Order, has remained a major player in the post-Suharto political landscape. This shows how New Order power relations, practices, and institutions have not been totally 'reformed' through *reformasi*, but have persisted even with the supposed end of the New Order regime. I will elaborate more on the background and ideology of these political parties in Chapter 6.

In order to accommodate growing regional and local demands for greater autonomy in the access to local resources and the control of local political machineries, the post-Suharto government also introduced regional decentralisation and local autonomy policies under two umbrella laws, Law No. 22/1999 and Law No. 25/1999. Under the decentralisation laws and regulations, significant administrative powers in industry, trade, investments, agriculture, public works, transport, cooperatives, labour, land, health care, education and culture, and environmental issues were transferred from the central government to regional and local governments (Heryanto and Hadiz 2005, 261; Hadiz and Robison 2005, 233). According to scholar-bureaucrat Ryaas Rasyid (2003), who was appointed by President Habibie to form a group known as the Team of Ten (Tim Sepuluh) to formulate the decentralisation laws and regulations, 'The [decentralisation] policy was intended to provide more scope for local creativity and initiative in making policy and promoting public participation' (64). Therefore, it can be said that in the context of Indonesia, one of the objectives of the regional decentralisation was to promote democratisation at the local level. This policy direction was

---

if violence continued to break out during local direct elections ('Local Elections are a Violent Business' 2013).

6. The PDI-P is a splinter party from the old PDI. It was formed by Megawati's faction in early 1999 (Suryadinata 2002a, 79, 84; Sherlock 2004, 25–26).

also strengthened by the introduction of direct elections for local government heads in 2005 (referred to as *pilkada*, or *'pemilihan kepala daerah'*; see Erb and Sulistiyanto [2009]). There have been numerous local direct elections since 2005. These elections saw the rise of several local government heads who were not associated with the Suharto regime, such as Joko Widodo, a.k.a. Jokowi; Basuki Tjahaja Purnama, a.k.a. Tjoeng Wan Hok (鍾萬學) (or better known by his affectionate Hakka nickname 'Ahok'); Tri Rismaharini; and Ganjar Pranowo.

One of the surprises of the decentralisation process, as pointed out by Henk Schulte Nordholt and Gerry van Klinken (2007), was the fragmentation of territories. In the space of 10 years, the number of provinces increased from 26 to 33 while the number of districts increased from 293 (1999) to 491 (2009) (Putri and Kusuma 2012). This fragmentation of administrative regions into smaller units is known as *pemekaran*, which literally means 'blossoming'. According to Schulte Nordholt and van Klinken (2007), the real objective of such administrative fragmentation was 'to increase bureaucratic jobs' (19). Interestingly, aspiring regional bureaucratic and political elites often mobilised ethnic sentiments in campaigns to establish new provinces or districts (Schulte Nordholt and van Klinken 2007, 2; Aspinall 2011, 306).

Although Indonesia went through a huge transition after the fall of Suharto, there are many who query whether this transition was a fully democratic one. As stated above, scholars such as Diamond (1999, 8–16) and Haynes (2001, 6–10) would classify post–New Order Indonesia as an 'electoral democracy' instead of a façade or pseudo-democracy, as was the case under the reign of Suharto, when elections were heavily controlled by the ruling party and legal alternative parties were denied a fair and authentic opportunity to compete for power.[7] However, there are other factors, as mentioned above, which are crucial to the emergence of a 'full democracy' by their definitions, and many reasons for questioning Indonesia's transition to a 'full democracy'. Although many scholars have shown optimism about Indonesia's democratisation process, because of electoral reforms, decentralisation, and the decline of the armed forces' role in politics (Abdulbaki 2008, Crouch 2010), there are also those who have pointed to serious flaws in Indonesia's democratisation process. For example, some scholars offer critical analyses of democratisation in post-Suharto Indonesia by highlighting the decay of state institutions, rampant corruption in the bureaucracy, and the capture of the new political parties and institutions by old as well as some new predatory interests in post-Suharto Indonesia. For example, both Marcus Mietzner (2008, 244–48) and Jamie S. Davidson (2009a, 294) point

---

7.   Diamond (1999, 15) regards such regimes as pseudo-democracies instead of non-democracies, since pseudo-democracies tolerate formally legal alternative parties and organisational pluralism to a certain extent. Such tolerance is absent in non-democracies.

out that corruption and internal mismanagement continue to characterise the bureaucracy in the country. Amy Freedman and Robert Tiburzi (2012) opine that, while Indonesia has made significant progress in the democratisation process, it is at the same time undermined by various hurdles such as rampant corruption and the poor enforcement of the rule of law. Howard Dick and Jeremy Mulholland (2011) coined the term *political marketplace* for the post–New Order Indonesian state, as the state was marked by money politics. Since membership dues and state subsidies for political parties are minimal, political parties and factions need slush funds to function. They obtain slush funds from ministries, agencies, and state enterprises competing for influence in the drafting and passage of laws as well as in the facilitating of favourable committee hearings through bribing parliamentarians. With regard to money politics within political parties, Dick and Mulholland point out that 'positions and parliamentary seats are allocated by internal auction, moderated by patronage and influence' (76).

In addition, Vedi R. Hadiz (2003; 2010) argues that, due to the absence of an effective, genuinely reformist party or political coalition, the predatory politico-business interests nurtured under the New Order managed to reconstitute and reorganise themselves successfully within the new political and economic regimes. Most of these predatory interests were previously entrenched at the lower layers of the New Order's vast and lucrative patronage network. This network extended from Jakarta all the way down to the provinces, cities, *kabupatens*, and villages. Although such a centralised system of patronage no longer exists after the fall of Suharto, its elements managed to reinvent and consolidate themselves in the new political parties and institutions. Such newly decentralised and competing predatory interests include ambitious political fixers, entrepreneurs and enforcers, state bureaucrats, newly ascendant business groups, and a wide range of political gangsters, hooligans, and thugs. They compete to gain ascendancy at the local level of politics, as regional decentralisation has created new rent-seeking opportunities for individuals in local governments. In other words, corruption—or what Indonesians generally call KKN (the Indonesian-language acronym for corruption, collusion, and nepotism)—has devolved from the central to local governments. Such incomplete democratisation, or democratisation without rule of law, has constrained what the ethnic Chinese have been able to do, particularly in business, and made their situation more complex. This will be further explored in the chapters to come.

According to Vedi R. Hadiz and Richard Robison (2005),[8] the absence of an effective, genuinely reformist party or political coalition in post-Suharto Indonesia is an important legacy of the New Order rule, which successfully

---

8. See also Hadiz (2000, 15; 2005b, 125).

disorganised civil society. During the New Order, mass-based social and political movements were systematically destroyed and paralysed in the name of eliminating the political Left, which was deemed a supporter and ally of the Indonesian Communist Party (PKI). As a result, the working class continued to be poorly organised and lacked political coherence. The emerging urban middle class and bourgeoisie, which largely basked in their position of privilege during the high economic growth period, grew increasingly conservative. This led to an extreme difficulty for reformist elements within civil society in organising coherently and effectively. Therefore, it is no surprise that when the structures of authoritarian rule finally came to an end, it was the predatory politico-business interests that included the ethnic Chinese *cukong*s and conglomerates nurtured by the New Order that were 'in the best position to take advantage of the opening up of political space' (Hadiz and Robison 2005, 232). Maxwell Lane (2015) makes a similar argument that the extreme political repression during the New Order era had eliminated 'all political traditions that may have provided an ideological basis for opposition—such as liberalism, liberal democracy, social democracy, socialism, and communism' (2). This resulted in the inability of the *reformasi* movement to develop a solid structure for competing with various political forces formerly nurtured under the New Order.

In fact, with regard to the relationship between democracy and civil society, Robert D. Putnam (1993; 1995) maintains that a strong and vibrant civil society is a precondition to the consolidation of democracy. According to Putnam (1993), strong bonds among civil society groups will generate social capital, i.e., 'features of social organization, such as trust, norms, and networks' (167). The social capital helps to facilitate coordinated actions among members of a community for mutual benefit and subsequently strengthens the state and the economy. This will bolster effective democratic governance. In order to foster wider cooperation, Putnam argues that networks of civil society groups should cut across salient social cleavages and be autonomous from politics. But Michael W. Foley and Bob Edwards (1996) criticise Putnam for focusing solely on the role of horizontally structured apolitical organisations and downplaying the ability of social-movement groups in advancing democracy. They also question the ability of such apolitical organisations to shape political participation and promote democracy 'without engaging in specifically political issues and without representing compelling social interests' (Foley and Edwards 1996, 41). They propose that 'social-movement organizations, grassroots interest groups, and grassroots political associations of all sorts' (Foley and Edwards 1996, 49) are more likely to advance citizens' interests and promote democracy. The more intensely a civil society engages in public and political issues as well as represents compelling social interests, the more likely it will be able to advance effective democratic governance.

I agree with Foley and Edwards's view because in the Indonesian case, the *reformasi* movement that played a crucial role in bringing down the Suharto regime comprised a cross-section of society, that is, university students, social activists, middle-class politicians, and intellectuals, all calling for the resignation of Suharto and his regime (Aspinall 2005). However, it should be noted that, although the movement succeeded in forcing Suharto to resign, the New Order regime did not enter into a thorough unravelling, as Hadiz, Robison, and Lane suggest. Golkar and most of Suharto's cronies remained powerful and influential in the political arena. The end of the Suharto regime did not lead to the consolidation of political opposition forces since the *reformasi* movement lacked a clear social base and effective organising vehicles that were crucial in establishing a viable alternative political choice to Indonesians.

J. Danang Widoyoko (2011) argues that the pervasive and systematic corruption in Indonesia 'is typical of a highly fragmented polity with a weak civil society' (165). The end of Suharto's highly centralised, autocratic regime led to the fragmentation of power and produced new power centres. This created mushrooming corruption throughout the entire country. Corruption flourishes in a new democracy because the wider society and organised interest groups are too weak to prevent it (Widoyoko 2011, 168–69). Interestingly, a recent volume on the illegal practices of state institutions in Indonesia, edited by Edward Aspinall and Gerry van Klinken (2011), argues that corruption and illegal activities by government officials in various sectors[9] are not just deviations from the normal operation of the state but also part of the state-formation process. Therefore, Aspinall and van Klinken emphasise that eradicating illegal practices in state institutions requires a new form of state that is embedded in a politically engaged citizenry (28).

Therefore, as Hadiz (2005a, 48) argues, the end of the New Order has not been followed by greater popular participation in politics. Movements and organisations representing the interests of lower classes such as labour and the urban poor have remained excluded from political contests. Hadiz and Robison (2005) further point out that political newcomers who genuinely promote reforms and do not associate with predatory networks 'often find themselves constrained in what they are able to achieve' (235). Most of them are academics and activists from various non-governmental organisations (NGOs). For their own survival in political contestations, they have little choice but to latch onto existing predatory coalitions with more established financial resources and an apparatus of violence.

---

9. Including election campaigns, the judiciary, the education sector, and the construction industry.

Mietzner holds a slightly different view with regard to civil society in post–New Order Indonesia. While emphasising that the democratisation process in Indonesia was undermined by anti-reformist elites, Mietzner (2012) nevertheless opined that civil society in the country 'has been vital in ensuring that recent elite attempts to overturn democratic reforms did not throw Indonesia into a full democratic recession' (217). For instance, when conservative elites attempted to take over the General Elections Commission (KPU, Komisi Pemilihan Umum), civil society organisations and the media actively resisted such an attempt and demanded that the KPU be freed from political party influence. Later, President Yudhoyono's Democratic Party (PD) began to oppose the inclusion of political parties into the KPU and, subsequently, the initial proposal to let political parties take over the commission has been shelved. Thus, Mietzner (2012) asserts that 'the impact of these elite manoeuvres has been mitigated by resistance from civil society, making Indonesia more a case of democratic stagnation than of full-blown regression' (211). He also notes that civil society in post–New Order Indonesia has its own internal problems that are closely related to the lack of coordination and cooperation between highly professional NGOs based in Jakarta and less developed civil society groups in the regions (Mietzner 2012, 222). This implies that civil society as a whole in post–New Order Indonesia is fragmented and unable to influence the government.[10]

Edward Aspinall (2010) asserts that the accommodation of predatory political forces nurtured by the New Order in Indonesia's new democracy forestalled their attempts to resist and destroy the democratic system from the outside. Therefore, the low quality of democracy is the price of Indonesia's steady democratic progress. He makes a paradoxical remark that 'the success of Indonesia's democracy and its poor quality are two sides of the same coin. It was precisely by achieving a low-quality outcome that Indonesian democratisation proceeded so smoothly' (Aspinall 2010, 32).

Apart from the corrupt and illegal practices that continue plaguing state institutions as well as the capture of the new political and economic regimes by the old (and some new) predatory interests, there are other hurdles that undermine the democratisation process. For instance, with regard to the military in post–New Order era, despite the positive official stances of the government and the military leadership towards military reform, the military remains powerful. Although some military officers indicted for human rights crimes in East Timor were prosecuted and found guilty, the sentences were later overturned (Kammen 2012, 111–12). Moreover, decentralisation reforms

---

10. Mietzner (2012, 222) therefore proposes that in order to protect democratic achievements in Indonesia, international donors should strengthen civil society by continuing to offer financial support to NGOs (based both in and outside Jakarta) instead of shifting the focus of aid to the Indonesian government.

have (ironically) opened up more opportunities for local military commanders to have more control over local budgets and decision-making processes (Croissant, Chambers, and Völkel 2011, 198). Harold Crouch (2010, 161) points out that the inability of the government to provide the military with adequate funding is the greatest hurdle to military reform. Since the end of the authoritarian regime, the military budget has remained very low. In 2000, a major-general was paid only Rp. 1.6 million (about US$200 at that time) every month, while the official basic monthly salary of a corporal was only Rp. 850,000 (about US$100) (Crouch 2010, 167). Therefore, most military (and police) officers relied on private semi-legal and illegal means to earn more funds to finance their daily operations. Some worked as security guards in commercial enterprises to earn extra income. In small towns, ethnic Chinese businesspeople make regular financial 'contributions' to local commanders to gain guaranteed military protection in the event of anti-Chinese violence. Besides that, local military and police units extract financial 'contributions' from both legal and illegal businesses such as logging, mining, and fishing in exchange for their 'protection' on those businesses. Military units are also involved in smuggling (Crouch 2010, 166).

In addition, efforts to bring an end to military-controlled businesses have, to date, largely failed. The military resisted the transfer of its business holdings to the government by selling a part of its stake to private commercial companies. Thereby, the assets could no longer be classified as military business enterprise and could not be transferred to the government (Crouch 2010, 168; Human Rights Watch 2010). Although the government later formed an inter-ministerial team in 2009 to oversee the partial reform of military-controlled businesses, the team does not have clear authority over the military and its businesses, and lacks independence because it is dominated by the ministry of defence (Human Rights Watch 2010, 1, 12). It can therefore be said that post–New Order governments have been half-hearted in pushing for reforms in the military.

In addition, the end of the New Order did not reduce the influence of *preman* (gangster/thug), paramilitary, and militia groups in Indonesia. These groups are closely related. The origins of the *preman* go back to the 1945–1949 revolution and the late 1950s. According to Ian Wilson (2010, 201), during the revolution, strongmen and toughs were at the forefront of the struggle for Indonesia's independence. Many of them were later incorporated into the new national military. In 1954, General Nasution, the head of the armed forces, 'deployed networks of gangsters and former militias as part of a campaign to pressure Sukarno into suspending parliamentary democracy, eventually ushering in the period known as "Guided Democracy"' (Wilson

2010, 201).[11] The Pancasila Youth (PP, Pemuda Pancasila), the largest quasi-official youth/crime organisation, was formed out of this alliance. In the mid-1960s, the military mobilised the PP and local gangsters to confront and crush suspected members of the communist party (Ryter 2000, 19; 2001; 2002; Hadiz 2004, 626). Former governor of North Sumatra Syamsul Arifin, as interviewed in *The Act of Killing*, a 2012 documentary film about the anti-communist genocide, acknowledged the important role of gangsters in eliminating communism in Indonesia: 'Communism will never be accepted here, because we have so many gangsters, and that's a good thing' (cited in the subtitles of *The Act of Killing*, 2012). Under Suharto, the institutionalisation of local gangsters was furthered intensified (Wilson 2011, 242). Apart from the PP, other quasi-official youth/crime organisations such as the Army Veterans' Youth (PPM, Pemuda Panca Marga) and the Armed Forces Sons' and Daughters' Communication Forum (FKPPI, Forum Komunikasi Putra-Putri Purnawirawan Indonesia) were formed to help maintain political order and stability through violence and intimidation (Ryter 2001; 2005, 22; Beittinger-Lee 2009, 164). These organisations are generally considered to be 'fronts for *preman* activity' (Hadiz 2003, 125–26), and were usually backed and protected by the military during the New Order period (Ryter 2000, 20). Thus, such organisations are also known as '*preman* organisations' (Wilson 2010, 200). (I will hereafter use the terms 'youth/crime organisations' and '*preman* organisations' interchangeably.) Therefore, it can be said that the distinction between *preman*, soldier, politician, and criminal is often blurry.

These quasi-official youth/crime organisations were particularly influential in Jakarta and North Sumatra (Ryter 2002). Members were mostly indigenous *preman* with criminal backgrounds. There are ethnic Chinese members in these organisations but their number is very small compared to that of indigenous members. Two well-known examples were Anton Medan, a.k.a. Tan Hok Liang (陳福良), and Yorrys Raweyai. Medan is a Chinese Muslim and Raweyai is a mixed Chinese-Papuan. Both used to be prominent figures in the criminal underworld, especially the early 1980s gambling scene in Jakarta. Medan was also allegedly involved in inciting the May 1998 riots and in burning down the house of Liem Sioe Liong, one of Suharto's cronies. Both Medan and Raweiyai were later racially targeted by their indigenous counterparts (Tsai 2011, 146n66; Ryter 2001, 125n4, 150, 150n76; Setyautama 2008, 357).

Preman also demanded to be given the opportunity to provide informal protection services in exchange for money (Beittinger-Lee 2009, 164). Many Chinese Indonesians were their clients. As cited by Ryter (2001), a field operative of the PP in Jakarta admitted that 'PP lives from the Chinese' (152).

---

11. For the background and characteristics of Guided Democracy, see Ricklefs (2008, 292–321).

After the unravelling of the New Order regime, despite losing their main backer, *preman* have survived by taking advantage of the inability of the post–New Order regimes to maintain security and the opportunities opened up by competitive electoral politics as well as regional decentralisation. Many political parties have established their own paramilitary wings or civilian militia known as *satgas parpol* (*satuan tugas partai politik*, i.e., political party militias). Members mostly come from youth/crime organisations such as the PP and '[mercenaries] of the disenfranchised urban milieu' (King 2003).[12] Moreover, *preman* still dominate the protection racket scene in Indonesia. According to Christian Chua (2008, 92–93), and as mentioned in an interview with an NGO activist in Medan (interview with Halim, in Indonesian, July 26, 2010), many well-established businesspeople (including ethnic Chinese) hire *preman* to protect their business, to break up strikes, or to intimidate business competitors and media that report negatively about them. In the 2009 general assembly of the PP, then Vice President Jusuf Kalla even openly defended the *preman* and emphasised their importance to Indonesia: 'We need a *preman* to run the economy, the market. We need adventurous people to engage in fair [economic] development' (cited in 'Kalla Says "Thug" Needed to Run Indonesia' 2009). Therefore, as Phil King (2003) observes, 'Reformasi was a liberalisation of both party politics and underworld criminal activities'. Some scholars have even opined that post–New Order Indonesia is becoming a '*preman* state' (Lindsey 2001; Schulte Nordholt 2002).

3.3 Democratisation, Decentralisation, and Ethnic Minorities in Indonesia

It is evident that the situation of ethnic minorities in Indonesia is varied. The Chinese represent a particular type of ethnic minority with quite different experiences than those of indigenous minority groups across the country. Edward Aspinall (2011) and Jacques Bertrand (2004; 2010) propose perspectives that focus on the agency of minority groups in dealing with democratisation and decentralisation since the end of the New Order. Aspinall opines that the opening up of democratic politics since the downfall of Suharto and the devolution of political and fiscal authority to local governments have provided opportunities for regional minorities to mobilise ethnicity in contesting for political power in local politics. Regional minority elites have been attempting to resuscitate tradition (*adat*) and traditional ethnic

---

12. The *satgas* were banned in 2004 but later revived in a less formal way (Wilson 2010, 204–5).

political institutions associated with particular ethnic identities.[13] In doing so, the elites are able to demonstrate that they are fit to rule when competing for political power. But Aspinall also notes that, as the new democratic system has settled into place (after 2001), the political salience of ethnicity has declined. Local politics has been marked by bargaining and cooperation between different ethnic groups. It can be said that the emergence of democratisation and decentralisation in Indonesia has opened up opportunities for regionally based indigenous minorities (as opposed to the ethnic Chinese, Arabs, and Indians) to compete for political power through inter-ethnic cooperation and this has, in turn, shaped pluralism in Indonesian politics.

Bertrand argues that the emergence of democratisation and decentralisation in post–New Order Indonesia opened up opportunities for certain minority groups to renegotiate their position in the country. Such renegotiation was made manifest in the form of violent conflicts involving various indigenous minority groups, particularly from 1999 to 2002. These included clashes between Muslims and Christians in Maluku (1999) and in Poso, Central Sulawesi (1999); Dayak-Madurese (1996–1997) and Dayak and Malay-Madurese (1999) conflicts in West Kalimantan; Dayak-Madurese conflicts in Central Kalimantan (2001); and the intensification of conflicts in East Timor, Aceh, and Papua (1999). Bertrand (2010) argues that ethnic relations in Indonesia were greatly influenced by the formation of an Indonesian national model 'characterized by the concept of a single nation and secular but religious state' (97).[14] Under the New Order regime, this model was reaffirmed, modified, and intensified primarily through repression. This process involved marginalising and creating tensions for certain minority groups. The downfall of the Suharto regime and the subsequent democratisation and decentralisation processes created uncertainties about future outcomes and opened up opportunities for certain minority groups to renegotiate their inclusion, or the terms of their inclusion, in the Indonesian national model. According to Bertrand (2010),

> Groups that had been integrated by force during the Suharto regime [i.e., East Timorese and Papuans] saw opportunities to remobilize and demand secession or significantly greater autonomy. Those that had been marginalized [such as the Dayaks of Kalimantan], either through repression or displacement in the name of development, could demand redress. Tensions among Muslims and Christians in some areas also were high, since the New Order regime had changed the balance of power between the two groups and demands were being made to revisit the status of Islam in the polity. These sets of tensions were embedded in the institutional structures that

---

13. For more details on the *adat* revivalism in post-Suharto Indonesia, see Davidson and Henley (2007).
14. See McVey (2003) for a detailed historical account of the formation of the Indonesian national model.

the New Order regime had established, as well as the way in which it had implemented its vision of Indonesia's national model. With its fall, the conditions were ripe for reopening terms of inclusion, in some cases through violent means. (97–98)

In other words, the collapse of the authoritarian regime and the emergence of democratisation as well as decentralisation opened opportunities for marginalised groups to seek 'better inclusion and more respect for their needs' (Bertrand 2010, 93), and for regionally based minority groups to demand greater autonomy or even independence. In this process, the minority groups shaped their destinies as well as the process of democratisation. Unlike regionally based minority groups, the Chinese could not mobilise their ethnicity in contesting for local political power because they do not have particular regions to identify with. However, they could appeal to their political ideals as a means to contest for political power. They also benefitted from the opening up of a relatively liberal socio-cultural environment following the end of the New Order because they could openly express and celebrate their ethnic and cultural identities. The open and active participation of the Chinese in the socio-political arena also contributed to multiculturalism and political activism in post-Suharto Indonesia.

Bertrand also points out that ethnic violence diminished significantly after Megawati Sukarnoputri became president in mid-2001. She was able to create a relatively stable institutional environment by forming a strong ruling coalition and establishing good relations with the armed forces. In addition, peace deals were reached in Maluku and Sulawesi. In Aceh and Papua, similar attempts to resolve existing crises were made with different degrees of success. East Timor was also officially separated from Indonesia in 1999 and became an independent state in 2002.

At first glance, Amy Chua's comments about democratisation bringing a backlash to deeply resented market dominant minorities seem to fit the situation of Indonesia in 1998, when Suharto stepped down from office and unleashed the forces of reform. The Chinese appeared to be a target for some of these forces, as was discussed above, with shops being burned and acts of atrocity being committed on Chinese individuals. However, as stated above, scholars' explanations of this violence have nothing to do with the actual process of reform or democratisation itself, but they argue that this violence served as an excuse for upheaval, or as camouflage, and was orchestrated by those in power, not by the resentful, poorer indigenous majority.

Although the position of the Chinese in Indonesian society may have restrained them in some ways, they still played an important role in shaping the reform process, which in turn contributed to their continuing ambivalent position. In fact, Mark R. Thompson (2011) attributes the weaknesses of the *reformasi* movement to the lack of support from the predominantly ethnic

Chinese capitalist class for the movement.[15] He points out that, due to its alien, 'pariah' status, the ethnic Chinese capitalist class in Indonesia has often been incapable of or reluctant to challenge the state. Hence, in 1998, the Chinese Indonesian bourgeoisie did not support the *reformasi* opposition movement that fought for the removal of Suharto from power. Had the capitalist class, including the ethnic Chinese, backed the reform movements, Indonesia might have seen a full-scale overthrow of the authoritarian regime and the rise of a new regime, like what happened in the Philippines and Thailand. In other words, in the case of Indonesia, a weak and alien bourgeoisie has made a half-hearted democracy more likely. In addition, Thompson argues that, due to the political passivity of the Chinese Indonesian bourgeoisie, the democratic system in post–New Order Indonesia has been relatively stable compared to that in the Philippines and Thailand, despite its many weaknesses.[16] This argument implies the significance of the agency of the Chinese Indonesian capitalist class in shaping the predatory nature of the new democracy and the incoherence of civil society in the *reformasi* era.

John Sidel (2006) and Jacques Bertrand (2004; 2010) point out that the period of reform and democratisation after the end of the authoritarian regime was actually marked by a considerable decline in anti-Chinese violence after May 1998. But they offer different explanations for this change. Sidel focuses on the role of state elites while Bertrand looks at the role of both the state and the Chinese minority. Sidel attributes the decline of anti-Chinese riots to state-dependent Muslim elites' engagement in straight religious competition, instead of using anti-Chinese violence to assume more political power. Bertrand offers a more comprehensive explanation, noting that the killings of May 1998, particularly the alleged mass rape cases, as well as the alleged involvement of the armed forces in the riots, shocked the political elite and Islamic politicians who had been most critical and vocal about Suharto's collusion with Chinese Indonesian big business groups. They began to sympathise with the Chinese minority and acknowledge that the Chinese had not been treated justly. Sarah Turner (2003) makes a similar remark: 'Since 1998 there has been an increased official and general

---

15. This does not mean the ethnic Chinese were totally absent from the reform movement. According to a newspaper interview with an ethnic Chinese social activist in Surabaya, and my interview with another ethnic Chinese social activist, in May 1998, there were a few ethnic Chinese social activists in Surabaya joining non-Chinese social activists and university students in street protests against Suharto and the New Order regime. Thus, they also played a role in bringing down the authoritarian regime ('Terlecut Kawan Jawa' 2009; interview with Dédé Oetomo, in English, December 24, 2010).

16. It should be noted that there were well-established Chinese businesspeople who backed reform-minded politicians such as Sofyan Tan in the 2010 Medan mayoral election and Dédé Oetomo in the 2004 legislative election. However, such businesspeople were rare. See Chapter 6 for more details.

acknowledgement within Indonesia that the ethnic Chinese community received gross injustices during the period of the riots' (347).

The reversal of attitudes towards the Chinese was also catalysed by capital flight and the 'exodus' of Chinese after the events of May 1998. In addition, some Chinese Indonesian tycoons had cooperated with post–New Order governments in investigations about corruption, which contributed further to the easing of resentment against the Chinese. Bertrand (2004) also notes that the prosecution and subsequent imprisonment of Bob Hasan (The Kian Seng 鄭建盛), Suharto's long-time crony and golf partner of Chinese descent, 'particularly pleased many Indonesians' (69). In other words, the end of Suharto's regime had removed Hasan, one of the most significant symbols of corruption in the Chinese minority.

Under the influence of a more sympathetic view from Indonesian political elites, Chinese Indonesians have begun to benefit from reforms introduced by subsequent governments. Many discriminatory measures against the Chinese were removed. Most significantly, Suharto's policy of forced assimilation was abandoned. In 2001, President Wahid sanctioned the publication of Chinese-language print media through the repeal of laws that had prohibited the local publication of Chinese characters in Indonesia since 1965; thus Chinese-language materials became more freely available. Many schools were allowed to conduct Chinese-language courses. Besides that, ethnic Chinese were allowed openly to celebrate Chinese festivals (Hoon 2008, 104; Giblin 2003, 347–48). In fact, in 2002, President Megawati Sukarnoputri announced that the Chinese New Year would be a state holiday from 2003 (Freedman 2003, 447). In July 2006, the Indonesian parliament passed a landmark bill on citizenship which took a step towards ending discrimination against ethnic Chinese Indonesians. The law did away with the distinction between 'indigenous' and 'non-indigenous' Indonesians—long cited by Chinese Indonesians as discrimination—by redefining 'indigenous Indonesian' to include all people born in Indonesia and/or to Indonesian parents, and who had never assumed foreign citizenship. Under the new law, Chinese Indonesians will no longer need to produce proof of their citizenship or undergo the naturalisation process as long as they were born to parents who are Indonesian citizens (Asmarani 2006, 1). They are also allowed to hold government posts, including the presidency, that were formerly closed to them.

Hence, the fall of Suharto in May 1998 was a turning point for the Chinese in Indonesia in terms of their open and active participation in the socio-political arena. The riots in May 1998 produced greater ethnic and political consciousness among ethnic Chinese Indonesians. They realised that if they wanted to defend themselves, they would have to become involved in the political process (Suryadinata 2001, 509).[17] Thus, a few Chinese have made use of the democratic environment to participate in national as well as local politics and to establish ethnic Chinese social and cultural organisations. The Chinese Indonesian Social Association (PSMTI) and the Chinese Indonesian Association (INTI) are two major ethnic Chinese organisations formed since the end of the New Order (Lembong 2008, 54). Both have branches in most provinces of the country. There are also Chinese Indonesians who actively participate in formal politics and run for public office under various political parties during general elections. This reflects the heterogeneous political views of the Chinese. Moreover, since the advent of democratisation, several Chinese Indonesians have taken the initiative to participate actively in political activities and social reform movements to fight for equal rights and an end to discriminatory practices. Hence, the Chinese minority enjoys a less vulnerable political position in the *reformasi* era.

But it is necessary to point out that, despite the abolition of several discriminatory policies and regulations, the position of the Chinese remains ambivalent in Indonesian society. The indigenous Indonesian population generally still perceives the Chinese as an alien minority because it does not have particular regions in the country to identify with and is associated with a homeland that is external to Indonesia. The stereotypes of Chinese Indonesians as wealthy, selfish, and exclusive are still common among indigenous Indonesians. Hence, although the Chinese enjoy more freedom in formal political participation, not many of them have been elected in general and local elections. The experience of Sofyan Tan in the opening story of this book clearly illustrates such an ambivalent position. In addition, the negative perceptions of the Chinese sometimes turn into overt hostility whenever there are high-profile cases involving illegal and semi-legal business practices committed by Chinese Indonesians.

For instance, in 2003, there were riots against the *Tempo* magazine headquarters by a group of *preman* supporting Tomy Winata (郭說鋒), a Chinese tycoon who owns the Artha Graha Group (GAG).[18] The riots happened a few days after *Tempo* published an article indicating that Winata might be behind a fire that struck the huge textile market in Tanah Abang, Jakarta. The article revealed that Winata had earlier made a Rp. 53 billion (about US$6.69 million) bid to renovate the market (Taufik, Rurit, and Junaedy, 2003a; 2003b). Winata allegedly sent his company's gang and the Indonesian Young Bulls (BMI, Banteng Muda Indonesia), a paramilitary organisation of the PDI-P, to the *Tempo* headquarters to demand the retraction of the article.

---

17. There were also Chinese Indonesians who moved to gated communities and hence retreated from the political process. See Tsai (2008; 2011) for more information on this issue.
18. The Artha Graha Group is a conglomerate that engages in banking as well as property and infrastructure development.

Chief editor Bambang Harymurti, editor Karaniya Dharmasaputra,[19] journalist Abdul Manan, and the journalist who wrote the article, Ahmad Taufik, were attacked and injured. Although several police were present during the riots, they did nothing to stop the attacks (Budiman and Manggut 2003; 'Law of the Concrete Jungle' 2003; Taufiqurrahman and Simanjuntak 2003). Winata also sued *Tempo* for defamation and biased reporting. *Tempo* lost the lawsuit and was ordered to pay Winata Rp. 500 million (about US$59,080 at that time) (Hantoro 2004).

According to Arief Budiman (2005, 95–96),[20] the brutal attack on *Tempo* resulted in public anger towards Winata, but this soon transformed into anger towards all Chinese Indonesians. As Budiman (2005) puts it,

> People felt that Winata's actions were 'typical Chinese' behaviour, especially for Chinese businessmen. They felt that the Chinese 'always' bribed state officials, particularly the police and the military. A considerable amount of commentary about the event was published on the Internet, including inflammatory anti-Chinese remarks. (95–96)

Fortunately, political and Muslim leaders such as former president Abdurrahman Wahid issued public statements that most Chinese Indonesians were decent and unlike Winata. This kept the anger under control (Budiman 2005, 96).

The utilisation of *preman* by Winata to intimidate *Tempo* not only threatened press freedom in the country but also reinforced negative stereotypes of Chinese Indonesians as corrupt, arrogant, and heartless. Most importantly, the incident clearly shows that the poor establishment of the rule of law in post-Suharto Indonesia allows well-established business elites to utilise thuggery and coercion provided by gangs and paramilitary groups for their personal gain.

Hence, I argue that the Chinese on the whole also play a role in shaping and perpetuating their continuing ambivalent position. In the following chapters, I will examine the strategies and tactics of local Chinese in post-Suharto Medan and Surabaya in gaining and safeguarding their interests in the aspects of business, the socio-cultural sphere, and electoral politics, and how these strategies and tactics at the same time shape and perpetuate the ambivalent position of the Chinese.

---

19. Karaniya Dharmasaputra is a Chinese Indonesian (Chinese name unknown). I would like to thank one of the reviewers for pointing this out.
20. Arief Budiman is a Chinese Indonesian. His Chinese name is Soe Hok Djin (史福仁). I would like to thank one of the reviewers for pointing this out.

3.4 Summary and Conclusion: Democracy in Indonesia

Amidst the diversity of views on Indonesia's democratisation in the post-1998 era, scholars generally agree that the post–New Order political system has offered more freedom for people to elect political leaders through free and relatively fair elections compared to previous regimes. As mentioned according to the typologies of Diamond (1999) and Haynes (2001), post-1998 Indonesia is considered an 'electoral democracy' because elections are conducted under 'meaningful rules and regulations' (Haynes 2001, 8). However, due to rampant corruption and internal mismanagement in state institutions, as well as the marginalisation of popular participation in political processes, Indonesia is still far from a 'full democracy' that promotes individual freedom, public participation in rule-making, and accountability of public officials to ordinary people (Haynes 2001, 10).

Based on the literature and debates above, it can be concluded that Indonesia has undergone significant institutional reforms and political liberalisation since the unravelling of Suharto's highly centralised, autocratic regime. The opening up of democratic politics has offered opportunities for the Chinese minority to participate directly in electoral politics and run for public office. The *reformasi* era has seen greater competition for state power and resources among political elites. The relatively liberal socio-cultural environment in the post–New Order era also allows the Chinese minority openly to express and celebrate their ethnic and cultural identities. However, the democratisation process has been marred by poor enforcement of the rule of law, the capture of state institutions and political parties by old as well as some new predatory interests, and rampant criminal gangs as well as political thuggery. In addition, civil society remains incoherent and too weak to function as a counterweight to the state. It can therefore be said that the end of the authoritarian regime has led to the emergence of a predatory, fragmented state and a fragmented, weak society. I argue that such a political environment allows some Chinese Indonesians to continue gaining wealth and protecting their personal interests through illegal or semi-legal means as well as opportunistic tactics. This contributes to the continuing, if not growing, ambivalent attitude held towards Chinese in Indonesia.

Part Two

Civil Society, Business, and Politics: The Ambivalent Position of the Chinese in Post-Suharto Indonesia

Part Two showcases how the mixed success of democratisation in post-Suharto Indonesia has created an even more ambivalent position for Chinese Indonesians. The end of the New Order regime has led to the emergence of democratisation and the removal of restrictions on Chinese cultural expression in Indonesia. The Chinese can openly and actively participate in the socio-political arena. However, due to the absence of an effective, genuinely reformist political force, democratisation in post–New Order Indonesia is undermined by various hurdles such as rampant corruption and the poor enforcement of the rule of law. In addition, the stereotype of Chinese Indonesians as wealthy, selfish, and exclusive is still common among indigenous Indonesians. Therefore, the Chinese remain the targets of extortion and corruption by power-holders and *preman*. But as I have shown in Part One, it is necessary to recognise that the Chinese on the whole are by no means passive bystanders in Indonesia's democratisation process, nor are they powerless victims of the problems of democratisation. They play an active and dynamic role in shaping their ambivalent position and the predatory nature of the new democracy. Part Two therefore suggests that in a newly democratised society without the establishment of good governance, the 'pariah' ethnic minorities tend to gain and protect their business and personal interests through illegal and semi-legal means as well as opportunistic tactics. These in return reinforce the negative stereotypes against them, and consequently reproduce their ambivalent position.

I show here how the bolstering of Chinese identity is manifested in the mushrooming of ethnic Chinese-based organisations and Chinese-language newspapers. Hence, Chinese ethnic and cultural identities have become increasingly visible in the post–New Order era. Moreover, the political liberalisation that has emerged since the unravelling of Suharto's highly centralised, autocratic regime allows the Chinese to get involved in politics and run for public office. However, in the face of the corrupt and muddy business environment in post-Suharto Indonesia, instead of backing genuine reform-minded electoral candidates during elections, some Chinese businesspeople support candidates who can promise them political favours and aid them in more corruption. Some Chinese businesspeople have become involved in politics to fight for the interests of their own business and not of the general public. They have resorted to money politics during their electoral campaigns. Therefore, the increasing visibility of the Chinese in sociocultural and political arenas has upset some indigenous Indonesians and has sometimes brought various threats and backlash against the Chinese. For instance, in the land seizures that involved three ethnic Chinese developers in North Sumatra that took place since November 2011, *Harian Orbit*, a local Indonesian-language newspaper in North Sumatra, referred to the three developers as 'slanted-eye businesspeople' (*pengusaha mata cipit* [*sic*]), clearly indicating their Chinese ethnicity. Furthermore, banners with provocative anti-Chinese words were displayed during the demonstrations against the land seizures.[1] Some Chinese community leaders are afraid of such possible threats and backlash if the Chinese are too visible. They therefore have urged the Chinese to keep a low profile and stay invisible.

At the same time, there are also Chinese Indonesians who chose to initiate and engage in cross-ethnic endeavours that seek to alter the indigenous Indonesians' perceptions of the Chinese. However, these endeavours are not well accepted by the majority of Chinese Indonesians. Therefore, the position of Chinese Indonesians as a whole is increasingly ambivalent and more complex in the post–New Order period.

---

1. I will elaborate more on the land seizures in Chapter 5.

4

Opening Up the Chinese Socio-cultural Sphere

The Ambivalence of Increasing Visibility*

The 2010 mayoral election in Medan not only featured Sofyan Tan as a mayoral candidate, as mentioned in the opening story in Chapter 1, but it also showcased Indra Wahidin (黃印華), another interesting Chinese Indonesian public figure. He is a well-known Chinese community leader in Medan, leading the North Sumatra branch of the Chinese Indonesian Association (INTI), as well as Perhimpunan Keluarga Besar Wijaya Medan, a Chinese surname clan association. These are two Chinese organisations that have recently focused on promoting Chinese culture among Chinese Indonesians. He is also the head of the North Sumatra branch of the Indonesian Buddhists Association (Walubi, or Perwakilan Umat Buddha Indonesia) and the China Committee of the North Sumatra Indonesian Chamber of Commerce and Industry. Wahidin is thus a Chinese with a strong ethnic identity. He studied in pre–New Order Chinese-medium schools and is Chinese-literate. Due to his literacy in Chinese, he is also in charge of *Medan Zao Bao*, a Chinese-language newspaper in Medan. Wahidin is an insurance agent by profession, though it is also rumoured that he is involved in paint distribution. Well connected to local power-holders in North Sumatra and state officials and businesspeople in China, he has been helping the North Sumatra provincial government to establish cultural and economic ties with China. He is therefore someone who strongly supports not only Chinese cultural identity, but also continuing ties to China.

However, Wahidin is an interestingly paradoxical figure. Although he appears to be in the forefront of new opportunities that the Chinese have in post-Suharto Indonesia to make their cultural and ethnic identities visible, he appears also to be frightened about what this visibility might mean for

---

* The names of informants in this chapter are pseudonyms except for the following public figures: Dédé Oetomo, Hendi Prayogo, Eddy Djuandi, Indra Wahidin, Ardjan Leo, William Rahardja, Liem Ou Yen, Alim Markus, Lim Ping Tjien, and Sofyan Tan.

attitudes towards the Chinese. Additionally, he continues to engage with gangster and criminal figures, as a way of ensuring the safety of his business, despite knowing that these connections put the Chinese in a bad light. As mentioned in the opening story of this book, during the 2010 Medan mayoral election, Wahidin led the North Sumatra branch of INTI in giving open support to Ajib Shah, a mayoral candidate who had been the head of the North Sumatra branch of the Pancasila Youth (PP), an influential youth/crime organisation in the province, important for business in Medan. It was alleged that Wahidin, who was close to *preman*, openly supported Ajib in exchange for political favours for his business. One informant's interpretation that puts this support in a different light, however, was that he supported Ajib in order to secure the safety of the local Chinese community. This is because Ajib was initially the candidate chosen by the Prosperous Peace Party (PDS), but they later revoked their support for Ajib in favour of Sofyan Tan, the only ethnic Chinese mayoral candidate in the election. Since Wahidin was afraid that Ajib would blame the local Chinese community for this matter and make trouble for them, he decided openly to support and campaign for Ajib.[1]

Later, when the brutal murder of a Chinese Indonesian couple took place in Medan in 2011, Wahidin urged the Chinese to keep a low profile and refrain from showing an extravagant lifestyle. This implies that Wahidin believed the murder of the couple could have been triggered by the perception of many local Chinese Indonesians as wealthy. This also clearly indicates his concern that the increasingly visible position of the Chinese minority might result in threats and backlash. He therefore thought it was better for the Chinese to stay invisible and refrain from moving too far beyond their (traditional) position.

Wahidin's imagining of Chinese ethnic and cultural identities is very different from that of Sofyan Tan. Wahidin is well aware of the paradoxical environment of the *reformasi* era. The emergence of a democratic and liberal socio-political environment was followed by increasing freedom and the opening of space for renewed cultural expression. As a result, the ethnic and cultural identities of the Chinese minority, which were hidden during the New Order period, have become increasingly visible. The Chinese have also become increasingly visible by actively getting involved in politics and running for public office. However, some Chinese community leaders such as Wahidin view such visibility with caution. To them, such visibility may mean becoming a potential target of backlash and creating more envy as well as hatred. They therefore see the visibility of Chinese ethnic and cultural

---

1. This interpretation was given by Surya, a media activist in Medan (interview in Indonesian, September 17, 2010).

identities in post-Suharto Indonesia as both a blessing and a curse, urging the Chinese to keep a low profile.

Tan, on the other hand, imagines Chinese ethnic and cultural identities in an entirely different way. He also adopts a different approach in dealing with the opening up of the socio-political space in post-Suharto Indonesia. Tan is far from a stereotypical Chinese. Unlike Wahidin, Tan did not have the opportunity to study in pre–New Order Chinese-medium schools because they were already closed down by the time he reached school age. His family usually spoke Indonesian at home and he had many indigenous Indonesian friends. Upon graduating with a medical degree in 1990, Tan decided not to open up his own clinic but to step out of his comfort zone and devote himself to the operation of an integrated school that aimed to promote inter-ethnic harmony. For Tan, the best way to combat prejudice and discrimination against the Chinese minority is through promoting cross-ethnic solidarity and understanding. Therefore, apart from establishing an integrated school, he also actively engages in fighting for the interests of SMEs (small and medium enterprises) in Indonesia, which in general are dominated by *pribumi*. In addition, he maintains a significant distance from China and never assists local governments in fostering cultural and business ties with China, unlike Wahidin and some Chinese organisation leaders. In the eyes of some Chinese Indonesians with a strong ethnic identity, Tan is closer to the indigenous population than to the Chinese community; they thus perceive him as culturally not 'Chinese' enough. This makes him a target of dislike among those Chinese. However, unlike Wahidin and some other Chinese Indonesians, Tan is not afraid of a potential backlash and threats against the Chinese for being too visible in the post-Suharto era. He insists that the Chinese have the right to get involved in politics without fearing any repercussion. As mentioned in Chapter 1, he set an example by running for a seat in the North Sumatra regional representatives council (DPD) in 2004 and contesting for the mayorship of Medan in 2010. He was committed to eliminating bureaucratic abuse and refrained from involvement in corruption, collusion, and nepotism (KKN). Therefore, unlike Wahidin, Tan is not close to power-holders and *preman*.

Wahidin and Tan thus represent two different Chinese ethnic and cultural identities in post-Suharto Indonesia. The former emphasises the revival of Chinese culture and the bolstering of Chinese ethnic identity. This often contributes to the view that the Chinese are very insular and exclusive and may result in a backlash from non-Chinese. The latter focuses on the integration of Chinese Indonesians into the wider Indonesian society through initiating and engaging in endeavours that seek to alter indigenous Indonesians' perceptions of the Chinese. I argue that the emergence of these different Chinese ethnic and cultural identities is due to different sociological characteristics of Chinese Indonesians. Wahidin, who represents the more conservative Chinese ethnic and cultural identities, studied in pre–New Order Chinese-medium schools and is Chinese-literate, whereas Tan, who represents the more inclusive Chinese ethnic and cultural identities, received his education in Indonesian-medium schools during the New Order and usually spoke Indonesian at home. Wahidin is actively engaged in business, whereas Tan is not involved in business activities. Wahidin is well connected to state officials and businesspeople in China, whereas Tan is closer to the indigenous Indonesian population, especially those from the grassroots community. Following Bourdieu's concept of habitus, both Wahidin and Tan are endowed with different kinds of cultural and social capital due to their different educational backgrounds and social networks; this results in two different habitus among them. These different habitus have led to the emergence of two different Chinese ethnic and cultural identities in post-Suharto Indonesia. These two different identities are manifested in two different approaches to opening up the Chinese socio-cultural sphere in post-Suharto Indonesia. One focuses on establishing ethnic-based, voluntary organisations that promote Chinese culture and socialisation activities among the Chinese. These organisations rarely engage in cross-ethnic initiatives that promote inter-ethnic solidarity and understanding. Some leaders of these organisations are afraid of potential threats and backlash if they go 'overboard' in celebrating their Chinese identity and culture. They therefore prefer to keep a low profile. Another approach focuses on reaching out to the wider society by establishing non-ethnic-based socio-cultural organisations to promote cross-ethnic understanding and solidarity. The leaders of these organisations believe such an approach is the best way to eliminate prejudice against the Chinese. They do not express fear of threats or a backlash for actively promoting their endeavours.

Following Giddens's structure-agency theory, this chapter examines how the opening up of a liberal socio-cultural environment in the post-Suharto era allows the two different approaches to opening up a Chinese socio-cultural sphere in post-Suharto Medan and Surabaya and how these approaches shape the socio-cultural environment in post-Suharto Indonesia, as well as contribute to ambivalent attitudes towards Chinese Indonesians. After giving a brief overview of the revival of ethnic and cultural identities in post-Suharto Indonesia, I introduce the major Chinese organisations and Chinese-language newspapers in post-Suharto Medan and Surabaya, and explore their activities that focus on promoting Chinese culture, assisting the local governments to establish cultural and business connections with China, philanthropy, and cross-ethnic understanding and solidarity. Then I discuss how indigenous Indonesians perceive the activities and endeavours of Chinese organisations, and explore how the Chinese in Medan and

Surabaya actively engage with and shape these attitudes through initiating and engaging in activities that shape the socio-cultural environment in post-Suharto Indonesia.

4.1 The Revival of Ethnic and Cultural Identities in Post-Suharto Indonesia

As detailed in the last chapter, the end of the New Order saw the revival of cultural expression and ethnic identity for minority groups across Indonesia. The cultural expression and ethnic identity of minority groups had been suppressed during the New Order period. According to Hoon Chang-Yau (2008),

> [T]he [cultural] plurality and pluralism fostered during the 1950s era of constitutional democracy were deemed by the New Order to threaten the nation's development and security, and so were suppressed through the introduction of SARA in the 1970s. SARA is an acronym that summarizes the sensitive issues of ethnicity (*suku*), religion (*agama*), race (*ras*) and interclass (*antar golongan*) differences. Under the banner of maintaining order and stability, all public discussions of issues related to SARA were prohibited. During the New Order, Indonesian citizens irrespective of their ethnicity, religion, class and gender were all imagined within a constructed homogeneous *Pancasila* national identity. Internally diverse identities were subsumed and overridden by this imagined and constructed national homogeneity. (16)

Jamie S. Davidson (2009b) also notes that 'The New Order discouraged public manifestation of SARA in any form, including organizations and discourse' (230n60).

The opening up of a liberal socio-cultural environment in post-Suharto Indonesia led to the revival of cultural expression and ethnic identity for minority groups across the country. David Henley and Jamie S. Davidson (2007) have noted that regional minorities have 'demanded the right to implement elements of *adat* or *hukum adat* (customary law) in their home territories' (1). As mentioned earlier in Chapter 3, regional minorities also mobilise ethnicity in contesting for political power in local politics.

Although the Chinese minority cannot mobilise their ethnicity in contesting for political power because they do not have particular regions to identify with, they have made use of the liberal socio-cultural environment openly to express and celebrate their ethnic and cultural identities. This is manifested in renewed cultural expression such as the open celebration of traditional Chinese festivals, the establishment of Chinese organisations and Chinese-language newspapers, and the opening of Mandarin learning centres as well as institutions. According to my informants in Medan and

Surabaya, after the abrogation of the Presidential Instruction no. 14/1967, which prohibited the practice of Chinese customs and religion in the public sphere in 2000, many Chinese Indonesians in both cities started openly to celebrate the Lunar New Year (interview with Surya, in Indonesian, September 1, 2012; interview with Dédé Oetomo, in English, December 24, 2010). The more open and liberal political environment has opened up an ideal breeding ground in which ethnic Chinese organisational activities can flourish. At the same time, the rise of China as an economic power has prompted the resurgence of ethnic identity among Chinese Indonesians.[2] As a result, post-Suharto Indonesia saw the mushrooming of ethnic Chinese–based organisations. Most ethnic Chinese organisations that were established or that re-emerged in the post-1998 period were Chinese clan organisations and alumni associations of pre-1965 Chinese-medium schools in Indonesia. Following the end of Suharto's rule, many Chinese organisations that were previously closed down re-emerged and those that had been converted to foundations dealing with health, religion, burial services, sports, or recreation began to include again socio-cultural activities that openly celebrate and promote Chinese traditions and culture in their routine activities. Two major ethnic Chinese mass organisations in post-Suharto Indonesia, i.e., the Indonesian Chinese Social Association (PSMTI) and the Chinese Indonesian Association (INTI), have branches that extend to various parts of Indonesia, including Medan and Surabaya. The objectives of both organisations are to

---

2. China has been experiencing significant economic growth since the implementation of its economic reform and its opening up to foreign direct investments in the late 1970s, as well as its entry into the World Trade Organisation in 2001. China is particularly competitive in labour-intensive industries due to its abundant supply of cheap labour (Leong 2006, 218). Some Chinese Indonesian businesspeople had taken advantage of the opportunities opened up by the booming Chinese economy to expand their business to China. However, as Leo Suryadinata (2006) and Michael Jacobsen (2007) argue, the rising mainland Chinese economy offers more opportunities only to large firms and conglomerates controlled by ethnic Chinese in Southeast Asian countries, including Indonesia, to expand their business abroad. Large firms and conglomerates are in a much better position to take advantage of the opportunities offered by the booming Chinese economy because they have access to huge amounts of capital and production assets, and are able to move their capital assets and production lines to China. In contrast, ethnic Chinese small and medium businesses do not benefit much from the expanding mainland Chinese market because they do not have sufficient capital assets to penetrate the Chinese market. Most small and medium businesses controlled by ethnic Chinese focus only on the domestic market and therefore are more dependent on local conditions such as the political environment and economic policy, combined with general perceptions of the Chinese in local communities. My fieldwork data corresponds to Suryadinata's and Jacobsen's argument as most of my informants who were owners of small and medium business focused only on the domestic market and did not market their products in China. To date, Chinese Indonesian businesspeople who have successfully expanded their business to China are mostly prominent business elites such as Liem Sioe Liong, a.k.a. Sudono Salim (owner of Salim Group); Mochtar Riady (李文正) and his son, James Riady (李白) (owners of Lippo Group); and Alim Markus (owner of Maspion Group) (Bolt 2000, 69–70; Chen 2005).

fight for the interests of Chinese Indonesians, to promote solidarity between ethnic Chinese and indigenous Indonesians, to promote social and cultural issues among Chinese Indonesians, and to advocate for the entry of Chinese Indonesians into electoral politics (Suryadinata 2001, 512–14; Giblin 2003, 357–58; Hoon 2008, 77–79).[3]

The existence of Chinese organisations dates back to the Dutch colonial period. Many were Chinese clan associations organised along surname, lineage, or dialect lines. The formation of Chinese clan associations is actually the direct result of the mass immigration of Chinese to Southeast Asia in the nineteenth and early twentieth centuries, as well as the minority status of the Chinese (Lim 1983, 3). Driven by poverty and political turmoil in China, many Chinese migrated to Southeast Asia to earn a better living and eventually a better life. These Chinese immigrants mostly originated from the coastal provinces of Fujian and Guangdong in southern China. Being in an alien land, early Chinese immigrants formed clan associations with the aim of providing help and support for the members. Some clan associations even provided financial assistance and bursaries for the children of their members. Such associations were (and are still) common within ethnic Chinese communities in Southeast Asian countries. Moreover, as mentioned in Chapter 2, in the midst of the Pan-Chinese Movement in the early twentieth century, the Chinese in the Indies formed organisations that promoted Chinese nationalism. These included the Tiong Hoa Hwe Koan (THHK), the Siang Hwee, and the Soe Po Sia. In addition, some Chinese organisations in Indonesia were alumni associations of pre-1965 Chinese-medium schools.

There were also Chinese triads or secret societies established in the Dutch East Indies but their activities were not widespread in the colony like their counterparts in British Malaya and Singapore.[4] According to Mary Somers Heidhues (1993), during the colonial period, ethnic Chinese in West Kalimantan, Bangka, and parts of Java formed triads or secret societies to fight against the Dutch regime. However, they were soon crushed by the colonial authorities. Bertil Lintner (2002) also suggests that since the number of the Chinese in the Dutch East Indies was much smaller than that in British Malaya, 'the East Indies Chinese were perhaps too dependent on Dutch goodwill to organise secret societies . . . [They] remained by and large

---

3. INTI is actually a breakaway faction of PSMTI. PSMTI established itself as an exclusively ethnic Chinese organisation in which only Chinese Indonesians could become full members. Non-Chinese Indonesians could only become honorary members. Some of the original members were uncomfortable with such a policy and subsequently left to form INTI. INTI accepts all Indonesian citizens who agree with the objective of the organisation to join as members (Giblin 2003, 357–58; Suryadinata 2001, 513–14).

4. For the origins and background of Chinese triads and secret societies in British Malaya and Singapore, see Mak (1981) and Comber (2009b).

faithful to the colonial masters who guaranteed their welfare and protected them against possible hostility from "the natives"' (293).

Apart from Chinese organisations, the Chinese in the Indies also established several Chinese-language newspapers. According to Leo Suryadinata (1997, 253–55), the emergence of Chinese-language newspapers was the direct result of the Pan-Chinese Movement in the early twentieth century. Early Chinese-language newspapers were all weeklies. The newspapers were either associated with the Soe Po Sia or the Siang Hwee. The first Chinese-language daily newspaper, *Xin Bao*, appeared in February 1921; it was followed by a few other Chinese-language dailies. When the Japanese invaded China in the 1930s, Chinese-language newspapers in the Indies were vocal in their opposition to the Japanese. Therefore, all Chinese-language newspapers were closed down during the Japanese occupation. After the end of the Second World War, some Chinese-language newspapers came back into circulation. A few new ones also came into being. Many of them were politically oriented towards the People's Republic of China (PRC) or the Republic of China (Taiwan) (Suryadinata 1997, 255–57).

After the military takeover in 1965, the Suharto regime imposed a social stigma on the Chinese minority as China- and communist-oriented (Hoon 2008, 37). Their culture and their very existence in Indonesia were branded by New Order politicians as 'the Chinese problem' (Allen 2003, 387). Consequently, the Suharto regime enforced assimilation policies to curtail Chinese culture and control the ethnic Chinese. Ethnic Chinese organisations were either closed down or converted to charitable foundations (*yayasan*) focusing on health, religion, burial services, sports, or recreation (Coppel 1983, 165).[5] Chinese-language newspapers were again prohibited, except for *Harian Indonesia* (印度尼西亞日報), produced by the government (Suryadinata 1997, 257).

The opening up of a liberal socio-cultural space since the end of the New Order has led to the 'revival' of Chinese organisations in Indonesia. There are several scholarly works on Chinese organisations in post-Suharto Indonesia. These include works by Leo Suryadinata (2001), Susan Giblin (2003), Hoon Chang-Yau (2008), and Aimee Dawis (2010). Their works introduce major Chinese-based or -led organisations that have emerged in Indonesia since the end of the Suharto regime. They also examine in detail the activities and endeavours of these major organisations in promoting Chinese culture and social activities among Chinese Indonesians, fighting discrimination and racism against the Chinese minority, and promoting

---

5. A similar mass suppression of Chinese organisations that were secret societies also took place in Singapore in 1958. However, the objective of the suppression was to eradicate criminal activities committed by secret societies rather than to eliminate communism like in Indonesia. See Goh (2002).

Opening Up the Chinese Socio-cultural Sphere 71

cross-ethnic understanding and solidarity. Two fairly recent endeavours by these organisations not covered extensively by these works involve assisting the local governments in establishing cultural and business connections with China, in addition to various philanthropic efforts.

After the end of the New Order, there were more than a hundred Chinese organisations established in Medan and Surabaya. Apart from the local branches of PSMTI and INTI, other major ethnic Chinese organisations in Medan include Medan Angsapura Social Foundation (Yasora Medan, or Yayasan Sosial Angsapura Medan, 棉蘭鵝城慈善基金會), a clan association for ethnic Chinese of Hui Chew origin;[6] and the North Sumatra Chinese Community Social and Education Association (MITSU-PSP, Perhimpunan Masyarakat Indonesia Tionghoa Sumatera Utara – Peduli Sosial dan Pendidikan, 印尼蘇北華社慈善與教育聯誼會), a coalition of Chinese organisations and Chinese community leaders in North Sumatra.

In Surabaya, after the May 1998 riots which brought significant losses and damage to many Chinese Indonesians and their businesses, a group of Chinese Indonesian activists formed the Committee of Social Concern of Surabaya (Kalimas, or Komite Aliansi Kepedulian Masyarakat Surabaya) with the objective of helping the victims of the riots and to promote racial harmony through inter-ethnic dialogues. According to its founder and chairperson, Hendi Prayogo (吳景賢) (interview in Indonesian, March 28, 2011), there were also some non-Chinese university students and social activists who joined the group. Kalimas ceased operation in 2000, as no serious riots had happened in Surabaya since 1998. Several Chinese members of Kalimas later joined the local branches of PSMTI or INTI (interview with Hendi Prayogo, in Indonesian, March 28, 2011).

Other major Chinese organisations in post-Suharto Surabaya include the Surabaya Chinese Association (PMTS, Paguyuban Masyarakat Tionghoa Surabaya, 泗水華裔聯誼會), a coalition of several Chinese organisations in the city; local branches of the Indonesian Chinese Entrepreneur Association (PERPIT, Perhimpunan Pengusaha Tionghoa Indonesia, 印尼中華總商會) and the Indonesian Chinese Entrepreneur Community (PERMIT, Perhimpunan Masyarakat and Pengusaha Indonesia Tionghoa, 印尼華商總會), two major ethnic Chinese entrepreneur associations; and Hwie Tiauw Ka Chinese Clan Association in Surabaya (PHTKS, Perkumpulan Hwie Tiauw Ka Surabaya, 泗水惠潮嘉會館), a clan association for Hakka-, Teochew-, and Cantonese-speaking Chinese.[7]

The post–New Order era also saw the unprecedented boom of Mandarin Chinese-language education, thanks to the strength of the People's Republic

---

6. Hui Chew is a city in Guangdong Province, China.
7. See Appendix II for a list of major Chinese organisations in post-Suharto Medan and Surabaya.

of China in the global economy and geopolitics. Many Chinese and non-Chinese Indonesians are keen to learn the language that was banned by the Suharto regime. In 1999, the Indonesian government approved Mandarin Chinese as an optional foreign language in national schools (Chia 2010, 454). Moreover, numerous Mandarin-language learning centres were established to meet demand. In 2004 alone, there were more than 3,000 Mandarin-language learning centres operating across Indonesia (Hoon 2008, 62). In the same year, the ministry of education in Indonesia began to cooperate with the Office of Chinese Language Council International (also known as the Confucius Institute Headquarters, or Hanban), a public institution affiliated with the ministry of education in China, to promote Mandarin-language education in Indonesia. In 2008, Hanban and the Ministry of Education in Indonesia recruited seventy-six teachers from China to teach Mandarin Chinese in Indonesia (Hoon 2008, 62–63; 'Hanban' 2013).

The removal of restrictions on Chinese cultural expression and the growing interest in the Chinese (Mandarin) language have led to media liberalisation and brought about a new beginning for Chinese-language newspapers in post-Suharto Indonesia. During Habibie's presidency, the House of Representatives passed a new law that abolished licensing requirements for the press and 'revoked the government's ability to ban publications' (Gazali, Hidayat, and Menayang 2009, 122). When the next president, Abdurrahman Wahid, came into power, he closed down the Ministry of Information, which implemented most of the New Order's restrictions on media (Sen 2011, 7). But soon after Vice President Megawati Sukarnoputri succeeded Wahid in 2001, a new Ministry of Communication and Information was established. Nevertheless, Ariel Heryanto and Vedi R. Hadiz point out that, compared to the former Ministry of Information, the new ministry 'has much less power and carries far fewer political responsibilities' (Heryanto and Hadiz 2005, 272n28). It is estimated that, after the fall of Suharto in 1998, the number of print media jumped from 300 to about 1,000 (Gazali, Hidayat, and Menayang 2009, 122), a number that includes a few Chinese-language newspapers. Chinese-language newspapers published in Jakarta and circulated across Indonesia include *The International Daily*, better known as *Guoji Ribao* (國際日報), a well-established Chinese-language newspaper in the country; *Indonesia Shang Bao* (印度尼西亞商報), a business newspaper; and *Harian Indonesia* (印尼星洲日報), formerly the only Chinese-language newspaper produced by the Suharto regime but later taken over by Sin Chew Media Corporation Berhad (星洲媒體集團) in Malaysia in 2007 (Hoon 2006a, 100–101, Table 4.1; 2008, 110–13; 'Harian Indonesia [Sin Chew]' 2013). *Guoji Ribao* cooperates with China's *People's Daily* (人民日報), Hong Kong's *Wen Wei Bo* (文匯報), and *Hong Kong Commercial Daily* (香港商報) in sharing news coverage. Therefore, *Guoji Ribao* includes these three foreign Chinese-language newspapers in its publication, making it the thickest Chinese-language newspaper in Indonesia. In general, the main reason behind the establishment of these newspapers is to revive the Chinese language and culture, which had been suppressed by the New Order regime for 32 years in Chinese Indonesian community.

In Medan, five Chinese-language newspapers were established after the end of the Suharto regime; all but one are still in print at the time of writing. In Surabaya, there were four Chinese-language newspapers established in the post-Suharto era but two ceased publication after a few years due to various factors.[8]

Despite the importance of these Chinese-language newspapers for the freedom of ethnic and cultural expression they afford the Chinese, those newspapers that are still in print in both cities are sustaining losses due to low readership. The trauma from the closure of all Chinese-language news-papers in 1965 and the anti-Chinese violence in May 1998 led to the practice of self-censorship by most Chinese-language newspapers in the post-Suharto era; they often refrain from venturing into political discussion. Most Chinese-language newspapers in Medan and Surabaya do not publish quality editori-als and commentaries on political issues. In addition, most of the editors and journalists of Chinese-language newspapers are older-generation Chinese aged 60 and above. The prohibition of Chinese-language education in New Order Indonesia produced a younger generation of Chinese who are mostly illiterate in Chinese. Therefore, there is no general readership beyond the older generation, leading to a diminishing market. Also younger Chinese are generally not interested in journalism, hence the editors are from the older generation. These editors and journalists are mostly not familiar with internet technology. Hence, unlike their Indonesian- and English-language counter-parts, most of the Chinese-language newspapers in Medan and Surabaya do not have well-established websites. These problems are an important legacy of the ban on the public usage of Chinese characters and Chinese-medium schools by the New Order regime. In order to survive, therefore, the newspapers need to rely on financial support from their shareholders and advertising revenue from local Chinese Indonesian businesspeople. These businesspeople use the newspapers as a venue for advertising and

---

8. In Medan, *Harian Promosi Indonesia* (印廣日報) ceased publication at the end of December 2014 due to low readership. It was later relaunched under a new name, *Zheng Bao Daily* (正報) in February 2015 (Wu 2015, 6). *Zheng Bao Daily* is currently a sister paper of *Harian Analisa*, a well-established Indonesian-language newspaper in Medan. In Surabaya, the closing down of *Rela Warta*, one of the local Chinese-language newspapers, is mainly due to the withdrawal of advertising by its main advertiser. I will elaborate more on this point in Chapter 5. The closing down of *Harian Naga Surya*, another local Chinese-language newspaper, is due to the low readership. For more details on this issue, see Huang (2005). See Appendix III for the list of Chinese-language newspapers in post-Suharto Medan and Surabaya.

relaying important news about their businesses. Some businesspeople who hold important positions in local Chinese organisations also utilise the newspapers as a cultural space for publicising the activities of their organisations. Therefore, many older-generation Chinese read Chinese-language newspapers to get updates on the social and cultural activities of local Chinese organisations, hence these newspapers feature more 'community news' than actual critical or informative news about what is happening in Indonesia. However, the Chinese-language newspapers in Medan and Surabaya give much coverage of news from China. Hence, Chinese who consider China as their cultural motherland rely on Chinese-language newspapers for news on China (interviews with people in charge and staff of local Chinese-language newspapers in Medan and Surabaya).

4.2 Promoting Chinese Culture: Socialising, Language, and Business

Most Chinese-based organisations in post-Suharto Medan and Surabaya actively engage in ethnic-based endeavours such as promoting Chinese culture and social activities among the Chinese, assisting the local governments in establishing cultural and business connections with China, reviving the Chinese language, and philanthropy. Such endeavours usually involve only limited interaction with non-Chinese.

In general, local Chinese organisations in Medan and Surabaya, particularly Chinese clan associations, function as a social hub for members who are mostly older-generation Chinese, through organising activities such as Chinese festival gatherings, dinner functions, choir and dance classes. Informants who are committee members of Chinese organisations in Medan and Surabaya relate that most Chinese organisations openly celebrate major Chinese festivals such as the Lunar New Year, Qingming Festival (a traditional Chinese festival in which celebrants remember and honour their ancestors), and Moon Cake Festival (interview with Amin, in Mandarin, November 2, 2010; interview with Susana, in Mandarin, January 14, 2011).[9] The vibrancy of such activities reflects the euphoria of the older generation of Chinese in openly celebrating their ethnic and cultural identities, the expression of which had been prohibited for more than 30 years during Suharto's rule. In addition, many Chinese Indonesian businesspeople also utilise Chinese organisations as a platform for meeting people, gaining access to business information, building business networks, and becoming better known. In fact, the leaders of local Chinese organisations in Medan and Surabaya (and Indonesia in general) are mostly businesspeople, as Chinese organisations

---

9. This is also mentioned by Cao Yunhua (2010) in his work on ethnic Chinese in Medan.

Opening Up the Chinese Socio-cultural Sphere

depend on financial support from the local Chinese business community for their operation.[10] It would be easier for an organisation to get money if the leaders are engaged in business. This point is emphasised in the following remark by the chairperson of INTI's Surabaya branch:

> Leading a Chinese organisation like INTI is not easy. We have to contribute not only our time and energy but also money. Without money, it is hard [for an organisation] to run activities. Chinese organisations in Indonesia do not receive any funds from the government. So, the funds of the organisations come mainly from the leaders. (interview with William Rahardja, in Indonesian, March 4, 2011)

Some Chinese organisations are also keen to revive and promote Chinese traditions and culture among young members who were born during Suharto's rule and did not have the opportunity to learn the Chinese languages. For instance, the PHTKS, a clan association founded by Hakka-, Teochew- and Cantonese-speaking Chinese, started a weekly Hakka-language class in 2008 with the aim of reviving and promoting the Hakka culture among the young members, who were mostly children of the elder members (most of the leaders and members of the organisation were from the Hakka clan) (*Sishui Huichaojia Huiguan* 2010, 98). In my interview with Susana, a committee member, she revealed that the instructor was a Hakka-speaking woman from Meizhou, China. She had been living in Surabaya for a long time and could speak Indonesian, too. Therefore, she conducted her lessons in both Hakka and Indonesian, so young students who previously had no basic knowledge of the Hakka language could follow her lessons (interview with Susana, in Mandarin, January 14, 2011).[11] Every year, the association also arranges a trip for a few young members to visit China and Taiwan in order to enhance their understanding of the Hakka culture (*Sishui Huichaojia Huiguan* 2010, 45).

During my fieldwork in Surabaya, the East Java branches of INTI, in collaboration with thirteen other ethnic Chinese religious and charitable organisations in East Java, jointly organised a talk on education in the Chinese tradition. They invited as the speaker Dr. Zhong Maosen (鍾茂森) from Pure Land Learning College (淨宗學院), a college that promotes Pure Land Buddhism in Australia. They also invited Master Chin Kung (淨空法師), head of the college who is also an eminent monk, to attend the event as a special guest (Deng and Xie 2011; Yandan 2011). I was invited by INTI to

---

10. See the tables in Appendix IV for the occupational backgrounds of local major Chinese organisations' leaders in Medan and Surabaya during the period of my fieldwork (2010–2011). All but one leader of those organisations were in business, implying the crucial role of Chinese businesspeople in running major Chinese organisations.

11. However, I did not have the opportunity to meet and interview the instructor, and therefore could not find out more about her background and her reasons for residing in Indonesia.

attend the event, which was attended by more than 1,000 people (Deng and Xie 2011; Yandan 2011). Here, I will include a detailed record of the event from my field notes:

> Before the talk began, a group of primary students in their school uniform from Metta School, which was a private school in Surabaya, went on stage and recited the teachings in *Di Zi Gui* (弟子規), an ancient book based on the teaching of Confucius that emphasises the basic requisites for being a good person and guidelines for living in harmony with others. After that, Mr. Wongso, chairperson of the organising committee, went on stage to deliver his speech in Mandarin, saying that the residents in Surabaya were very blessed because they had the opportunity to listen to Dr. Zhong Maosen's sharing. Interestingly, his speech was not translated into Indonesian, indicating that it was addressed more for the benefit of the speaker than the audience, since most of the audience did not understand Mandarin.
>
> When Dr. Zhong started to deliver his speech, there was an interpreter who translated it all into Indonesian. In his view, Chinese traditional culture consisted of the concepts of morality and ethics as well as karma. He advised that those who were keen to learn Chinese traditional culture should start with reading and practising the teachings of *Di Zi Gui*, which had been recited by the primary school students before the talk began. He emphasised that all could live a happy life if they practised the teachings of *Di Zi Gui*. He concluded with a saying of Mencius, another Chinese philosopher, 'Everyone can be a sage'. (field notes, January 14, 2011)

It was evident that the organisers and attendees perceived the event as an opportunity for the Chinese to celebrate their ethnic and cultural identity, promoting both what was considered Chinese philosophy of a good life as well as the Mandarin language. However, there was still an evident gap because of the lack of Mandarin proficiency among the audience.

In Medan, local Chinese organisations have made a significant contribution to promoting Chinese-language education by establishing the Asian International Friendship Foreign Language College (STBA-PIA, Sekolah Tinggi Bahasa Asing Persahabatan Internasional Asia), a Chinese-language tertiary institution that offers a bachelor degree programme in Chinese language. The establishment of such a college would have been unimaginable during the New Order period, during which the public usage of the Chinese language was forbidden and all Chinese-medium schools were closed down. The institution is located in the quiet neighbourhood of Glugur, in the northwest part of Medan. I had the opportunity to visit the campus when Ardjan Leo (廖章然), vice president of the institution, walked me around the campus after my interview with him.[12] The library had many Chinese books that were

---

12. The environment of STBA-PIA reminded me of New Era College (NEC) (新紀元學院), a Chinese-language tertiary institution funded by the Chinese community in Kajang, Malaysia. The environments of both colleges were very similar as their signboards and notice boards were in both Chinese and Indonesian/Malay languages. Classes were conducted in

mostly donated by Chinese community leaders, Chinese Indonesian writers, the Office of Chinese Language Council International (Hanban) in China, and the Chinese Language and Culture Education Foundation of China (a foundation established by the Chinese government to promote Chinese-language education outside China) (North Sumatra's Chinese Community Social and Education Association n. d., 6).

STBA-PIA was founded in 2008 by the North Sumatra Chinese Community Social and Education Association (MITSU-PSP), headquartered in Medan. The objectives of the institution are to promote Chinese language and culture, and to train local Mandarin Chinese language teachers (Wu 2009, 185). In order to have a better understanding of the background and activities of MITSU-PSP, it is essential first to look at the background of the North Sumatra Chinese Community Relief Committee (PTSUPBA, *Panitia Tionghoa Sumatera Utara Peduli Bencana Alam*, 蘇北華社賑災委員會), the predecessor of MITSU-PSP (interview with Ardjan Leo, in Mandarin, November 12, 2010).

PTSUPBA was an ad hoc relief committee formed in December 2004 to provide relief aid to tsunami victims from Aceh and Nias, North Sumatra. The victims were sheltered in Medan. PTSUPBA consisted of sixty-five Chinese organisations in North Sumatra, including PSMTI, INTI, and Yasora Medan. During the relief period, PTSUPBA encountered leaders from Sin Chew Media Corporation Berhad, the largest Chinese publishing group in Malaysia, who went to Medan to help the tsunami victims. The leaders from the publishing group were touched by the efforts of PTSUPBA in providing relief aid to the victims. The group later donated RM500,000 (about US$131,579) to the relief funds of PTSUPBA. According to Leo, the relief committee also received a donation of RM10 million (about US$1.2 million) from the Chinese government (interview with Ardjan Leo, in Mandarin, November 12, 2010).

Later, a reader of *Sin Chew Jit Poh* (星洲日報), a leading Chinese-language newspaper in Malaysia owned by Sin Chew Media Corporation Berhad, donated RM4.5 million (about US$1.2 million) to the publishing group. The reader requested the group to build an institution in disaster areas such as Sri Lanka, Cambodia, or Aceh. The group decided to pass the funds to PTSUPBA and requested the leaders to build a college at Aceh. But the relief committee eventually set up the institution at Medan instead of Aceh due to some unforeseen circumstances, as told by Leo, the leader of the relief committee at that time:

> As one of the leaders of PTSUPBA, I went to Banda Aceh to discuss with the local Chinese community leaders and the governor of Aceh regarding

Mandarin and most students were ethnic Chinese. For the historical background of the New Era College (NEC), see the website of the college ('History of NEC' 2013).

the proposal to set up an institution in their city. Although the governor was supportive of the proposal and willing to offer a piece of land in the province without any charge, the Chinese community leaders there were reluctant to build an institution in their city because they were afraid that it would be tough to maintain the operation of such an institution. After all, not many students in Aceh were able to pay the tuition fees. After four unfruitful meetings with them, I decided to give up the plan to build in Aceh.

Later, I went to Kuala Lumpur, Malaysia, to meet the leaders of Sin Chew Media Corporation Berhad. I told them frankly the difficulties of setting up an institution in Aceh and proposed to establish the institution in Medan instead. They immediately agreed with my proposal and asked me to proceed with the plan. In fact, it only took 15 minutes for me to inform the leaders about the difficulties of opening an institution in Aceh and get the approval of the publishing group to change the location of the proposed institution to Medan. (interview with Ardjan Leo, in Mandarin, November 12, 2010)

Leo and other leaders of PTSUPBA decided to form MITSU-PSP together with a few Chinese community leaders in North Sumatra, in order to establish and manage the proposed institution. The association decided to build STBA-PIA at the site of an abandoned sugar factory in Glugur, Medan. The site was found and introduced by Tansri Chandra (陳明宗), one of the founders of MITSU-PSP. The construction of the institution started on May 27, 2007 and was completed on August 20, 2008 (North Sumatra Chinese Community Social and Education Association n. d., 2). The establishment of STBA-PIA cost about US$3.5 million. About one-third of the amount came from Sin Chew Media Corporation Berhad (RM4.5 million or about US$1.2 million), the largest Chinese publishing group in Malaysia, and another two-thirds was donated by several Chinese organisations in North Sumatra (interview with Ardjan Leo, in Mandarin, November 12, 2010).

The South China Normal University (華南師範大學) in Guangdong, China, assisted the college in preparing the syllabus of Chinese-language courses and sending over a few lecturers to teach in the institution. The China Overseas Exchange Association (中國海外交流協會) and the Overseas Exchange Association of Guangdong Province (廣東省海外交流協會) assisted in recruiting lecturers in China to teach the Chinese language in STBA-PIA (North Sumatra Chinese Community Social and Education Association n. d., 6–7). All Chinese lecturers sent to teach in the institution were paid by the Chinese government ('Yazhou Guoji Youhao Xueyuan' 2011). Therefore, the Chinese government plays an active role in the operation of the institution. The institution also offers a bachelor's degree in English language. The English-language courses are taught by lecturers from the State University of Medan (UNIMED, Universitas Negeri Medan) (interview with Ardjan Leo, in Mandarin, November 12, 2010). Therefore, the founding and operation of the college involves international collaboration between Indonesia, Malaysia, and China.

Students who pursue the Chinese language programme in STBA-PIA can choose to specialise in teacher-training, business, or tourism. They can pursue the whole programme at the STBA-PIA campus, or spend the first two years in the campus and proceed with their third and fourth years at South China Normal University (North Sumatra Chinese Community Social and Education Association n. d., 7–8). MITSU-PSP offers financial aid to students, regardless of ethnic background, who are interested to study at STBA-PIA and become Chinese-language teachers in the future but are unable to pay the tuition fees (interview with Ardjan Leo, in Mandarin, November 12, 2010).

Leo revealed that the founders of STBA-PIA hope the institution will play a role in reducing indigenous Indonesians' hostility towards the Chinese. They hope to draw more indigenous Indonesians to study in the institution and believe indigenous students would understand the Chinese better and have less prejudice towards the Chinese if they studied and interacted with Chinese students in the institution (interview with Ardjan Leo, in Mandarin, November 12, 2010). However, during my fieldwork in Medan, I noticed that very few indigenous Indonesians studied at the institution. Less than 10% of the student population were indigenous Indonesians (interview with Ardjan Leo, in Mandarin, November 12, 2010). The institution is generally perceived as a *Chinese* college by indigenous people. In fact, a journalist from *Tribun Medan* (an Indonesian-language newspaper in Medan) commented that the campus was like 'the bamboo curtain country, China', when he saw many Chinese characters and Chinese-style furniture in the institution (Azmi 2011, my translation from Indonesian original).[13] The management of the institution might see the Chinese-style decoration and the accentuation of Chinese characters in the campus as a revival and public acknowledge-ment of Chinese culture and identity. The comments made by the journalist, however, suggest that such representations only reproduce the perception of the Chinese as an unchanging alien minority. Therefore, not many indig-enous Indonesians study in the institution.

Local Chinese-language newspapers in Medan and Surabaya play an active role in promoting Chinese culture within local Chinese communities. Most Chinese-language newspapers in Medan and Surabaya cover Chinese cultural features like Chinese classics, literature, and calligraphy. In order to promote the learning of Chinese language and culture among young Chinese children, *Xun Bao*, a Chinese-language newspaper in Medan, began

---

13. The 'Bamboo Curtain' is a Cold War euphemism for the political demarcation between China and non-communist countries.

producing a children's magazine in 2010. As the person in charge of the newspaper recounted:

> Our newspaper designed and added *Xun Bao Youth*, a children's magazine, to *Xun Bao* since February 4, 2010 to attract more young readers. *Xun Bao Youth* publishes information about learning Chinese and English, general knowledge in science and technology, as well as children's comics. The contents are designed by our editors, hired from China, and are suitable for primary school students. We still keep the same price of the newspaper although *Xun Bao Youth* had been added to it. We also offer discounts for schools that subscribe to *Xun Bao*. (interview with Joe, in Mandarin, November 5, 2010)

Besides that, Chinese-language newspapers in Medan and Surabaya give extensive coverage on China in their news reports. According to a journalist from *Harian Nusantara*, a Chinese-language newspaper in Surabaya, the newspaper cooperates with *Indonesia Focus* (印尼焦點), a bi-annual Chinese-language news magazine founded by the Hong Kong Society for Indonesian Studies, China News Agency (中新社), and Xinhua News Agency (新華社) in sharing news coverage (interview with Musa, in Mandarin, May 19, 2011). Other Chinese-language newspapers that do not have any cooperative relations with China News Agency and Xinhua directly download and appropriate news on China from both news agencies. The heavy focus on China in Chinese-language newspapers is due to two factors. First, older-generation Chinese Indonesians who can read Chinese are generally interested in news on China because they consider China as their cultural motherland. Second, China's economy is booming and there is a rising demand for news about the Chinese economy.

Moreover, with the exception of *Rela Warta*, Chinese-language newspapers in Medan and Surabaya actively support the activities of local Chinese organisations. They publish news about the social and cultural as well as philanthropic activities of local Chinese organisations. In fact, Vincent, the adviser to *Sishui Chenbao* in Surabaya, told me that the newspaper was founded in 2004 with the aim of covering events and activities of the Chinese organisations in East Java (interview in Mandarin, April 7, 2011).

So why did *Rela Warta* not provide extensive coverage of activities organised by local Chinese organisations? This had much to do with the political ideology of its founder and chief editor. *Rela Warta* was a Chinese-language newspaper founded in 2001 by a group of local ethnic Chinese social activists. Since the founder and the chief editor of *Rela Warta* were progressive-minded, left-leaning social activists, the newspaper stood in sharp contrast to other Chinese-language newspapers in Surabaya (and Medan) in the sense that it gave more coverage of political issues rather than dinner functions and socio-cultural activities. The founder and the chief editor of the newspaper considered such events to be lacking in substance (interview with Samas H. Widjaja, in Mandarin, May 5, 2011). As *Rela Warta* did not cover many social and cultural activities held by local Chinese organisations in the city, it did not get much support from leaders of local Chinese organisations. Moreover, the leftist and progressive stand of the newspaper was also in conflict with the interests of local Chinese capitalists such as Alim Markus (林文光), owner of the Maspion Group, a Surabaya-based conglomerate that manufactures household appliances. Therefore, many well-established local Chinese businesspeople did not support the newspaper (interview with Vincent, in Mandarin, April 7, 2011).

The emergence of various institutions specialising in Chinese language and culture point to the increasing business connections Indonesia has opened with China. According to Zhao Hong (2013), Indonesia-China relations began to improve significantly after 1998 due to 'dramatic changes in Indonesia's domestic politics' after the demise of the New Order regime (3). Post–New Order governments no longer perceive China as an ideologically threatening country. Instead, they see China 'as an economic powerhouse providing positive spillovers to its cash-strapped neighbours in Southeast Asia' (4). The Indonesian government is keen to attract more Chinese businesses to invest and set up enterprises as well as factories in Indonesia in order to accelerate and expand economic development and the building of infrastructure in the country. These efforts of the Indonesian government have coincided with China's pursuit of friendly relations with Southeast Asian countries. A few Chinese organisations in Indonesia are in a good position to help the government establish cultural and economic ties with China since the leaders are well connected to state officials and businesspeople in China. They are thus able to utilise their intra-ethnic linkages and social networks in China to assist the government in establishing cultural and business connections with China.

In Medan, INTI's North Sumatra branch plays an important role in helping local governments form cooperative relations with China. With the help of Indra Wahidin, then chairperson of INTI's North Sumatra branch, and other leaders of the organisation who have strong social networks in China, North Sumatra and Guangdong have become sister provinces. There are also a few cities and towns in North Sumatra that have become twinned with certain cities or towns in China. Those sister cities or towns are Medan and Chengdu, Binjai and Nan'an, Samosir and Changdao, Deli Serdang and Shanwei, and Karo and Yunnan (Wu 2009, 223–24; 'Jida Dongnanya Yanjiusuo' 2009, B7).

In Surabaya, the Surabaya Chinese Association (PMTS) and East Java branches of both PSMTI and the Indonesian Chinese Entrepreneur Association (PERPIT) are major Chinese organisations that have been active in such initiatives. PMTS and PERPIT's East Java branches help the local government in developing cooperative relations with China by entertaining officials or special guests from that country (interview with Liem Ou Yen, in Mandarin, March 23, 2011; interview with William Rahardja, in Indonesian, March 4, 2011). PMTS offered a warm reception to then vice president of China Hu Jintao (胡錦濤), who visited Surabaya in July 2000, and former president Li Peng (李鵬), who visited Surabaya in April 2002 (interview with Liem Ou Yen, in Mandarin, March 23, 2011). PERPIT's East Java branch, on the other hand, often receives businesspeople from China who are visiting Surabaya to seek business opportunities in the city. Since its foundation, the branch has offered a warm reception to businesspeople from Shandong and Yunnan provinces (interview with Liem Ou Yen, in Mandarin, March 23, 2011). During my fieldwork, PMTS took a lead in entertaining the representatives of Nanchang University in Jiangxi, China, who visited on February 26, 2011. Leaders of PMTS accompanied the representatives on their visit to the State University of Surabaya and invited them for dinner in a restaurant (Zeng 2011a). PMTS also helped facilitate the cultural performance tour presented by the representatives of Nanchang University the next day (Zeng 2011b).

In addition, with the help of Samas H. Widjaja (黃三槐), vice chairperson of PSMTI's East Java branch, who has good relations with local power-holders and strong social networks in China, Surabaya has become a sister city of Xiamen and Guangzhou (interview with Hendi Prayogo, in Indonesian, March 28, 2011; interview with Samas H. Widjaja, in Mandarin, May 5, 2011).

The cultural and business connections between local governments and China have resulted in some significant investments from China in both East Java and North Sumatra. For instance, the Industrial and Commercial Bank of China (ICBC), a prominent Chinese bank, set up branches in Surabaya (2007) and Medan (2010), creating job opportunities for local Indonesians as well as promoting trade and investment in East Java and North Sumatra (Zhao 2007; 'Zhongguo Gongshang Yinhang' 2010). Chinese companies also invested in significant infrastructure projects in these Indonesian provinces. For example, two Chinese companies, China Road and Bridge Corporation and China Harbour Engineering Company, cooperated with two Indonesian companies, PT Adhi Karya and PT Waskita Karya, to build the Surabaya-Madura Bridge, a cable-stayed bridge that connects Surabaya and Madura Island. The project cost Rp4.5 trillion (about US$440 million); most of the funding came in the form of a soft loan from China. The construction began in 2003 and ended in 2009. The bridge was inaugurated by President Yudhoyono on June 10, 2009 ('The Suramadu Bridge' 2009; Witular 2009; 'Ekonomi Perdagangan Jadi Jembatan Persahabatan Tiongkok-RI' 2013). In North Sumatra, two Chinese companies, China Harbour Engineering and China State Construction Engineering Company, cooperated with an Indonesian company, PT Hutama Karya Persero, to jointly construct a toll road (with a total length of 17.8 km) connecting Medan and Kuala Namu, where the new airport that replaced the Polonia International Airport in Medan is located. The project cost Rp1,507 trillion (about US$165 million) and was funded by the Indonesian government and the Export-Import Bank of China ('Kontrak Tol Medan-Kualanamu Ditandatangani' 2011; Ridin 2012). The construction began in 2012 and is estimated to be completed by 2014 ('Tol Medan-Kuala Namu Siap 2014' 2011). These infrastructure projects promote regional economic and social growth in East Java and North Sumatra. In addition, China's direct investment in East Java increased significantly from Rp0.32 trillion (about US$353 million) in 2011 to Rp1.56 trillion (about US$1.6 billion) in September 2012[14] ('Primadona PMA' 2013; 'Minat Negara Asal PMA s/d Triwulan III – 2012' 2013).[15, 16]

In short, in the post-Suharto era, leaders of local major Chinese organisations in Medan and Surabaya have been making use of their intra-ethnic networks in China to assist local governments in establishing business and cultural connections with China that have resulted in the increase in China's direct investments in both East Java and North Sumatra. China's significant investments in some local major infrastructure projects have helped promote regional economic and social development in both provinces.[17] The initiative of Chinese organisation leaders in helping to build bridges between Indonesia and China has at the same time strengthened their relationship with local governments in Indonesia.

4.3 Cross-ethnic Endeavours

As can be seen above, there are many activities in the post-Suharto era that have helped to strengthen Chinese ethnic identity, as well as Chinese Indonesian links to the People's Republic of China. Some Indonesian Chinese are aware of how these activities appear to separate the Chinese from *pribumi* Indonesians and concertedly take steps to temper the impression that the Chinese in Indonesia are insular and inward-looking, one of the negative stereotypes of the Chinese that has lasted over the centuries. One way to reach out to *pribumi* Indonesians is through philanthropic efforts, in which many of the Chinese organisations are involved. Another way is the establishment

---

14. This is the latest official data available at the time of writing. Official data for the period before 2011 are unavailable.
15. 'PMA' is the acronym of '*penanaman modal asing*' (foreign investment).
16. Official data on China's investment in North Sumatra are unavailable.
17. For a more critical view of the actual benefits of China's direct investments in Indonesia, see Lee (2013).

of organisations that attempt to cut across ethnic ties. There are a few ethnic Chinese community leaders and social activists who are willing to reach out to the wider society by establishing socio-cultural organisations that are not ethnic-based, to promote cross-ethnic understanding and solidarity.

In general, Chinese organisations in Indonesia (and other Southeast Asian countries) actively engage in philanthropy. They offer financial assistance to members of their organisation who are poor and in need, and also provide financial assistance and bursaries to children of their members who excel in academic performance. Besides that, these Chinese organisations often provide financial assistance to poor indigenous Indonesians. In Medan and Surabaya, most local Chinese organisations contribute food and daily necessities to the local poor, mostly indigenous Muslims, during the Ramadan fasting month every year. Leaders of local Chinese organisations hope that helping indigenous Indonesians who are in need will reduce prejudice and hostility towards the Chinese. In other words, the participation in philanthropy is a strategy for reducing racial hostility and prejudice towards the Chinese among the indigenous population. As told by Lim Ou Yen (林武源), the executive chairperson of the PMTS, 'We contribute to society by helping those in need. Since most of them are indigenous Indonesians, offering assistance to them could also eliminate racial hostility toward the Chinese' (interview in Mandarin, March 23, 2011).

Some Chinese organisations also offer assistance to local people who are in need of medical care. For instance, according to the chairperson of INTI's Surabaya branch, the organisation offers free medical aid for the poor on a regular basis at the secretariat office and rural areas (interview with William Rahardja, in Indonesian, March 4, 2011). Similarly, since 1999, INTI's North Sumatra branch has been working before Independence Day every year with North Sumatra Local Daily Council 45 (Dewan Harian Daerah 45 Sumatera Utara) to provide free medical aid for the poor in Medan (Waristo 2010; 'Pengobatan Gratis' 2010). In addition, according to an executive committee member of PERMIT's East Java branch, in early 2011, the branch had donated blood bags to the Indonesian Red Cross in Surabaya and mobile medical vehicles to the East Java provincial government to conduct cervical screening tests in local communities (interview with Susana, in Mandarin, January 14, 2011). In April 2011, the PMTS and PERPIT's East Java branch had decided to work with the East Java Entrepreneur Charitable Foundation and the East Java High Prosecution Office to jointly set up a clinic at a village in Jambon, about 200 kilometres away from Surabaya (Yaoyin 2011).

INTI's Surabaya branch offers free legal consultations at the secretariat office (interview with William Rahardja, in Indonesian, March 4, 2011). PSMTI's East Java branch, on the other hand, participated in the establishment of Kampung Ilmu (Knowledge Village), a business area where petty traders, mostly indigenous Indonesians, can sell both old and new reading materials, at Jalan Semarang, Surabaya. This endeavour offers business opportunities for petty traders and promotes the reading habit among residents in Surabaya (interview with Hendi Prayogo, in Indonesian, March 28, 2011).

The major Chinese organisations in both cities often offer relief aid to victims of disasters in the country. They usually initiate fundraising campaigns through local Chinese-language newspapers. For example, MITSU-PSP and PMTS provided relief aid to tsunami victims in Aceh and Nias, North Sumatra, in December 2004. Some leaders of both organisations even went to the disaster areas to provide material aid (interview with Ardjan Leo, in Mandarin, November 12, 2010; interview with Liem Ou Yen, in Mandarin, March 23, 2011). MITSU-PSP also helped shelter several victims in Medan (Jian 2009, 202–3). In October 2009, a strong earthquake hit Padang, the capital of West Sumatra, destroying scores of buildings and leaving many helpless victims. PHTKS launched a fundraising campaign to help the victims (*Sishui Huichaojia Huiguan Chengli 190 Zhounian Jinian Zhuanji* 2010, 96). During my fieldwork in Medan, PSMTI's North Sumatra and Medan branches launched a fundraising campaign through local Chinese-language newspapers to help victims of flash floods that hit Wasior, West Papua, in October 2010. In less than one month, both branches had raised Rp110,430,000 (about US$12,357) for the victims ('Subei Ji Mianlan Yinhua Baijiaxing Xiehui' 2010). In the same month, the Mentawai Islands in West Sumatra were struck by a 7.7-magnitude earthquake and tsunami. The disaster took more than 400 lives and about 20,000 people lost their homes. MITSU-PSP initiated a similar fundraising campaign through local Chinese-language newspapers to assist the victims (Youying 2010).

The leaders of most major Chinese organisations are businesspeople; funds raised to help those in need are mostly contributed by other local Chinese Indonesian businesspeople. Thus, it can be said that Chinese Indonesian businesspeople have played a significant role in helping the poor and other people in need. As a Chinese Indonesian journalist in Medan remarked, 'Actually, Chinese Indonesian businesspeople have been offering a lot of help to those in need all this while. In fact, so far I never heard of any non-Chinese businessperson who is actively involved in philanthropy' (interview with Andi, in Indonesian, September 10, 2010).

Apart from these philanthropic endeavours, some Chinese Indonesians have attempted to go further, establishing organisations that reach out more directly to the *pribumi* community. Sofyan Tan, the 2010 mayoral candidate in Medan, already mentioned, was previously a physician and has become a social activist. Instead of donating cash or consumer goods to local poor indigenous Indonesians, as most Chinese Indonesian community leaders have done, he has tried to promote inter-ethnic understanding and to rectify the negative stereotypes about Chinese Indonesians through education. In 1987, when he was still studying medicine at the Medan Methodist University of Indonesia (UMI Medan, or Universitas Methodist Indonesia Medan), he founded an integrated school (*sekolah pembauran*)[18] known as the Sultan Iskandar Muda Educational Foundation (YPSIM, or Yayasan Perguruan Sultan Iskandar Muda) in Sunggal, Medan. The school promotes integration among students from various ethnic-religious backgrounds.

There have been a few works written about the school. Tan (2004) himself introduces the objectives and programmes of the school in detail, in a book he wrote about building a society that is free from discrimination. The works of Judith Nagata (2003), C. W. Watson (2006), J. Anto (a former journalist and media activist in Medan) (2009), and an article in the independence-day English edition of *Tempo* in 2004 ('Schools without Boundaries' 2004) also cover the background of the school but are not as detailed as Tan's book. Tan, as well as others who write about the school, explain the background of the school by telling Tan's own story.

Being from a poor family of tailors, Tan was far from a stereotypical Chinese. His family usually spoke Indonesian at home and he had many indigenous Indonesian friends. While Tan's father was still alive, he repeatedly pushed his son to mingle and integrate with fellow citizens of other ethnic groups ('Schools without Boundaries' 2004). Tan's family successfully fostered good relationships with indigenous Indonesians. Through the episodic ethnic violence of the 1960s and the 1990s in Medan, when many Chinese homes in Tan's neighbourhood were attacked and burned, Tan's family survived, miraculously free from attack (Nagata 2003, 375).

After his father passed away in 1980, Tan had to finance his own medical training by tutoring upper secondary school students. As a result, he needed to spend a longer time than usual (12 years) to get a medical degree (Anto 2009, 63, 66–73; Nagata 2003, 375; Gunawan 2004). Upon graduating with a medical degree in 1990, Tan decided not to open up his own clinic but to devote himself to the operation of YPSIM (Gunawan 2004; 'Schools without Boundaries' 2004). Tan funded the operation of the school by securing a bank loan and borrowing money from a few friends. Later, a few international NGOs, including Caritas Switzerland and Pan Eco Foundation, financed the facilities of the school ('Sejarah Singkat' 2014; Anto 2009, 104–5). Using the Indonesian language as its medium of instruction, the school offers education from kindergarten up to upper secondary levels. Apart from Indonesian and English, students can also learn Chinese (as an elective subject) (interview with Sofyan Tan, in Indonesian, August 23, 2010). In 1988, the school

---

18. An integrated school is a school with students from different ethnic groups.

Opening Up the Chinese Socio-cultural Sphere   87

had only 171 students. But the number has been increasing from year to year and reached 2,200 in 2013 ('Sejarah Singkat' 2014).

In order to encourage cross-ethnic sympathy and inter-ethnic understanding, and in addition to provide financial aid to students who are smart but of limited means, Tan had devised a programme of fosterage (*program anak asuh*) whereby every student was financially supported by a wealthy patron of a different ethnic and religious group. Chinese patrons would sponsor non-Chinese students and vice versa (Tan 2004, 29–33; Nagata 2003, 375; 'Schools without Boundaries' 2004; Watson 2006, 179). The school would arrange monthly meetings between patrons and their protégés. The school also made it compulsory for protégés to send greeting cards to their patrons on the latter's birthdays and during festivals related to the latter's religious beliefs ('Program Anak Asuh', 2014). Through these arrangements, the programme has produced better inter-ethnic relations among patrons and protégés. Since the launch of this programme in 1990, the number of protégés has generally been increasing from year to year.[19]

The programme of fosterage has generated some good, strong relationships between patrons and protégés. According to Tan himself (2004, 30), patrons who are Chinese businesspeople can employ their protégés to work in their companies upon graduation. The protégés can also learn about entrepreneurial skills and work ethics from their patrons. For protégés of Chinese descent who are sponsored by indigenous Indonesian patrons, their family would be protected by their patrons in the event of racial riots breaking out (Tan 2004, 30).

The programme of fosterage was followed in 1997 by another project, i.e., the building of places of worship in the school. According to J. Anto (2009, 199), who wrote the Tan's biography, Tan hoped this project would lead to religious solidarity among students. The first place of worship built was a mosque, but this aroused suspicion and opposition among non-Muslim parents, especially those who were Chinese. They questioned Tan on why a mosque was built before other places of worship. Tan replied that it was because Muslims needed to pray every day. Unfortunately, his reply led to more misunderstanding among non-Muslim parents; they accused Tan of attempting to change YPSIM into an Islamic school and convert students to Islam. There were also rumours circulating in Sunggal (where the school was situated) that Tan and his family had converted to Islam. This resulted in the withdrawal of a few non-Muslim students by their parents (Anto 2009, 201–2; Watson 2006, 180). Despite these challenges, Tan persisted. Later, other places of worship, a Buddhist temple and a Christian church, were built in the school as well (Anto 2009, 202–5; Watson 2006, 180). Tan revealed that the

---

19. See Appendix V for numbers of protégés at YPSIM from 1990/1991 to 2011/2012.

building of a mosque in the school had also unexpectedly made the school a 'safe' place during the outbreak of anti-Chinese violence in early May 1998. Many local Chinese parked their cars in the school compound because they believed the rioters would not dare to attack the school since it had a mosque (interview with Sofyan Tan, in Indonesian, August 23, 2010).

Every year, the school has organised a 'Unity in Diversity Night' (Malam Perayaan Bhineka Tunggal Ika), an annual event combining the celebration of festivals related to the five official religions of Indonesia, i.e., Islam, Protestantism, Catholicism, Buddhism, and Hinduism. Students present various cultural performances such as Chinese lion dance, Indian dance, Malay poetry recitation, Batak *gondang* musical performance, and the like. Students also prepare various ethnic dishes and cuisines. Tan (2004, 36) asserts that by participating in such activities, students have the opportunity to learn about the cultural richness and diversity in the country.

The YPSIM has made some headway in altering negative stereotypes of the indigenous Indonesians as those who extort money from the Chinese and of the Chinese as wealthy and exclusive. It has blurred what Barth (1969, 15) calls 'the ethnic boundary' among students of various ethnic groups. This is vividly illustrated in the following excerpts from an article on the school taken from the independence-day English edition of *Tempo* in 2004:

> "I used to think that all Chinese were rich!" said Mona, a grade five student in Medan, speaking to *TEMPO* two weeks ago. Classmate Maggie weighs in, "In the village, my older brother would often be asked for money [by indigenous Indonesian gangsters]. I was afraid of them," said this small girl with the slanted eyes, reminiscing.
>
> But that's all in the past now. Since attending school together at the Sultan Iskandar Muda School in the area of Sunggal, Medan, these two girls, of Batak and Chinese origin, have come to see that their traditional view of social relationships regarding the Chinese and other ethnic groups—always a thorny point—does not correspond to reality. These days they can play together; there is no feeling of awkwardness or fear. "What's more, is that here we can tease each other," jokes Maggie. ("Schools without Boundaries" 2004)

Tan claims that his devotion to promoting inter-ethnic solidarity and understanding through education has earned him the respect of many Medanese, particularly the indigenous Indonesians from grassroots communities (interview with Sofyan Tan, in Indonesian, August 23, 2010). He has been called 'an integrator between the different ethnic groups' in Medan ('Schools without Boundaries' 2004).[20] His popularity was also reflected in

---

20. However, data from my field study implied that Tan was not actually very popular among local Chinese with a strong ethnic identity. According to these Chinese, Tan identified more with the indigenous population than the Chinese community. He was also perceived not to care much about issues related to the Chinese community (interview with Farid, in

Opening Up the Chinese Socio-cultural Sphere

the result he and his running mate achieved in Medan's mayoral election in 2010. As I related at the beginning of the book, there were ten pairs of candidates and Tan was the only Chinese.

However, as Tan admitted when interviewed by *Tempo*, the students of the school are mostly indigenous Indonesians. Many Chinese parents refuse to send their children to integrated schools such as YPSIM because they consider schools dominated by ethnic Chinese a better choice. Some do not want their children to enrol in integrated schools due to the trauma they experienced in riots directed against the Chinese ('Schools without Boundaries' 2004). My observation of the school during my visit in 2010 corresponds to Tan's information, since I saw very few Chinese students in the school. Most were indigenous Indonesians.

An organisation with a similar goal to YPSIM, to fight against ethnic and racial discrimination, was opened in Surabaya by a group of Chinese and indigenous Indonesian social activists and university students after the May 1998 riots. This organisation is called the Committee of Social Concern of Surabaya (Kalimas, or Komite Aliansi Kepedulian Masyarakat Surabaya). Hendi Prayogo, the founder of Kalimas, shares a similar background with Sofyan Tan. Both are Chinese Indonesians who did not have the opportunity to study in pre–New Order Chinese-medium schools because they had already been closed down by the time they reached school age. Both of them usually speak Indonesian at home and have many indigenous Indonesian friends. Moreover, unlike most Chinese Indonesians, neither is involved in business activities. Prayogo works as a marketing executive for a private company ('Hendi Prayogo, Ketua Komite Tionghoa Indonesia Peduli Pemilu' 2009).

In September 1999, Kalimas and a few institutes as well as NGOs, such as the Institute of Ethnic and Racial Unity Studies in Indonesia (INSPIRASI, or Institut Studi Persatuan Etnis dan Ras di Indonesia) and the Indonesian Anti-Discrimination Movement (GANDI, or Gerakan Perjuangan Anti Diskriminasi), jointly organised a conference that focused on ending all forms of ethnic and racial discrimination in Indonesia. About a hundred social activists from various ethnic and religious backgrounds attended the event ('Ratusan Produk Hukum di Indonesia Diskriminatif' 1999). They made several demands to the government. These included making amendments to certain articles in the 1945 constitution that discriminate against non-indigenous Indonesians and introducing an anti-ethnic and racial discrimination law (*Stop Rasisme* 1999; 'Tionghoa Serukan DPR Buat UU Diskriminasi Etnis' 2000).

Hokkien, July 15, 2010; interview with The Lie Hok, in Mandarin, October 31, 2010). I will elaborate on this point in Chapter 6.

Although Kalimas later ceased operation in 2000, its efforts and those of its fellow organisers and participants in the anti-racism conference resulted in some positive outcomes: the government later removed the term *pribumi* from Article 6 in the constitution, pertaining to the eligibility of candidates running for president and vice president. This implies that all Indonesian citizens, regardless of whether they are indigenous or non-indigenous, are eligible to run for president and vice president (Indrayana 2008, 434). Moreover, in 2008, the House of Representatives passed a bill that criminalised ethnic and racial discrimination. According to a news report in *The Jakarta Post*, 'Under the new law, leaders of public institutions found guilty of adopting discriminatory policies would face jail terms one-third more severe than those stipulated in the Criminal Code' ('Bill Against Racial Discrimination Passed' 2008). The passing of the anti-discrimination law is a breakthrough in dealing with racial discrimination at the bureaucratic level, although it is by no means able to end the prejudice and discrimination against Chinese at the grassroots level.

Following Bourdieu's concept of habitus, I argue that the orientation of the activities and endeavours of major local Chinese organisations and Chinese-led cross-ethnic organisations in post-Suharto Medan and Surabaya has much to do with the backgrounds of their leaders. Leaders of major local Chinese organisations are mostly engaged in business and are well connected with local power-holders in Indonesia as well as state officials and business-people in China. Some of them studied in pre–New Order Chinese-medium schools and therefore have a strong ethnic Chinese identity. Hence, their organisations focus on the interests and needs of ethnic Chinese (including Chinese businesspeople) and support continuing ties to China, but rarely engage in cross-ethnic initiatives that promote inter-ethnic solidarity and understanding. Conversely, Chinese Indonesians who founded and lead cross-ethnic organisations received their education in Indonesian-medium schools during the New Order and have many indigenous Indonesian friends. Hence, they have more inclusive ethnic and cultural identities and favour the integration of Chinese Indonesians into the wider Indonesian society. They believe that reaching out directly to the indigenous Indonesian community is the most effective way to promote inter-ethnic understanding and rectify the negative stereotypes about Chinese Indonesians. Moreover, these leaders are not involved in business activities. Therefore, unlike other major Chinese organisations, their organisations do not serve as a platform for Chinese businesspeople to establish business networks but instead focus on promoting cross-ethnic understanding and solidarity.

4.4 The Perceptions of Indigenous Indonesians

Despite the efforts of the Chinese to gain favour with indigenous Indonesians, through philanthropic efforts or the creation of various cross-ethnic organisations, the perceptions of many indigenous Indonesians of the Chinese often remain rather negative. For example, a university lecturer who is also an executive committee member of a few ethnic Chinese organisations in Surabaya pointed out that most of these organisations' events, particularly dinners celebrating Chinese festivals organisational anniversaries, are often too extravagant and reinforce negative perceptions of the Chinese:

> Many Chinese organisations often hold Chinese festival dinners and other events at high-class hotels and upscale [Chinese] restaurants. Seriously, I think this is too extravagant. Waiters and waitresses serving at these hotels and restaurants are mostly indigenous Indonesians. Don't they know how to calculate how much has been spent each time a Chinese organisation holds a dinner? They will certainly see the Chinese as wealthy, extravagant and loving to show off their wealth. After all, the Chinese are generally economically better off compared to the indigenous population. (interview with Susana, in Mandarin, January 14, 2011)

My informant's concern was not without basis. Although to date there is no official data on the financial condition of Chinese Indonesians, they are generally perceived as economically dominant compared to indigenous Indonesians. As long as the uneven distribution of wealth, which is perceived to be along racial lines, remains unresolved, in addition to the negative perceptions of Chinese businesspeople that still exist among indigenous people, the more extravagant the events of Chinese organisations the more they reproduce the negative stereotypes of the Chinese.

In addition, an indigenous NGO activist in Medan commented that the charitable activities carried out by major Chinese organisations were not sufficient to reduce the racial prejudice among the indigenous population towards the Chinese. He argued that Chinese organisations should tackle racism by promoting political education about ethnic and cultural diversity among indigenous Indonesians:

> [The Chinese community] could promote the political awareness [about ethnic and cultural diversity] among indigenous Indonesians by facilitating training workshops on political awareness [about ethnic and cultural diversity for the indigenous population]. They should do that. They [the Chinese community] also have several social organisations but these organisations are mostly charitable. They only donate groceries [to the poor] but never promote political awareness [about ethnic and cultural diversity among the non-Chinese]. The poor just accept whatever is given [by Chinese organisations] but they still have the mindset of 'Chinese versus non-Chinese'.... So their charity endeavours should be followed by contributions that are more

concrete in raising the awareness of the non-Chinese about the contributions of the Chinese. (interview with Usman, in Indonesian, July 30, 2010)

A reader of *Guoji Ribao* made a similar remark on the limitations of philanthropic activities in eliminating anti-Chinese sentiments that are deeply rooted among the non-Chinese:

> Although the Chinese often offer relief aid to victims of disasters, provide free medical aid and distribute food for the needy, it only scratches the surface of the anti-Chinese problem and can hardly solve the root causes. The only way is through cultural and educational initiatives as well as introducing the historical background of ethnic Chinese in Indonesia. (Peng 2010)

The above comments imply that the reader was not confident that the philanthropic activities and endeavours of Chinese organisations could reduce the prejudice of the indigenous Indonesians against the Chinese. He believed the indigenous Indonesians' perceptions of Chinese Indonesians would change only if they understood the historical background of Chinese Indonesians. This can only be accomplished through cultural and educational initiatives.

On May 15, 2012, *Koran Tempo*, a mainstream Indonesian-language newspaper, published a letter from a reader who called for all ethnic Chinese organisations in Indonesia to be disbanded. According to the letter, the reader was not comfortable with the official visit of the chief and a few officers of the Overseas Chinese Affairs Office in Beijing to Indonesia and their meeting with several Chinese Indonesian community leaders in Jakarta in April 2012. The following is my translation of the full text of the letter:[21]

Disband Ethnic Chinese Organisations

Recently, on April 20, the delegation of the Overseas Chinese Affairs Office in Beijing visited Jakarta and met with the Indonesian Chinese Entrepreneur Association. The chief of the Office Li In Zhe remarked that the ethnic Chinese from around the world have built good 'foreign relations' with China. This is an advantage that other ethnic groups do not have. At present, China has become the second largest economy in the world, thanks to the great contribution of the Chinese/Chinese overseas.

He also said that the objective of the visit was to offer assistance to solve the problems of learning the Chinese language among young Chinese/Chinese overseas. Learning the Chinese language

---

21. See Appendix VI for the original text of the letter.

> and understanding Chinese culture are important for strengthening the unity of the ethnic Chinese. Therefore, he hoped young Chinese overseas would master the Chinese language, strengthen their communication with young Chinese in China, and strengthen their ethnic identity.[22]
>
> This kind of visit was also made in other cities outside Jakarta. In order to safeguard the interest of our nation, the Indonesian nation, especially in the aspects of nation and character building, as well as to prevent the utilisation of 'Chinese organisations' as a fifth column for China, we should disband and prohibit organisations that are exclusively 'Chinese'. The public and social organisations play a crucial role in this matter because without pressure from the public, the government will certainly not take any action! Do not let foreign interests manipulate our reformation.
>
> Sastrawinata
> Jalan Benda, Cilandak Timur
> Pasar Minggu, Jakarta Selatan

Although we are not sure if the writer of the letter is an indigenous Indonesian since the name could also be of that of a Chinese Indonesian,[23] this letter did highlight the displeasure of some Indonesians at the resurgence of ethnic Chinese organisational activities in the *reformasi* era, as well as their deep concern about the close ties between Chinese organisations and China. If the letter was written by an indigenous Indonesian, it also implies that the close ties between Chinese organisations and China has aroused suspicion about Chinese Indonesians' loyalty to Indonesia among some indigenous Indonesians. They are worried that the Chinese government will utilise Chinese organisations in Indonesia as a communist 'fifth column' to interfere in the domestic affairs of Indonesia, although there is no evidence to show that China has such an intention. As discussed in Chapter 2, late in the Sukarno era, some Indonesian anti-communist leaders perceived the Chinese minority as a potential 'fifth column' of China, considering the local Chinese to be oriented towards China and loyal to the Chinese government (Suryadinata 1992, 167); this attitude became even stronger during the Suharto era. It is interesting that this fear has resurfaced in the post-Suharto era precisely because of the issues discussed in this chapter, the revival of

---

22. This incident also reveals insensitivity on the part of the Overseas Chinese Affairs Office in Beijing.
23. I would like to thank one of the reviewers for pointing this out.

Chinese language and tradition and the development of closer business ties with China.

The letter drew the attention of a few Chinese Indonesians. Yu Zhusheng (余竹生), a commentator on Indonesia's Metro TV's Chinese-language programme, as interviewed by *Lianhe Zaobao* (Singapore's mainstream Chinese-language newspaper), opined that Chinese organisations should position themselves as local Indonesian organisations and refrain from being too close to China. He pointed out that many Chinese organisations were too close to the Chinese embassy in Indonesia and some of them even invited officers from the embassy to interfere in the internal disputes among their members (Yu 2012).[24] ChanCT (2012), a member of a Chinese Indonesian online Yahoo discussion group known as *Budaya Tionghoa* (Chinese Culture), argued that the freedom to organise was a basic human right and Chinese Indonesians should not be barred from setting up organisations based on ethnicity. This individual opined that, instead of making a provocative statement by calling for the disbandment of all ethnic Chinese organisations in Indonesia, the writer of the letter should urge the organisations to put on more meaningful social activities that could benefit the wider society. ChanCT's suggestion is relevant because the activities and events organised by ethnic Chinese organisations mostly cater to the interests and needs of ethnic Chinese and rarely include non-Chinese, as I mentioned earlier in this chapter. Most ethnic Chinese organisations in the post-Suharto era have merely established a limited interaction with the wider local society. The letter that calls for the disbandment of all ethnic Chinese organisations shows that some Indonesians are uncomfortable with the existence of organisations that are exclusively Chinese in terms of their membership and activities, as well as their close relationships with China. This is mainly due to the negative perceptions of Chinese Indonesians as clannish, exclusive, opportunistic, and oriented towards China instead of Indonesia.

4.5 Discussion and Conclusion

The emergence of a more open and liberal socio-political environment in post-1998 Indonesia has opened up opportunities for Chinese Indonesians to establish and participate in various ethnic- and non-ethnic-based organisations. In addition, the rise of China as an economic power has played a part in the revival of ethnic identity among Chinese Indonesians. This has resulted in the mushrooming of ethnic Chinese–based organisations in post-1998 Indonesia. Most of these organisations have been established by

---

24. Yu, however, did not reveal the names and other details of these organisations. During my fieldwork in Medan and Surabaya, I never heard of any factions in local ethnic Chinese organisations that invited the Chinese embassy to interfere in their internal affairs.

Chinese Indonesians with a strong ethnic identity. These Chinese are keen to revive and bolster Chinese ethnic and cultural identities, which were suppressed and hidden during the New Order period. They utilise their intra-ethnic linkages to safeguard Chinese ethnic and cultural identities by promoting Chinese cultural and social activities among the Chinese, consequently contributing to multiculturalism in post-Suharto Indonesia. Using Giddens's concept of structure and agency, I argue that the more open and liberal socio-political environment in post-Suharto Indonesia is both the medium and the outcome of Chinese Indonesians' actions in opening up the Chinese socio-cultural sphere. However, the activities and events organised by these organisations are mostly focused on the interests and needs of ethnic Chinese and rarely include non-Chinese. Hence, most ethnic Chinese organisations in the post-Suharto era have merely established a limited interaction with the wider local society. This often feeds into the view that the Chinese are very insular and exclusive. Moreover, several Chinese organisations are well connected with China, where Chinese Indonesians have their ancestral roots. In addition, some Chinese organisations often hold their events in an excessively extravagant way. All these factors have a tendency to reproduce and perpetuate stereotypes of the Chinese as exclusive, clannish, loving to show off their wealth, opportunistic, and oriented towards China instead of Indonesia.

At the same time, there are also Chinese Indonesians who favour integration into the wider Indonesian society; some have formed socio-cultural organisations that promote cross-ethnic understanding and solidarity. The integrated school founded by Sofyan Tan in Medan and Kalimas in Surabaya are such organisations. By introducing the programme of fosterage, Tan's school has to some extent reduced the negative stereotypes that indigenous and Chinese Indonesian students and parents hold towards each other, as well as generated some good and strong relationships between patrons and protégés from different ethnic and religious backgrounds. Students have the opportunity to learn about ethnic and cultural differences in the country, and thus have better understanding of other ethnic groups. The initiatives of Kalimas resulted in changes in the constitution pertaining to the eligibility of presidential candidates and the passing of a bill that criminalised ethnic and racial discrimination. However, to date, Chinese Indonesian community leaders and activists who actively engage in cross-ethnic initiatives are rare and have achieved only limited success in altering the generally negative perceptions of the Chinese within the wider society. The approaches of Tan's school and Kalimas are still not popular among Chinese organisations in Medan and Surabaya.

Although Chinese Indonesians are free openly to express and celebrate their ethnic and cultural identities in the post-Suharto era, their position in Indonesian society, on the whole, remains ambivalent because they are generally still perceived by the indigenous Indonesians as an alien minority that is exclusive, extravagant, opportunistic, and oriented towards China. Therefore, the increasing visibility of Chinese ethnic and cultural identities does sometimes result in threats and backlash against the Chinese. It is therefore not surprising that some Chinese community leaders such as Wahidin think it is best for the Chinese to keep a low profile and not to be too visible.

Nevertheless, the experience of Tan's school suggests that the education system of Indonesia could encourage more people, including Chinese Indonesians, to become actively involved in cross-ethnic initiatives if the schools introduced programmes and activities that promote inter-ethnic understanding and solidarity.

On the other hand, the above discussion also shows that Chinese Medanese have a relatively stronger ethnic identity compared to their counterparts in Surabaya. The ethnic Chinese socio-cultural life in Medan is more vibrant than that of Surabaya. This can be seen from the fact that the Chinese Medanese community established STBA-PIA, the first Chinese-language tertiary institution in Indonesia to offer a bachelor's degree programme in the Chinese language. In fact, to date STBA-PIA is the only such Chinese-language tertiary institution in the country. Such differences between Chinese Medanese and Chinese Surabayans are due to the historical and geographical factors that I mentioned in Chapter 1. Hence, it can be said that the historical and geographical differences between Chinese Medanese and Chinese Surabayans made it easier for the latter to resist the attractions of the freedom to openly express their ethnic identity and to have greater access to China, Chinese-language newspapers, and ethnic Chinese organisations in the post-Suharto era.

5
Local Ethnic Chinese Business*

Susanto, a Chinese Indonesian, lives in Medan and is a stuffed toy distributor. He runs his business from a shophouse located in the central city area. He started his business in 2003; in these past 10 years the business has remained small in scale. He brings in the stuffed toys from Jakarta and sells them to customers in Medan. He has fifteen employees working for him, most of whom are indigenous Indonesians.

Susanto revealed to me that, since the end of the New Order regime, the central government has become stricter in collecting taxes from business enterprises. Business owners need to declare their revenues, calculate the taxes they have to pay, and make the payment accordingly. Tax officers later visit these companies to check their actual revenues. If tax officers find that business owners have under-reported their revenues, instead of penalising the business owners, they usually ask for bribes to cover up the tax fraud. Susanto emphasised, however, that even if a business owner has paid all the necessary taxes, tax officers usually create fictive taxes and charges and request the business owner to pay accordingly. Moreover, tax officers often demand higher bribes from businesspeople who are ethnic Chinese as they are deemed by others to be doing better in business. For this reason, Susanto and many local Chinese businesspeople have found it expedient not to declare their actual revenues, knowing that being honest does not pay. They will have to pay even more taxes and bribes. Instead, they wait for the officers to visit and negotiate with them the rates of the taxes and bribes requested and only then pay their taxes. In my interview with him, Susanto said, 'Although many businesspeople and I feel bad about it, we

---

* Part of this chapter was published earlier in Chong (2015). The names of informants in this chapter are pseudonyms except for the following public figures: Mely G. Tan, Hasyim, Sofyan Tan, Johan Tjongiran, Anuar Shah, Dirk A. Buiskool, Dédé Oemoto, Yap Juk Lim, Anton Prijatno and Samas H. Widjaja.

have no choice but to pay them [the bribes] since we have to survive' (interview in Mandarin, August 4, 2010). Susanto also revealed that he and many Chinese businesspeople prefer not to fight against extortion because they are 'afraid of running into trouble' (in Mandarin, *pa mafan* 怕麻煩) by doing so. Therefore, they would rather pay bribes to avoid any further problems. This also indicates that these Chinese businesspeople possess enough economic capital (money) to pay the bribes in order to protect their business.

Susanto's story indicates the ambivalent value, for the Chinese, of democratisation in post-Suharto Indonesia. Although democratisation has opened space for them to live their culture and express their ethnicity, it has not led to the emergence of good governance promoting the rule of law, transparency, and accountability; corruption remains endemic in state institutions. This poorly developed democratisation creates, therefore, an even more ambivalent situation for Chinese Indonesian businesspeople. On the one hand, they remain targets of extortion by power-holders; on the other hand, they also play a role in perpetuating the corrupt, predatory political-business system. In this chapter, following Giddens's structure-agency theory, I look at how the corrupt and muddy business environment of the post–New Order era has influenced the ways by which Chinese Indonesian businesspeople in Medan and Surabaya gain and safeguard their business interests, as well as deal with illegal practices by government officials, police, and *preman*. I argue that due to the fear of the hassle of fighting back, as well as the economic and social capital they possess, Chinese Indonesian businesspeople tend on the whole to give in to the illegal requests of government officials, police, and *preman*, and resort to illegal or semi-legal means as well as opportunistic tactics to gain wealth and protect their business interests. Although there are Chinese businesspeople who fight against illegal practices, such businesspeople are rare. Therefore, this collusion with corrupt practices in turn reinforces the negative stereotypes against the Chinese and consequently reproduces their ambivalent position.

5.1 The Economic Role of the Ethnic Chinese in Post–New Order Medan and Surabaya

Sofyan Wanandi (1999), Michael Backman (2001), and Charles A. Coppel (2008) point out that it is commonly asserted that ethnic Chinese control 70% of Indonesia's economy, although official data for the economic domination of the Chinese in Indonesia are unavailable. These authors, however, emphasise that such a view is an exaggeration because a large portion of Indonesia's economy (such as the oil and gas industry) has always been under the control of the state, not the Chinese. In addition, sociologist Mely G. Tan argues that it is impossible for the Chinese minority, who constitute less than 3% of the total population in Indonesia, to control 70% of the national economy (personal communication with Mely G. Tan, in English, June 8, 2010). Wanandi (1999, 132) suggests that Chinese Indonesian businesses constitute only 25% of the national economy, while Backman (2001) estimates that Chinese Indonesians 'control 70 per cent of the private, corporate, domestic capital' (88).

In the post-Suharto era, Chinese Indonesians continue to play a crucial role in the economic development of Medan and Surabaya. Since there are no available official data specifically on the economic domination of Chinese Indonesians, I have had to rely on individual interviews to obtain information on this aspect. According to an NGO activist in Medan, Chinese Indonesians in the city dominate businesses medium-sized and above. At the same time, domination of businesses that are medium-sized and below is almost split evenly between Chinese and indigenous businesspeople. Businesses that are small and micro are dominated by indigenous businesspeople (interview with Halim, in Indonesian, July 26, 2010). In addition, three other NGO activists disclosed that Chinese businesspeople engage in nearly all sectors of the economy in Medan except the construction industry, which is dominated by indigenous Batak businesspeople and members of youth/crime organisations (interview with Daniel, in Indonesian, September 17, 2010; interview with Surya, in Indonesian, September 17, 2010; interview with Halim, in Indonesian, July 26, 2010). A local economic analyst in Surabaya remarked that Chinese businesspeople dominate 100% of manufacturing and about 90% of real estate business in the city. In addition, more than 60% of bankers and about 70% of advertisers in Surabaya are Chinese Indonesian (interview with Wahyu, in Indonesian, May 18, 2011). In short, Chinese Indonesians continue to dominate the private economies of Medan and Surabaya in the post–New Order era.

5.2 The Business Environment in Post–New Order Indonesia

Since the advent of democratisation in Indonesia, international and domestic organisations such as the SMERU Research Institute, the World Bank, and the United States Agency for International Development (USAID) have been actively offering policy advice on the decentralisation of state authority in the country. The SMERU Research Institute sees regional decentralisation as a huge administrative operation that could improve weaknesses in the administration of central and local governments (Usman 2002). The World Bank Group (2010) believes that decentralisation would break up stifling central government authority, reduce complex bureaucratic procedures and administrative bottlenecks, as well as 'increase government officials' sensitivity to local conditions and needs'. A USAID publication argues that decentralisation would stimulate the development of democratic, accountable, and effective local governance (USAID Office of Democracy and Governance 2000, 7). In particular, the Asia Foundation assists local governments in addressing inefficiencies in the business licensing process and reducing the cost of doing business in Indonesia through developing the One Stop Shops (OSS) programme. The OSS are service centres that handle applications of various business permits (Steer 2006). As stated in an article that introduces the programme, '[The OSS] are new institutions that merge authority from disparate technical departments into one office where licenses and permits can be obtained quickly' (Steer 2006, 7).

However, during my fieldwork in Medan, it was observed that the OSS, established with the aim of addressing the licensing process and reducing the burden on business, actually created more burdens for local businesspeople. According to a news report in *Harian Orbit*, a local Indonesian-language newspaper in Medan, officials at the centre often demanded bribes by asking for 'service charges' from applicants. If applicants refused to pay, they would wait for a long time before getting their permits ('Pungli Berdalih Uang Jasa' 2010). For instance, applicants for a business permit (SIUP, *Surat Izin Usaha Perdagangan*) needed to pay an extra Rp150,000 (about US$17) of unofficial 'service charge' to the officials in order to get the permit on time ('Pungli Berdalih Uang Jasa' 2010). Such incidents have been highlighted in local newspapers. The mayor, Rahudman Harahap, said he would summon the persons in charge of the OSS ('Kepala dan Sekretaris BPPT Medan Diduga Pungli' 2010). As of December 2013, the local government had not yet investigated the problem and such corrupt practices were still rampant in the OSS of Medan ('Tak Mampu Stop Pungli di BPPT Medan' 2013).

In addition, scholars have noted that the implementation of regional decentralisation in Indonesia has produced many regional heads who behave like 'little kings' (*raja-raja kecil*) in the sense that they perceive decentralisation and regional autonomy to mean more power to control local resources and raise revenues rather than as more responsibility to offer better public services to their local constituencies. These 'little kings' are unaccountable to central authorities, local legislatures, or local citizens (Hofman and Kaiser 2004, 26; Hofman and Kaiser 2006, 97; Azis 2003, 3; Firman 2009, 148). Since the decentralisation law went into effect, local governments in Indonesia have had more power to tax the local population. According to my informants, the imposition of new taxes has increased burdens on the business community (interview with Johan Tjongiran, in Mandarin, August 3, 2010; interview with Sofyan Tan, in Indonesian, August 23, 2010; interview with Harianto, in Mandarin, November 23, 2010). The local governments in Medan and Surabaya have been levying new taxes and charges on businesses as a means to increase direct revenues, as well as to extract indirect revenues in the form of bribes. Moreover, officials at all levels of governments, i.e., central, provincial, and local, claim ultimate authority over many kinds of investment activity (Hadiz and Robison 2005, 235–36). This increases unpredictability in the business environment and perpetuates the common practice of bribing officials for licenses and the like.

At the end of 2010, the Committee for the Monitoring of Regional Autonomy (KPPOD, or Komite Pemantau Pelaksanaan Otonomi Daerah), an NGO in Indonesia that monitors the implementation of regional autonomy in the country, announced that North Sumatra and East Java, where Medan and Surabaya are located, had more problematic local regulations issued by the city and *kabupaten* governments than all other provinces. The committee proposed that 315 local regulations in North Sumatra and 291 local regulations in East Java should be abolished because they were deemed to hamper business activities in the provinces. Nevertheless, as of 2011, the city and *kabupaten* governments of North Sumatra and East Java had repealed only ninety-eight and ninety-one of the problematic regulations respectively ('Evaluasi Perda Penghambat Investasi Diperketat' 2011).[1]

Medan is notorious for the prominence and influence of its gangsters or *preman*. It is known as 'gangster city' (*kota preman*) (Honna 2011, 266). As ethnic Chinese are often deemed wealthier than others in Medan, they always become targets of extortion for *preman* (Hadiluwih 1994, 159). It is also common for local Chinese Indonesian businesspeople in the city to rely on extra-legal resources such as *preman* for their security and protection (Purdey 2006, 117). *Preman* in Medan are mostly members of major New Order–nurtured youth/crime organisations such as Pancasila Youth (PP, or Pemuda Pancasila), Work Service Youth Association (IPK, or Ikatan Pemuda Karya), and Armed Forces Sons' and Daughters' Communication Forum (FKPPI). When the Indonesian Democratic Party of Struggle (PDI-P) became the ruling party after winning a majority of national parliamentary seats in the 1999 elections, it formed Satgas PDI-P as the paramilitary arm of the party to compete with other, more established youth/crime organisations in Medan in controlling local state and private resources (Hadiz 2003, 128).[2] Although the *satgas* was banned in 2004, it was later revived in a less formal way (Wilson 2010, 204–5). In other words, there are more *preman* organisations in Medan now than before the fall of Suharto.

Indeed, according to Hadiz (2004, 626), the collapse of the Suharto regime did not reduce the influence of local *preman* linked to youth/crime organisations in Medan, but instead brought new opportunities for them

---

1. These are the latest data available. There is no further update after 2011.
2. According to Wilson (2010, 204), among all political parties, PDI-P has the largest number of members with a *preman* background. The party greatly appeals to *preman* through its populist approach and pro-'little people' rhetoric.

to exploit. These *preman* are able to provide muscle for candidates during election periods and to fund political bids since they dominate lucrative underworld businesses (Hadiz 2003, 128). In addition, many leaders of such youth/crime organisations are given opportunities to run local branches of political parties. Some even hold local parliamentary seats and some top executive body positions in local government (Hadiz 2003, 125–26). For instance, for the 1999–2004 period, three members of the Medan city council—Bangkit Sitepu (Golkar), Moses Tambunan (Golkar), and Martius Latuperissa (Justice and Unity Party)—were leaders of the local branches of *preman* organisations. Sitepu, Tambunan, and Latuperissa led the Medan branches of PP, IPK, and FKPPI respectively (Hadiz 2005a, 47; Ryter 2000, 19–21; Soed 2002). Besides that, Ajib Shah, the former chairperson of PP's North Sumatra branch, is a member of the North Sumatra provincial legislature affiliated with Golkar for the 2009–2014 period (Bangun 2013; 'DPRDSU: Pemasok Narkoba' 2012; 'Menuju Parpol Terbaik di Sumut' 2013). He was also a mayoral candidate in Medan's 2010 mayoral election ('H. Anif Shah dan Keluarga' 2010). Therefore, it can be said that members and leaders of local youth/crime organisations in Medan have captured the new local state institutions and political vehicles in the *reformasi* era.

Some of my informants who are local Chinese businesspeople in Medan say they have encountered more harassment and extortion from *preman* in the post-Suharto era, especially during Megawati's presidency (2001–2004) (interview with Susanto, in Mandarin, August 4, 2010; interview with Eddie, in Mandarin, November 10, 2010). A few disclosed that *preman* often ask for 'protection money' from businesspeople who own factories or shophouses; otherwise these places are vandalised (interview with Hasyim, in Indonesian, August 11, 2010; interview with Sofyan Tan, in Indonesian, August 23, 2010; interview with Halim, in Indonesian, July 26, 2010; interview with Joko, in Indonesian, November 11, 2010). To further squeeze money from these businesses, when goods are unloaded in front of shophouses, *preman* force their loading or unloading services on the businesses. Usually they charge from Rp500 (about US$0.06) to Rp1,000 (about US$0.12) per item. Even if such services are refused, the business owners still need to pay the *preman* not to vandalise their shophouses (interview with Johan Tjongiran, in Mandarin, August 23, 2010; interview with Andi, in Indonesian, September 20, 2010). In addition, *preman* ask for between Rp300,000 (about US$33) and Rp500,000 (about US$56) when a businessperson opens a new company in their area; if a shophouse is renovated, the owner also needs to pay a certain amount of money to *preman* (interview with Johan Tjongiran, in Mandarin, August 23). Moreover, whenever *preman* organisations have installation events, they send an 'invitation' with a proposal for expenses to be paid by businesspeople and ask for 'donations'. Normally businesspeople need to pay them at least Rp10,000 (about US$1.12) to Rp20,000 (about US$2.24) (interview with Daniel, in Indonesian, September 17, 2010; interview with Johan Tjongiran, in Mandarin, August 23, 2010). Some Chinese businesspeople need to pay *uang keamanan* (protection money) to more than one *preman* if there is more than one youth/crime organisation that claims authority over that particular area (interview with Andi, in Indonesian, September 20, 2010). As a 'service' to industrialists, *preman* also help to break up strikes (interview with Halim, in Indonesian, July 26, 2010).

It is important to point out that *preman* also demand *uang keamanan* from indigenous businesspeople.[3] But my informants disclosed that they often ask for more *uang keamanan* from businesspeople who are ethnic Chinese as the latter are deemed by others to be doing better than their non-Chinese counterparts (interview with Susanto, in Mandarin, August 4, 2010; interview with Sofyan Tan, in Indonesian, August 23, 2010).

Why do *preman* ask for money from the business community? According to the chief of PP's North Sumatra branch, there are too many unemployed citizens in Indonesia. If they join 'youth' organisations like the PP, these organisations arrange for them to help enforce the safety of business areas, letting them collect money from businesspeople (interview with Anuar Shah, in Indonesian, October 30, 2010). Sociologist Usman Pelly and criminologist Mohammad Irvan Olii, as interviewed by *Gatra* and *The Jakarta Globe* respectively, made a similar argument, that poverty and unemployment are the main causes of *premanism* (Sujatmoko et al. 1995; Nirmala 2012). According to another source, the unemployment rate in Indonesia reached 6.8% in 2011, while more than half the population was living on less than US$2 per day in the same year. In addition, more than 65% of workers in the country were employed informally (Brooks 2011).[4] Poverty and the failure of the Indonesian government to create sufficient employment opportunities for its citizens are seen by many as the main causes of the rampant nature of such extortion.

Informants told me that *preman* have become less active since President Susilo Bambang Yudhoyono (2004–2014) came to power because the police have become more powerful and have started to arrest *preman* who extort money from the business community (interview with Johan Tjongiran, in Mandarin, August 3, 2010; interview with Susanto, in Mandarin, August 4,

---

3. For instance, an indigenous businesswoman who owned a restaurant in Medan was beaten by two *preman* on November 4, 2010, when she refused to pay the 'protection money' worth Rp500,000 (about US$56), which she deemed too high. See 'Tidak Beri Uang Keamanan, Preman Pukul Ibu Rumahtangga' (2010, 4). In addition, *preman* often extort money from owners of small- and medium-sized businesses, including street vendors (*pedagang kaki lima*), who are mostly indigenous Indonesians, in exchange for 'protection'. See Tan (2004, 134–36).

4. These are the latest data available at the time of writing.

2010; interview with Dirk A. Buiskool, in English, July 14, 2010). This corresponds to findings by other scholars working on Indonesia (Aspinall, Dettman, and Warburton 2011, 33; Wilson 2011, 257–58). According to Wilson (2011, 257), high-profile 'anti-*preman*' campaigns were initially run by the police in 2001 and were limited to Jakarta, but they became national in scope by 2004. Aspinall and his co-authors on the other hand, remark that the influence of the Work Service Youth Association (IPK), once a dominant youth/crime organisation in Medan, has declined since the death of its founder, Olo Panggabean, in 2009 (Aspinall, Dettman, and Warburton 2011, 33).[5] The diminution of the power of IPK is also due to a police crackdown on illegal gambling run by the organisation. Although the power of *preman* organisations in the city has markedly declined, it is alleged that business enterprises in certain areas such as Jalan Asia and Jalan Gatot Subroto still encounter harassment and extortion from *preman* (interview with Andi, in Indonesian, September 20, 2010).

In Surabaya, on the other hand, youth/crime organisations are much less prominent and influential. The *preman* who offer 'protection' for Chinese business premises in Surabaya are often unorganised Madurese *preman*. According to Dédé Oetomo, an ethnic Chinese social activist in Surabaya, there is a system of mutual dependence between Chinese businesspeople and Madurese *preman* in Surabaya. Chinese businesspeople usually pay about Rp500,000 (US$56) each month to Madurese *preman* in exchange for protection of their business (interview with Dédé Oetomo, in English, December 24, 2010). Such a system of mutual dependence existed in the city even before the demise of the New Order regime. Although unorganised, the Madurese *preman* normally allocate territories among themselves so that each area only has one *preman* in charge of 'safety'. The *preman* make sure that the business premises in their territories are free of burglary, theft, robbery, and vandalism (interview with Dédé Oetomo, in English, December 24, 2010).

In Surabaya, underworld activities are controlled by the military and police units. According to Hadiz (2010, 140), it is alleged that the military, rather than *preman* from youth/crime organisations, acts as immediate protectors and bodyguards for illegal gambling operations controlled by Chinese Indonesians in Surabaya. Furthermore, the navy and marine units in the city are said to have direct links with local prostitution.

It is ironic, therefore, that in attempting to control *preman* activities, the police have started acting like *preman*. According to an NGO activist in Medan, local police officers often extort money from businesspeople in the city, especially those who own factories; such incidents have become more

---

5. See also Dedy (2009).

rampant especially throughout the 'anti *preman*' campaigns (interview with Joko, in Indonesian, November 11, 2010). The police officers will pay a visit to a factory and ask for money. If the business owner refuses to pay, the police coerce him or her to admit to offences which he or she did not commit, threatening to close down the factory. Sometimes the police will even confiscate some machines in a factory if the business owner refuses to pay them money (interview with Joko, in Indonesian, November 11, 2010). Wilson (2011) suggests that such phenomena indicate that some police 'have used the campaigns as an opportunity to reclaim sources of illegal rent extraction taken from them by street level racketeers' (257). A well-established Chinese businessperson in Medan has even remarked that

> During Suharto's reign, the military was the most powerful institution. Since the fall of Suharto, the military is not as powerful as before. Now the police are more powerful. They often ask for money from businesspeople and will give us a hard time if we refuse to pay them. So the police are no different from a select group of scoundrels. (interview with Erik, in Mandarin, August 25, 2010)

Similarly, in Surabaya, the police often ask for money from local businesspeople, who are mostly ethnic Chinese. According to an informant who used to work in a real estate company in Surabaya's Chinatown, whenever the police have an event, they ask for 'contributions' from businesspeople in their area. If the businesspeople refuse to pay, the police give them a hard time if they ask for police help (personal communication with Yati, in Indonesian, April 8, 2011). In addition, Junus, a university professor in Surabaya, told me that the police often visit nightclubs and discos (mostly run by Chinese businesspeople) and ask for a 'protection fee'. If the owners refuse to pay, the police will conduct a raid and threaten to close down their premises (interview with Junus, in Indonesian, January 11, 2011).

In this difficult business environment, some Chinese businesspeople resort to illegal or semi-legal business practices to gain wealth and safeguard their business interests.

5.3 Dealing with Power-holders, Police, and Military Commanders

As mentioned earlier, according to some of my informants, most of the Chinese businesspeople in Medan and Surabaya usually just pay the money or bribes requested by government officials in order to get their business permit or other related documents issued on time. Most of them give in to police officers' illegal requests in order to prevent any further problems. Sometimes they try to negotiate with the people who ask for money if the amount requested is too large (interview with Daniel, in Indonesian, July 13,

2010; interview with Johan Tjongiran, in Mandarin, August 3, 2010; interview with Susanto, in Mandarin, August 4, 2010; interview with Atan, in Mandarin, February 28, 2011). As I mentioned at the opening of this chapter, it is alleged that even if a businessperson pays all taxes and charges levied on his or her business accordingly, tax officers will still pay a visit to check his or her business and ask for bribes; even when they do pay their taxes honestly, they will have to pay more. So, most Chinese businesspeople will pay only some of the taxes and charges. Then when tax officers pay a visit to their companies, they will usually just bribe the officers as requested (interview with Johan Tjongiran, in Mandarin, August 3, 2010; interview with Susanto, in Mandarin, August 4, 2013). Johan Tjongiran, an ethnic Chinese social activist in Medan, explained this practice by giving an example:

> For instance, if a businessperson needs to pay Rp500 million [about US$55,788] of taxes, the officers would normally ask him or her to pay only Rp250 million [about US$27,894] and they would keep Rp220 million [about US$24,547] for themselves, and submit only Rp30 million [about US$3,347] to the government. (interview with Johan Tjongiran, in Mandarin, August 3, 2010)

Susanto, the ethnic Chinese toy distributor in Medan mentioned in the opening story of this chapter, argues:

> The wealthiest people in Indonesia are in fact not ethnic Chinese business-people but indigenous bureaucrats in the central and local governments like Gayus Tambunan.[6] They become extremely rich after getting many bribes from businesspeople. Their children often spend time shopping in Singapore and bringing back many branded luxury goods to Indonesia. (interview with Susanto, in Mandarin, August 4, 2010)

Following Bourdieu's concept of habitus and field, I argue that most Chinese businesspeople choose to give in to the illegal requests of government officials, police, and *preman* not only due to their reluctance to run into more trouble and the fear of the hassle of fighting back, but also because they have enough economic capital to pay the bribes and extortion to protect their business and save them from further troubles. This is in line with Bourdieu's notion of habitus and field: social actors well endowed with capital tend to defend the status quo of the field (social structure) they are in, in order to safeguard their capital.

Although there are also Chinese businesspeople who refuse to be extorted by the police and who organise and protest against the extortion,

---

6. Gayus Tambunan is a former tax official who was arrested by police on March 30, 2010 for alleged tax evasion of Rp25 billion (about US$272,659). See Abdussalam (2010) and 'Gayus Tambunan Arrested' (2010). Although Tambunan is of Batak origin, a minority ethnic group, his ethnicity is never problematised by the public because the Batak are an indigenous group in the country.

such businesspeople are rare. These businesspeople often do not have the necessary economic capital to pay bribes. They therefore decide to protest against the extortion in order to safeguard their business. This is in line with Bourdieu's notion of habitus and field, that the social actors least endowed with capital are the most inclined to challenge the status quo of the field (social structure) they are in. One well-known example is Yap Juk Lim (葉鬱林), a local Chinese businessperson engaged in the snack production industry near Jalan Metal, Medan. Yap used to have to pay the police between Rp300,000 (about US$33) and Rp400,000 (about US$45) every time they visited his factory. Eventually, in 2007, he could not bear the extortion and refused to pay the police. As a result, the police alleged that his factory had used expired ingredients and detained him for eight days (interview with Yap Juk Lim, in Mandarin, November 16, 2010). As noted in a news report in *Waspada*, the Medan branch of the Regional Forum of Small and Medium Enterprises (FORDA UKM, or Forum Daerah Usaha Kecil dan Menengah) supported Yap and, on March 25, 2008, launched a public protest together with other owners of small- and medium-sized businesses from different ethnic backgrounds ('Hari Ini Ratusan Pelaku UKM Unjukrasa Keprihatinan' 2008). The protest took place in front of the North Sumatra Police Headquarters, the governor's office, the mayor's office, the provincial legislature, and the Medan city council. About 2,000 people joined the protest, demanding that the police stop targeting the owners of small- and medium-sized businesses (interview with Yap Juk Lim, in Mandarin, November 16, 2010). According to Yap, after the protest, the police officers stopped harassing the factories around Jalan Metal for a long time. From 2010, however, they again began to visit some factories in that area, asking for payments; Yap's factory, however, remained free from harassment (interview with Yap Juk Lim, in Mandarin, November 16, 2010). This indicates that the police recognised Yap would fight back if they tried to extort him.

Sofyan Tan, the 2010 mayoral candidate in Medan, revealed that many local Chinese businesspeople viewed Yap's action positively although it was not a common practice among Chinese businesspeople (interview with Sofyan Tan, in Indonesian, May 7, 2013). Yap spoke of the reluctance of most Chinese businesspeople to fight against extortion by government officials and police, and their reluctance to spend time getting themselves organised:

> We have to get ourselves organised if we want to fight against such illegal requests. Many Chinese businesspeople regard this as time-consuming and would rather give in to illegal requests of government officials and police to avoid any further problems. (interview with Yap Juk Lim, in Mandarin, November 16, 2010)

Another Chinese businessperson made a similar remark: 'The Chinese are generally afraid of trouble. If paying money to those extorting them can save them from further troubles, they will just pay the money instead of fighting back' (interview with Ivan, in Hokkien, July 16, 2010).

In short, most Chinese businesspeople prefer to give in to the illegal requests of government officials and police because they are afraid of the hassle of fighting back and the trouble it is likely to cause them. Moreover, they have the necessary economic capital to pay the bribes. Very few choose to fight against the extortion because they consider that getting themselves organised to fight back is time-consuming. By giving in to the illegal requests, Chinese businesspeople continue to make themselves the targets of extortion, and perpetuate a corrupt, predatory political-business system.

Additionally, many well-established Chinese Indonesian businesspeople in Medan and Surabaya have utilised their social capital to establish close relationships with the heads of security forces. The following quotation from an interview and the excerpts from a Chinese-language newspaper report on a dinner for the East Java Regional Military Command in 2010 illustrate such political-business relationships between local Chinese Indonesian business elites and heads of security forces in both cities.

> The ceremony of North Sumatra police chief transfers was held recently [in March 2010]. I was there too. [Do you] want to know who most of the attendees were? About 90% of them were big Chinese businesspeople! (interview with Usman, in Indonesian, July 30, 2010)

> The East Java Entrepreneur Charitable Foundation, the Surabaya Chinese Association [PMTS] and Chinese community leaders jointly organised a welcome and farewell dinner for the East Java Regional Military Command on October 6 at 7 p.m. The event was held at the Grand Ballroom of Shangri-La Hotel, Surabaya.
> During the dinner, Alim Markus [president of the East Java Entrepreneur Charitable Foundation and PMTS] delivered his speech with enthusiasm: 'Thanks to the mercy of the Lord, tonight we have the opportunity to get together with the former and new military commanders of East Java. On behalf of the Chinese community in Surabaya, I would like to wish our former military commander [Suwarno] all the best in his future endeavours. I would also like to call upon the Chinese community to cooperate with the new military commander [Gatot].' (Chen 2010, my translation from Chinese original)

As referred to in the excerpts above, the local Chinese business community in Surabaya, led by Alim Markus, organised a dinner for the former and new regional military commanders of East Java in 2010. Junus, one of my informants who is a university professor in Surabaya, revealed that Markus used to be well connected to President Suharto during the New Order. After the collapse of the Suharto regime, Markus established close ties with Imam Utomo, then governor of East Java (interview with Junus, in Indonesian, January 11, 2011). Markus is the owner of Maspion Group, a Surabaya-based conglomerate that manufactures household appliances. Besides its core business, the group is involved in trade, financial services, real estate, and the production of construction material.[7]

Many well-established Chinese businesspeople in Surabaya have established close relationships with the governor, the regional police chief (Kapolda, or Kepala Polisi Daerah) and the regional military commander (Pangdam, or Panglima Daerah Militer), all of whom are paid money on a regular basis (interview with Junus, in Indonesian, January 11, 2011). Bambang, a Chinese businessperson whom I interviewed, disclosed that he is a good friend of Soekarwo, the governor of East Java. Bambang owned a ceramic tile factory (interview in Indonesian, March 3, 2011). Junus, who knows many local Chinese businesspeople, commented that Bambang is free from harassment and extortion by the police due to his good relationship with the governor (interview with Junus, in Indonesian, January 11, 2011). Moreover, a few well-established Chinese businesspeople who run night-clubs in the city are well connected to the mayor and local police. Therefore, their businesses are well protected and their clubs are not subject to police raids (interview with Junus, in Indonesian, January 11, 2011).

It is alleged that some Chinese businesspeople who run big businesses in Surabaya are well connected to Anton Prijatno (王炳金), a Golkar member who served during the Suharto era in the East Java provincial legislature and the national legislature (DPR, or Dewan Perwakilan Rakyat), and later, after the end of the New Order, became a prominent businessman and political patron of many Chinese businesses in Surabaya (interview with Junus, in Indonesian, January 11, 2011).[8] In my interview with him, Prijatno revealed that he had left Golkar in May 1998 because he was very disappointed with the rampant corruption within the Suharto regime (interview with Anton Prijatno, in Indonesian, February 24, 2011). Unlike most local Chinese politicians with business backgrounds, Prijatno only became actively engaged in business activities after spending many years in politics. He became the chairperson of an asphalt distribution company in 2003 (interview with Anton Prijatno, in Indonesian, February 24, 2011). Since Prijatno is close to the governor, his business flourishes and is protected from harassment and

---

7. The Maspion Group was formerly known as UD Logam Jawa. It was established in 1962 by Markus's father, Alim Husin (林學善), and his business partner, Gunardi Go ('Brief History' 2013). By 2010, the group had branched out to Singapore, Hong Kong, the People's Republic of China, Japan, France, and Canada (Chen 2005). At the time of writing, Markus and two of his brothers, Alim Mulia Sastra and Alim Satria, are members of the group's board of directors. Alim Prakasa, another brother of Markus, is a member of the group's board of commissioners ('BOC & BOD' 2013; 'Brief History' 2013).

8. Prijatno was a member of the East Java provincial legislature from 1977 to 1987 and a member of the national legislature from 1987 to 1997 (interview with Anton Prijatno, in Indonesian, February 24, 2011).

extortion by the police. He is also a business partner of Sudomo Mergonoto (吳德輝), who owns Kapal Api Group, a coffee production company, and Bambang (the ceramic tile factory owner) (interview with Junus, in Indonesian, January 11, 2011). In addition, Prijatno is a supplier of asphalt for many well-established Chinese real estate developers and contractors in the city (interview with Anton Prijatno, in Indonesian, February 24, 2011; interview with Atan, in Mandarin, February 28, 2011). Since he is a prominent politician and close to the governor, it is alleged that he also acts as a political patron for most well-established Chinese businesses in Surabaya, except Markus's Maspion Group, the largest conglomerate in Surabaya (interview with Junus, in Indonesian, January 11, 2011).

Similarly, in Medan, according to a local media activist who knew many local businesspeople of Chinese descent, in order to obtain protection and privileged access to permits and contracts from local power-holders, many well-established Chinese Indonesian businesspeople in the city established close relationships with local power-holders and heads of security forces who hold the most power in North Sumatra, i.e., the governor, the regional police chief, and the regional military commander. They often group together to 'contribute' money to those power-holders and heads of security forces in exchange for protection and permits (interview with Daniel, in Indonesian, September 17, 2010). Another NGO activist disclosed that it is common for Chinese businesspeople that operate big businesses in the city to group together and form close ties with local police officers. They pay money to the police regularly in exchange for protection (interview with Joko, in Indonesian, November 11, 2010).

Benny Basri (張保圓) is a good example of a well-connected Chinese businessman in Medan. Running a well-established real estate company in the city, Basri is said to be close to regional military officers and local police officers (interview with Usman, in Indonesian, July 30, 2010; interview with Christopher, in Indonesian, August 18, 2010; interview with Joko, in Indonesian, November 11, 2010). He also holds the position of treasurer in the North Sumatra branch of the Democratic Party (PD) since 2003 (interview with Sofyan Tan, in Indonesian, August 23, 2010; interview with Joko, in Indonesian, November 11, 2010). It is alleged that, because of his close relationship with local power-holders, he could purchase land previously owned by the Indonesian Air Force in Polonia, Medan, for a real estate development (interview with Usman, in Indonesian, July 30, 2010).

While Chinese businesspeople who run large-scale businesses often establish close ties with local power-holders and heads of security forces because they have strong social networks, those who own small- and medium-scale businesses generally do not have the ability and opportunity to establish close ties with local power-holders or potential power-holders.

5.4 Relations with *Preman*

In Medan, some local Chinese businesspeople who run large-scale businesses have established close relationships with youth/crime organisations to get more protection for their business. Apart from paying 'protection money' regularly to members of those organisations, some of them have also become their advisers. For instance, one of my informants disclosed that Vincent Wijaya, a local Chinese businessperson engaged in the frozen seafood industry, was an advisor of PP's North Sumatra branch, a major youth/crime organisation in the province, hence his business was well protected by the PP (interview with Joko, in Indonesian, November 11, 2010). In addition, according to the person in charge of *Harian Promosi Indonesia* (印廣日報), a Chinese-language newspaper in Medan, the founder of the newspaper, Hakim Honggandhi (關健康), had been the treasurer of IPK, a youth/crime organisation based in Medan. Honggandhi was also connected to the North Sumatran military because he used to distribute consumer goods to them (interview with Setiawan, in Mandarin, November 8, 2010).[9]

Another good example is the support given by Indra Wahidin, then chairperson of INTI's North Sumatra branch, and a group of Chinese community leaders (who were mostly businesspeople) to Ajib Shah-Binsar Situmorang, one of the candidate pairs in Medan's 2010 mayoral election, as mentioned in Chapter 4 (Purnama 2010; '150 Tokoh Masyarakat Tionghoa Siap Menangkan Ajib-Binsar' 2010; '150 Tokoh Masyarakat Tionghoa' 2010). Wahidin, as already mentioned, is an insurance agent and paint distributor (interview with Christopher, in Indonesian, August 18, 2010) who openly supported Ajib-Binsar because of his connections with Ajib, the former chairperson of PP's North Sumatra branch. Wahidin and several other Chinese businesspeople, some said, believed Ajib would offer more protection to their business if he was elected (interview with Farid, in Hokkien, July 15, 2010; interview with Ivan, in Hokkien, July 16, 2010), as opposed to Sofyan Tan, who as I mentioned in the opening of Chapter 1, refused to promise any favours to those who supported his candidature.[10] However, Wahidin's open support for Ajib-Binsar upset a few local Chinese community leaders who supported Sofyan Tan, the only ethnic Chinese mayoral candidate. He subsequently became less popular among his fellow Chinese community leaders after the mayoral election (interview with Hasan, in Mandarin, August 19,

---

9. As *Harian Promosi Indonesia* had been running at a loss due to low readership, Honggandhi eventually lost all of the capital he had invested in the newspaper. He later moved to Jakarta and worked in a hotel (interview with Setiawan, in Mandarin, November 8, 2010).

10. As mentioned in Chapter 4, one informant suggested however that Wahidin supported Ajib as mayor in order to protect the Chinese community and not because of his hope for business favours.

2010; interview with Rudy, in Mandarin, August 25, 2010; interview with Erik, in Mandarin, August 25, 2010).[11]

Besides that, according to some of my informants, the local governments of post–New Order Medan/North Sumatra often allocate local state projects to indigenous contractors who are members of youth/crime organisations (interview with Ivan, in Hokkien, July 16, 2010; interview with Halim, in Indonesian, July 26, 2010). But it is also not uncommon for them to subcontract some of their projects to Chinese contractors who are their friends. An indigenous contractor may subcontract his projects to his Chinese friends at 20% less than his original tender cost. What this means is that the contractor would get a 20% cut from the contract (interview with Halim, in Indonesian, July 26, 2010). In other words, some local Chinese businesspeople who are well connected with youth/crime organisations also work on local state projects informally.

5.5 Financial Coercion against the Media

As mentioned in Chapter 4, the advent of democratisation and the removal of restrictions on Chinese cultural expression have brought about press freedom and a new beginning for Chinese-language newspapers in Indonesia. Several Chinese-language newspapers have been established across the country since the end of the New Order. However, it is worth noting that press freedom appears to be a double-edged sword for Chinese businesspeople. On the one hand, they can establish Chinese-language newspapers to promote Chinese culture and discuss issues related to the ethnic Chinese in Indonesian society. They can also use the newspapers as a cultural space to showcase themselves and their business. But, on the other hand, press freedom also allows the media to expose the corrupt practices of Chinese businesspeople and the politicians to whom they are connected.

As mentioned in the previous chapter, Chinese-language newspapers in Medan and Surabaya are generally making a loss due to low readership. The newspapers need to depend on the financial support of local Chinese businesspeople in order to survive. Some well-established Chinese businesspeople support Chinese-language newspapers in Medan and Surabaya by becoming their shareholders or advertisers. In this way, they make sure that the newspapers report in their favour. Such patrimonial power relations between local Chinese-language newspapers and well-established Chinese businesspeople have deterred the newspapers from reporting negative news about local Chinese business. Therefore, news about corrupt business

---

11. It appeared that the local Chinese community leaders' dislike of Wahidin did not affect their perception of INTI, as I heard only of their complaints about Wahidin but not INTI during my fieldwork.

practices that involve Chinese businesspeople has rarely been reported in the local Chinese-language newspapers. For instance, in October 2010, while local Indonesian-language newspapers in Medan such as *Waspada* and *Harian Orbit* covered the alleged tax evasion by PT Indo Palapa, a real estate company owned by Benny Basri, an ethnic Chinese real estate tycoon in the city, most local Chinese-language newspapers did not report about the case. PT Indo Palapa allegedly submitted false information to tax offices in the city about the number of shophouses built by the company, so as to avoid paying taxes.[12] When *Xun Bao* later published a news report on the case, they did not mention Benny Basri by name ('Jianzu Xingjian Xukezheng Xingpian' 2010).

Moreover, the Chinese businesspeople who fund these Chinese-language newspapers are mostly well connected to national and local level power-holders. In order to survive, these newspapers must refrain from being critical of these power-holders; otherwise, they might encounter withdrawal of their sponsorship as a form of punishment. The fate of *Rela Warta* (誠報) in Surabaya vividly illustrates such carrot-and-stick methods. As mentioned in the previous chapter, *Rela Warta* was the only Chinese-language newspaper in Surabaya that did not cover many of the socio-cultural activities held by local Chinese organisations. It was also the only Chinese-language newspaper that often published in-depth and critical editorials and opinion pieces on current affairs and politics in Indonesia. The newspaper published a few editorials and opinion pieces on the general election and the role of Chinese Indonesian voters during the 2004 legislative election.[13] It also published news on Dédé Oetomo, an ethnic Chinese social activist in Surabaya who stood in the East Java regional representative council (DPD) election in 2004 ('Buyao Xuan Ceng Yanzhong' 2004).

Shortly after the 2004 election, *Rela Warta* suddenly announced that it would turn into a weekly paper due to low readership and the increase in printing price ('Gao Jingai De Duzhe Shu' 2004; Li 2008, 360). But according to the person formerly in charge of the newspaper, the change was actually due to the main advertiser's decision to stop advertising in the newspaper after the editorial team refused to openly support Susilo Bambang Yudhoyono, the soon-to-be presidential candidate at that time, as requested by the main advertiser. The main advertiser was an elite Chinese businessperson who ran various types of business in East Java. He had been contributing Rp2 million (about US$223) in advertising fees to the newspaper every month. Prior to the polls, the main advertiser, who was close to Yudhoyono, urged *Rela Warta* to support Yudhoyono openly and to call upon the local Chinese

---

12. See 'Bekukan Aset Bos PT Indo Palapa, "Tangkap Benny Basri"' (2010) and Suwandi (2010).
13. For examples, see 'Yao Zhengque Shiyong Women De Xuanjuquan (1)' (2004); 'Yao Zhengque Shiyong Women De Xuanjuquan (2)' (2004); 'Xuanmin Yao Jizhu' (2004); 'Huazu Xuanmin' (2004).

community to support Yudhoyono. But the newspaper's editorial team refused to do so because they maintained that the Chinese community had the right to support any electoral candidate they liked. In addition, the newspaper published a few news articles that were critical of Yudhoyono prior to the election. The main advertiser was upset and subsequently decided to withdraw his regular contribution of advertisements to the newspaper. Moreover, he urged other local Chinese business elites to boycott the newspaper. Consequently, *Rela Warta* lost many subscribers and a considerable amount of advertising revenue. Shortly after the legislative election, the founders decided to turn *Rela Warta* into a weekly paper (interview with Samas H. Widjaja, in Mandarin, May 5, 2011). But even after the weekly circulation of the paper was reduced to 2,000 copies, it was still losing money. Later, in June 2007, *Rela Warta* was taken over by PSMTI's East Java branch, led by Jos Soetomo (江慶德), and became the bulletin of the organisation (Li 2008, 360). In 2009, the paper ceased publication as it was no longer supported by PSMTI's East Java branch (interview with Samas H. Widjaja, in Mandarin, May 5, 2011).

The decline of *Rela Warta* clearly shows that some Chinese business elites do not hesitate to resort to financial coercion against a media outlet in order to safeguard their business interests. It also shows that it is extremely difficult to establish and maintain a Chinese-language newspaper without financial support from the Chinese business community. Without this money, it is impossible for a newspaper to survive in the long term. This illustrates the ambivalence of press freedom for the Chinese in the post-Suharto era. The patrimonial power relations between local Chinese-language newspapers and Chinese business elites in Medan and Surabaya have also played an important role in shaping local politics, which is infused with corruption.

5.6 Land Disputes in Medan and Threats against Chinese Indonesians

Due to the absence of a well-established rule of law both before and after the end of the New Order, there have been several cases of land disputes involving the illegal seizure of state and residential land by real estate developers who are mostly Chinese Indonesians. However, as I will discuss later in this section, land disputes in Medan tend to turn into violent conflicts and threats against Chinese Indonesians. Conversely, violent conflicts and threats against Chinese Indonesians related to land disputes rarely occur in Surabaya, for two reasons. The first has much to do with the interethnic relationships between Chinese and indigenous Indonesians in these two cities. I mentioned in the first chapter that Medan has a long history of tensions between local Chinese and local indigenous groups, whereas

Chinese in Surabaya generally maintain a good relationship with indigenous Indonesians. A second reason has much to do with the way the local government and developers in Surabaya deal with land disputes. As Howard W. Dick notes in his book on Surabaya, the local government and developers in the city prefer negotiation to violence in dealing with land disputes. Prompt resettlement with a higher rate of compensation is the usual compromise (Dick 2003, 406). In other words, residents in Surabaya enjoy better institutional protection compared to those in Medan. Hence, land disputes in Surabaya seldom turn into threats against ethnic Chinese Indonesians.

There are a few land disputes involving Chinese Indonesian real estate developers in Medan that I want to showcase here to show how some Chinese Indonesian developers have willingly resorted to illegal practices to further their business interests. These cases received fairly high coverage in the local and national newspapers and have kept alive the general national view of Chinese Indonesians as collusive and willing to engage in corruption to maintain their wealth.

In November and December 2011, Indonesian-language newspapers in Medan reported that three ethnic Chinese tycoons were implicated in the illegal seizure of state and residential land in the city. The tycoons involved were Benny Basri, Tamin Sukardi, and Mujianto (鄭祥南). All of them were real estate developers ('Warga Sari Rejo Iri dengan Benny Basri' 2011; 'Mafia Tanah Hilangkan Nurani' 2011; 'Tangkap Tamin Sukardi' 2011; "Tangkap Tamin, Mujianto & Benny Basri' 2011; 'Mafia Tanah Sengsarakan Rakyat' 2011; 'Mujianto Dituding Mafia Tanah' 2011). It was alleged that they managed to take over the land by bribing local government bureaucrats. Basri, the owner of PT Central Business District (CBD), was alleged to have obtained the land title for Sari Rejo Sub-district (Kelurahan Sari Rejo) through illegal means. The land was previously under the ownership of the Indonesian Air Force but it later became a residential area. However, residents who had been living in Sari Rejo for decades did not get their land title while Basri managed to get it within a short period of time and planned to turn the land into a commercial property. In other words, the ownership of the land had been transferred from the air force to Basri's company.

As mentioned earlier in this chapter, Basri was a real estate tycoon well connected to local power-holders and local military as well as police officers. He had also been the treasurer of PD's North Sumatra branch since 2003. So, it was quite possible that Basri managed to take over the land in Sari Rejo within a short period of time because of his close association with local power-holders and officers at the local air force base.

Both Sukardi and Mujianto were also implicated in land seizures at Helvetia, Deli Serdang district (*kabupaten Deli Serdang*), North Sumatra. Sukardi, owner of PT Erniputra Terari, had taken over former state land in Helvetia for commercial purposes. The land had earlier been given by the state to the residents of Helvetia. Sukardi was allegedly involved in the hiring of gangsters to kidnap and assault an NGO activist who led residents of Helvetia to defend their land rights. The activist was later released after being assaulted by gangsters repeatedly for several hours. Mujianto, the owner of Agung Cemara Realty, was implicated in the seizure of another piece of former state land in Helvetia. The land had been given to residents of Helvetia in 1968, and they later turned it into a football field. According to a local social activist, as cited in *Harian Orbit*, Mujianto suddenly claimed the ownership of the land in 2011 with a title deed. Although the title deed did not show the correct address of the land, Mujianto still fenced the land off with the help of the police to prevent residents from entering. Therefore, the activist believed the incident was 'a game of land mafia' with the collusion of government officials ('Mujianto Dituding Mafia Tanah' 2011, my translation from Indonesian original). As a result, the residents could no longer use the field for leisure and exercise. This angered them and they subsequently demolished the fence, setting up a clash between the residents and gangsters hired by Mujianto. Police officers showed up during the clash but, instead of protecting the residents, they joined the gangsters in attacking the residents as well. Several residents were injured in the confrontation.

The land disputes in Helvetia drew the attention of a few North Sumatra provincial legislators, who later paid a visit to the location of the land disputes on April 9, 2013. They promised to hold a meeting with the residents to discuss the issue and to look for solutions. In June 2013, the promise had not yet been fulfilled, so on June 7, 2013, the Islamic organisation Al Washliyah, which owned land in Helvetia taken over by Sukardi, officially lodged a complaint with the Corruption Eradication Commission (KPK) about Sukardi's seizure of land in Helvetia. Apart from protesting against Sukardi in front of his office, members of Al Washliyah also held demonstrations in front of the North Sumatra chief attorney's office and the North Sumatra High Court, urging law enforcement to take action against Sukardi ('Penyerobotan Tanah Negara di Helvetia Menuai Kemarahan' 2013). The protesters carried a coffin when they protested again outside Sukardi's office on June 24, 2013 ('Lagi, Al-Washliyah Beri Tamin Keranda Mayat' 2013).

Harian Orbit referred to the three developers as 'slant-eyed businesspeople' (*pengusaha mata cipit* [*sic*]), clearly indicating their Chinese ethnicity ('Tangkap Tamin, Mujianto & Benny Basri' 2011). To some extent, the alleged involvement of the three Chinese developers in land disputes reinforced stereotypes of Chinese businesspeople as being heartless, corrupt, and opportunistic.

On another occasion, PT Jatimasindo, a real estate company owned by Arsyad Lis, another ethnic Chinese tycoon in Medan, was involved in the demolition of the Raudhatul Islam Mosque in Medan on April 11, 2011 ('Terkait Perubuhan Masjid Raudhatul Islam' 2013). The mosque was situated behind the Emerald Garden Hotel, also owned by Lis. According to the chairperson of the Muslim People's Forum (FUI, or Forum Umat Islam),[14] Indra Suheri, as interviewed by *The Jakarta Post*, the demolition of the mosque was to make way for the establishment of a shopping mall and a housing complex ('Protest Against Mosque Relocation Turns Wild' 2012). The company carried out the demolition after obtaining approval from Medan's Council of Indonesian Islamic Scholars (MUI, or Majelis Ulama Indonesia). Suheri accused the Medan MUI of gaining material benefits at the expense of a mosque ('Perubuhan Masjid Raudhatul Islam' 2012). Since then, FUI and several local Islamic activists have staged demonstrations in front of the Emerald Garden Hotel from time to time. In early February 2012, banners with provocative words '[*Kalau*] *1 mesjid lagi digusurr.1000 rumah cina kami bakarr.!*' (If one more mosque is demolished, we will burn 1,000 Chinese houses!) were even displayed during the demonstrations. It was also rumoured that the protesters had carried out sweeping raids on every car passing the area and asked the drivers to lower the car window. Although the sweep never really happened, the rumour, circulated via mobile phone text messages in Medan, caused panic among local Chinese in the city ('Sweeping di [Em]erald Garden tidak Benar' 2012).

Later, in February 2013, PT Jatimasindo promised to rebuild the mosque at the same location. But, as of March 2013, the company had not yet provided the rebuilding funds and was perceived by local Islamic activists as breaking its promise. So, they continued to stage open demonstrations in front of Emerald Garden Hotel ('Massa Ancam Bakar Hotel Emerald Garden' 2013). As of May 2014, the company had still not provided the rebuilding funds. So the activists continued to stage open demonstrations in front of the hotel ('Massa Ancam Bakar Hotel Emerald Garden' 2013; 'BKM Tuntut Emerald Garden Robohkan Tembok Pembatas' 2014).

At the time of writing, there is still no further news on land disputes involving the abovementioned Chinese tycoons.

Chinese businesspeople's involvement in these land disputes have not only violated the land rights of local communities, but also perpetuated the corrupt, predatory political-business system in Medan. In addition, their alleged corrupt business practices have reinforced negative perceptions of ethnic Chinese among indigenous Indonesians, which has sometimes led to violence and threats against Chinese Indonesians.

---

14. Muslim People's Forum is an Islamic organisation in Indonesia.

5.7 Discussion and Conclusion

The democratisation that is not accompanied by the emergence of good governance in post-Suharto Indonesia reinforces the ambivalent position of Chinese Indonesian businesspeople. On the whole, they are both victims and perpetuators of the muddy and corrupt business environment. On the one hand, they remain targets of extortion and corruption by power-holders, police, and *preman*. On the other hand, in the process of utilising their economic and social capital to gain and safeguard their business and personal interests, most Chinese businesspeople actually play an active role in perpetuating and reproducing the corrupt, predatory political-business system. By giving in to the illegal requests of power-holders, police, and *preman*, Chinese businesspeople have connived in and indirectly perpetuated such corrupt practices, as well as reinforced the notion that the Chinese can pay, will pay, and should pay for everything, including a peaceful business environment. By establishing collusion with local power-holders, the heads of security forces, and youth/crime organisations to get protection and access to permits and contracts, Chinese businesspeople have become an integral part of the problematic political-business relationship. Although there are a few Chinese businesspeople who refuse to become victims of extortion and choose to fight back, these appear to be rare.

By resorting to various illegal and semi-legal means such as bribing bureaucratic officers and hiring *preman* to intimidate local residents during land disputes, the Chinese businesspeople have not only perpetuated organised crime and corruption in both cities but also reinforced the negative perceptions of the Chinese as corrupt, opportunistic, arrogant, and heartless. This has therefore worsened ethnic relations between Chinese and non-Chinese, and exacerbated the ambivalent position of the Chinese in Indonesian society. By intimidating critical media through financial coercion, Chinese businesspeople have seriously threatened press freedom in post-Suharto Indonesia. Such a problematic political-business system is a vicious circle: following Giddens's structure-agency theory, the corrupt and muddy business environment in post-Suharto Indonesia prompts Chinese business-people to resort to various illegal and semi-legal business practices to gain and protect their business and personal interests. Such business practices in turn perpetuate and reproduce this business environment, as well as reinforce and reproduce the ambivalent position of ethnic Chinese in Indonesian society. I therefore argue that the corrupt, predatory political-business system continues to exist in the *reformasi* era not only because of the capture of new political vehicles and institutions by New Order–nurtured predatory interests, but also due to the active role of many Chinese businesspeople in perpetuating the system. Many, if not most, Chinese businesspeople in post-Suharto Medan and Surabaya are agents of the status quo instead of agents of change. To encourage more Chinese Indonesian businesspeople to refuse to be extorted and to refrain from resorting to illegal and semi-legal means of gaining wealth and protecting their business interests, a better enforced rule of law must certainly be put in place.

6
Electoral Politics and the Chinese in Post-Suharto Indonesia*

Since the end of the New Order, there has been more participation of Chinese Indonesians in electoral politics. However, as suggested in earlier chapters, the Chinese have been considered economically strong, and a move into politics is believed by some Chinese to risk the anger of *pribumi* Indonesians. Moreover, although the more democratic and liberal political environment in post-Suharto Indonesia allows, on the one hand, Chinese Indonesians to become actively involved in politics, on the other hand, the consequential explosion of costs for election campaigning has constrained the political achievements of those Chinese Indonesians with high political ideals but who are least endowed with money. I would now like to look more closely at the tensions between the high political ideals of some Chinese Indonesian politicians, such as Sofyan Tan, and the more personally oriented agendas of some other Chinese Indonesians, and the way these respective groups have a differing view of the democratisation process in Indonesia and the changing landscape of electoral politics. I suggest that these different political behaviours and political views are due to the different habitus of Chinese Indonesian politicians.

I will first examine some of the political-institutional changes at the national level in post-Suharto Indonesia in order to set the context for understanding the local level in Medan and Surabaya. Understanding Indonesian politics means taking a look at the spread of money politics in post-Suharto Indonesia; I suggest that Chinese businesspeople have had an important instigating role in this regard. Well-established Chinese businesspeople often back electoral candidates who can promise them political favours, while refusing to support those with anti-corruption political ideals. Candidates

---

* The names of informants in this chapter are pseudonyms except for the following public figures: Eddy Gunawan Santoso, Dédé Oetomo, Hasyim, Simon Lekatompessy, Hendi Prayogo, Samas H. Widjaja, Anton Prijatno, Sofyan Tan, Nelly Armayanti, Indra Wahidin, Eddy Djuandi, Christianto Wibisono, and Brilian Moktar.

who promise political favours to anyone who backs them are usually not committed to push for positive changes in Indonesia by fighting against all forms of corruption and bureaucratic abuse. This is in line with Bourdieu's notion of habitus and field, in which social actors who control considerable capital are inclined to defend the status quo of their field in order to safeguard their interests. However, there are also a few wealthy Chinese Indonesian businesspeople who support genuinely reform-minded Chinese Indonesian electoral candidates without expecting any political favours in return. I argue that these businesspeople choose of their free will to challenge the status quo of the Indonesian political environment because they perceive the promotion of good governance as more important than their personal interests. This is in line with the concept of free will in Giddens's structure-agency theory. There has been increasing political participation of the Chinese in post-Suharto Indonesia; looking at the political participation and achievements of the Chinese in Medan and Surabaya will help us focus on the tensions between high political ideals and personal agendas. Following Giddens's structure-agency theory, I argue that the active agency that Chinese Indonesians in Medan and Surabaya have demonstrated in their political participation has helped to shape the political environment and also contributed to exacerbating their ambivalent, contradictory position in post-Suharto Indonesia.

6.1 Politics at the National Level

The fall of Suharto in May 1998 led to the opening up of a more democratic and liberal political space in Indonesia. As noted earlier in Chapter 1, post-Suharto governments allowed the formation of political parties based on any principle and aspiration that did not conflict with the *Pancasila*. Responding to this newly found political freedom, people began to organise themselves and establish political parties. It was reported that more than 200 political parties were registered in 1999, but only forty-eight were qualified to contest in the 1999 election (King 2000, 92). According to the new election law, in order to contest in the election, a political party must have established management (*pengurus*) in more than half of the provinces and in more than half of the districts and special regions in Indonesia (Suryadinata 2002a, 91). Parties that were qualified to contest in the 1999 election ranged from major *Pancasila*-based secular parties such as Golkar (the dominant party of the New Order), the Indonesian Democratic Party of Struggle (PDI-P), the National Awakening Party (PKB), the National Mandate Party (PAN) to Islamic parties such as the United Development Party (PPP) and the Justice Party (PK, or Partai Keadilan).

The PDI-P was led by Sukarno's daughter, Megawati Sukarnoputri. The party was formed out of internal conflict within the Indonesian Democratic Party (PDI) in the closing years of the New Order regime. As Stephen Sherlock (2004) notes, '[PDI] was split between those supporting the leadership of Megawati Sukarnoputri and a leadership imposed on the party by the government' (25). Megawati's faction formed PDI-P in early 1999. The party identifies itself as a secular party that focuses on defending the unity and integrity of Indonesia as well as safeguarding the interests of the common people (Suryadinata 2002a, 79, 84; Sherlock 2004, 25–26).

The PKB was established after the fall of Suharto in 1998 by Abdurrahman Wahid, the leader of Nahdlatul Ulama (NU), the largest mass-based Muslim organisation in Indonesia.[1] Although the party is strongly identified as an 'Islamic party', its ideological basis is *Pancasila*, the official philosophical foundation of the Indonesian state, and not Islam (Sherlock 2004, 31). During Wahid's presidency, PKB put considerable effort into improving inter-religious relations and safeguarding minority rights. Therefore, PKB is seen as a tolerant and inclusive political party by non-Muslim and minority groups (Ananta, Arifin, and Suryadinata 2005, 49). The party had a strong base in East Java, a province that is dominated by members of NU (Ananta, Arifin, and Suryadinata 2005, 48).

PAN was formed after the fall of Suharto in 1998 by Amien Rais, the leader of Muhammadiyah, the second-largest mass-based Muslim organisation in Indonesia (Suryadinata 2002a, 85). Leaders and members of the party are mostly modernist Muslims. However, in order to establish a wider basis of support, the party adopts *Pancasila* instead of Islam as its ideological basis (Sherlock 2004, 34).

The PPP was a forced amalgam of Islamic parties created by the New Order regime in 1973. It was also one of the three legal political parties during the New Order era (Sherlock 2004, 32). PPP takes Islam as its ideology and restricts its membership to Muslims only (Suryadinata 2002a, 76). After the fall of Suharto in 1998, PPP was led by Hamzah Haz, a member of NU (Suryadinata 2002a, 77).

The PK was formed in July 1998 as an Islamic party adopting Islam as its ideological basis. The party was led by Nur Mahmud Ismail, an intellectual (Ananta, Arifin, and Suryadinata 2005, 13). PK has been active on university campuses in the post–New Order years and therefore is influential among Muslim students and intellectuals (Suryadinata 2002a, 75; Ananta, Arifin, and Suryadinata 2005, 13).

The 1999 election also saw the participation of the People's Democratic Party (PRD, or Partai Rakyat Demokratik), the only participating political

---

1. For the historical background and politics of NU, see Bush (2009).

party that had adopted socialism as its ideology (Suryadinata 2002a, 78–84, 205). According to Edward Aspinall (2005, 130), the party was originally established as an NGO known as the People's Democratic Union (PRD, or Persatuan Rakyat Demokratik) in 1994. The founders of PRD were a group of university student activists influenced by Marxist ideology and by leftist student movements in the Philippines and South Korea. The objective of the organisation was to fight against the New Order regime and to push for democratisation in the political, economic, and cultural aspects (Aspinall 2005, 131). According to Leo Suryadinata (2002a), PRD 'has a large following among university students and urban youths' (70). In addition, PRD activists mobilised workers to join numerous labour protests and strikes during the New Order period (Aspinall 2005, 131). As Aspinall (2005) notes, '[PRD activists'] capacity to organize large mass actions, plus their discipline and programmatic boldness, gave them a dramatic visibility in the developing democratic movement' (131). Despite the prohibition of additional political parties by the New Order regime, PRD publicly launched itself as a political party and was renamed the People's Democratic Party in 1996 (Aspinall 2005, 189). PRD's political activity ultimately marked it out for repression by the New Order regime. Senior military officers denounced PRD 'as a reincarnation of the PKI [Indonesian Communist Party]' (Aspinall 2005, 192) and many PRD members were later hunted down. Budiman Sudjatmiko, the leader of PRD, was tried for subversion and sentenced to 13 years in prison. But he was later released in December 1999 after Abdurrahman Wahid became president (Amri and Hasits 2008). PRD played a major role in the *reformasi* movement. Its members actively organised students' demonstration that played an important role in pressuring Suharto to step down in May 1998 (Suryadinata 2002a, 70). Therefore, it can be said that the party is genuinely reformist, with high political ideals, and favours rapid change. After the fall of Suharto, PRD contested in the 1999 election but only received 0.07% of the total votes, failing to pass the 2% electoral threshold that was required to secure a seat in parliament (Suryadinata 2002a, 223). It is plausible that many voters did not vote for PRD because it was a socialist party and deemed by many Indonesians as pro-communist. It is also possible that PRD did not get much support from the business community because the party opposes the capitalist system, which it believes exploits workers (See 'Sekilas Tentang PRD' [2010] for more details on the ideology of PRD). After failing to get a parliamentary seat in the 1999 election, PRD has not contested in subsequent elections.

Another radical political change undertaken after the end of the New Order was the move to decentralise power. The laws put in place also changed the process for electing regional heads, which during the New Order had always been appointed by the central government. It was expected that,

124 *Chinese Indonesians in Post-Suharto Indonesia*

with the removal of intervention from the central government, local governments would freely elect the best and most suitable leaders to lead them (Choi 2004, 282; Rasyid 2003, 65). Although both laws included a clause that postponed their implementation until early 2001, in the wake of the general election held in June 1999, newly elected members of local legislative assemblies immediately began to implement the law's provisions on the election of local government heads. Such actions did not face many obstacles from the national government 'under the lame-duck presidency of B. J. Habibie, and subsequently the weak leadership of Abdurrahman Wahid' (Malley 2003, 110). Consequently, local government leaders were elected by local assembly members after late 1999. However, it was later alleged that local government leaders could win elections by bribing local assembly members (Rasyid 2003, 66). In response to such allegations, international and domestic civil society organisations called for a direct election system in which local government heads are elected directly by the people. In late 2002, the national assembly eventually agreed to adopt direct elections for government heads at all levels of governance, including at the local level (Choi 2005, 7). The first direct election of local government heads, better known as *pilkada*,[2] was held in June 2005 (Sulistiyanto and Erb 2009, 17).

Initially, only political parties or party coalitions that gained 15% of the vote or parliamentary seats in their respective electoral areas could nominate candidates for the direct elections. Independent candidates were not allowed to contest (Mietzner 2009, 127). Later, in 2008, under Law No. 12/2008 on regional government, independent candidates were allowed to contest in local executive government elections without the nomination of a political party or coalition of political parties by posting an election bond and by garnering a certain number of signatures from residents in their territory as a proof of the support they enjoyed (Buehler 2010, 271, 273). They have to get signatures from at least 'between 3 and 6.5 per cent of the residents in their territory, with the exact figure depending on population size' (Buehler 2010, 273).

In addition, a new institution known as the regional representative council (DPD) was established in 2001 (Crouch 2010, 61). The DPD and the national parliament (DPR, or Dewan Perwakilan Rakyat) constitute the new national assembly (MPR, or Majelis Mermusyawaratan Rakyat). The DPD has the right to draft bills and offer advice on bills proposed by the DPR.

---

2. *Pilkada* is the Indonesian acronym for *pemilihan kepala daerah* (election of local government heads). The *pilkada* were initially called *pilkadasung* or *pilkada langsung* (direct election of local government heads) in order to distinguish them from the previous elections of local government heads through local legislative assemblies. But now *pilkada* is the more common acronym used for direct election of local government heads.

However, it cannot pass, reject, or amend legislation (Sherlock 2010, 161). DPD members were elected by the voters, for the first time, in 2004.

Besides that, a closed party list ranking system was initially adopted in the 1999 legislative elections, whereby voters were given only the opportunity to elect the party of their choice as the names of the candidates were unavailable on the ballot paper. The political party would later decide who the actual candidate occupying the seat would be (Sherlock 2004, 7). Later, in the 2004 election, the closed party list ranking system was replaced by an open party list ranking system, in which parliamentary candidates were named on the ballot paper. Voters could, for the first time, vote for a candidate of their choice as well as the party that nominated the chosen candidate (Ananta, Arifin, and Suryadinata 2005, 5). The party list ranking system was later abolished in late December 2008. From the 2009 election onwards, an electoral candidate can gain a seat in parliament as long as he or she obtains the most votes in the constituency being contested (Buehler 2010, 272).

In short, from the 2004 election onwards, voters could directly elect the president and vice-president, members of parliaments at national (DPR), provincial (DPRD 1, or Dewan Perwakilan Rakyat Daerah 1), and local (DPRD 2, or Dewan Perwakilan Rakyat Daerah 2) levels as well as their DPD representatives. They could also directly elect local government heads from 2005 onwards.

The political landscape in Indonesia, therefore, since the advent of democratisation is entirely different from during the New Order period, when Golkar had always been the dominant party in electoral politics. The 1999 legislative election saw the rise of the PDI-P, which obtained the most votes and seats at the national level, defeating Golkar, the long-time ruling party. Other major parties that gained seats in the national parliament included PKB, PAN, and PPP (Suryadinata 2002a).

In the 2004 election, however, the dominance of PDI-P declined significantly at the national level; it lost to Golkar, which again emerged as the strongest and largest party in Indonesia (Ananta, Arifin, and Suryadinata 2005, 18).[3] The election also saw the emergence of the Prosperous Justice Party (PKS) and two new major parties, i.e., the Democratic Party (PD) and the Prosperous Peace Party (PDS). PKS is actually the reconstitution of the Justice Party (PK). PK contested in the 1999 election but gained only 1.8% of the votes, failing to pass the 2% electoral threshold required to contest in the 2004 legislative election (Hellmann 2011, 125–26). In order to appeal to broader constituencies, PK, as Olli Hellmann (2011) puts it, 'was thus not only reconstituted as the Prosperous Justice Party but . . . downplayed its Islamic goals and, instead, campaigned mainly on *bersih* (clean, meaning

---

3. For the factors behind the PDI-P's poor performance, see Ananta and colleagues (2005, 46–48).

non-corrupt, government) and *peduli* (caring, meaning concern for social welfare)' (126). This strategy proved to be successful. According to Aris Ananta and colleagues (2005), PKS's campaign, which focused on the eradication of corruption and poverty, appealed to many urban voters. They supported PKS 'not because they wanted an Islamic state but because they supported the anti-corruption and anti-poverty promises that PKS highlighted' (24). PKS gained 7.34% of the votes in 2004 (Ananta, Arifin, and Suryadinata 2005, 22, Table 1.3).

However, in the 2014 election, PDI-P again garnered the majority of popular votes (18.95%) and became the largest party ('KPU Sahkan Hasil Pemilu' 2014). Furthermore, the party's presidential candidate, Joko Widodo, was elected in the presidential election.

The PD is the political vehicle of retired general Susilo Bambang Yudhoyono. Within a short period of time, the party was able to create branches within all major provinces. PD is a secular party that promotes democracy and advocates popular political participation, multiculturalism, as well as a professional armed forces (Ananta, Arifin, and Suryadinata 2005, 23–24). Due to the attraction of these various principles, although Yudhoyono's party was not so successful in the legislative elections, he himself, as a fairly charismatic leader, was later elected as president in Indonesia's first direct presidential election in 2004.

The PDS was formed in 2001 by Ruyandi Hutasoit, a Christian pastor and a doctor in Jakarta. The party is based on *Pancasila* and Christians are its main constituents, making it a primarily Christian party (Ananta, Arifin, and Suryadinata 2005, 17, 25). PDS gained 2.13% of the votes in the 2004 election and was allotted twelve seats in the national parliament (Ananta, Arifin, and Suryadinata 2005, 22, Table 1.3).

In the legislative election of 2009, the PD gained the most votes and seats at the national level and became the largest party in parliament (Sukma 2010, 56–57), due to the influence and charisma of President Yudhoyono. As Dirk Tomsa (2010) points out, the huge gains of PD in 2009 'were much more a reflection of the president's popularity than the performance of the party as such' (149–50). The 2009 election also saw the emergence of two new secular parties founded and led by controversial former generals, i.e., the Great Indonesian Movement Party (Gerindra), founded and led by ex-general Prabowo Subianto, and the People's Conscience Party (Hanura), founded and led by ex-general Wiranto. Both ex-generals have respectively been accused of human rights violations in East Timor and of fomenting anti-Chinese violence in May 1998 ('Profile: General Wiranto' 2004; Tomsa 2009). Their parties were formed shortly after the 2004 election. Their formation was inspired by PD's successes due to the influence and charisma of President Yudhoyono. Tomsa (2010) has noted that '[t]he only function of these parties was to provide a political vehicle for their ambitious leaders' (150). Both Gerindra and Hanura passed the electoral threshold and gained seats in the national parliament (Tomsa 2010, 144, Table 7.1). However, Tomsa (2010) also points out that Gerindra and Hanura did not emulate the achievements of PD. Both parties obtained less than 5% of the votes, while PD gained more than 20% (150). Nevertheless, in the 2014 election, PD received only 10.90% of the votes, dropping from first place in 2009 to fourth place in 2014. Conversely, there were increases in the votes gained by Gerindra and Hanura. The vote share garnered by the former was 11.81%, more than double its vote share in 2009. Gerindra's vote share was also larger than that of PD in 2014. At the same time, Hanura gained 5.26% of the votes, slightly higher than in 2009. But its vote share was still much smaller than that of PD and Gerindra ('KPU Sahkan Hasil Pemilu' 2014).

Without a doubt, the Indonesian political system since the end of the New Order has been much more democratic than in the past. The opening up of political space has created opportunities for Indonesians, including the Chinese minority, to get involved in politics by joining political parties other than Golkar. Voters also have more choices to elect their political representatives during elections. However, as pointed out by Suryadinata (2002a), most of the new major parties that have emerged since the fall of Suharto 'are conservative and do not favour rapid change' (214). The PRD, which favours rapid reform, could not become an effective, strong force because it got little support from voters in the 1999 election. Moreover, as I will discuss later in this chapter, the opening up of political space has been followed by the explosion of the costs of election campaigning, which in turn has led to the rise of money politics. This implies a paradox of democratisation in post-Suharto Indonesia. On the one hand, the advent of democratisation brings more opportunities and choices for Indonesians to get involved in politics. On the other hand, genuine reformist forces such as the PRD are marginalised. Moreover, the rise of money politics excludes those lacking financial resources from political contests. Therefore, as I mentioned in Chapter 3, the end of the New Order has not been followed by greater popular participation in political contests.

6.2 The 2014 Presidential Election

The year 2014 was a historic turning point for post-Suharto Indonesia. Joko Widodo (better known by his nickname, Jokowi), who had been the governor of Jakarta from 2012 to 2014 and the mayor of Solo from 2005 to 2012, was elected as the seventh president of Indonesia. For the first time, a businessman-turned-politician not related to the usual clutch of political and business dynasties was elected as president. Jokowi had been a humble furniture entrepreneur. He only got involved in politics in 2005 when he was elected to the mayorship of Solo, a modest-sized city in central Java. Jokowi is pragmatic and 'has a good record of dealing with the concerns of ordinary Indonesians' ('Competing Visions' 2014). During his mayorship in Solo and governorship in Jakarta, he regulated street hawkers and renovated traditional markets ('Indonesia's Joko Searches for Honest Men' 2014). He also implemented a health card programme that gave residents free access to public health care (Aspinall and Mietzner 2014, 351). Furthermore, he improved bureaucratic performance by conducting spot checks on government offices and brought in measures such as transparent online tax collection as well as e-procurement schemes (Aspinall and Mietzner 2014, 351; 'Indonesia's Joko Searches for Honest Men' 2014). Therefore, he is popularly known as a pragmatic and uncorrupt political leader.

6.3 The Political Landscape in Post-Suharto Medan and Surabaya

In the post–New Order era, the election results for the city councils of both Medan and Surabaya (Dewan Perwakilan Rakyat Daerah Kota Medan and Dewan Perwakilan Rakyat Daerah Kota Surabaya) have not always been the same as for the national and provincial legislatures.[4] In the 1999 legislative election, the North Sumatra provincial legislature and the Medan city council were both dominated by PDI-P, led by Megawati (*Perhitungan Perolehan Kursi DPRD I*, 1999). But five years later, the dominance of PDI-P had declined significantly at both the provincial and local levels in North Sumatra. Most of the electoral candidates elected into the North Sumatra provincial legislature were from Golkar but, interestingly, the Medan city council was dominated by representatives from the PKS, an Islamic party that sought to solve the problems of people's lives via Islam (Apriyanto 2007, 36, 39). This was due to the party's anti-corruption and anti-poverty promises that had impressed many Medanese voters. In East Java, although the provincial legislature was dominated by PKB in the 1999 and 2004 legislative elections, the Surabaya city council was dominated by PDI-P in the same period ('Perbandingan Kursi DPRD Jatim Antara Pemilu 1999 dan 2004' 2004; 'PPP, PBB, PBI, PKP Dapat 1 Kursi' 1999; Apriyanto 2007, 334, 336). PKB was closely associated

---

4. The politics of Medan and Surabaya is best reflected in the election results for the city councils of both cities, because all members of the city councils are elected by voters in both cities and they represent the people in both cities. Members of the North Sumatra and East Java provincial legislatures are respectively elected not only by voters in Medan and Surabaya but also by voters in other parts of North Sumatra and East Java. Therefore, I suggest that one has to refer to the election results for the city councils of Medan and Surabaya instead of the North Sumatra and East Java provincial legislatures to get a better understanding of politics in Medan and Surabaya.

with the NU and since East Java was the birthplace and stronghold of NU, it was not surprising to see the domination of PKB in the provincial legislature. However, the secular nationalist party, PDI-P, had a strong base in Surabaya, the capital city of the province (Wibowo 2001, 141), thus the city council was dominated by PDI-P representatives.

Nevertheless, the 2009 legislative election saw the rise of PD, led by President Yudhoyono, at both the national and local levels. The party won most seats in the provincial legislatures of North Sumatra and East Java, as well as the city councils of Medan and Surabaya (Central Statistics Agency of North Sumatra 2013; East Java Provincial Legislature 2013; '50 Calon Anggota DPRD Medan Terpilih Periode 2009–2014' 2009; 'Anggota DPRD Surabaya 2009–2014' 2009, 29). The outstanding performance of PD was closely related to the influence and charisma of President Yudhoyono (Harahap 2010).

However, in the 2014 legislative election, due to the 'Jokowi effect' as well as voters' disappointment at President Yudhoyono's performance, at the national level, the performance of PD declined significantly and PDI-P moved into first place in the city councils of Medan and Surabaya, and second place in the provincial legislatures of North Sumatra and East Java ('Daftar Calon Terpilih Anggota DPRD Kota Medan Periode 2014–2019' 2014; 'Ini Dia 50 Anggota DPRD Kota Surabaya Periode 2014–2019' 2014; 'Anggota DPRD Sumut Periode 2014–2019 Resmi Dilantik' 2014; 'Inilah 100 Anggota DPRD Jatim 2014–2019 Terpilih' 2014). In fact, the total number of seats gained by the PDI-P in both provincial legislatures was only one seat less than that of the best-performing parties.[5]

6.4 The Rise of Money Politics and the Role of Chinese Businesspeople

The opening up of political space in post-1998 Indonesia and the consequent explosion of the costs of election campaigning have led to the rise of what has been called money politics. There are two different types of money politics: one involves the electoral candidates and the party 'vehicles' that candidates hope will support them, and the other involves direct payment to voters. I will discuss these different types here, and the role that Chinese businesspeople have come to play in this evolving post–New Order political landscape.

Changes in the election procedures have not eradicated the use of money and bribes but have only changed how and to whom money is given.

---

5. In North Sumatra, Golkar and PDI-P gained seventeen and sixteen parliamentary seats respectively while in East Java, PKB and PDI-P gained twenty and nineteen parliamentary seats respectively ('Anggota DPRD Sumut Periode 2014–2019 Resmi Dilantik' 2014; 'Inilah 100 Anggota DPRD Jatim 2014–2019 Terpilih' 2014).

When a closed party list ranking system was adopted in the 1999 legislative elections, in order to be placed at the top of the list and selected by party leaders to fill the seats after the elections, some electoral candidates resorted to bribing their party leaders (Choi 2009, 125). As mentioned earlier in this chapter, the party list ranking system was later abolished in 2008.

At the local level, according to Sukardi Rinakit (2005), candidates who contested in elections needed to pay for campaign expenses as determined by the local election commission and the political vehicles, i.e., the political parties that nominated them. Each candidate must pay an average of up to 20% of their campaign funds for the use of the political vehicles (2). Moreover, the cut in state subsidies for political parties in 2005 brought severe financial difficulties to most parties in the country (Mietzner 2007, 238–63). According to Marcus Mietzner (2009), in order to consolidate their finances, local party branches tended to overlook their own cadres and offer nominations to external candidates with vast financial resources (128–29). In most nominations across the country, parties were more concerned about the financial resources of the nominees and their preparedness to contribute their wealth to the party than about their loyalty to the party and ideological affinity (Mietzner 2009, 128). Therefore, the process of being elected to regional office has become increasingly expensive in the *reformasi* era. The country's anti-corruption watchdog, Indonesia Corruption Watch (ICW), as reported in *Jawa Pos*, revealed that the total amount spent on all 244 direct elections for local government heads (*pilkada*) in 2010 alone had exceeded Rp14 trillion (about US$1.55 billion). This included Rp3.5 trillion (about US$387.1 million) spent by local election commissions on the operation of elections and Rp10.9 trillion (about US$1.21 billion) spent by all candidates on campaign activities ('Pilkada 2010 Telan Rp14 Triliun Lebih' 2011, 2).

Another type of money politics involves vote-buying. Syarif Hidayat (2009, 128, 142) points out that, during *pilkada*, most voters tend to base their political decisions on pragmatic considerations; for instance, what material benefits can be obtained directly from the candidates for local government head, and who and what societal figures the candidates are affiliated with. It is therefore not surprising that the practice of vote-buying (in the form of cash or goods) marks the process of *pilkada*.

As elections in post-Suharto Indonesia involve a huge expenditure, aspiring politicians need to seek the support of rich businesspeople who can make considerable financial contributions to their political activities and campaign funds. As noted by Syarif Hidayat and Gerry van Klinken (2009), the democracy that has emerged in post-Suharto Indonesia requires money (149). Chinese Indonesian businesspeople are therefore important sources of income for electoral candidates who need significant electoral campaign funds to get elected. In return, they often expect to get political protection,

Electoral Politics and the Chinese in Post-Suharto Indonesia · 131

kickbacks, state projects, or other benefits, should the candidate get elected. In this way, Chinese businesspeople continue to establish corrupt and patrimonial relationships with aspiring politicians in exchange for political favours. By using Bourdieu's concept of habitus and field, I argue that these well-established Chinese businesspeople have played a part in maintaining the existing corrupt political environment. The advent of competitive electoral politics has also created new incentives for Chinese businesspeople to sponsor politicians from parties other than Golkar. Some hedge their bets by sponsoring more than one candidate, thus creating a higher chance that they will have supported someone who will be elected into office. For example, according to Christian Chua (2008, 126), during the 2004 presidential elections, it was alleged that Tomy Winata, owner of the Artha Graha Group, financed the campaigns of both Megawati and Yudhoyono.[6] Chua (2008) also reveals that certain Chinese business family members 'carefully split their political loyalties' (126). For instance, Sofjan Wanandi, the owner of the Gemala Group,[7] backed Yudhoyono while his brother, Jusuf Wanandi, a board member of *The Jakarta Post*, used the newspaper to secure support for Megawati. Mochtar Riady, the founder and owner of the Lippo Group,[8] backed opposition leaders while his son, James Riady, supported the actual power-holders. A news report in *Gatra* discloses that Djoko Tjandra, a.k.a. Tjan Kok Hui, owner of the Mulia Group, and Prajogo Pangestu, a.k.a. Phang Djun Phin, owner of the PT Musi Hutan Persada, sponsored the campaign of Megawati in the 2004 presidential elections (Pamuji, Arifin, and Febriana 2004).[9]

The division of political loyalties within the Poo family, which owns the Cipta Cakra Murdaya (CCM) Group, is another good example of hedging among Chinese businesspeople. The CCM Group was founded and owned by Murdaya Widyawimatra Poo, a.k.a. Poo Tjie Goan (傅志寬), and his wife, Siti Hartati Cakra Murdaya, a.k.a. Chow Li Ing (鄒麗英) (Setyautama 2008, 38, 312).[10] Poo joined the PDI-P, led by Megawati, and became the treasurer and financial backer of the party. He also ran in the 2004 and 2009 elections and was elected to the national parliament in both elections, thanks

---

6. There were five pairs of candidates contesting in the 2004 presidential election: Wiranto-Solahuddin Wahid (Golkar), Megawati Sukarnoputri-Hasyim Muzadi (PDI-P), Amien Rais-Siswono Yudo Husodo (PAN), Susilo Bambang Yudhoyono-Jusuf Kalla (PD), and Hamzah Haz-Agum Gumelar (United Development Party, PPP) (Ananta, Arifin, and Suryadinata 2005, 71–74). The Yudhoyono-Kalla pair was elected.
7. The Gemala Group is a conglomerate engaging in automotive and property development.
8. The Lippo Group is a conglomerate engaging in retail, media, real estate, health care, and financial businesses.
9. The Mulia Group is a commercial property developer while the PT Musi Hutan Persada is a forestry company.
10. The CCM Group is a conglomerate engaging in electric utilities, footwear, plantations, furniture, and the plywood industry.

to his financial status as a wealthy businessman and to support from well-established Chinese businesspeople in Surabaya (Yunianto 2004a; Li 2007, 195; Li 2010, 122; 'Murdaya Poo Dipecat dari PDIP dan DPR' 2009).[11] Siti, on the other hand, joined PD, led by Yudhoyono, and became his benefactor (Prakoso 2012). In other words, the Poo family members split their political loyalties and financial support between PDI-P and PD. But after the presidential election in 2009, where Yudhoyono was re-elected as president, Poo was stripped of his party membership and his office in parliament by PDI-P, as he had allegedly channelled his support to Yudhoyono, the incumbent, instead of Megawati during the presidential election ('Murdaya Poo Dipecat dari PDIP dan DPR' 2009).[12]

In Surabaya, Yahya, a university professor, disclosed that Alim Markus, owner of the Maspion Group in the city, funded three out of the five pairs of candidates during the first direct gubernatorial election in 2008, although he was well connected to only one candidate pair, i.e., Soekarwo-Saifullah Yusuf. The other two candidate pairs were Soenarjo-Ali Maschan Moesa and Kholifah Indar-Mudjiono (interview with Yahya, in Indonesian, December 31, 2010). The gubernatorial election was eventually won by the Soekarwo-Saifullah Yusuf pair.

These examples show that some Chinese businesspeople play a crucial role in perpetuating the corrupt and predatory characteristics of Indonesian politics. They support certain politicians and expected to be paid back. This leads to corrupt practices. Therefore, these businesspeople are key players in the prevalence of money politics and the perpetuation of corruption; ultimately, they are part of the problem.

6.5 Political Achievements of Chinese Indonesians

After the end of the New Order, Chinese Indonesians have themselves become increasingly involved in politics. This has been the case both in terms of appointed positions as well as elected ones. At the time of writing, Chinese Indonesians appointed to high office since the *reformasi* era include Kwik Kian Gie (郭建義), coordinating minister for the economy, finance, and industry from October 1999 to August 2000 and state minister/head of the national planning board from July 2001 to October 2004; Mari Elka Pangestu (馮惠蘭), minister of trade from October 2004 to 2011 and minister of tourism and creative economy from 2011 to 2014; Amir Syamsudin, a.k.a. Tan Toan

---

11. In fact, to date, Poo is the only Chinese Indonesian conglomerate owner elected into public office since the end of the Suharto regime.
12. There were three pairs of candidates contesting in the 2009 presidential election: Jusuf Kalla-Wiranto (Golkar), Susilo Bambang Yudhoyono-Boediono (PD) and Megawati Sukarnoputri-Prabowo (PDI-P) (Sukma 2010, 61).

Sin, minister of justice and human rights from 2011 to 2014; Thomas Trikasih Lembong, minister of trade from August 2015 to July 2016 and head of the Investment Coordinating Board since July 2016; Ignasius Jonan (楊賢靈), minister of transportation from October 2014 to July 2016; and Enggartiasto Lukita (盧尤英), minister of trade since July 2016 (Coppel 2008, 120; Primanita and Daslani 2012; 'Minister Mari Elka' 2011; 'Yinni Lijie Zhengfu Neige You Duoshao Huaren Buzhang' 2016; Parlina and Widhiarto 2014; Amindoni 2016).

Many Chinese have run for elected positions, mostly in various local-level constituencies, and not at the national level. Those who have been elected include Hasan Karman, a.k.a. Bong Sau Fan (黃少凡), mayor of Singkawang, West Kalimantan, from November 2007 to September 2012; Christiandy Sanjaya, deputy governor of West Kalimantan since November 2007; Basuki Tjahaja Purnama, a.k.a. Tjoeng Wan Hok, better known by his affectionate Hakka nickname, Ahok, chief of the East Belitung regency from 2005 to 2006, deputy governor of Jakarta from October 2012 to November 2014, and governor of Jakarta from November 2014 to May 2017;[13] Basuri Tjahaja Purnama (Ahok's younger brother), chief of the East Belitung regency from 2010 to 2015; Eliezer Yance Sunur, a.k.a. Eliezer Yantje Sunur, chief of Lembata regency, East Nusa Tenggara, from 2011 to 2014;[14] Alvin Lie Ling Piao (李寧彪), national parliamentarian for Semarang from 1999 to 2004 and Central Java I from 2004 to 2009; and Murdaya Widyawimatra Poo, a.k.a. Poo Tjie Goan, national parliamentarian for East Java I from 2004 to 2009 and Banten II in 2009 (Hui 2011, 299; Tambun 2012; 'Pasangan Awang-Abdul Pemenang Pilkada Singkawang' 2012; Primanita and Daslani 2012; Suryadinata 2002a, 241; Li 2007, 195–96; 2010, 122; 'Kepala Daerah'

---

13. Ahok resigned as chief of the East Belitung regency in December 2006 to run for the governorship of Bangka Belitung in 2007. However, he was not elected ('Basuki Tjahaja Purnama' 2014). He later contested for a national parliamentary seat in the 2009 legislative election and was elected (Kuwado 2014). Ahok was appointed governor of Jakarta by President Joko Widodo, who was the former governor of Jakarta, on November 19, 2014 (Elyda and Sundaryani 2014). But during his tenure as the governor, Ahok made a controversial speech when he introduced his administration's fish farming programme in the Thousand Islands, in which he referenced a Quranic verse. He rather boldly told Muslim voters that they should not be misled by some religious leaders who were using the verse to justify the claim that Muslims should not elect a non-Muslim political leader (Huda 2017). An edited version of Ahok's speech was later uploaded online by people who disliked him, with several words removed, making it seem as though he was humiliating the religion. Although Ahok later apologised, his remarks angered many Muslim citizens. He was subsequently charged with blasphemy ('Jakarta Governor Ahok Stands Trial for Blasphemy' 2016; Lamb 2016). When the case was still under trial, Ahok contested in the 2017 Jakarta gubernatorial election but was defeated by his Muslim rival ('Jakarta Election Official Results' 2017). He was later sentenced to two years in prison on May 9, 2017 (Huda 2017; Lamb 2017). For a detailed analysis of Ahok's downfall, see Setijadi (2017).
14. Sunur was suspended by the Lembata regency parliament in February 2014 for his alleged involvement in extortion and fraud against a local state project contractor (Seo 2014).

2014; 'Bupati Lembata Dilantik Kamis' 2011; Seo 2014; Setyautama 2008, 312–13). Several ethnic Chinese electoral candidates who are popular among Chinese and non-Chinese Indonesians, including Dédé Oetomo, a.k.a. Oen Tiong Hauw, a well-known social activist in Surabaya, were not elected in past parliamentary and local elections. Karman and Ahok were previously members of the New Indonesia Party of Struggle (PPIB, or Partai Perjuangan Indonesia Baru) but they later switched to other parties.[15] Having lost in the Singkawang mayoral election in 2012, Karman joined Gerindra in 2013 and ran for the national parliament in the 2014 election as a Gerindra candidate ('Gerindra Usung Hasan Karman' 2013). However, he was not elected. Ahok switched to Golkar in 2009 but left the party and joined Gerindra in 2012. However, he left Gerindra in September 2014 in protest, after the party attempted to eliminate direct elections for local government heads (Li 2010, 185; 'Pengurus Baru Gerindra' 2012; 'I have officially left Gerindra: Ahok' 2014).[16] Since then he has not joined any political party. Ahok's brother, Basuri, is affiliated with Golkar (Widianto 2010). Sanjaya was previously affiliated with PDS but later switched to PD in 2011 (Xunjian 2010; Handoko 2011). Sunur, Poo, and Tan were members of PDI-P, while Lie was affiliated with PAN ('Bupati Lembata Dilantik Kamis' 2011; Li 2007, 195–96; Anto 2009, 261). Oetomo ran for a seat in the national parliament as a PRD candidate in 1999 (interview with Dédé Oetomo, in English, December 24, 2010).

6.6 The Political Participation of Chinese Indonesians in Post-Suharto Medan and Surabaya: High Political Ideals versus Personal Agendas

Although the numbers of ethnic Chinese Indonesians in Medan and Surabaya that contested in the 1999, 2004, 2009, and 2014 legislative elections are unavailable, according to my interviews with a few ethnic Chinese politicians and social activists in both cities, as well as news reports and advertisements

---

15. The PPIB was formed as the New Indonesia Alliance Party (Partai Perhimpunan Indonesia Baru) in 2002. It is a secular party oriented towards justice, democracy, and welfare (Ananta, Arifin, and Suryadinata 2005, 16, Table 1.2). The party gained only 0.59% of popular votes in 2004 and failed to pass the 2% electoral threshold required to contest in the 2009 election (Ananta, Arifin, and Suryadinata 2005, 16, Table 1.3). It was later renamed the New Indonesia Party of Struggle and ran in the 2009 election. For the background of the PPIB, see 'Partai Perjuangan Indonesia Baru (10)' (2008).
16. In September 2014, the Red-and-White coalition (KMP, or Koalisi Merah Putih), led by Gerindra chairperson Prabowo, voted in parliament to abolish direct elections for local government heads. The bill was passed since KMP dominated parliament at that time. The passing of the bill sparked outrage among Indonesians and then-president Susilo Bambang Yudhoyono repealed the legislation by issuing a government regulation before leaving office (Kwok 2014; Tomsa 2015, 168–70).

in some local newspapers, in 1999, at least one candidate in Medan and five candidates in Surabaya contested in legislative elections. Five years later, there were at least seventeen candidates in Medan and seven candidates in Surabaya in legislative elections. In 2009, there were at least sixteen candidates in Medan and seventeen candidates in Surabaya who contested in legislative elections. In the 2014 legislative elections, there were at least ten and nine Chinese Indonesian electoral candidates in Medan and Surabaya respectively (see Appendix VII for a compiled list of ethnic Chinese candidates in Medan and Surabaya). In 2009, the first Chinese Indonesian legislative candidates in Medan were elected. There were four ethnic Chinese elected into the fifty-member Medan city council and another two Chinese from Medan elected into the hundred-member North Sumatra provincial legislature. Five years later, Medan had five ethnic Chinese elected as legislators, one to the national parliament, two to the provincial legislature, and another two to the city council. Surabaya, on the other hand, already had two Chinese Indonesian candidates elected as legislators in 1999. One was elected to the forty-member Surabaya city council and another one was elected to the hundred-member East Java provincial legislature. Five years later, Surabaya saw another two Chinese candidates elected as legislators, one to the national parliament and another one to the city council. In 2009, there were three ethnic Chinese candidates elected in Surabaya. One was elected to the national parliament and another two were elected to the city council. In 2014, Surabaya saw two Chinese Indonesians elected to the national parliament, one elected to the provincial legislature, and another two elected to the city council.

As I will illustrate below with several case studies, I believe that the participation of Chinese Indonesians in electoral politics in post-Suharto Medan and Surabaya reflects tensions between the admirable political ideals of certain politicians and the personal agendas of businesspeople who support them or who themselves become involved in electoral politics. On the one hand, some Chinese Indonesian politicians who put themselves forward as electoral candidates are reform-minded and often have admirable political ideals, being committed to bringing positive change to society by fighting against corruption, collusion, and nepotism in state institutions as well as against all forms of discrimination. On the other hand, the Chinese Indonesian businesspeople who support them often want to further their own agendas, expecting political favours from the candidates they back should they get elected. They therefore prefer to establish corrupt and patrimonial relationships with politicians in exchange for patronage and protection. This misfit between expectations and ideals is the best example of the tension between the roles played by Chinese businesspeople and Chinese politicians in Indonesia. Politicians with anti-corruption ideals reject financial offers from

136 *Chinese Indonesians in Post-Suharto Indonesia*

those who expect political favours from them, but, very few get elected. This is because they cannot fund the massive electoral campaigns needed to win nor hire reliable election witnesses to prevent fraud and irregularities during the polling process. Some Chinese businesspeople, such as Murdaya Widyawimatra Poo mentioned earlier, and Simon Lekatompessy, also in Surabaya, become actively involved in politics and run for public office with the aim of gaining political protection for their business. Because they have the money to launch extensive campaign activities to influence voters, they are able to get elected.

I will now explore the experiences of a few Chinese Indonesian politicians who have run for public office in post-Suharto parliamentary and local direct elections. Their stories vividly illustrate the tensions between high political ideals and personal agendas. I include their stories in this chapter because I had the opportunity to interview them and they were willing to share with me many details of their experience. I was also able to obtain more information about them from other informants and the media, as well as other printed sources.[17]

Hasyim, a.k.a. Oei Kien Lim

Hasyim, a.k.a. Oei Kien Lim (黃建霖), an ethnic Chinese who was elected to the Medan city council in 2009, comes from a family involved in politics, rare among Chinese families. In the pre–New Order era, his granduncle, younger brother of his grandfather, had been an active member of the Indonesian National Party (PNI, or Partai Nasional Indonesia), which was founded and led by President Sukarno. After Suharto came into power, his uncle, younger brother of his father, joined the Indonesian Democratic Party (PDI), a party that was created out of PNI and a few non-Islamic parties. From his participation in the party, he became connected with Megawati, Rachmawati, and Sukmawati Sukarnoputri, the daughters of Sukarno and leaders of PDI. However, he did not play an active role in the party since PDI was the major opposition party during the New Order era and those who were well connected to its leaders were subject to close supervision by the New Order regime, suffering various forms of subtle harassment. Hasyim revealed that his interest in politics was mainly due to the influence of his uncle's political participation:

> When I was in my upper secondary years, I was always with my uncle. We were very close. He liked to talk to me about politics. Perhaps because of that, my interest in politics gradually grew. When I enrolled in the UDA

---

17. These politicians are all men. Although there are also Chinese women politicians in Medan and Surabaya, I did not have the opportunity to interview any of them during my fieldwork.

[University of Darma Agung, Medan], I joined the Indonesian National Students' Movement [GMNI, *Gerakan Mahasiswa Nasional Indonesia*], a student organisation that had historical connections with PNI.[18] From then on, I participated in the activities of that organisation. Besides that, I often accompanied my uncle to meet his friends who also participated in politics. From them I heard and learnt a lot about politics. (interview with Hasyim, in Indonesian, August 11, 2010)

Hasyim graduated with a bachelor's degree in economics (accounting) in 1991. However, he did not immediately enter formal politics. Instead, he worked as chief financial officer at a tapioca flour mill in Pematangsiantar, North Sumatra. After two years, he resigned and started a business with his wife distributing office stationery (Wahyudi 2009). At the same time, he was also socially active and held important positions in local branches of the PSMTI and the Lions Club (Wahyudi 2009). Therefore, he was well known within the local community in Medan. Later, Hasyim was encouraged by his uncle to run in the legislative election of 2009. He then contested for a Medan city council seat as a PDI-P candidate. His campaign team consisted of both Chinese and non-Chinese Indonesians. He was financially supported by a few local Chinese businesspeople in Medan (interview with Hasyim, in Indonesian, August 11, 2010). Hasyim received 2,937 votes and was elected ('50 Calon Anggota DPRD Medan Terpilih Periode 2009–2014' 2009). He was happy both Chinese and non-Chinese Indonesians voted for him. He revealed that about 30% of the votes he gained were from non-Chinese voters (interview with Hasyim, in Indonesian, August 11, 2010). In comparison with Sofyan Tan's defeat in the 2010 mayoral election, it is possible that Hasyim was elected as a city councillor because a city councillor represents a smaller number of voters than a mayor. Moreover, legislators at the national, provincial, and local levels have only legislative power and are not as powerful as mayors, who hold executive power. Hence, it is relatively more difficult to be elected as a mayor than as a legislator.

As a city councillor, Hasyim always spent time visiting and helping victims of misfortunes, such as fires, approaching a few social organisations and requesting them to help the victims. Therefore, a news report in *Harian Mandiri*, a local Indonesian-language newspaper in North Sumatra, described Hasyim as a dedicated political leader and complimented him as the 'Ahok of Medan' ('Hasyim Sosok Ahok Medan' 2013). Therefore, it is not surprising that he was re-elected in the 2014 legislative election ('2 Etnis Tionghoa Akan Duduk Di DPRD Medan' 2014).

---

18. GMNI was affiliated with PNI in the 1960s (Aspinall 2005, 120).

Simon Lekatompessy

Simon Lekatompessy was an ethnic Chinese member of the Surabaya city council for the period 2009–2014. He ran for the first time in 2009 as a PDS candidate and was elected. He was born and raised in Maluku but later moved to Surabaya to study accounting at the Surabaya Academy of Accounting (Akademi Akuntansi Surabaya), a private institute of higher learning in the city. He was active in a few student organisations during his college years. After graduation, Lekatompessy stayed in Surabaya and started his billboard business (interview with Simon Lekatompessy, in Indonesian, May 5, 2011).

Although Lekatompessy does not know Mandarin or Chinese dialects, he identifies himself as an ethnic Chinese. After the end of the New Order regime, he joined the Indonesian Unity in Diversity Party (PBI, or Partai Bhinneka Tunggal Ika), a political party founded by Nurdin Purnomo, a.k.a. Wu Nengbin (吳能彬), a Chinese Indonesian businessperson who ran a travel company in Jakarta. Although PBI was a multi-ethnic political party, about 85% of its committee members were Chinese. Lekatompessy in an interview mentioned that he decided to be involved in politics in order to fight for the abolition of discriminatory policies against Chinese Indonesians (interview with Simon Lekatompessy, in Indonesian, May 5, 2011). Nevertheless, if one examines the circumstances surrounding his motives for entering politics (which I will recount below), one can speculate that he may have been more concerned with the interests of his own business and of the local big business community than the interests of the general public.

PBI was disbanded in 2004 due to lack of interest and support. As a Chinese Indonesian Christian, Lekatompessy decided to join PDS, which was led and dominated by Christians, becoming the head of the party's Surabaya branch. In 2009, he ran for the Surabaya city council and was elected (interview with Simon Lekatompessy, in Indonesian, May 5, 2011). However, Lekatompessy was not generally well known among Chinese Indonesians in Surabaya because he never joined any Chinese organisations. It was alleged that he was elected because he had spent a huge amount of money (Rp500 million or about US$41,754 at that time) on his campaign activities (interview with Eddy Gunawan Santoso, in Indonesian, May 6, 2011).

After getting elected to the city council, Lekatompessy was active in fighting for the interests of the local big business community, but not of the general public. In November 2010, Tri Rismaharini, the mayor of Surabaya, issued the Mayor Regulations No. 56 and No. 57, which increased the tax rates on large-sized (8 m^2 and above) outdoor advertisement billboards in the city by 100 to 400%. The aim of increasing the taxes was to reduce the number of large-sized billboards in the city, which were considered dangerous to the public should they collapse. At the same time, the taxes on small-sized outdoor advertisement billboards were to be reduced by 40% ('Tri Rismaharini' 2011). The regulations upset many producers of large-sized billboards.[19] They wrote to Lekatompessy and other members of Surabaya City Council complaining about the regulations (Kusumadewi and Martudji 2012). Lekatompessy and a few other city councillors opposed the regulations because they affected not only local businesspeople but also politicians who installed large-sized billboards.[20] Lekatompessy and his fellow city councillors proposed to file an impeachment proceeding against Rismaharini during the city council session (Effendi 2010a, 2010b; 'Tri Rismaharini' 2011; Kusumadewi and Martudji 2012). They accused the mayor of not following proper procedures in issuing the regulations because she did not involve the Local Government Working Unit (SKPD, or Satuan Kerja Perangkat Daerah) in the debate nor in the proper procedures for the drawing up of the regulation (Hakim and Taufiq 2011). But hundreds of locals backed Mayor Rismaharini by demonstrating in front of Surabaya city council on January 24, 2011, urging the city councillors to stop bothering the mayor with the issue. The demonstrators argued that the increase in the taxes on large-sized billboards affected only some businesspeople and not the general public. Therefore, the city councillors should not waste time fighting with the mayor on this matter ('Wali Kota Disidang Pansus Angket' 2011). Despite the protest, the city council still launched an impeachment proceeding against the mayor and suspended her on January 31, 2011 (Taufiq and Abidien 2011; 'Konflik Wali Kota dengan DPRD Surabaya' 2011). However, as reported in *The Jakarta Globe*, Home Affairs Minister Gamawan Fauzi later interfered in the matter and defended Rismaharini, saying that the reasons behind the impeachment of Rismaharini were not strong enough ('Surabaya Deputy Mayor Tenders Resignation' 2011). Eventually, the city council annulled the plan to oust Rismaharini (Hakim 2011).

In April 2013, not long after PDS was disqualified from the 2014 election, Lekatompessy left PDS and joined Hanura, led by former military officer Wiranto, planning to run for the 2014 election as a Hanura candidate ('Batal Maju DPD RI' 2013; 'DPRan PDS Pertanyakan Posisi Simon Lekatompessy' 2013). His salary as a member of the Surabaya city council was suspended from May 2013, because according to city regulations city councillors are considered withdrawn from their posts if they switch political parties (Hakim 2013). However, for unknown reasons, Lekatompessy later cancelled his

---

19. The regulations also upset many businesspeople who installed large-sized billboards. In an interview, my informant who is an ethnic Chinese ceramic tile factory owner in Surabaya complained about the regulations and criticised the mayor for not being considerate of businesspeople's interests (interview with Bambang, in Indonesian, March 3, 2011).
20. It was alleged that Lekatompessy opposed the increase because it also affected his own business (interview with Eddy Gunawan Santoso, in Indonesian, May 6, 2011).

plans to run in the election and decided to return to PDS. PDS, however, did not accept his return because, according to the leader of PDS's Surabaya branch, as interviewed by D-onenews.com (an online Indonesian-language news site based in Surabaya), Lekatompessy never cared about his party cadres in the Surabaya branch ('DPRan PDS Pertanyakan Posisi Simon Lekatompessy' 2013). In other words, leaders of PDS's Surabaya branch did not like Lekatompessy and therefore refused to let him return to the party. Nevertheless, the party eventually accepted his return but he did not contest in the 2014 legislative election.

Lekatompessy's experience shows that he is an ambitious, opportunistic politician. In order to pursue his political ambitions, he chose to leave PDS and join Hanura, led by the notorious Wiranto, who is still influential in the political arena. This upset leaders of PDS's Surabaya branch. But he later changed his mind for some unknown reasons and decided to return to PDS. No matter what reasons prompted Lekatompessy to switch parties, his actions give the impression that he is an opportunistic politician with no loyalty to any party. In addition, he does not seem concerned for the safety and good of the masses nor the views of the public but only his own business.

Eddy Gunawan Santoso

In 2010, Eddy Gunawan Santoso (吳繼平), an ethnic Chinese businessman engaged in the cargo industry and business consultation, was keen to contest in the mayoral election of Surabaya. As a devoted Protestant Christian, Santoso was active in the Christian society of his university during his varsity years. Since his graduation, he had been active in inter-religious activities. He held important positions in the East Java Inter-Religious Harmony Association (Ikatan Kerukunan Umat Beragama Jawa Timur) and the Surabaya Inter-Religious Harmony Forum (Forum Kerukunan Umat Beragama Surabaya). However, according to Wahyu, an economic analyst, Santoso was popular only within the local Christian community and not well known in the wider local community in Surabaya. He was also not popular among the local Chinese because he never joined any Chinese organisations (interview with Wahyu, in Indonesia, May 18, 2011). Suhaimi, a university lecturer, made a similar remark that, although Santoso was a wealthy businessman, he was not a popular public figure (interview with Suhaimi, in Indonesian, April 27, 2011).

Santoso revealed that he wanted to run in the mayoral election because he wanted to bring positive change to the city and do away with all forms of discrimination against Indonesian citizens regardless of their ethnicity and class. He was also encouraged by some religious leaders in Surabaya to run (interview with Eddy Gunawan Santoso, in Indonesian, May 6,

2011). Santoso was not affiliated with any political party at that time and intended to run as an independent candidate. According to Law No. 12/2008 on regional government, for districts or cities with more than one million residents, independent candidates keen to run for district head or mayor without the nomination of a political party or a coalition of political parties are obliged to garner signatures from at least 3% of the residents in their territory. According to a news report in *Surabaya Post*, the population in Surabaya in 2010 was about 2.9 million. Therefore, each independent mayoral candidate had to get at least 90,000 signatures (Arfani 2010). In my interview with him, Santoso revealed that he managed to get about 400,000 signatures (interview with Eddy Gunawan Santoso, in Indonesian, May 6, 2011). But later he thought it would be difficult to get elected as an independent candidate. Thus, he announced that he was keen to get the support of political parties in the election ('Eddy Gunawan Tunggu Pinangan Parpol' 2010). Possibly due to his financial status as a wealthy businessman, the Surabaya branches of PDS and PD initially offered to nominate Santoso as the deputy mayoral candidate ('PDS Gandeng Eddy Gunawan' 2010, 33; 'PAC Demokrat Dukung Eddy Gunawan' 2010). However, PDS and PD later decided not to nominate him because he did not have enough money to 'pay' for the nominations. Santoso revealed that PD had requested him to pay the party Rp50 billion (about US$417,536) as the 'nomination fee' but he rejected the request (interview in Indonesian, May 6, 2011). At the same time, PDS offered the nomination to Fandi Utomo, an indigenous Muslim entrepreneur who had allegedly contributed Rp5 billion (about US$41,754) to the party. Having been 'abandoned' by PDS and PD, Santoso decided not to run (interview with Eddy Gunawan Santoso, in Indonesian, May 6, 2011).

Santoso later joined Gerindra, founded and led by Prabowo Subianto, a former military officer accused of inciting anti-Chinese riots in May 1998. He decided to join the party because he saw Prabowo as an influential and powerful leader (interview with Eddy Gunawan Santoso, in Indonesian, May 6, 2011). Santoso ran for the Surabaya city council in 2014 as a Gerindra candidate but was not elected ('Daftar Calon Tetap' 2013). With regards to accusations against Prabowo, Santoso, who was closely connected to Prabowo, defended the former military officer by saying that Prabowo was not involved in the anti-Chinese riots. According to Santoso, the perpetrators were actually former president Habibie and Wiranto, another former military officer, who has been accused of crimes against humanity in East Timor. In reporting on a conversation he had with Prabowo, Santoso related that Prabowo had said, 'How could I possibly kill the Chinese? My mother is a Chinese-Manadonese and I was born from a Chinese womb' (interview with Eddy Gunawan Santoso, in Indonesian, May 6, 2011). According to Santoso, Prabowo had also told him that he would make public the evidence of the involvement of Habibie and Wiranto in the anti-Chinese violence should Habibie and Wiranto 'push him too hard [in the political arena]' (interview with Eddy Gunawan Santoso, in Indonesian, May 6, 2011). Nevertheless, at the time of writing, there is still no concrete evidence that can prove the validity of Santoso's (and Prabowo's) statement regarding Habibie and Wiranto's involvement in the anti-Chinese violence.

By joining Prabowo's party, therefore, Santoso has chosen to collaborate with a controversial former military officer who is influential and powerful in the political arena. This indicates that he believes he can achieve his political ambition with the help of Prabowo's influence and power. It does not matter if Prabowo is accused of perpetrating violence against the Chinese because Santoso believes that Prabowo is innocent.

Dédé Oetomo, a.k.a. Oen Tiong Hauw

Dédé Oetomo, a.k.a. Oen Tiong Hauw, is a pro-*reformasi* social activist and a university lecturer based in Surabaya. He is also a leading activist for LGBT (lesbian, gay, bisexual, and transgender) rights in Indonesia.

Oetomo was born in 1953 to a *peranakan* Chinese family in Pasuruan, East Java (Li 2004a, 356; Lev 2011, 18). He is the eldest child and has two younger brothers and one younger sister (Oetomo 2001, xxvii). According to Oetomo, his father owned a soap factory but it ceased operations in 1957 because he was betrayed by his wife's relative. He then opened an automobile repair shop, thanks to the skills he had obtained from the mechanic training course he took in Surabaya before getting married (interview with Dédé Oetomo, in English, August 31, 2016). An article in the *New York Times* notes that Oetomo's father was 'a left-leaning nationalist and strong supporter of Indonesia's founding president, Sukarno' (Emont 2016). He was a member of the Indonesian National Party (PNI), which was founded and led by President Sukarno (Li 2004a, 356). He was also close to a few pro-Sukarno officials and bureaucrats. Hence, most of his customers were pro-Sukarno officials and bureaucrats during the Sukarno presidency (1950– 1965). However, his business again folded in 1967 as most of his customers who were officials or bureaucrats were either replaced or purged during the 1965–1966 anti-communist purge led by Major-General Suharto, who later replaced Sukarno as president of the country (interview with Dédé Oetomo, in English, August 31, 2016).

Oetomo's mother then took over the family economy by making and selling snacks, preserved foods, and children's clothes. She and her husband also went to Surabaya to get some small items and peddled it to women sugar factory workers in Oosthoek, which consists of the Pasuruan and Besuki residencies. They opened a grocery shop in 1970. It became a clothing shop five years later (interview with Dédé Oetomo, in English, August 31, 2016).

It can be said that Oetomo's father played an essential role in shaping his political ideology. He bought Oetomo Chinese and Soviet comic books that dignified the proletariat. Due to the influence of his father, who was left-leaning and pro-Sukarno, Oetomo began to develop a leftist ideology and had also become interested in Sukarno's Independence Day speeches in 1964 and 1965, when he was still in primary school (interview with Dédé Oetomo, in English, August 31, 2016).

Oetomo studied in Catholic private schools during his primary and secondary years (interview with Dédé Oetomo, in English, September 1, 2016). He became a Roman Catholic at the age of 17 (Oetomo 2001, xxxi). In an interview with me, he revealed that he felt the Suharto regime had purged communists and the left unfairly. Thus, he 'often tried to read about the "forbidden" (namely materials about communism and left-wing politics)' during his upper secondary years (1969–1971) (interview with Dédé Oetomo, in English, August 31, 2016).

After completing his secondary education, Oetomo enrolled at the Institute of Teaching and Education (IKIP, or Institut Keguruan dan Ilmu Pendidikan) in Surabaya, in the English as a Second Language (ESL) programme. He revealed that one of his favourite lecturers, Mrs. Thea Kusuma, was the daughter of the mayor of Pasuruan, with whom his parents were close. Mrs. Kusuma's husband was a political activist who had been with the Socialist Party of Indonesia (PSI, or Partai Sosialis Indonesia), a leftist party that was banned by the Sukarno regime in 1960. He was detained in 1974 after the Malari incident, where during a state visit by the Japanese prime minister, Kakuei Tanaka, a group of university students held a demonstration in Jakarta protesting corruption, high prices, and inequality in foreign investments.[21] Mrs. Kusuma 'often rattled away criticisms about the Soeharto regime' (interview with Dédé Oetomo, in English, August 31, 2016). Thus, it can be said that the influence of his father and his favourite lecturer as well as the injustice imposed by the Suharto regime on the communists and the left significantly shaped his left-leaning political ideology and also his rejection of the Suharto regime as well as Golkar.

At the same time, Oetomo also began to realise that he was homosexual. Despite being told by many people that homosexuality was a 'sin' and abnormal, Oetomo eventually accepted his sexual orientation in 1977 after spending a long time contemplating the issues of sexual orientation, religion, and God, as well as reading a book that gave a positive perspective on homosexuality (Oetomo 2001, xxvii–xxxiv). One year later, he got a

---

21. For more details of the Malari incident, see Vickers (2005, 166–67).

scholarship to do his PhD in linguistics at Cornell University, in the United States (Oetomo 2001, xxxiv–xxxv; Setyautama 2008, 281). In Cornell, Oetomo began to explore gay liberation literature and 'was re-introduced to Marxist thinking' in that literature (interview with Dédé Oetomo, in English, August 31, 2016). In his book, Oetomo points out that the gay rights movement in the United States and other parts of the West was initiated by the left and hence was leftist in nature (Oetomo 2001, 156). Such experience further strengthened his leftist political ideology.

Oetomo's intellectual development made him feel that it is important to practise what he had learned. Therefore, after completing his PhD and returning to Indonesia, Oetomo founded GAYa Nusantara, an organisation that promotes LGBT rights, in Surabaya (Oetomo 2001, 155–56). He was inducted as an Ashoka Fellow in 1991 for his work in fighting for the rights of sexual minorities (*Ashoka at 30* 2011, 73). At the same time, he lectured at the University of Airlangga, Surabaya. In Airlangga, he came across a group of students 'who framed their thinking and study along Marxist lines' (interview with Dédé Oetomo, in English, August 31, 2016). In 1994, this group of students established the People's Democratic Union (PRD)—already mentioned as a leftist NGO—with the objective to fight against the Suharto regime and to push for democratisation in the political, economic, and cultural aspects (Aspinall 2005, 131). Two years later, the organisation publicly launched itself as a political party and was renamed the People's Democratic Party in 1996, despite the prohibition of additional political parties by the Suharto regime (Aspinall 2005, 189).

PRD was the only political party in Indonesia that had consistently been defending the rights of various marginalised groups, including sexual minorities (Oetomo 2001, 126). Hence, Oetomo decided to join the party in 1999 after being invited by some of PRD's leaders, including his students (interview with Dédé Oetomo, in English, August 31, 2016). He also ran for public office during the 1999 legislative elections under the banner of PRD. Oetomo decided to contest in the elections in order to 'build a more democratic Indonesia where everyone regardless of any identity or status can reach an optimal level of well-being in work, education and health' (interview with Dédé Oetomo, in English, August 10, 2012). However, he was not elected because the party received only 0.07% of the total votes, failing to pass the 2% electoral threshold required to secure a seat in the parliament (Suryadinata 2002a, 223). It is plausible that many voters did not vote for PRD because it was a socialist party and was deemed by many to be pro-communist. It is also possible that PRD did not get much support from the business community because the party opposes the capitalist system, which it believes exploits workers.[22] After failing to get a parliamentary seat in the 1999 election, PRD has not contested in subsequent elections.

In 2004, Oetomo ran for the East Java regional representative council (DPD), whereby members are elected on their individual merits and not on their party affiliation. Oetomo's election platform in 2004 focused on the promotion of pluralism in the society (interview with Dédé Oetomo, in English, August 10, 2012). According to Oetomo and Hendi Prayogo, a member of Oetomo's campaign team, a few local Chinese business elites offered to sponsor Oetomo; most of them had the motive of getting business favours from him should he get elected (interview with Dédé Oetomo, in English, December 24, 2010; interview with Hendi Prayogo, in Indonesian, March 28, 2011). But Oetomo made no promises to anyone who backed him. He rejected the approaches of some Chinese businesspeople whom he considered to be close to corrupt local power-holders and the military. He even told a Chinese Indonesian tycoon who approached him outright that the latter should not collude with corrupt politicians and military to get business favours (interview with Dédé Oetomo, in English, December 24, 2010). Oetomo spent nearly Rp65 million (about US$7,615) on his election campaign; most of the funds were contributed by a well-established local Chinese business elite who kept a significant distance from local power-holders and military (interview with Dédé Oetomo, in English, December 24, 2010).

Oetomo was openly supported by local branches of PSMTI, because he was the adviser to PSMTI's East Java branch. He was also popular among local Chinese who strongly identified with their ethnic background since he could speak and read Mandarin. In addition, during the New Order era, he had written positively about Chinese culture and China when he was a columnist of the *Surabaya Post* in the 1980s and 1990s (interview with Dédé Oetomo, in English, December 24, 2010). Oetomo was also openly supported by GAYa Nusantara; Persatuan Waria Kota Surabaya (PERWAKOS), a *waria* (male-to-female transgender) organisation in Surabaya; PRD; and the New Indonesia Alliance Party (PPIB) (interview with Dédé Oetomo, in English, September 24, 2013). However, Oetomo was not elected. According to Samas H. Widjaja, the chairperson of PPIB's East Java branch at that time, Oetomo could not win a seat due to the intentional misrecording of votes he obtained by the legislative election commission officials who were bribed by his rivals.[23] This happened because Oetomo did not have enough money to hire enough reliable witnesses to prevent such fraud from taking place (interview with Samas H. Widjaja, in Mandarin, May 5, 2011).

---

22. See 'Sekilas Tentang PRD' (2010) for more details on the ideology of PRD.
23. It is also possible that Oetomo was not elected because he is an openly gay man and a LGBT rights activist.

After failing to get elected in the 2004 election, Oetomo became busy with 'work on sexuality training and other SOGI (sexual orientation and gender identity)- and HIV (human immunodeficiency virus)-related issues, both at the local, national and regional levels' (interview with Dédé Oetomo, in English, September 3, 2016). Thus, he has not contested in subsequent elections.

Oetomo's story shows that his passion for pushing for positive change and fighting for a less discriminatory society in Indonesia is strongly influenced by his habitus, which is shaped by his family upbringing, his experience during his school and university, as well as his social network comprising friends and students who are passionate about social justice.

Anton Prijatno

Apart from Dédé Oetomo, Anton Prijatno was another ethnic Chinese candidate who ran for an East Java regional representative council (DPD) seat in 2004 (Li 2004b, 104). He was one of the very few Chinese Indonesian former parliamentarians affiliated with Golkar during the Suharto era (interview with Anton Prijatno, in Indonesian, February 24, 2011). As mentioned in Chapter 5, Prijatno left Golkar in May 1998 as he was very disappointed with the rampant corruption within the New Order regime. He then turned to the asphalt distribution business. According to Junus, a university lecturer, due to Prijatno's close connection with the governor, his business is protected from harassment and extortion by the police. He has also become a patron of many well-established Chinese businesses in Surabaya. Chinese businesses under his patronage are free from harassment and extortion by the police (interview with Junus, in Indonesian, January 11, 2011). In addition, Prijatno served as rector (till 2003) and later chairperson of the University of Surabaya (interview with Anton Prijatno, in Indonesian, February 24, 2011).

In my interview with him, Prijatno revealed that he had decided to run in the 2004 election in order to serve the people (interview with Anton Prijatno, in Indonesian, February 24, 2011).[24] It was alleged that he was not popular among Chinese Indonesians with a strong ethnic identity because he did not understand Chinese at all and did not join any ethnic Chinese organisations (interview with Dédé Oetomo, in English, December 24, 2010). However, due to his background in politics and business, he was supported by many well-established businesspeople. Prijatno was allegedly backed by many wealthy Chinese business elites who contributed altogether about Rp3.5 billion (about US$410,015) to his campaign fund (interview with Hendi Prayogo, in Indonesian, March 28, 2011).

---

24. It is also possible that he ran for office in order to gain political protection for his business.

Electoral Politics and the Chinese in Post-Suharto Indonesia   147

However, Prijatno was not elected. Wahyu, an economic analyst in Surabaya, revealed that this was due to Prijatno's lack of popularity among rural and grassroots communities in East Java (interview with Wahyu, in Indonesian, May 18, 2011). He has not run in subsequent elections.

Sofyan Tan, a.k.a. Tan Kim Yang, and Indra Wahidin

I have already said much about these two interesting and important figures, who have been very influential in the Chinese community in Medan. I would now like to discuss more of the background of these two individuals as a way of highlighting the tension between different ideas and desires in the Chinese community in Indonesia.

In the 2004 legislative election, two local Chinese Indonesians ran for the North Sumatra regional representatives council (DPD).[25] These two candidates were Indra Wahidin, then chairperson of INTI's North Sumatra branch, and Sofyan Tan, who served on the advisory board of PSMTI's North Sumatra branch. As discussed in Chapter 4, both INTI and PSMTI are major Chinese organisations in Indonesia. Both Tan and Wahidin were not affiliated with any political party at that time.

Tan's passion for social activism and politics was motivated by his family upbringing and the racial discrimination he encountered during his entrance examination to the University of North Sumatra (USU, or Universitas Sumatera Utara) and later during the oral examination for all final year medical students. As mentioned earlier in Chapter 4, Tan's father had many indigenous Indonesian friends and had always pushed his son to mingle and integrate with Indonesians of other ethnic backgrounds. After graduating from high school, Tan wished to pursue his medical studies at USU, the most prominent public university in Medan. However, he was not given a place due to the unwritten quota system in Indonesia's public universities during the Suharto era that restricted the number of ethnic Chinese students admitted. There were also corrupt practices in the process of examination administration (Anto 2009, 57–59).[26] It was alleged that Tan's parents could not pay Rp4 million (about US$9,049) as requested by the examination committee to pass him in the examination (Anto 2009, 58–59). Therefore, he had to pursue his medical studies at Medan Methodist University of Indonesia (UMI Medan, or Universitas Methodist Indonesia Medan), a private university founded by the Indonesian Methodist Church (Anto 2009, 61).

---

25. There were forty-eight DPD candidates in North Sumatra (Pemilu.Asia 2012).
26. According to Tan's biographer, it was alleged that USU's Faculty of Medicine accepted only a hundred new students for every intake and only 2% were of ethnic Chinese origin (Anto 2009, 57–58).

Later, during the oral examination in his final year, Tan encountered a racist indigenous Indonesian examiner who often failed him just because he was ethnic Chinese. Tan decided to get a friend to help him bring up this issue to the dean of USU's Faculty of Medicine. Eventually, Tan passed the examination after taking it again in front of the dean (interview with Sofyan Tan, in Indonesian, 23 August 2010).

Hence, it can be said that Tan's family upbringing and his experience of racial discrimination are two main factors that motivated him to get involved in social activism and, later, politics to push for positive changes in Indonesia.

In 2004, Tan decided to run for the North Sumatra DPD because he was keen to enter the political system without joining any political party and to bring changes to society (Anto 2009, 238–39). He also wanted to 'break the political silence within Chinese community' and 'set an example to show that the Chinese have the right to be elected and they do not have to be afraid of politics' (Anto 2009, 239, my translation from Indonesian original). Wahidin, on the other hand, ran for office because he wanted to try 'something new' (*mencoba 'barang baru'*) (Anto 2009, 242, my translation from Indonesian original).[27] It so happens that both Wahidin and Tan possess medical degrees but no longer practise as physicians. Wahidin obtained his medical degree from the Islamic University of North Sumatra while Tan graduated from UMI Medan ('Calon DPD Sumut No. 12 dr Indra Wahidin' 2004; Anto 2009, 61). As earlier mentioned, Wahidin was an insurance agent while Tan was a social activist and the founder of the Sultan Iskandar Muda integrated school in Medan.

As a well-known Chinese community leader in Medan, Wahidin has been actively assisting the provincial government to introduce and promote investment from Malaysia, South Korea, Thailand, and China. In 2003, he was honoured by the Karo-Batak Protestant Church in Medan with a 'Ginting' Karo-Batak surname in recognition of his contributions to North Sumatra (Li 2004a, 337–38). He is also well connected to several political elites and high-ranking military officers, thanks to the six-month training he received at the Indonesian National Defense Institute (LEMHANNAS RI, or Lembaga Ketahanan Nasional Republik Indonesia) in Jakarta in 2001 (Wu 2009, 224; 'Calon DPD Sumut No. 12 dr Indra Wahidin' 2004). In addition, as mentioned in Chapter 5, it is alleged that Wahidin is well-connected to gangsters in Medan (interview with Sofyan Tan, in Indonesian, August 23, 2010).

Tan, on the other hand, is very popular among many local grassroots indigenous Indonesians because he actively promotes inter-ethnic harmony through education work and engages in fighting for and safeguarding the

---

27. 'Something new' refers to the DPD, which was established in 2001 (Crouch 2010, 61).

Electoral Politics and the Chinese in Post-Suharto Indonesia 149

interests of SMEs (small and medium enterprises), which are dominated by indigenous Indonesians. Although PSMTI and INTI always claim to take a neutral stance on partisan politics, they openly supported and campaigned for their specific candidates, who held important positions in their organisations. Wahidin was strongly supported by ethnic Chinese from INTI while Tan was openly supported by those from PSMTI. As a result, the local Chinese community was divided between support for these two Chinese electoral candidates (interview with Sofyan Tan, in Indonesian, August 23, 2010). As it turned out, neither of them were elected.[28]

According to Wu Yiguang (2009), although Wahidin was popular among political elites and high-ranking military officers in North Sumatra, not many people from the grassroots community and working class knew him (221). On the other hand, although Tan was an outstanding public speaker and gained strong support from the working class, he was not supported by many well-established Chinese business elites. As mentioned earlier in this chapter, running for the DPD is by no means less expensive although candidates do not need party backing. Candidates need to conduct massive electoral campaigns throughout the province in order to get elected. Since Tan did not get much financial support from the local Chinese business community, he could not conduct the massive electoral campaign needed to win. His campaign fund was only about Rp400 million (about US$46,859), which was much lower than of many other candidates, whose funds might reach billions of rupiah (Wu 2009, 221; Anto 2009, 243–44).

After failing to get elected in 2004, Tan later joined PDI-P, led by former president Megawati Sukarnoputri, in 2008. He chose PDI-P because, in his view, the party 'is more accepting of ethnic Chinese members compared to other political parties' (interview with Sofyan Tan, in Indonesian, August 23, 2010). He was the treasurer of PDI-P's North Sumatra branch from 2005 to 2010 (Anto 2009, 465). Tan was enthusiastic to participate in politics as he was very keen to promote the well-being of the people in Medan regardless of their ethno-religious background and to end all sorts of corruption and malpractice in the bureaucracy. Apart from focusing on his education work, which promoted inter-ethnic harmony, as already mentioned in Chapter 5, he also actively engaged in fighting for and safeguarding the interests of SMEs in Indonesia, which are dominated by *pribumi*. He was the head of the National Forum of Small and Medium Enterprises (FORNAS UKM, or Forum Nasional Usaha Kecil dan Menengah) from 1998 to 2004. FORNAS UKM is an NGO that promotes the interests of SMEs in the country by speaking out against the policies of the government and banks that unfairly discriminate against SMEs. Tan assists owners of SMEs to expand their business network

---

28. Even if there was only one ethnic Chinese contested for the seat, that alone would not have been sufficient to ensure the victory of the Chinese candidate in the race.

through the programmes of FORNAS UKM. As the head of FORNAS UKM, Tan was instrumental in introducing ethnic Chinese businesspeople to indigenous owners of SMEs. He also managed to get a few Chinese businesspeople to join the leadership of the organisation ('Pemilihan Wali Kota Medan Geliat Politik Etnis Tionghoa di Medan' 2010). Besides that, Tan was also very active in helping poor people from the local grassroots community, most of whom were *pribumi*. In my interview with him, Tan felt that his work for the poor had made him popular among the *pribumi* in the city's grassroots community (interview with Sofyan Tan, in Indonesian, August 23, 2010). In fact, prior to the first round of the 2010 mayoral election, Tan was also honoured by the local Karo-Batak community leaders with a 'Ginting' surname. The honour was in recognition of his social work and contributions to helping Batak Karo small and medium entrepreneurs ('dr Sofyan Tan Dianugerahi Marga Ginting' 2010).[29]

Contesting against one another in the 2004 DPD elections appears to have destroyed the friendship between Indra Wahidin and Sofyan Tan.[30] Although neither got elected, as mentioned, tension between these two candidates started to surface, and their differences in opinions and ideologies drove a wedge in their relationship, which became even more strained during the later mayoral election of 2010. Tan decided to join the race in order to participate in the country's development with his ideas ('Pemilihan Wali Kota Medan Geliat Politik Etnis Tionghoa di Medan' 2010). In addition, he wanted to 'test the response of the people regarding their acceptance for an ethnic Chinese in the nation and character building' (Gunawan 2010). Tan initially was nominated as a deputy mayoral candidate, pairing with Rahudman Harahap, the incumbent acting mayor. At that time, both of them agreed to work together in the race with the support of Golkar and PDI-P. But four days before the registration deadline with the local election committee, Rahudman left Tan and paired with Dzulmi Eldin, the Medan regional secretary.[31] Both Rahudman and Dzulmi were supported by Golkar and PD, the political party of President Yudhoyono. Tan disclosed that Rahudman and Dzulmi were paired at the instruction of Syamsul Arifin, the governor

---

29. Tan later drew on his 'Ginting' surname when he campaigned in the first round of the 2010 mayoral election (Aspinall, Dettman, and Warburton 2011, 43).
30. Sofyan Tan disclosed to me how Wahidin became hostile to him and they were no longer on as good terms after the 2004 elections (interview with Sofyan Tan, in Indonesian, August 23, 2010). Moreover, three informants confirmed for me that Wahidin did not like Tan (interview with Farid, in Hokkien, July 15, 2010; interview with Hasan, in Mandarin, August 19, 2010; interview with Rudy, in Mandarin, August 25, 2010). In fact, during my fieldwork in Medan, I was advised by a few Chinese Medanese friends not to talk about Tan when I interviewed Wahidin.
31. According to Law No. 32/2004 on regional government, the regional secretary is in charge of assisting the regional head in drawing up policies as well as coordinating regional government offices (*dinas daerah*) and regional technical institutions (*lembaga teknis daerah*).

Electoral Politics and the Chinese in Post-Suharto Indonesia   151

of North Sumatra, who was also the chairperson of Golkar's North Sumatra branch. Syamsul and other leaders in Golkar intended to eliminate any contestant of Chinese origin in the mayoral election (interview with Sofyan Tan, in Indonesian, August 23, 2010).

Subsequently, PDI-P split with Golkar and decided to nominate Tan as a mayoral candidate, since they believed there was no other better candidate from the party. The party managed to get PDS, a party led by Christians, to form a coalition in nominating Tan as the mayoral candidate. As mentioned in Chapter 1, Tan later decided to pair with Nelly Armayanti, a Muslim woman of Minangkabau ethnicity, as the deputy mayoral candidate. Armayanti was the former head of the General Elections Commission (KPU) of Medan (2003–2008) and also an activist for women's issues. She was a lecturer at the State University of Medan (UNIMED) at the time she ran for election. Tan recounted the reasons for choosing Armayanti as his running mate:

> I was sure that I would be attacked by my rivals because of my religious background [as a non-Muslim]. So I picked a woman with a headscarf. I did not mention whether she was a Muslim but people surely would say, 'Oh, she is a Muslim.' And I picked a woman because I thought women would probably vote for a woman candidate. (interview with Sofyan Tan, in Indonesian, August 23, 2010)

Armayanti, on the other hand, decided to join Tan because of her interest in politics and the fact that they shared the same political ideology and vision:

> When I was still the head of the KPU in Medan, I found that power was something very important. . . . When we have power, it becomes something very significant for us. We can then come out with various policies in public decision-making. . . . I have known Dr. Sofyan Tan for a long time. We first met and became friends in an NGO. He is also an idealist like me. So I know him well. Prior to the mayoral election, he asked me to be his running mate and I wondered why did he choose me. Then he explained that he was looking for a running mate who was different from him in terms of gender and religious background. But the most important factor for him in looking for a running mate at that time was gender. He said the gender of his running mate must be different from his. . . . Then I thought both of us had met the person who shared the same vision [i.e., committed to bringing positive change to society]. Both of us had the same will. We joined the race to bring change to Medan. (interview with Nelly Armayanti, in Indonesian, August 12, 2010)

In short, Tan picked Armayanti in order to draw more votes from Muslim and women voters but clearly also because both of them were committed to bringing positive change to society.

It should be noted that, initially, Wahidin had intended to run in the election as well. He sought PDS's nomination and registered with the party's Medan branch as a candidate for mayor or deputy mayor ('Daftarkan Diri ke DPC PDS' 2010). But later Wahidin decided to pull out from the race as he could not get enough support from the members of the party and there was 'a lack of basis for cooperation with PDS' (Huang 2010, my translation from the original Chinese newspaper commentary article).[32] In addition, some indigenous friends told him that it was still not a good time for an ethnic Chinese to run for the mayoral election, as he recounted:

> Yes, initially I was keen to participate in the election. But later many of my indigenous friends and Islamic religious leaders advised me to withdraw as it was still not a good time for me to run for the post. They said the indigenous population generally still could not accept an ethnic Chinese to be their mayor. Many indigenous Indonesians feel that since May 1998, the Chinese already have the freedom to openly express their ethnic and cultural identities, to run businesses, and to establish Chinese-language newspapers. So, why should we fight for more political power? Therefore, I eventually decided to pull out from the contest. (interview with Indra Wahidin, in Mandarin, October 19, 2010)

It can be said that a feeling that there was suspicion and prejudice among the indigenous Indonesians against the ethnic Chinese was one important factor behind Wahidin pulling out of the race.

Initially, when Tan became the mayoral candidate, he was concerned that he would not have enough money to fund a massive electoral campaign. When he had been paired with Rahudman, many wealthy businesspeople offered to sponsor the pair since Rahudman as the incumbent was deemed to have a higher chance of winning. But later when they found that he would not be paired with Rahudman, those businesspeople withdrew their offers and channelled their support for Rahudman-Eldin. As Tan recounted:

> I did not want to be the number one [mayoral] candidate because I knew I would need a large amount of money to campaign.[33] When I was nominated to be the number one candidate, I was not happy but sad because all the people [wealthy businesspeople] had left me. No [well-established] businesspeople supported me because they believed I would lose. . . . I did not borrow money from other people. If I was paired with Rahudman, I am sure I would win and all people would give us their money. [Initially, when Golkar intended to pair Rahudman with me], one of them said, 'Wow, I will sponsor you with Rp15 billion [about US$163,595]!' But later when he knew

---

32. My understanding of the phrase 'a lack of basis for cooperation with PDS' is that, since most members of the PDS did not support the nomination of Wahidin as a candidate for the mayoral election, there was no basis for him to cooperate with the party.

33. Here, the number one candidate refers to mayoral candidate while deputy mayoral candidate is known as the number two candidate. Usually, it is the mayoral candidate who carries more responsibility for seeking funds.

Electoral Politics and the Chinese in Post-Suharto Indonesia

that I would not pair with Rahudman . . . , he just disappeared! I tried to call him but could not get through. (interview with Sofyan Tan, in Indonesian, August 23, 2010)

According to a news report, Tan initially did consider pulling out from the race but later changed his mind after getting encouragement from his family: 'At that time, I really wanted to withdraw from the nomination. But my eldest daughter told me that the biggest mistake a person makes is that he or she never tries' (Cited in 'Tokoh Thionghoa Salut Kepada Sofyan Tan' 2010, my translation from Indonesian).

Tan recalled how he tried his very best to campaign despite the lack of funds in the first round of the election:

> People ridiculed me by uttering words like 'Forget it, just withdraw from the race. You won't win'. How did I respond? I woke up every morning and walked to traditional markets. I greeted women in shabby and stinking clothes. I greeted the hawkers, shoppers, trishaw drivers, people who lived beside railway tracks, people who lived at slums, trash areas and along rivers. I could stand it! I often appeared dirty with bad smell when I went home then. . . . Wealthy Chinese organised campaign events for Rahudman, Maulana Pohan, and Ajib Shah in hotels and restaurants because they were confident that these candidates would win. But they never held such events for me [in the first round]. [PSMTI] did help in campaigning for me but they did not have enough money. So we could only have simple and moderate campaign events. (interview with Sofyan Tan, in Indonesian, August 23, 2010)

The local Chinese in Medan were once again divided in their support for Tan. PSMTI actively campaigned for Tan and mobilised the Chinese voters while INTI's members, led by Wahidin, his long-time rival, openly supported Ajib Shah. Shah was an indigenous Indonesian who had been the head of the North Sumatra branch of the Pancasila Youth (PP), an influential youth/crime organisation in the province. Besides that, Tan also received financial support from the Tan surname clan associations in Medan and Jakarta (interview with Halim, in Indonesian, July 26, 2010). According to Halim, an NGO activist in Medan, Tan was also supported by many indigenous social activists and intellectuals with a progressive mindset because they saw him as a 'symbol of change'. In contrast, Rahudman was generally perceived as a New Order bureaucrat and symbol of the entrenchment of the old oligarchy-style bureaucrats. Thus, voters who wanted change did not support him (interview with Halim, in Indonesian, July 26, 2010).

During the electoral campaign, Tan promised to pay more attention to people from the lower class. He also promised to provide loans for local SMEs as well as to simplify the application procedures for the loans if he was elected. He stated his commitment to improve urban infrastructure such as electricity, water supply, and roads in Medan so that the city would be as progressive as Penang in Malaysia (Xiaoxing 2010).

In the first round of the mayoral election, held on May 12, 2010, there were ten pairs of candidates and Tan was the only Chinese contestant. Tan-Armayanti unexpectedly defeated eight other candidate pairs by gaining 140,676 votes (20.72%). Rahudman-Eldin received the highest number of votes, i.e., 150,671 (22.20%).[34] Aspinall and colleagues, in an analysis of this election, point out that the result was probably due to a split in Muslim community's vote because of the large number of candidates (Aspinall, Dettman, and Warburton 2011, 46). Since none of the pairs gained the 30% minimum of the total valid votes, a second round of polls was needed; both Rahudman-Eldin and Tan-Armayanti were qualified to enter the second round (Edward 2010). According to Aspinall and colleagues (2011, 45), Tan-Armayanti gained a majority vote in eleven *kecamatan*s (subdivisions), i.e., Medan Area, Medan Kota, Medan Maimum, Medan Sunggal, Medan Petisah, Medan Barat, Medan Timur, Medan Perjuangan, Medan Polonia, Medan Baru, and Medan Tuntungan.[35] In most of these districts, the Chinese are the largest or second-largest ethnic group. In fact, the pair managed to defeat Sigit Pramono Asrie, who was paired with Nurlisa Ginting, a Batak Karo candidate, in Medan Sunggal, a Batak Karo area ('Pemilihan Wali Kota Medan Geliat Politik Etnis Tionghoa di Medan' 2010).

Tan disclosed that after he entered the second round, many wealthy businesspeople began to offer sponsorship to him as they believed he had a chance to win:

> [Originally,] many people did not expect that I could contest against Rahudman in the second round. Therefore, I received very little funds [from businesspeople] in the first round. In the second round, I began to get more funds. Many people gave [me their money]. People began to see there was hope [for me to win] because all the trishaw drivers and parking attendants said they would vote for Sofyan Tan to make a change. (interview with Sofyan Tan, in Indonesian, August 23, 2010)

These businesspeople included a well-established real estate tycoon in the city. Tan disclosed that they intended to fund him and his running mate in order to obtain business favours if the pair was elected (interview with Sofyan Tan, in Indonesian, August 23, 2010). But as I mentioned earlier in Chapter 1, Tan rejected financial offers from businesspeople who hoped to get favours from him. Tan openly claimed that if he won and became the mayor, he would not be involved in corruption, collusion, and nepotism.

---

34. I obtained this data from the General Elections Commission (KPU) of Medan.
35. I obtained this data from the General Elections Commission (KPU) of Medan. There are twenty-one *kecamatan*s in Medan. Rahudman-Eldin gained a majority vote in nine *kecamatan*s while Ajib Shah-Binsar Situmorang won in one *kecamatan*.

Therefore, he would not grant any favours to businesspeople who sponsored him during the election (interview with Sofyan Tan, in Indonesian, August 23, 2010). Furthermore, on one occasion, Tan even displayed a gallows to the audience and claimed that he was ready to be hanged if found guilty of corrupt practices ('Zaoshihui Renchao Ruyong' 2010; 'Pendukung Pasangan No 10 "Menyemut" di Lapangan Merdeka' 2010).

According to Armayanti, the campaign fund for the candidate pair was Rp5 billion (about US$547,709) in the first round and Rp8 billion (about US$870,665) in the second round (interview with Nelly Armayanti, in Indonesian, August 12, 2010). There were some Chinese businesspeople who offered genuine support to Tan without expecting any favours in return. For instance, two prominent wealthy Chinese entrepreneurs, Djuandi, who runs a food and beverage production company and is also the chairperson of PSMTI's North Sumatra branch, and Rudy, who is engaged in the metal-grinding industry, openly supported and campaigned for Tan (interview with Eddy Djuandi, in Mandarin, August 25, 2010; interview with Sofyan Tan, in Indonesian, August 23, 2010). According to Djuandi, Tan had been the adviser to PSMTI's North Sumatra branch. Djuandi had known Tan for a long time and found that he was knowledgeable and capable enough to be a political leader. Therefore, Djuandi decided to support and campaign for him together with other members of the organisation (interview with Eddy Djuandi, in Mandarin, August 25, 2010). In addition, Tan-Armayanti were also supported by several local Chinese owners of SMEs who did not ask for 'kickbacks' or other business privileges in return (interview with Sofyan Tan, in Indonesian, August 23, 2010; interview with Nelly Armayanti, in Indonesian, August 12, 2010; interview with Halim, in Indonesian, July 26, 2010). In addition, my informant Erik, a local Chinese businessperson engaged in the iron and plastics industry, claimed that he had made the highest financial contribution to Tan-Armayanti, but kept a low profile and remained in the background during the election (interview with Erik, in Mandarin, August 25, 2010). Both Rudy and Erik decided to support Tan because they perceived Tan to be an honest and clean politician. They believed he would be able to bring positive change to Medan if elected (interview with Rudy, in Mandarin, August 25, 2010; interview with Erik, in Mandarin, August 25, 2010). Djuandi, Rudy, and Erik decided to support Tan because they saw the promotion of good governance as more important than their personal interests. They therefore chose of their free will to challenge the existing muddy and corrupt political environment.

Tan perceived Rudy as a good and honest Chinese big businessman. During his electoral campaign, Rudy told Tan not to allocate any state project to him if he got elected. He only demanded that Tan not to commit corrupt acts and bring disgrace to the Chinese community. He also requested that Tan create more employment opportunities to the grassroots community in Medan, which comprised mainly *pribumi*, in order to improve their living conditions. He believed that when the *pribumi* enjoyed better living conditions, they would not be as hostile to the ethnic Chinese, who have often been seen as wealthier than the *pribumi* (interview with Sofyan Tan, in Indonesian, August 23, 2010).

Tan-Armayanti's good performance in the first round and entry into the second round had not been expected by most of their rivals. The second round saw a contest between a Muslim candidate who was an incumbent and a non-Muslim Chinese candidate who was 'a relative political outsider' (Aspinall, Dettman, and Warburton 2011, 46). According to my interview with Armayanti (interview in Indonesian, August 12, 2010) as well as to Aspinall and colleagues (2011, 29–30, 46–51), the second round of the election saw the dramatic escalation of communal tension and an increased emphasis on religious identity. Tan's non-Muslim background became a target of attack for his opponents. Rahudman's campaign teams and supporters, including leaders of the Council of Indonesian Islamic Scholars (MUI) and a few famous Muslim preachers, undermined Tan's legitimacy as a mayoral candidate by manipulating the issue of religious identity. They launched a concerted campaign urging Muslim voters to support Rahudman, claiming it was against the teachings of Islam to vote for a *kafir* (infidel) (interview with Yopie, in Indonesian, July 27, 2010; interview with Halim, in Indonesian, July 26, 2010; interview with Sofyan Tan, in Indonesian, August 23, 2010). The Rahudman camp even used the city's mosques to spread such messages. According to Yopie, a lecturer at the University of North Sumatra, on every Friday prior to polling day, preachers at many of the city's mosques called upon Muslims to vote for a Muslim candidate (interview with Yopie, in Indonesian, July 27, 2010). Many conservative Muslim voters were influenced by such propaganda and decided not to support Tan (interview with Yopie, in Indonesian, July 27, 2010; interview with Halim, in Indonesian, July 26, 2010). It is also possible that conservative Muslims did not support Tan-Armayanti because they were not happy with a woman running for public office. In addition, according to Tan, local Muslims were intimidated by rumours that if Tan was elected, he would turn Medan into a 'Chinatown' and build many Chinese temples instead of mosques (interview with Sofyan Tan, in Indonesian, August 23, 2010).

In response, Tan's campaign team came out with a campaign that aimed to portray Tan as a pluralist figure (Aspinall, Dettman, and Warburton 2011, 49). Most controversially, they had photographs taken of Tan with Islamic preachers who wore *peci* (a cap widely worn by Muslim men in Indonesia) and long robes, and used them extensively in the campaign. Nevertheless, according to Usman, an NGO activist in Medan, as well as to Aspinall et

Electoral Politics and the Chinese in Post-Suharto Indonesia 157

al., the use of these photographs backfired as many voters felt that Tan manipulated religious symbols for political motives (interview with Usman, in Indonesian, July 30, 2010; Aspinall, Dettman, and Warburton 2011, 49). Usman further commented:

> Then he [Sofyan Tan] took photographs with a few Islamic preachers, right? Some of the preachers were, excuse me, not known to the public in many places. These were *ustaz dadakan*.[36] They suddenly became preachers. [They were] *ustaz tukang*.[37] Yes, for political ends, all of a sudden I wear a *peci* and a long robe. I can become [such a] preacher too. There are many of these people nowadays in Indonesia. . . . For me, this is fatal. . . . The Sofyan camp was trapped [with such religious issues]. They enlarged the photos and put them on billboards and around the city. [Tan was seen] [s]haking hands with those preachers [in the photos]. Many people found these photos very strange. [The preachers] [j]ust appeared all of a sudden. As if they were forced to [take photos with Tan in that way]. It looked so unnatural.[38] (interview with Usman, in Indonesian, July 30, 2010)

Usman's comments indicate that the attempts by Sofyan Tan's camp to counter the attacks from the Rahudman camp were apparently ineffective, as it upset many voters who had no knowledge of the preachers in these photos.

Moreover, Halim and Usman, two local NGO activists in Medan, disclosed that although Tan was popular among many *pribumi* in the grassroots community, most *pribumi* urban voters in the city did not support him due to his being ethnic Chinese. In their view, the ethnic Chinese exercised considerable domination over the economy and they were afraid that, if Tan was elected, the Chinese would become more powerful both in the economy and politics, and this would subsequently threaten the position of the *pribumi* (interview with Halim, in Indonesian, July 26, 2010; interview with Usman, in Indonesian, July 30, 2010). In fact, prior to polling day, a Chinese Indonesian who worked in a local Chinese-language newspaper heard some racist remarks against Tan while riding on a public minivan in the city:

> I remember during the election period, one evening, as usual, I took a public minivan to go home after work. Then I suddenly heard an indigenous passenger angrily utter, 'The Chinese are indeed greedy. They have controlled the economy and now they want to control the political arena as well. This is terrible! We must not support the Chinese candidate in the coming mayoral

---

36. The expression refers to Islamic preachers who were previously not known to many people but appeared 'all of a sudden'.
37. In Indonesia, *uztaz tukang* refers to people who are paid to disguise themselves as preachers, usually for political reasons. There is no direct English equivalent for this term. It can be translated as 'instant preachers', which has the nearest meaning.
38. Unfortunately, I did not have an opportunity to see the photos. The photos are also not included in Aspinall and colleagues' article (2011) on the mayoral election.

election!' (personal communication with Janice, in Mandarin, November 12, 2010)

According to Usman, racial prejudice against the Chinese among the *pribumi* was so great that, during the campaign, some *pribumi* were unhappy when they heard ethnic Chinese members of Tan's team speaking in Hokkien:

> In a few public events, such as visiting patients who were fire victims in hospitals . . . they [members of Tan's team] spoke Hokkien and some non-Chinese heard it. I think they did not purposely speak the language [in public] but even if they only uttered a very few words in Hokkien, the consequences were serious. After that, I heard some non-Chinese commenting, 'These people have not come into power but they are already bold enough to speak Chinese wherever they like.' (interview with Usman, in Indonesian, July 30, 2010)

In addition, although Tan was supported by many Chinese voters in the first round, data from my field study implied that he was actually not very popular among some local Chinese with a strong ethnic identity. In the view of these Chinese, Tan identified himself more with the indigenous population than with the Chinese community. As a Chinese businessman engaged in garment production commented:

> Sofyan Tan's biggest mistake is that prior to his participation in the mayoral election, he never established a close relationship with the local Chinese community in Medan although he held an advisory position in PSMTI's North Sumatra branch. All this while, he was closer to the indigenous community. (interview with Farid, in Hokkien, July 15, 2010)

It was also alleged that Tan was ideologically an assimilationist and this made him seem unfavourable in the eyes of some Chinese in Medan. Another informant pointed out, 'Sofyan Tan advocated for the assimilation of the Chinese population into the indigenous communities. He shared the same ideology with Junus Jahja. Therefore, many Chinese did not like him and did not support him in the mayoral election' (interview with The Lie Hok, in Mandarin, October 31, 2010).[39] As mentioned in Chapter 2, Junus Jahja was one of the key figures of the assimilation movement in the 1960s. His open advocacy for the assimilation of the Chinese had upset some Chinese Indonesians, especially those with a strong ethnic identity.

---

39. But it should be noted that Tan's advocacy for Chinese assimilation was probably made prior to his candidacy in the mayoral election and not during the mayoral election as the newspapers did not report any such remarks during the election period. After all, it would be unwise for Tan to promote such an ideology during the election as he needed support from the local Chinese community. Anyway, given that Chinese assimilation is a sensitive issue among Chinese with a strong ethnic identity, many Chinese could not forget Tan's advocacy for the idea although it took place prior to the election.

Moreover, according to a journalist of *Yazhou Zhoukan* (亞洲週刊), a Chinese-language international affairs magazine, when anti-Chinese riots broke out in Indonesia in May 1998, Tan openly expressed his disapproval of China's intervention as he deemed it a domestic matter. This upset many Chinese Indonesians who considered China as their cultural motherland and thought China should express her concern for the Chinese victims in Indonesia. They still could not forgive Tan on this matter (Lin 2010).

A commentary article in *Guoji Ribao* even stated that

> [Sofyan Tan] is a controversial figure in the Chinese community. Therefore, local Chinese who did not vote at all on the day of the election were actually also making their choice [as there were no suitable candidates whom they wanted to support]. It does not necessarily mean that they were politically apathetic. (Mingyanren 2010, my translation from Chinese original)

The ambivalent feelings towards Tan within the Chinese community reflect, therefore, the diversity of ideas among the Chinese in Medan. Although Tan was the only ethnic Chinese mayoral candidate, some Chinese refused to support him because he was very close to the indigenous population, but not to the Chinese community. In addition, some Chinese with a strong ethnic identity considered Tan as culturally 'not Chinese enough' because he spoke Indonesian instead of Hokkien with his family members and did not identify China as his cultural motherland. Moreover, he had allegedly advocated for the assimilation of the Chinese population years previously and this had upset many Chinese in Medan. But at the same time, there were also Chinese, including leaders and members of PSMTI, who strongly supported and campaigned for Tan because he was the adviser to the North Sumatra branch of that organisation. Moreover, they saw Tan as an honest and clean politician. To them, the relatively 'weak' ethnic identity of Tan was not an issue.

Many local wealthy Chinese businesspeople did not support Tan because of two reasons. First, Tan came from a poor family and was not part of the Chinese business elite community in Medan (interview with Halim, in Indonesian, July 26, 2010). Second, Tan refused to grant favours to businesspeople who funded him should he get elected. As a result, many Chinese businesspeople who intended to get favours and patronage from local power-holders decided not to support Tan, who would not help and protect them in their business (interview with Daniel, in Indonesian, July 13, 2010).

In addition, some Chinese did not support Tan because they were not confident that Tan, as an ethnic Chinese, would be able to work effectively with local government officials, who were mostly indigenous Indonesians (interview with Daniel, in Indonesian, July 13, 2010). In an opinion piece, a reader of a local Chinese-language newspaper disclosed remarks that he or she had encountered, 'Baseless rumours in coffee shops [that I heard]: "If the Chinese [Sofyan Tan] is elected, if anything goes wrong, all Chinese will be in trouble. A Chinese mayor is unable to lead non-Chinese government officials"' ('Jingxuan Zhong De Fengyu' 2010, my translation from Chinese original). It seems many people in Medan believe that if a Chinese mayor made a mistake, all Chinese in the city would be blamed. In other words, if something happens that people do not like about one Chinese, then all Chinese become victims, an idea held also by Indra Wahidin, as mentioned in Chapter 4.

In short, not all Chinese in Medan approved of Tan. Indeed, during my interview with Christianto Wibisono (黃建國), a noted Chinese Indonesian economist in Jakarta, prior to the second round polling day, he told me frankly that he was not confident Tan would be elected as not all Chinese in Medan supported him (interview with Christianto Wibisono, in English, June 18, 2010).

Prior to polling day, many Chinese voters were also intimidated by rumours and mobile phone text messages warning that if Tan won the election, there would be riots in the city against the Chinese (interview with Brilian Moktar, in Mandarin, July 16, 2010; interview with Sofyan Tan, in Indonesian, August 23, 2010; interview with Ivan, in Hokkien, July 16, 2010; interview with Rudy, in Mandarin, August 25, 2010; interview with Hasan, in Mandarin, August 19, 2010). The rumours and text messages were mostly spread by Tan's competitors but it was alleged that some were also sent out by local Chinese who disliked Tan (interview with Rudy, in Mandarin, August 25, 2010; interview with Hasan, in Mandarin, August 19, 2010). Many Chinese were frightened and did not vote for Tan on polling day; some did not vote at all. According to Eddy Djuandi, the chairperson of PSMTI's North Sumatra branch, who observed the polling process with other leaders and activists of the organisation, there were probably only 30 to 40% of the Chinese who came out to cast their votes in the second round (interview with Eddy Djuandi, in Mandarin, August 25, 2010). Aspinall and colleagues (2011) also note that there was 'a lower turnout in booths in Chinese districts that had voted strongly for Sofyan in round one' (52).

It was also alleged that there were a lot of violations and irregularities committed by the Rahudman camp, who were mainly bureaucrats of the local government in Medan. They bribed all *kecamatan* and *kelurahan* (village) heads and instructed them to ensure that Rahudman-Eldin won in their districts. Otherwise they would be removed from their position. According to a newspaper report and also mentioned in an interview with Sofyan Tan, many voters in the *kecamatan*s where Tan-Armayanti gained most votes in the first round were consequently de-listed and could not vote in the second round (Hutabarat 2010; interview with Sofyan Tan, in Indonesian, August 23, 2010). In addition, according to Budiman P. Nadapdap, the head of Tan's campaign team, all *kecamatan* and *kelurahan* heads in the city received a mobile phone text message from H. M. Fitryus, the regional secretary of Medan, which read, '*Demi menjaga nama besar Partai Demokrat-Golkar, demi menjaga nama baik Presiden SBY dan Gubernur Syamsul Arifin, maka kami meminta agar memenangkan Rahudman-Eldin pada Pilkada 19 Juni 2010*' (For the sake of the reputation of Democratic Party-Golkar, President SBY [Susilo Bambang Yudhoyono] and Governor Syamsul Arifin, we request you to ensure the victory of Rahudman-Eldin in the mayoral election on June 19, 2010) ('KPU Medan dan Panwas Dituding Berpihak ke Pasangan Rahudman-Eldin' 2010, my translation from Indonesian original). Tan disclosed that, in fact, two witnesses from PDI-P who were supposed to inspect the polling process were bribed by his opponents. Tan had paid each of them Rp100,000 (about US$11) to inspect the polling process but later they were bribed Rp300,000 (about US$33) respectively by the rival's camp to 'disappear' from the polling station and thus did not prevent fraud from taking place (interview with Sofyan Tan, in Indonesian, August 23, 2010).

Eventually, Tan-Armayanti lost the second round. They received only 251,435 votes (34.12%), while Rahudman-Eldin gained 485,446 votes (65.88%). The former managed to win in only four *kecamatan*s, i.e., Medan Tuntungan, Medan Baru, Medan Sunggal, and Medan Petisah.[40]

PDI-P and Tan's campaign team later filed a lawsuit at the Constitutional Court on June 24, 2010, citing rampant violations and irregularities during the campaign period and on polling day. But three of their key witnesses, i.e., the heads of Medan Tuntungan and Medan Baru as well as an officer at the mayor's office, did not turn up to testify (Hutabarat 2010). According to Tan, the witnesses were 'kidnapped' (meaning they were bribed) by people who did not want them to testify in court (interview with Sofyan Tan, in Indonesian, August 23, 2010). Eventually, the court turned down the lawsuit on July 20, 2010 ('MK Tolak Gugatan Sofyan Tan' 2010). It is worth noting that Rahudman later removed a few *kecamatan* and *kelurahan* heads who had failed to ensure his victory in their districts. They were the heads of Medan Baru, Medan Tuntungan, Medan Polonia, Medan Barat, and Aur (a *kelurahan* under Medan Maimun) ('Dinilai Tidak Dukung Saat Pilkada' 2010). Tan-Armayanti won a majority of votes in these *kecamatan*s and *kelurahan*s during the first or second round of the election.

It can be concluded that Tan lost in the second round because of multiple factors associated with the position of the Chinese in Indonesia: low turnout among ethnic Chinese voters (and also the fact that not all Chinese supported him), the lack of support from the Muslim indigenous community, and massive electoral fraud. Tan, however, was not disappointed with the

---

40. I obtained this data from the General Elections Commission (KPU) of Medan.

162   *Chinese Indonesians in Post-Suharto Indonesia*

result, since he had managed to enter the second round of the race, defeating eight other pairs. Despite the defeat, he was happy that, to a certain extent, his participation in the race, especially in the first round, had indicated a reduction of anti-Chinese antagonism among *pribumi*:

> I felt that I had won when I was able to enter the second round. I was satisfied as I had partially achieved the objective of reducing hostility toward the Chinese. [After entering into the second round,] I began to campaign in villages and poor areas, where the residents tended to hate and kill the Chinese when riots broke out.[41] [The circumstances had] [c]hanged. I won in strongholds of PKS, *Partai Keadilan Sejahtera*, which was the Islamic party. I think this was amazing because it clearly showed that the Chinese had become more acceptable to indigenous communities. What happens today should become an example and model for Chinese in Indonesia. [They should] [d]o the same as me so that they will be free from being killed or hated. That is my advice. (interview with Sofyan Tan, in Indonesian, August 23, 2010)

Indeed, his idealism has not disappeared, nor his political ambition; in the 2014 parliamentary election, Tan contested for a national parliamentary seat in North Sumatra 1 that covered Medan, Deli Serdang, Serdang Bedagai, and Tebing Tinggi, and was elected. In fact, his vote tallies were the highest among all of the ten elected parliamentarians in the constituency. ('Sofyan Tan dan Hasyim Raih Suara Terbanyak di Medan' 2014).

The process of the 2010 Medan mayoral election clearly shows that, due to the relative lack of democratic behaviour among state and societal actors, Indonesia's formal democratic institutions remain vulnerable to patrimonial manipulation by entrenched and well-financed elites. In the opinion of a university lecturer, the election also shows that identity politics that focuses upon race, ethnicity, and religion are still very influential among Indonesians (interview with Yopie, in Indonesian, July 27, 2010). Although Tan was popular among many *pribumi* from the grassroots, most *pribumi* from other social classes in Medan, especially those who were conservative Muslims, still could not accept a non-indigenous Indonesian as their leader. This factor also prompted Wahidin to pull out of the race. Therefore, the mayoral election implies that, despite the opening up of an open and liberal democratic environment in post-1998 Indonesia, it is still not easy for ethnic Chinese Indonesians to make a significant breakthrough in electoral politics.

The mayoral election also reflects the diversity of ideas within the Chinese community in Medan. Some Chinese with a strong ethnic identity did not support Tan because they considered him as not 'Chinese' enough and not close to the Chinese community. They were also upset with Tan's alleged advocacy of assimilation into the indigenous society. However, at

---

41. This is probably in reference to the riots against the Chinese in May 1998.

the same time, there were also Chinese who perceived Tan as an honest and clean politician despite his relatively 'weak' ethnic identity. Thus, they fully supported and even campaigned for him.

The stories of the abovementioned Chinese Indonesian politicians imply that Chinese Indonesians have made use of the liberal and democratic political environment in the post–New Order era to become actively involved in electoral politics. Politicians with high ideals such as Tan and Oetomo ran in order to bring positive change to Indonesian society. They also tried to do away with the corrupt and opportunistic role the Chinese have played behind the scenes by rejecting financial offers from Chinese businesspeople who expected political favours in return. At the same time, however, the rise in electoral campaign costs means that, without a great amount of money, it is difficult for a Chinese Indonesian politician to run for public office or get elected in elections. Santoso's failure to be nominated by political parties to run in Surabaya's mayoral election clearly shows that, without enough money, a politician does not stand a chance. Besides that, Chinese Indonesian candidates who encounter smear campaigns attacking their ethnicity and religious background (such as Tan during the 2010 Medan's mayoral election) need more funds to counter those attacks. Chinese Indonesians who are keen to enter electoral politics have no choice but to abide by the new rules of Indonesia's political game. Some Chinese electoral candidates receive financial support from Chinese businesspeople who expect political protection and other benefits in return. In this way, Chinese businesspeople establish corrupt and patrimonial relationships with aspiring Chinese politicians in exchange for political favours. Some Chinese businesspeople have become directly involved in politics and contested in elections with the aim of gaining political protection for their business. Some like Lekatompessy have allegedly resorted to money politics during their campaigns. This has in turn reproduced the predatory characteristics of Indonesian politics. In other words, economic clout undermines high political ideals and aids in producing more corruption.

It is interesting to note that, according to the stories discussed above, only Sofyan Tan was attacked by his opponents for being Chinese. Indra Wahidin also encountered suspicion and prejudice from indigenous Indonesians when he intended to contest in the same mayoral election. The experience of Tan and Wahidin is similar to that of Christiandy Sanjaya, the ethnic Chinese deputy gubernatorial candidate who was paired with a Dayak during the election of November 2007. Sanjaya was elected and became the first ethnic Chinese deputy governor of West Kalimantan. As mentioned in Chapter 1, the Malays, the second-largest indigenous group after the Dayaks in West Kalimantan, were upset that they had been denied representation in the highest office of the province. Later, riots broke out in Pontianak, the capital of West Kalimantan, in which Malay rioters attacked and vandalised properties owned by Chinese Indonesians. The riots were an externalisation of the anger and disappointment of Malays at the increasing political ascendancy of the Chinese. However, other Chinese Indonesian politicians running for legislative office, i.e., Hasyim, Simon Lekatompessy, Dédé Oetomo, and Anton Prijatno, did not encounter attacks on their ethnicity. This might be due to the fact that legislators have only legislative power and are not as powerful as mayors/deputy mayors and governors/deputy governors, who hold executive power. Hence, indigenous Indonesians do not feel so threatened if Chinese contest for legislative office. Thus, one can suggest that Chinese Indonesians running for legislative office face less racial hostility compared to those running as regional or local government heads. Hence, it is relatively easier for a Chinese Indonesian to be elected as a legislator than as a regional or local government head.

On the other hand, the affiliation of Chinese Indonesian politicians with different political parties clearly demonstrates the heterogeneous political views of the Chinese as well as the presence of both pro-reform and pro-predatory forces within the local Chinese communities in both cities. Chinese politicians who were reform-minded such as Tan and Hasyim chose to join PDI-P, a major party that was relatively less connected to the predatory forces incubated under the New Order regime. However, at the same time, there were also Chinese politicians who were willing to be affiliated with political parties led by former generals who were implicated in human rights violations (Gerindra and Hanura) in order to pursue their personal agendas and political ambitions. To them, those predatory forces were still very influential and powerful in Indonesia's political arena. Hence, they believed they would have the chance to break through in politics if they cooperated with these predatory forces. By establishing close connections with predatory forces, these Chinese politicians have played a significant role in reproducing and perpetuating negative perceptions of the Chinese as a corrupt and opportunistic minority group, as well as reinforcing the predatory characteristics of Indonesia's new democracy.

6.7 Discussion and Conclusion

This chapter has discussed the new democratic environment in post-Suharto Indonesia and the agency of Chinese Indonesians in engaging in electoral politics in Medan and Surabaya. The advent of a democratic and liberal political environment has led to the political involvement of several Chinese Indonesians in both cities. Such political activism was unimaginable during the New Order era.

In general, there are two kinds of Chinese Indonesian politician. Some are reform-minded and have admirable political ideals. They get involved in politics in order to push for positive changes in Indonesia by fighting against corruption, collusion, and nepotism in state institutions as well as all forms of discrimination. However, others become actively involved in politics with the aim of gaining political protection for their business. Such politicians are not concerned about the interests of the general public. As I mentioned earlier, these different political behaviours and views are due to different habitus of Chinese Indonesian politicians. Those with anti-corruption political ideals are mostly social activists who are not well endowed with money, whereas those who get involved in politics for their personal agendas are mostly well-established businesspeople. In the face of the explosion of the costs of election campaigning since the advent of democratisation, very few Chinese Indonesian politicians with high political ideals get elected because they often reject financial offers from Chinese Indonesian businesspeople who expect political favours from them. As a result, they cannot fund the massive electoral campaigns needed to get elected, nor can they hire reliable witnesses to prevent fraud and irregularities during the polling process. In other words, their political ideals are undermined by their lack of economic clout. Conversely, those getting involved in politics for personally oriented agendas often have a higher chance of being elected because they have the money to launch extensive campaign activities to influence voters. In order to pursue their political ambitions, some even join political parties that are associated with the predatory forces incubated under the New Order regime. Hence, it can be said that the marginalisation of genuinely reform-minded Chinese Indonesian politicians and the rise of Chinese Indonesian politicians with personally oriented agendas in post-Suharto Indonesia is mainly due to differences in their habitus, which is shaped by their family upbringing, education, and social networks, as well as the lack of an effective enforcement of the rule of law.

The explosion of the costs of election campaigning has also created opportunities for some Chinese Indonesian businesspeople to offer financial backing to electoral candidates with the motive of obtaining favours in return. They prefer to establish corrupt and patrimonial relationships with politicians in exchange for patronage and other benefits. Thus, they have been playing an instigating role in money politics. This has consequently perpetuated the corrupt and predatory characteristics of Indonesian politics, as well as reinforced perceptions of the Chinese as corrupt and opportunistic. I argue that the tensions between the anti-corruption political ideals of certain Chinese Indonesian politicians and the more collusive personal agendas of some Chinese Indonesian businesspeople who support them or who are themselves involved in electoral politics have made the democratisation process and the dynamics of electoral politics in Indonesia more complex.

It is also worth noting that, despite the opening up of a democratic political environment in post-Suharto Indonesia, it is still not easy for Chinese Indonesians to make a significant breakthrough in electoral politics, especially when they run for executive positions as regional or local government heads, which have more power than legislative offices. Indigenous Indonesians often feel more threatened if Chinese contest for positions as regional or local government heads. Therefore, Chinese candidates for these positions tend to face more backlash and racial hostility from indigenous Indonesians.

Another interesting issue that electoral politics helps to highlight is how some Chinese in post-Suharto Indonesia have become very protective and assertive in terms of their cultural roots and ethnic identity. As mentioned in Chapter 4, the freedom of cultural expression opened up in the reform era has allowed these strong ethnic feelings to surface and become more visible. Interestingly, Chinese with a strong ethnic identity do not support Chinese politicians whom they consider as not 'Chinese' enough and not close to the Chinese community. There are, however, other ideals that have emerged in the post-Suharto era, such as the combating of corruption and the attempt to foster good governance. These different ideals do sometimes clash in the political choices of the Chinese Indonesians. Thus there are also Chinese who are more concerned with other qualities of a Chinese politician and do not consider his or her ethnic identity as the deciding issue. They are willing to support a Chinese politician with a relatively 'weak' ethnic identity as long as he or she has good qualities such as being honest and clean, therefore furthering the goal of promoting good governance in Indonesia. This implies tensions between two different Chinese ethnic and cultural identities due to the different habitus of Chinese Indonesians mentioned in Chapter 4. One emphasises the revival of Chinese culture and the bolstering of Chinese ethnic identity; another focuses on the integration of Chinese Indonesians into the wider Indonesian society. Those who strongly support Chinese ethnic and cultural identities often perceive those who focus on integration as identifying more with the indigenous population than with the Chinese community. The ambivalent feelings towards Sofyan Tan within the Chinese community in the 2010 mayoral election in Medan clearly reflect such tensions. Tan's reformist political ideals did not appeal to some local Chinese with a strong ethnic identity because they considered him as not 'Chinese' enough and not close to the Chinese community. Only the Chinese who considered the integrity of a politician as the most important criterion were willing to support him, despite his relatively 'weak' ethnic identity.

Hence, it can be said that, under the democratisation process in post-Suharto Indonesia, the situation of the Chinese has become more ambivalent and complex. In order to pursue their political ambitions, some Chinese politicians resort to money politics during their electoral campaigns. Some even cooperate with New Order–linked predatory forces. In order to obtain protection and other benefits for their business, some Chinese businesspeople prefer to back politicians who can promise them political favours. All these factors have reinforced perceptions of the Chinese as corrupt and opportunistic. Although there are also genuinely reform-minded Chinese Indonesian politicians and Chinese businesspeople who support them without expecting any political favours in return, these appear to be rare. In other words, they are 'a minority within a minority'.

I suggest that, in a society that experiences incomplete democratisation or democratisation without the rule of law, the resented economically dominant minorities on the whole tend to resort to money politics and cooperate with predatory forces in order to pursue their political agendas. They also tend to prioritise ethnic identity over the integrity or political ideals of a politician when they decide whom to support during elections. This in return perpetuates the negative stereotypes against them, and consequently reinforces their ambivalent position. Thus, if one wishes to see more Chinese Indonesians participating in the role of reformers in politics, a better enforced rule of law that eliminates money politics is a prerequisite.

7
Conclusion

My stories of the various individuals who live and work in post-Suharto Medan and Surabaya have attempted to illustrate the paradoxes of democratisation for ethnic minorities. As mentioned in Chapter 1, many scholars have reservations about considering democracy as a political system that necessarily guarantees minority rights. Some argue that democratisation tends to bring a backlash against minorities, especially those who play a dominant role in the economy. Some opine that democratisation may marginalise or even eliminate the culture of minorities. However, this study shows that such views appear to be too simplistic. As I discussed in the previous chapters, in the case of Indonesia, the Chinese minority has enjoyed certain positive outcomes of democratisation since the unravelling of the authoritarian regime. Most significantly, anti-Chinese violence has declined considerably and many discriminatory measures against the Chinese have been removed. The Chinese are allowed openly to express and celebrate their ethnic and cultural identities by establishing Chinese organisations and Chinese-language presses. They are also free to become involved in electoral politics and to run for public office. On the other hand, the Chinese minority is still perceived by many indigenous Indonesians as a wealthy, selfish, exclusive, corrupt, and opportunistic alien minority. They remain the perfect target of extortion and corruption by government officials, police, and *preman*. The increasing visibility of the Chinese in the socio-cultural sphere and politics has also resulted in suspicion and anger from indigenous Indonesians. From the perspective of constructivism, proposed by Anderson (1998), this is the outcome of the divide-and-rule policy of the Dutch colonial period and the stigmatisation of Chinese Indonesians as an economically dominant minority group by post-independence regimes, especially during Suharto's rule. Therefore, it is more accurate to say that the situation of the Chinese minority has become increasingly ambivalent and more complex since the advent of democratisation in Indonesia.

Conclusion

169

This study has shown that the situation of minorities in a newly democratised society depends largely on how democratised the society has become, how well established the rule of law, and how the minorities respond to and shape the democratisation process. According to the typologies of Diamond (1999) and Haynes (2001), minority rights are only fully guaranteed under a 'liberal' or 'full' democracy that promotes individual freedom, public participation in the political process, and the rule and accountability of public officials to ordinary people. This means that if a society has not yet developed into a 'liberal' or 'full' democracy, the interests of minorities are not necessarily guaranteed. To date, Indonesia has not become a 'liberal' or 'full' democracy that truly safeguards the interests of minorities. On the one hand, a relatively democratic and liberal political environment has emerged; but on the other hand, the new political parties and institutions have generally been captured by old as well as some new predatory interests. Moreover, corruption and internal mismanagement have continued to plague state institutions.

In the foregoing, I have explored and shown, through a combination of Anthony Giddens's structure-agency theory as well as Pierre Bourdieu's notion of habitus and field, that Chinese Indonesians are by no means merely passive bystanders of the (incomplete) democratisation process in Indonesia and powerless victims of their increasingly ambivalent and complex position. Although the Chinese are constrained by various conditions, they have also played an active and dynamic role in responding to and shaping the new political, business, and socio-cultural environment in post-Suharto Indonesia. In the aspects of business and politics, due to the hassle of fighting back and also the fact that they have enough economic capital to pay bribes and extortion money, most Chinese prefer to give in to the illegal requests of government officials, police, and *preman* in order to prevent any further problems. Some Chinese businesspeople have willingly resorted to illegal practices to further their business interests. Some make use of their social capital to establish corrupt and patrimonial relationships with power-holders, heads of security forces, aspiring politicians, and youth/crime organisations who can promise them protection and other benefits for their business. Some become involved in politics and run for public office with the aim of gaining political protection for their business instead of fighting for the interests of the general public. In the socio-cultural aspect, due to their strong ethnic identity and their well-established social networks in China, many Chinese Indonesian organisation leaders strongly support not only Chinese cultural identity, but also continuing ties to China. All these factors have kept alive the general perception of Chinese Indonesians as corrupt, collusive, opportunistic, insular, and oriented toward China. At the same time, there are also Chinese Indonesians such as Sofyan Tan who focus on the integration of Chinese Indonesians into the wider Indonesian society. They work relentlessly to rectify the negative perceptions of Chinese among indigenous Indonesians. They play an active role in initiating and engaging in cross-ethnic endeavours that promote inter-ethnic solidarity and understanding. However, these Chinese are fewer in number than those who continue to reinforce such negative perceptions. Moreover, they are often perceived as culturally not 'Chinese' enough by some Chinese with a strong ethnic identity, and therefore become a target of dislike among those Chinese. In this way, Chinese Indonesians as a whole have played a part in shaping the incomplete democratisation process as well as their increasingly ambivalent and more complex position in post-Suharto Indonesia.

It is hoped that the case studies in this book constitute a cutting-edge representation of Chinese Indonesian communities in the urban centres of post-Suharto Indonesia, primarily Medan and Surabaya, since both cities are large and have a relatively high percentage of ethnic Chinese. The dynamics of Chinese Indonesian communities in post-Suharto urban Indonesia is therefore apparent in this study.

In broader theoretical terms, this study argues that, in order to have a better understanding of the relationship between democratisation and minority rights, one cannot ignore the agency of the minorities themselves. The situation of minorities in a newly democratised society depends not only on the historical development of ethnic relations and the various policies of governments, but also how the minorities themselves respond to the democratisation process. With regard to the position of resented, economically dominant minorities, such as the Chinese in Indonesia, this study suggests it is only possible to see a significant improvement in their position if the majority of the minority plays an active role in fighting against corrupt practices in state institutions, initiating and engaging in cross-ethnic initiatives that seek to alter the negative perceptions against them, and supporting genuinely reform-minded politicians regardless of their ethnic identity. Otherwise, their position will only become increasingly ambivalent and more complex under democratisation.

To encourage more people from the resented, economically dominant minorities to refuse to be extorted, to refrain from engaging in illegal and semi-legal business practices, to actively engage in cross-ethnic endeavours, as well as to participate as reformers in politics, effective enforcement of the rule of law is certainly a prerequisite. In addition, the experience of YPSIM, the private school founded by Sofyan Tan that promotes integration among students from various ethnic-religious background (mentioned in Chapter 4), indicates that the education system could also promote more open- and reform-minded people if schools introduce programmes and activities that promote inter-ethnic understanding and solidarity. This would certainly bring a significant positive impact on democratisation in society.

Appendix I
List of Informants

Public Figures

Jakarta

Mely G. Tan (陳玉蘭) (sociologist), June 8, 2010.
Christianto Wibisono (黃建國) (noted economist), June 18, 2010.

Medan

Dirk A. Buiskool (historian), July 14, 2010.
Brilian Moktar (莫粧量) (member of North Sumatra provincial legislature, 2009–present), July 16, 2010.
Johan Tjongiran (章生榮) (ethnic Chinese activist; electoral candidate in 2004 and 2009 elections), August 3, 2010.
Hasyim, a.k.a. Oei Kien Lim (黃建霖) (Medan city councillor, 2009–present), August 11, 2010.
Nelly Armayanti (deputy mayoral candidate in 2010 Medan's mayoral election; woman activist), August 12, 2010.
Sofyan Tan (陳金揚) (mayoral candidate in 2010 Medan's mayoral election; electoral candidate in 2004 election; Medan parliamentarian, 2014–present; social activist; founder and chairperson, Sultan Iskandar Muda Educational Foundation [YPSIM]), August 23, 2010; October 13, 2010; May 7, 2013 (online).
Eddy Djuandi (莊欽華) (ethnic Chinese businessperson engaged in food and beverage industry; chairperson, Chinese Indonesian Social Association's [PSMTI] North Sumatra branch), August 25, 2010.
Indra Wahidin (黃印華) (ethnic Chinese businessperson engaged in insurance industry; chairperson, Chinese Indonesian Association's [INTI] North Sumatra branch; electoral candidate in 2004 election), October 19, 2010.
Anuar Shah (chairperson, Pancasila Youth's [PP] North Sumatra branch), October 30, 2010.
Ardjan Leo (廖章然) (director, Medan Angsapura Social Foundation [Yasora Medan]; vice president, North Sumatra Chinese Community Social and Education Association [MITSU-PSP]), November 12, 2010.
Yap Juk Lim (葉鬱林) (ethnic Chinese businessperson engaged in snack production industry; chairperson, Medan Deli Regional Forum of Small and Medium Enterprises [FORDA UKM Medan Deli]), November 16, 2010.

Surabaya

Dédé Oetomo (溫忠孝) (social activist; electoral candidate in 1999 and 2004 elections), December 24, 2010; August 10, 2012 (online); September 24, 2013 (online); August 31, 2016 (online); September 1, 2016 (online); September 3, 2016 (online).

Anton Prijatno (王炳金) (ethnic Chinese businessperson engaged in distribution of asphalt; chairperson, University of Surabaya Foundation; former member of the East Java provincial legislature, 1977–1987; former member of the national legislature, 1987–1997; electoral candidate in 2004 election), February 24, 2011.

William Rahardja (江國榮) (chairperson, Chinese Indonesian Association's [INTI] Surabaya branch; travel agent; supplier of consumer goods), March 4, 2011.

Henky Kurniadi (遊經善) (ethnic Chinese businessperson engaged in real estate industry; electoral candidate in 2009 election; Surabaya parliamentarian, 2014–present), March 9, 2011.

Liem Ou Yen (林武源) (executive chairperson, Surabaya Chinese Association [PMTS]; vice president, Indonesian Chinese Entrepreneur Association's [PERPIT] East Java branch; ethnic Chinese businessperson engaged in distribution of water pipes), March 23, 2011.

Alim Markus (林文光) (president director/chief executive officer, Maspion Group; chairperson, Surabaya Chinese Association [PMTS]; vice president 1-cum-executive president, Indonesian Chinese Entrepreneur Association [PERPIT]), March 23, 2011.

Hendi Prayogo (吳景賢) (vice chairperson, Chinese Indonesian Social Association's [PSMTI] East Java branch; founder and chairperson, Committee of Social Concern of Surabaya [Kalimas]; social activist; founder of *Rela Warta* [誠報]), March 28, 2011.

Harry Tanudjaja (陳國樑) (chairperson, Indonesian Democratic Party of Devotion's [PKDI] Surabaya branch; electoral candidate in 1999 and 2009 elections; lawyer), March 31, 2011; May 26, 2011.

Lim Ping Tjien (林秉正) (chairperson, Indonesian Chinese Entrepreneur Community's [PERMIT] East Java branch; ethnic Chinese businessperson engaged in glass production and processing industry), April 13, 2011.

Simon Lekatompessy (surabaya city councillor, 2009–2014), May 5, 2011.

Samas H. Widjaja (黃三槐) (vice chairperson, Chinese Indonesian Social Association's [PSMTI] East Java branch; former chief editor, *Rela Warta*; former adviser, *Harian Naga Surya* [龍陽日報]; former chairperson, New Indonesia Alliance Party's [PPIB] East Java branch, 2002–2006), May 5, 2011; May 28, 2011.

Eddy Gunawan Santoso (吳繼平) (ethnic Chinese businessperson engaged in cargo industry; activist for inter-religious harmony), May 6, 2011.

Other Informants (with Pseudonyms)

Jakarta

Timothy (university lecturer), January 31, 2011.

Adam (person in charge, *Harian Nusantara*'s [千島日報] Jakarta branch office), May 25, 2011.

Appendix I 173

Medan

Daniel (deceased) (former media activist), July 13, 2010; September 17, 2010.

Farid (ethnic Chinese businessperson engaged in garment production industry), July 15, 2010.

Ivan (ethnic Chinese businessperson engaged in real estate), July 16, 2010.

Halim (NGO activist), July 26, 2010.

Yopie (university lecturer), July 27, 2010.

Syarfi (person in charge, *Medan Bisnis*), July 29, 2010.

Usman (NGO activist), July 30, 2010.

Robertus (journalist), August 2, 2010.

Susanto (ethnic Chinese businessperson engaged in distribution of toys), August 4, 2010.

Christopher (ethnic Chinese businessperson engaged in frozen seafood industry), August 18, 2010.

Hasan (ethnic Chinese businessperson engaged in printing industry; writer), August 19, 2010.

Rudy (ethnic Chinese businessperson engaged in metal-grinding industry), August 25, 2010.

Erik (ethnic Chinese businessperson engaged in iron and plastics industry), August 25, 2010.

Surya (media activist), September 17, 2010.

Andi (journalist), September 20, 2010.

Melani (person in charge, *Medan Zao Bao* [棉蘭早報／*Subei Ribao* (蘇北日報)]), October 22, 2010.

Janice (staff, *Medan Zao Bao／Subei Ribao*; former staff, *Huashang Bao* [華商報]), November 12, 2010.

The Lie Hok (veteran writer), October 31, 2010.

Amin (committee member, Medan Angsapura Social Foundation [Yasora Medan]), November 2, 2010.

Joe (person in charge, *Xun Bao* [訊報]), November 5, 2010.

Setiawan (person in charge, *Harian Promosi Indonesia* [印廣日報]), November 8, 2010.

Eddie (ethnic Chinese businessperson engaged in distribution of mechanical power-transmission products), November 10, 2010.

Joko (NGO activist), November 11, 2010.

Patrick (person in charge, *Hao Bao* [好報]), November 15, 2010.

Surabaya

Harianto (ethnic Chinese businessperson engaged in beverage production industry), November 23, 2010.

Yahya (university professor), December 31, 2010.

Junus (university professor), January 11, 2011.

Susana (university lecturer; committee member, women's division of Chinese Indonesian Association's [INTI] East Java branch; committee member, Hwie Tiauw Ka Chinese Clan Association in Surabaya [PHTKS]), January 14, 2011; February 13, 2012.

Atan (ethnic Chinese businessperson engaged in real estate industry; developer-cum-contractor), February 28, 2011.

Bambang (ethnic Chinese ceramic tile factory owner), March 3, 2011.
Vincent (advisor, *Sishui Chenbao* [泗水晨報]), April 7, 2011.
Yati (former staff of a real estate company in Surabaya's Chinatown), April 8, 2011.
Suhaimi (university lecturer), April 27, 2011.
Wahyu (economic analyst; university lecturer), May 18, 2011.
Musa (journalist, *Harian Nusantara*), May 19, 2011.

Appendix II

Major Ethnic Chinese Organisations in Post-Suharto Medan and Surabaya

Table IIa: Major Ethnic Chinese Organisations in Post-Suharto Medan

Organisation	Year of Establishment	Remarks
Medan Angsapura Social Foundation (Yasora Medan, or Yayasan Sosial Angsapura Medan)	1895	Formerly known as Hui Chew Indonesia in the pre–New Order period. Converted during the New Order era to a charitable foundation that provided burial services. Yasora Medan again began to include socio-cultural activities that promoted Chinese culture after the demise of the New Order regime.
Local branches of the Indonesian Chinese Social Association (PSMTI, or Paguyuban Sosial Marga Tionghoa Indonesia)	1999	
Local branches of the Chinese Indonesian Association (INTI, or Perhimpunan Indonesia Tionghoa)	1999	
North Sumatra Chinese Community Social and Education Association (MITSU-PSP, or Perhimpunan Masyarakat Indonesia Tionghoa Sumatera Utara – Peduli Sosial dan Pendidikan)	2007	A coalition of Chinese organisations and Chinese community leaders in Medan.

Table IIb: Major Ethnic Chinese Organisations in Post-Suharto Surabaya

Organisation	Year of Establishment	Remarks
Hwie Tiauw Ka Chinese Clan Association in Surabaya (PHTKS, or Perkumpulan Hwie Tiauw Ka Surabaya)	1820	Converted during the New Order era to a charitable foundation that provided burial services. PHTKS began again to include socio-cultural activities that promoted Chinese culture after the demise of the New Order regime.
Surabaya Chinese Association (PMTS, or Paguyuban Masyarakat Tionghoa Surabaya)	1985	A coalition of several Chinese organisations in Surabaya. Carried out its activities with a low profile during the New Order period but became more active after the demise of the Suharto regime.
Committee of Social Concern of Surabaya (Kalimas, or Komite Aliansi Kepedulian Masyarakat Surabaya)	1998	A coalition of Chinese and non-Chinese Indonesian social activists and university students. Ceased operation in 2000.
Chinese Indonesian Social Association (PSMTI, or Paguyuban Sosial Marga Tionghoa Indonesia)'s local branches	2003	
Chinese Indonesian Association (INTI, or Perhimpunan Indonesia Tionghoa)'s local branches	2005	
Indonesian Chinese Entrepreneur Association (PERPIT, or Perhimpunan Pungusaha Tionghoa Indonesia)'s local branches	2010	
Indonesian Chinese Entrepreneur Community (PERMIT, or Perhimpunan Masyarakat and Pengusaha Indonesia Tionghoa)	2010	

Appendix III
Chinese-Language Newspapers in Post-Suharto Medan and Surabaya

Table IIIa: Chinese-Language Newspapers in Post-Suharto Medan

Newspaper	Year of Establishment	Remarks
Harian Promosi Indonesia (印廣日報)	1999	Ceased publication at the end of 2014.
Subei Ribao (蘇北日報)	2002	Previously known as *Huashang Bao* (華商報) and later *Medan Zao Bao* (棉蘭早報). It is a subsidiary paper of *Guoji Ribao* (國際日報), a well-established Chinese-language newspaper in Indonesia.
Xun Bao (訊報)	2007	A sister paper of *Kwong Wah Yit Poh* (光華日報), a Chinese-language newspaper in Malaysia.
Hao Bao (好報)	2008	A sister paper of *Harian Analisa*, a well-established Indonesian-language newspaper in Medan. First published as a weekly paper in 2008 and later converted to a daily paper in 2010.
Zheng Bao Daily (正報)	2015	A sister paper of *Harian Analisa*, a well-established Indonesian-language newspaper in Medan.

Table IIIb: Chinese-Language Newspapers in Post-Suharto Surabaya

Newspaper	Year of Establishment	Remarks
Harian Naga Surya (龍陽日報)	2000	Ceased publication in 2001.
Harian Nusantara (千島日報)	2000	
Rela Warta (誠報)	2001	Ceased publication in 2009.
Sishui Chenbao (泗水晨報)	2008	A subsidiary paper of *Guoji Ribao* (國際日報), a well-established Chinese-language newspaper in Indonesia.

Appendix IV
Occupational Backgrounds of the Leaders of Local Major Chinese Organisations in Medan and Surabaya, 2010–2011

Table IVa: Occupational Backgrounds of the Leaders of Local Major Chinese Organisations in Medan, 2010–2011*

Organisation	Chairperson	Occupation of Chairperson
Indonesian Chinese Social Association's (PSMTI) North Sumatra branch	Eddy Djuandi (莊欽華)	Businessperson engaged in food and beverage industry
Indonesian Chinese Social Association's (PSMTI) Medan branch	Joko Dharmanadi (楊果奮)	Electrical products supplier
Chinese Indonesian Association's (INTI) North Sumatra branch	Indra Wahidin (黃印華)	Insurance agent; paint distributor
Chinese Indonesian Association's (INTI) Medan branch	Hartimin	Dentist
Medan Angsapura Social Foundation (Yasora Medan)	Hakim Tanjung (曾來金)	Businessperson engaged in wood-making industry
North Sumatra Chinese Community Social and Education Association (MITSU-PSP)	Fajar Suhendra (蘇用發)	Businessperson engaged in steel industry

Sources: Interview with Hasyim, in Indonesian, August 11, 2010; interview with Christopher, in Indonesian, August 28, 2010; interview with Eddy Djuandi, in Mandarin, August 25, 2010; interview with Indra Wahidin, in Mandarin, October 19, 2010; interview with Ardjan Leo, in Mandarin, November 12, 2010; 'Hakim Tanjung Kembali Pimpin Yasora Medan' (2012); 'Surat Palsu Muluskan Illegal Logging di Tapsel' (2009).

---

* The names of informants in this appendix are pseudonyms except for the following public figures: Hasyim, Eddy Djuandi, Indra Wahidin, Ardjan Leo, William Rahardja, Liem Ou Yen, Alim Markus, Hendi Prayogo, and Lim Ping Tjien.

Appendix IV

Table IVb: Occupational Backgrounds of Leaders of Local Major Chinese Organisation in Surabaya, 2010–2011

Organisation	Chairperson	Occupation of Chairperson
Indonesian Chinese Social Association (PSMTI)'s East Java branch	Jos Soetomo (江慶德)	Businessperson engaged in logging industry
Indonesian Chinese Social Association's (PSMTI) Surabaya branch	Tirto Wardono	Pharmacy owner
Chinese Indonesian Association's (INTI) East Java branch	Aliptojo Wongsodihardjo (黃奮立)	Traditional Chinese medicine shop owner
Chinese Indonesian Association's (INTI) Surabaya branch	William Rahardja (江國榮)	Travel agent; supplier of consumer goods; social activist
Surabaya Chinese Association (PMTS)	Alim Markus (林文光)	Maspion Group owner
Hwie Tiauw Ka Chinese Clan Association in Surabaya (PHTKS)	Benny Saiful (黃奮鵬)	Owner of a pharmaceutical factory, a restaurant, and a travel agency
Indonesian Chinese Entrepreneur Association's (PERPIT) East Java branch	Chen Yituan (陳宜團)	Businessperson engaged in plastics production and real estate
Indonesian Chinese Entrepreneur Community's (PERMIT) East Java branch	Lim Ping Tjien (林秉正)	Businessperson engaged in glass production and processing industry

Sources: Interview with William Rahardja, in Indonesian, March 4, 2011; interview with Liem Ou Yen, in Mandarin, March 23, 2011; interview with Alim Markus, in Mandarin, March 23, 2011; interview with Hendi Prayogo, in Indonesian, March 28, 2011; interview with Lim Ping Tjien, in Mandarin, April 13, 2011; interview with Susana, in Mandarin, February 23, 2012.

Appendix V
Numbers of Protégés of Sultan Iskandar Muda Educational Foundation, 1990/1991–2011/2012

Table V: Numbers of Protégés of Sultan Iskandar Muda Educational Foundation, 1990/1991–2011/2012

No.	Academic Year	Number of Protégés	Category	
			Non-Chinese	Chinese
1	1990/1991	17	9	8
2	1991/1992	30	14	16
3	1992/1993	60	34	26
4	1993/1994	90	57	33
5	1994/1995	86	54	32
6	1995/1996	119	71	48
7	1996/1997	131	90	41
8	1997/1998	95	49	46
9	1998/1999	98	52	36
10	1999/2000	112	67	45
11	2000/2001	98	64	34
12	2001/2002	77	42	35
13	2002/2003	78	54	24
14	2003/2004	76	62	14
15	2004/2005	89	Not available	Not available
16	2005/2006	91	Not available	Not available
17	2006/2007	86	Not available	Not available
18	2007/2008	113	Not available	Not available
19	2008/2009	107	Not available	Not available
20	2009/2010	115	Not available	Not available
21	2010/2011	183	Not available	Not available
22	2011/2012	204	Not available	Not available

Sources: Tan (2004, 33); 'Program Anak Asuh' (2014).

Appendix VI
Original Text of Letter in *Koran Tempo* (May 15, 2012)

Bubarkan Perkumpulan Tionghoa

Pada 20 April lalu, delegasi rombongan Kantor Urusan Overseas Chinese dari Beijing berkunjung ke Jakarta, dan melakukan pertemuan dengan Perkumpulan Dagang Tionghoa Indonesia. Dalam sambutannya, Kepala Bidang Overseas Chinese Li In Zhe antara lain mengucapkan: orang Tionghoa yang tersebar di semua pelosok telah menciptakan untuk Tiongkok "hubungan overseas" yang baik. Inilah kelebihan yang tidak dimiliki bangsa mana pun. Saat ini ekonomi Tiongkok telah menjadi terbesar kedua di dunia. Ini tidak terlepas dari sumbangsih besar yang dilakukan oleh orang Tionghoa/Chinese overseas.

Dia juga mengatakan maksud kunjungan kali ini adalah membantu generasi muda Tionghoa/Chinese overseas dalam hal mempelajari bahasa Tionghoa. Belajar bahasa Tionghoa dan memahami budaya Tionghoa akan menjadi penting dalam meningkatkan kemasifan bangsa Tionghoa. Maka dia berharap kaum muda Tionghoa di luar negeri belajar bahasa Tionghoa dengan baik, memperkuat kontak hubungan dengan kaum muda di dalam negeri (Tiongkok), dan memperkuat pengakuan rasa kebangsaan bersama.

Kunjungan-kunjungan seperti itu juga didapati di kota-kota di luar Jakarta. Untuk kepentingan nasional kita, bangsa Indonesia, terutama dalam pembangunan bangsa dan character building, juga untuk mencegah penggunaan "perkumpulan-perkumpulan Tionghoa" sebagai alat kolone kelima. Sudah sepantasnya kita membubarkan dan melarang perkumpulan yang bersifat eksklusif "Tionghoa". Peranan ormas-ormas menjadi sangat penting untuk menyikapi hal ini, karena pemerintah pasti akan melakukan pembiaran, tanpa adanya tuntutan yang kuat dari masyarakat! Jangan biarkan reformasi kita ditunggangi kepentingan asing,

Sastrawinata
Jalan Benda, Cilandak Timur
Pasar Minggu, Jakarta Selatan

Appendix VII

List of Chinese Indonesian Candidates Running for Legislative Elections in Medan and Surabaya, 1999–2014*

Table VIIa: List of Chinese Indonesian Candidates Running for Legislative Elections in Medan, 1999–2014†

Year	Name	Gender	Political Party	Occupational Background	Level of Legislative Election Contested/ Achievement
1999	Haryanto (吳其生)	Male	PKPI	Businessperson engaged in coconut industry	Provincial/Not elected
2004	Uton Utomo	Male	PNBK	Lawyer	National/Not elected
	Frans Tshai (蔡華喜)	Male	PD	Physician	National/Not elected
	Indra Wahidin (黃印華)	Male	–	Insurance agent; businessperson engaged in palm oil industry; paint distributor	Regional Representative Council/Not elected
	Sofyan Tan a.k.a. Tan Kim Yang (陳金揚)	Male	–	Social activist; chairperson of Sultan Iskandar Muda Educational Foundation (YPSIM)	Regional Representative Council/Not elected
	Haryanto (吳其生)	Male	PKPI	Businessperson engaged in coconut industry	Provincial/Not elected

---

* The names of informants in this appendix are pseudonyms except for the following public figures: Sofyan Tan, Dédé Oemoto, Anton Prijatno, William Rahardja, Henky Kurniadi, Hendi Prayogo, Harry Tanudjaja, Simon Lekatompessy and Samas H. Widjaja.

† For legislative elections at national, provincial, and local levels, only constituencies that cover Medan are included, i.e., North Sumatra 1 (Medan, Deli Serdang, Serdang Bedagai, and Tebing Tinggi) for national legislative elections, Medan City for provincial legislative elections, and all constituencies in Medan for city council elections.

Appendix VII   183

Year	Name	Gender	Political Party	Occupational Background	Level of Legislative Election Contested/ Achievement
	Sonny Firdaus (黃新榮)	Male	PPIB	Businessperson engaged in conducting management and training workshops	Provincial/Not elected
	Sudarto	Male	Golkar	Not available	Provincial/Not elected
	Karya Elly	Male	Pancasila Patriot Party	Social activist	Provincial/Not elected
	Amin (陳建銘)	Male	PPIB	Not available	City/Not elected
	Johan Tjongiran (章生榮)	Male	PPIB	Social activist; businessperson engaged in distribution of automotive synthetic leather	City/Not elected
	Sumandi Widjaja (黃貴財)	Male	PPIB	Lawyer	City/Not elected
	Lily Tan (陳俐簆)	Female	PPIB	Tax accountant	City/Not elected
	Ek Kiong (黃弈强)	Male	PPIB	Not available	City/Not elected
	Suherman Gatot (吳振雄)	Male	PPIB	Tax accountant	City/Not elected
	Sukiran (蘇志忠)	Male	PPIB	Lawyer	City/Not elected
	Kwik Sam Ho (郭三和) (Dharwan Widjaja)	Male	Golkar	Real estate businessperson	City/Not elected
	Tjia Susanto Wijaya	Male	PAN	Businessperson	City/Not elected
2009	Rusmin Lawin (劉德華)	Male	PAN	Real estate businessperson	National/Not elected
	Hartono (Ang Ching Peng)	Male	Gerindra	Not Available	National/Not elected

Year	Name	Gender	Political Party	Occupational Background	Level of Legislative Election Contested/ Achievement
	Lim Aho	Male	PRN	Not available	National/Not elected
	Brilian Moktar (莫粧量)	Male	PDI-P	Businessperson engaged in vehicle trading and servicing	Provincial/Elected
	Sonny Firdaus (黃新榮)	Male	PPIB	Businessperson engaged in conducting management and training workshops	Provincial/Elected
	Kwik Sam Ho (郭三和) (Dharwan Widjaja)	Male	Golkar	Real estate businessperson	Provincial/Not elected
	Haryanto (吳其生)	Male	PKPI	Businessperson engaged in coconut industry	Provincial/Not elected
	Kie Hock Kweng	Male	PPRN	Not available	Provincial/Not elected
	Lily Tan (陳俐簗)	Female	PPIB	Tax accountant	City/Elected
	Janlie (饒潔莉)	Female	PPIB	Tax accountant	City/Elected
	Hasyim a.k.a. Oei Kien Lim (黃建霖)	Male	PDI-P	Businessperson engaged in distribution of office stationery	City/Elected
	A Hie (王天喜)	Male	PD	Hotel owner	City/Elected
	Johan Tjongiran (章生榮)	Male	PDI-P	Social activist; businessperson engaged in distribution of automotive synthetic leather	City/Not elected
	Rudi Arif	Male	Golkar	Physician	City/Not elected
	Rudy Wu	Male	PKPI	Not available	City/Not elected
	Wong Chun Sen (Tarigan)	Male	PKPI	Not available	City/Not elected

Appendix VII

Year	Name	Gender	Political Party	Occupational Background	Level of Legislative Election Contested/Achievement
2014	Sofyan Tan a.k.a. Tan Kim Yang (陳金揚)	Male	PDI-P	Social activist; chairperson of Sultan Iskandar Muda Educational Foundation (YPSIM)	National/Elected
	Yenni Meilina Lie	Female	PDI-P	Legal consultant	National/Not elected
	Rusmin Lawin (劉德華)	Male	PAN	Real estate businessperson	National/Not elected
	Brilian Moktar (莫粔量)	Male	PDI-P	Incumbent provincial legislator	Provincial/Elected
	Sonny Firdaus (黃新榮)	Male	Gerindra	Incumbent provincial legislator	Provincial/Elected
	Haryanto (吳其生)	Male	PKPI	Businessperson	Provincial/Not elected
	Lily Tan (陳俐策)	Female	Gerindra	Incumbent city councillor	City/Not elected
	Janlie (饒潔莉)	Female	Gerindra	Incumbent city councillor	City/Not elected
	Hasyim a.k.a. Oei Kien Lim (黃建霖)	Male	PDI-P	Incumbent city councillor	City/Elected
	Wong Chun Sen (Tarigan)	Male	PDI-P	Not available	City/Elected

Data obtained from: '10 Cara memilih Anggota DPRD Sumut' (2004); Go (2004); 'Bakom PKB Medan Tempatkan Empat Kadernya Sebagai Calon Legislatif' (2004); 'Karya Elly, SH' (2004); 'Ketua Pimpinan Cabang Partai PIB Kota Medan Sumandi Wijaya' (2004); 'Mohon Doa Restu Partai Perhimpunan Indonesia Baru' (2004); 'Partai Pilihan Kami!' (2004); 'Warga Tionghoa Harus Manfaatkan Peluang yang Dibuka Gubsu' (2004); Indonesian Electoral Commission (2008b); 'PDI Perjuangan Serahkan 2,8 Ton Kayu' (2008); 'Caleg DPRD Sumut dari PPRN Kie Hock Kwen[g]' (2009); 'Daerah Pemilihan Sumut 1 DPRD Sumut' (2009); 'Golput Bukan Solusi' (2009); 'Gunakan Akal Sehat, Pilih Partai PIB' (2009); 'Kepedulian terhadap Masyarakat Harus Ditumbuhkan' (2009); 'Partai Keadilan dan Persatuan Indonesia' (2009); 'Peluang Kursi Caleg DPRD Dapil 1 Medan' (2009); 'Peluang Kursi Caleg DPRD Dapil 3 Medan' (2009); 'Peluang Kursi Caleg DPRD Dapil 4 Medan' (2009); 'Pilihlah kami!!!' (2009); 'Rusmin Lawin dan Kepedulian terhadap Musik Tradisional' (2009); 'Wong Cung Sen Tak Bayar Sate' (2009); 'Xuanmin Bushi Huayi Houxuanren' (2009); 'Ketua DPP Golkar' (2009); Harahap (2010); 'Sofyan Tan-Nelly Dapat Dukungan 19 Parpol' (2010); interview with Ivan, in Hokkien, July 16, 2010; interview with Syarfi, in Indonesian, July 29, 2010; interview with Christopher, in Indonesian, August 18, 2010; interview with Sofyan Tan, in Indonesian, October 13, 2010; '030406-Yenni Meilina Lie' (2014); Damanik (2014); '48 Anggota DPRD Medan Maju Lagi di Pileg 2014' (2013); Cui (2014).

186   Appendix VII

Table VIIb: List of Chinese Indonesian Candidates Running for Legislative Elections in Surabaya, 1999–2014‡

Year	Name	Gender	Political Party	Occupational Background	Level of Legislative Election Contested/ Achievement
1999	Dédé Oetomo, a.k.a. Oen Tiong Hauw (溫忠孝)	Male	PRD	Social activist; university lecturer	National/Not elected
	Harry Tanudjaja (陳國樑)	Male	PBI	Lawyer	National/Not elected
	Fajar Budianto	Male	PBI	Grocery shop owner	Provincial/Elected
	Rosita Tumbelaka	Female	PDI-P	Not available	City/Elected
	Bambang Handoko	Male	PBI	Physician	City/Not elected
2004	Murdaya Widyawimatra Poo, a.k.a. Poo Tjie Goan (傅志寬)	Male	PDI-P	Owner of Central Cipta Murdaya (CCM) Group	National/Elected
	Sundoro Sasongko	Male	PKS	Businessperson engaged in coal mining	National/Not elected
	Dédé Oetomo, a.k.a. Oen Tiong Hauw (溫忠孝)	Male	–	Social activist; university lecturer	Regional Representative Council/Not elected
	Anton Prijatno (王炳金)	Male	–	Businessperson engaged in distribution of asphalt; chairperson of the University of Surabaya Foundation; former member of the East Java provincial legislature (1977–1987); former parliamentarian, (1987–1997)	Regional Representative Council/Not elected

‡ For legislative elections at national, provincial, and local levels, only constituencies that cover Surabaya are included, i.e., East Java 1 (Surabaya and Sidoarjo) for national legislative elections, Surabaya City for provincial legislative elections, and all constituencies in Surabaya for city council elections.

Appendix VII

Year	Name	Gender	Political Party	Occupational Background	Level of Legislative Election Contested/ Achievement
	Soetanto Adi (陳紀雄)	Male	PPIB	Private employee	Provincial/Not elected
	Agoes Suryadjaja G. (倪政煌)	Male	PPIB	University lecturer; businessperson engaged in distribution of corn seeds	City/Not elected
	Arifli Harbianto Hanurakin (韓明理)	Male	PDS	Bakery shop owner	City/Elected
2009	Harry Tanudjaja (陳國樑)	Male	PKDI	Lawyer	National/Not elected
	Arifli Harbianto Hanurakin (韓明理)	Male	PDS	Bakery shop owner	National/Not elected
	Johan Tedja Surya (鄭文英)	Male	Golkar	Real estate businessperson	National/Not elected
	Indah Kurnia	Female	PDI-P	Former branch manager of Bank Central Asia (BCA); branch manager of Maspion Bank; amateur singer	National/Elected
	Henky Kurniadi (遊經善)	Male	PDI-P	Businessperson engaged in real estate and mining industry	National/Not elected
	M. Soka (胡賜嘉)	Male	PRN	Lawyer	National/Not elected
	Charles Honoris	Male	PAN	Businessperson engaged in automotive industry in Jakarta and China	National/Not elected
	Nyoto Wijaya (楊富盛)	Male	PKPI	Not available	National/Not elected
	Abdul Chalim MZ. H. (李光霖)	Male	–	Tobacco supplier	Regional Representative Council/Not elected

Year	Name	Gender	Political Party	Occupational Background	Level of Legislative Election Contested/Achievement
	Adhinata Wira Diputro	Male	PKDI	Businessperson engaged in distribution of cosmetic products	Provincial/Not elected
	Bagus Raharja (張豪仁)	Male	PKDI	Travel agent	Provincial/Not elected
	Agoes Suryadjaja G. (倪政煌)	Male	People's Conscience Party (Partai Hanura)	University lecturer; businessperson engaged in distribution of corn seeds	Provincial/Not elected
	Simon Lekatompessy	Male	PDS	Billboard entrepreneur	City/Elected
	Elisawati Wonohadi (林進娘)	Female	PKDI	University lecturer; pharmacy owner	City/Not elected
	Merta Pangestu	Female	PKDI	Staff of a real estate company	City/Not elected
	Herlina Harsono Njoto	Female	PD	Not available	City/Elected
	Susilo Vivi A.	Female	Sovereignty Party (Partai Kedaulatan)	School teacher	City/Not elected
2014	Indah Kurnia	Female	PDI-P	Incumbent parliamentarian	National/Elected
	Henky Kurniadi (遊經善)	Male	PDI-P	Businessperson engaged in real estate and mining industry	National/Elected
	Antonius Iwan Dwi Laksono	Male	PKB	Not available	National/Not elected
	Johan Tedja Surya (鄭文英)	Male	Golkar	Real estate businessperson	National/Not elected
	Minarto Tjandra (潘偉民)	Male	Gerindra	Not available	National/Not elected
	Benjamin Kristianto, a.k.a Benyamin Kristianto	Male	Gerindra	Physician	Provincial/Elected

Appendix VII

Year	Name	Gender	Political Party	Occupational Background	Level of Legislative Election Contested/ Achievement
	Herlina Harsono Njoto	Female	PD	Incumbent city councillor	City/Elected
	Vinsensius Awey	Male	NasDem	Businessperson	City/Elected
	Eddy Gunawan Santoso (吳繼平)	Male	Gerindra	Businessperson engaged in cargo industry	City/Not elected

Data obtained from Li (2004b, 104); introductory advertisement of PIB's East Java candidates contested in the 2004 legislative election (2004); Surabaya City Government (2011); 'Yinhua Guanxin Puxuan Lishihui' (2004); Yunianto (2004a; 2004b; 2004c); 'Geng Shenceng Di Renshi Zheng Wenying (Johan Tedja Surya)' (2009); 'M. Soka, DRS., SH., MH' (2009); Indonesian Electoral Commission (2008a); interview with Dédé Oetomo, in English, December 24, 2010; interview with Yahya, in Indonesian, December 31, 2010; interview with Anton Prijatno, in Indonesian, February 24, 2011; interview with William Rahardja, in Indonesian, March 4, 2011; interview with Henky Kurniadi, in Indonesian, March 9, 2010; interview with Hendi Prayogo, in Indonesian, March 28, 2011; interview with Harry Tanudjaja, in Indonesian, March 31, 2011; May 26, 2011; interview with Simon Lekatompessy, in Indonesian, May 5, 2011; interview with Samas H. Widjaja, in Mandarin, May 26, 2011; '2014–2019 Niandu Guohui Yiyuan Huayi Houxuanren (Si)' (2014); '2014–2019 Niandu Guohui Yiyuan Huayi Houxuanren (Wu)' (2014); 'Daftar Cawali Surabaya, Ketua Kesira Jatim dr Benyamin Kristianto MARS Tantang Risma' (2015); 'Daftar Calon Tetap Anggota Dewan Perwakilan Rakyat Daerah Kabupaten/Kota Dalam Pemilihan Umum Tahun 2014' (2013); Cui (2014).

Notes:

Gerindra: Great Indonesia Movement Party (*Partai Gerakan Indonesia Raya*)

Golkar: Party of Functional Groups (*Partai Golongan Karya*)

PAN: National Mandate Party (*Partai Amanat Nasional*)

PBI: Indonesian Unity in Diversity Party (*Partai Bhinneka Tunggal Ika Indonesia*)

PD: Democratic Party (*Partai Demokrat*)

PDI-P: Indonesian Democratic Party of Struggle (*Partai Demokrasi Indonesia-Perjuangan*)

PDS: Prosperous Peace Party (*Partai Damai Sejahtera*)

PKDI: Indonesian Democracy Devotion Party (*Partai Kasih Demokrasi Indonesia*)

PKPI: Indonesian Justice and Unity Party (*Partai Keadilan dan Persatuan Indonesia*)

PKS: Prosperous Justice Party (*Partai Keadilan Sejahtera*)

PNBK: Indonesian National Populist Fortress Party (*Partai Nasional Benteng Kemerdekaan*)

PPIB: New Indonesia Alliance Party (*Partai Perhimpunan Indonesia Baru*)/New Indonesia Party of Struggle (*Partai Perjuangan Indonesia Baru*)

PPRN: National People's Concern Party (*Partai Peduli Rakyat Nasional*)

PRD: People's Democratic Party (*Partai Rakyat Demokratik*)

PRN: Republic of Indonesia Party (*Partai Republika Nusantara*)

Abbreviations and Glossary

Adat	Tradition
Akademi Akuntansi Surabaya	Surabaya Academy of Accounting
Bahasa Melajoe Tionghoa	Sino-Malay language
BAPERKI	Badan Permusjawaratan Kewarganegaraan Indonesia (Consultative Body for Indonesian Citizenship)
BMI	Banteng Muda Indonesia (Indonesian Young Bulls)
BPS	Badan Pusat Statistik (Central Statistics Agency)
Cantonese	A Chinese dialect originating from Guangdong Province in southern China
CBD	PT Central Business District
CCM	Cipta Cakra Murdaya Group
cukong	A Hokkien term for Chinese Indonesian capitalists who collaborate with members of the Indonesian power elite
DEPDAGRI	Departemen Dalam Negeri (Ministry of Home Affairs)
DPD	Dewan Perwakilan Daerah (Regional Representatives Council)
DPR	Dewan Perwakilan Rakyat (Parliament/National Legislature)
DPRD 1	Dewan Perwakilan Rakyat Daerah 1 (Provincial Legislature)
DPRD 2	Dewan Perwakilan Rakyat Daerah 2 (Local Legislature)
dwi fungsi	The Indonesian armed forces' 'dual' defence and political function
FKPPI	Forum Komunikasi Putra-Putri Purnawirawan Indonesia (Armed Forces Sons' and Daughters' Communication Forum)
FORDA UKM	Forum Daerah Usaha Kecil dan Menengah (Regional Forum of Small and Medium Enterprises)

Abbreviations and Glossary

FORNAS UKM	Forum Nasional Usaha Kecil dan Menengah (National Forum of Small and Medium Enterprises)
Forum Kerukunan Umat Beragama Surabaya	Surabaya Inter-Religious Harmony Forum
FUI	Forum Umat Islam (Muslim People's Forum)
GAG	Artha Graha Group
GANDI	Gerakan Perjuangan Anti Diskriminasi (Indonesian Anti-Discrimination Movement)
GAYa Nusantara	A lesbian, gay, bisexual, and transgender (LGBT) rights organisation in Indonesia
Gerindra	Partai Gerakan Indonesia Raya (Great Indonesia Movement Party)
GMNI	Gerakan Mahasiswa Nasional Indonesia (Indonesian National Students Movement)
Golkar	Partai Golongan Karya (Party of Functional Groups)
Hainanese	A Chinese dialect originating from Hainan Province in southern China
Hakka	A Chinese dialect originating from Guangdong and Fujian provinces in southern China
Hanban	Office of Chinese Language Council International in China, also known as the Confucius Institute Headquarters
Hanura	Partai Hati Nurani Rakyat (People's Conscience Party)
Hokkien	A Chinese dialect originating from Fujian Province in southern China
ICBC	Industrial and Commercial Bank of China
ICMI	Ikatan Cendekiawan Muslim Se-Indonesia (All-Indonesian Association of Islamic Intellectuals)
ICW	Indonesia Corruption Watch
Ikatan Kerukunan Umat Beragama Jawa Timur	East Java Inter-Religious Harmony Association
IKIP	Institut Keguruan dan Ilmu Pendidikan
INSPIRASI	Institut Studi Persatuan Etnis dan Ras di Indonesia (Institute of Ethnic and Racial Unity Studies in Indonesia)
INTI	Perhimpunan Indonesia Tionghoa (Chinese Indonesian Association)
IPK	Ikatan Pemuda Karya (Work Service Youth Association)
kabupaten	district
Kalimas	Komite Aliansi Kepedulian Masyarakat Surabaya (Committee of Social Concern of Surabaya)

kapitan Cina	The headman of the Chinese community in each locality of the Dutch East Indies (lit., Chinese captain)
Kapolda	Kepala Polisi Daerah (Regional Police Chief)
kecamatan	subdivision
kelurahan	village
KKN	korupsi, kolusi dan nepotisme (corruption, collusion and nepotism)
KMP	Koalisi Merah Putih
KPK	Komisi Pemberantasan Korupsi (Corruption Eradication Commission)
KPPOD	Komite Pemantau Pelaksanaan Otonomi Daerah (Committee of Monitoring for Regional Autonomy)
KPU	Komisi Pemilihan Umum (General Elections Commission)
LEMHANNAS RI	Lembaga Ketahanan Nasional Republik Indonesia (Indonesian National Defense Institute)
LPT	Laskar Pemuda Tionghoa (Chinese Youth Irregulars)
LGBT	Lesbian, gay, bisexual, and transgender
MITSU-PSP	Perhimpunan Masyarakat Indonesia Tionghoa Sumatera Utara – Peduli Sosial dan Pendidikan (North Sumatra Chinese Community Social and Education Association)
MPR	Majelis Mermusyawaratan Rakyat
MUI	Majelis Ulama Indonesia (Council of Indonesian Islamic Scholars)
NEC	New Era College
NU	Nahdlatul Ulama
OSS	One Stop Shops (service centres that handle applications for various business permits in Indonesia)
pa mafan	A Mandarin term that literally means 'afraid of running into trouble'
PAN	Partai Amanat Nasional (National Mandate Party)
Pancasila	The official philosophical foundation of the Indonesian State
Pangdam	*Panglima Daerah Militer* (Regional Military Commander)
Pao An Tui/Poh An Tui	Chinese self-defence corps during the Revolution (1945–1946) in Indonesia
Partai Kedaulatan	Sovereignty Party
PBI	Partai Bhinneka Tunggal Ika Indonesia (Indonesian Unity in Diversity Party)

Abbreviations and Glossary

PD	Partai Demokrat (Democrat Party)
PDI	Partai Demokrasi Indonesia (Indonesian Democratic Party)
PDI-P	Partai Demokrasi Indonesia Perjuangan (Indonesian Democratic Party of Struggle)
PDS	Partai Damai Sejahtera (Prosperous Peace Party)
pedagang kaki lima	street vendors
pemekaran	The fragmentation of administrative regions into smaller units (lit., blossoming)
peranakan	A term referring to acculturated Chinese who have little or no command of Chinese languages or dialects and who practise culture and customs that are neither purely Chinese nor purely indigenous Indonesian. Some *peranakan* Chinese are descendants of intermarriage between Chinese male immigrants and local indigenous women.
PERMIT	Perhimpunan Masyarakat and Pengusaha Indonesia Tionghoa (Indonesian Chinese Entrepreneur Community)
PERPIT	Perhimpunan Pengusaha Tionghoa Indonesia (Indonesian Chinese Entrepreneur Association)
PERWAKOS	Persatuan Waria Kota Surabaya, a *waria* (male-to-female transgender) organisation in Surabaya
PHTKS	Perkumpulan Hwie Tiauw Ka Surabaya (Hwie Tiauw Ka Chinese Clan Association in Surabaya)
pilkada	The Indonesian acronym for *pemilihan kepala daerah* (election of local government heads).
PK	Partai Keadilan (Justice Party)
PKB	Partai Kebangkitan Bangsa (National Awakening Party)
PKDI	Partai Kasih Demokrasi Indonesia (Indonesian Democracy Devotion Party)
PKI	Partai Komunis Indonesia (Indonesian Communist Party)
PKPI	Partai Keadilan dan Persatuan Indonesia (Indonesian Justice and Unity Party)
PKS	Partai Keadilan Sejahtera (Prosperous Justice Party)
PMA	*penanaman modal asing* (foreign investment)
PMTS	Paguyuban Masyarakat Tionghoa Surabaya (Surabaya Chinese Association)
PNBK	Partai Nasional Benteng Kemerdekaan (Indonesian National Populist Fortress Party)

PNI	Partai Nasional Indonesia (Indonesian National Party)
PP	Pemuda Pancasila (Pancasila Youth)
PPIB	Partai Perhimpunan Indonesia Baru (New Indonesia Alliance Party)/Partai Perjuangan Indonesia Baru (New Indonesia Party of Struggle)
PPM	Pemuda Panca Marga (Army Veterans' Youth)
PPP	Partai Persatuan Pembangunan (Development Unity Party)
PPRN	Partai Peduli Rakyat Nasional (National People's Concern Party)
PRD	Partai Rakyat Demokratik (People's Democratic Party) / Persatuan Rakyat Demokratik (People's Democratic Union)
preman	gangster/thug
pribumi	indigenous Indonesian
PRN	Partai Republika Nusantara (Republic of Indonesia Party)
PSI	Partai Sosialis Indonesia
PSMTI	Paguyuban Sosial Marga Tionghoa Indonesia (Chinese Indonesian Social Association)
PTSUPBA	*Panitia Tionghoa Sumatera Utara Peduli Bencana Alam (*North Sumatra's Chinese Community Relief Committee*)*
reformasi	A term referring to the post-Suharto reform period in Indonesia
satgas parpol	*satuan tugas partai politik* (political party militias)
SBKRI	*Surat Bukti Kewarganegaraan Republik Indonesia* (Citizenship Letter)
Sekber Golkar	Sekretariat Bersama Golongan Karya (Joint Secretariat of Functional Groups)
sekolah pembauran	Integrated school
singkeh	A Hokkien term used by the *peranakan* to refer to *totok* (lit., new guests)
SIUP	*Surat Izin Usaha Perdagangan* (Business Permit)
SKPD	Satuan Kerja Perangkat Daerah (Local Government Working Unit)
SMEs	small and medium enterprises
STBA-PIA	Sekolah Tinggi Bahasa Asing Persahabatan Internasional Asia (Asian International Friendship Foreign Language College)
Teochew	A Chinese dialect originating from Guangdong Province in southern China

THHK	Tiong Hoa Hwe Koan
totok	A term originally meaning pure-blooded Chinese who migrated to Indonesia more recently than the *peranakan*. In the present day, it is used to refer to Chinese Indonesians who have a China-oriented upbringing and who have command of some Chinese languages or dialects.
uang keamanan	protection money
UDA	Universitas Darma Agung (University of Darma Agung)
ustaz dadakan	A term referring to Islamic preachers who were previously not known to many people but appeared all of a sudden
ustaz tukang	A term referring to people who are paid to disguise themselves as preachers
UMI Medan	Universitas Methodist Indonesia Medan
UNIMED	Universitas Negeri Medan (State University of Medan)
USAID	United States Agency for International Development
USU	Universitas Sumatera Utara
VOC	Dutch East India Company
Walubi	Perwakilan Umat *Buddha* Indonesia (Indonesian Buddhists Association)
waria	male-to-female transgender
wayang	shadow puppetry
Yasora Medan	Yayasan Sosial Angsapura Medan (Medan Angsapura Social Foundation)
yayasan	'charitable' foundations used for political funding and rent extraction
YPSIM	Yayasan Perguruan Sultan Iskandar Muda (Sultan Iskandar Muda Educational Foundation)

Glossary of Personal Names

A Hie	王天喜
Adi, Soetanto	陳紀雄
Alim Husin	林學善
Alim Markus	林文光
Amin	陳建銘
Basri, Benny	張保圓
Budiman, Arief, a.k.a. Soe Hok Djin	史福仁
Chalim MZ. H., Abdul	李光霖
Chandra, Tansri	陳明宗
Chen Yituan	陳宜團
Chin Kung, Master	淨空法師
Dharmanadi, Joko	楊果奮
Djuandi, Eddy	莊欽華
Ek Kiong	黃弈强
Firdaus, Sonny	黃新榮
Gatot, Suherman	吳振雄
Hanurakin, Arifli Harbianto	韓明理
Haryanto	吳其生
Hasan, Bob, a.k.a. The Kian Seng	鄭建盛
Hasyim, a.k.a. Oei Kien Lim	黃建霖
Honggandhi, Hakim	關健康
Hu Jintao	胡錦濤
Jahja, Junus, a.k.a. Lauw Chuan Tho	劉全道
Janlie	饒潔莉
Jonan, Ignasius	楊賢靈
Kang Youwei	康有為
Karman, Hasan, a.k.a. Bong Sau Fan	黃少凡
Kurniadi, Henky	遊經善
Kwik Kian Gie	郭建義

Glossary of Personal Names

Kwik Sam Ho, a.k.a. Dharwan Widjaja	郭三和
Lawin, Rusmin	劉德華
Leo, Ardjan	廖章然
Li Peng	李鵬
Lie Ling Piao, Alvin	李寧彪
Liem Ou Yen	林武源
Lim Ping Tjien	林秉正
Lukita, Enggartiasto	盧尤英
Medan, Anton, a.k.a. Tan Hok Liang	陳福良
Mergonoto, Sudomo	吳德輝
Moktar, Brilian	莫粧量
Mujianto	鄭祥南
Murdaya, Siti Hartati Cakra, a.k.a. Chow Li Ing	鄒麗英
Oetomo, Dédé, a.k.a. Oen Tiong Hauw	溫忠孝
Onghokham, a.k.a. Ong Hok Ham	王福涵
Pangestu, Mari Elka	馮惠蘭
Poo, Widyawimatra, a.k.a. Poo Tjie Goan	傅志寬
Prayogo, Hendi	吳景賢
Prijatno, Anton	王炳金
Purnama, Basuki Tjahaja, a.k.a. Tjoeng Wan Hok, 'Ahok'	鍾萬學
Purnomo, Nurdin, a.k.a. Wu Nengbin	吳能彬
Rahardja, William	江國榮
Raharja, Bagus	張豪仁
Riady, James	李白
Riady, Mochtar, a.k.a. Lie Mo Tie	李文正
Saiful, Benny	黃奮鵬
Salim, Sudono, a.k.a. Liem Sioe Liong	林紹良
Sanjaya, Christiandy	黃漢山
Santoso, Eddy Gunawan	吳繼平
Sindhunatha, K.	王宗海
Soerjadjaja, William, a.k.a. Tjia Kian Liong	謝建隆
Soetomo, Jos	江慶德
Soka, M.	胡賜嘉
Suhendra, Fajar	蘇用發
Sukiran	蘇志忠
Sun Yat-sen	孫逸仙／孫中山
Surya, Johan Tedja	鄭文英
Suryadjaja G., Agoes	倪政煌
Tan, Lily	陳俐簫

Tan, Mely G.	陳玉蘭
Tan, Sofyan, a.k.a. Tan Kim Yang	陳金揚
Tanjung, Hakim	曾來金
Tanudjaja, Harry	陳國樑
Tjandra, Minarto	潘偉民
Tjongiran, Johan	章生榮
Tshai, Frans	蔡華喜
Wahidin, Indra	黃印華
Wibisono, Christianto	黃建國
Widjaja, Samas H.	黃三槐
Widjaja, Sumandi	黃貴財
Wijaya, Nyoto	楊富盛
Winata, Tomy	郭說鋒
Wongsodihardjo, Aliptojo	黃奮立
Wonohadi, Elisawati	林進娘
Yap Juk Lim	葉鬱林
Yu Zhusheng	余竹生
Zhong Maosen	鍾茂森
Zhou Enlai	周恩來

References

Official Sources

Apriyanto, Pemi. 2007. *Database Pemilu 2004: Peta Daerah Pemilihan Perolehan Suara dan Kursi untuk DPR RI, DPRD Propinsi dan DPRD Kabupaten/Kota Se-Indonesia* [Database of 2004 general election: Election results at national, provincial, and local levels in Indonesia]. [Place of publication unknown]: Spirit Research and Database.

Badan Koordinasi Masalah Cina – BAKIN. 1979. *Pedoman Penyelesaian Masalah Cina di Indonesia, Buku 1* [Handbook for the resolution of the Chinese problem in Indonesia, Volume 1]. Jakarta: Badan Koordinasi Masalah Cina – BAKIN.

Central Statistics Agency of East Java. 2001. *Penduduk Jawa Timur: Hasil Sensus Penduduk Tahun 2000* [Population of Jawa Timur: Results of the 2000 population census]. Jakarta: Central Statistics Agency.

Central Statistics Agency of North Sumatra. 2001. *Karakteristik Penduduk Sumatera Utara: Hasil Sensus Penduduk 2000* [Characteristics of the population of North Sumatra: Results of the 2000 population census]. Medan: Central Statistics Agency of North Sumatra.

Central Statistics Agency of North Sumatra. 2013. 'Tabel-tabel Pemerintahan' [The government's tables]. Central Statistics Agency of North Sumatra's website. Accessed September 30, 2013. http://sumut.bps.go.id/?qw=stasek&ns=02.

'Daftar Calon Terpilih Anggota DPRD Kota Medan 2014–2019' [List of elected city councillors of Medan 2014–2019]. 2014. General Elections Commission of Indonesia's website. Accessed April 16, 2015. http://www.kpu.go.id/koleksigambar/DATA_ANGGOTA_DPRD_KOTA_MEDAN_edit.pdf.

'Daftar Calon Tetap Anggota Dewan Perwakilan Rakyat Daerah Kabupaten/Kota Dalam Pemilihan Umum Tahun 2014' [List of regent/city councillor candidates for 2014 general election]. 2013. The Surabaya General Elections Commission website. Accessed August 29, 2016. https://2aa82ce6a79aee1d818d42435e9da5b0e60173a6.googledrive.com/host/0BxtMeYDB9flKQ1I5SjNjOXQ5Sjg/DATA%20PEMILU/Pemilu%20DPR,%20DPD,%20dan%20DPRD/Tahun%202014/Daftar%20Calon%20Tetap%20DPRD%20Kota%20Surabaya%202014/DCT%20Calon%20Anggota%20DPRD%20Kota%20Surabaya%202014.pdf.

Department of Statistics Malaysia. 2010. 'Population Distribution and Basic Demographic Characteristic Report 2010'. Department of Statistics Malaysia website. Accessed June 14, 2014. http://www.statistics.gov.my/portal/index.php?option=com_content&id=1215.

East Java Provincial Legislature. 2013. 'Daerah Pemilihan [Constituencies]'. East Java Provincial Legislature's website. Accessed September 30, 2013. http://dprd.jat-improv.go.id/dapil.

Embassy of the Republic of Indonesia, Washington D.C. 2008. 'National Symbols'. Embassy of the Republic of Indonesia, Washington D.C. website. Accessed April 2, 2013. http://www.embassyofindonesia.org/about/natsymbols.htm.

'Hanban'. 2013. Confucius Institute Headquarters website. Accessed December 7, 2013. http://english.hanban.org/node_7719.htm.

Indonesian Electoral Commission. 2008a. 'Daftar Calon Tetap Anggota Dewan Perwakilan Rakyat Dalam Pemilihan Umum Tahun 2009, Provinsi: Jawa Timur, Daerah Pemilihan: Jawa Timur 1' [List of candidates of 2009 national legislative election, province: East Java, constituency: East Java 1]. Pemilu Asia. Accessed March 20, 2011. http://www.pemilu.asia/images/DCT/DPR/Jatim%20I.pdf.

Indonesian Electoral Commission. 2008b. 'Daftar Calon Tetap Anggota Dewan Perwakilan Rakyat Dalam Pemilihan Umum Tahun 2009, Provinsi: Sumatera Utara, Daerah Pemilihan: Sumatera Utara 1' [List of candidates of 2009 national legislative election, province: North Sumatra, constituency: North Sumatera 1]. Pemilu Asia. Accessed November 21, 2012. http://www.pemilu.asia/images/DCT/DPR/Sumut%20I.pdf.

The Joint Fact-Finding Team (TGPF). 2013. 'The Final Report of the Joint Fact-Finding Team (TGPF) on the May 13–15, 1998 Riot Executive Summary'. Accessed November 12, 2013. http://www.our21.com/Indo/TGPF.html.

'Kepala Daerah' [Local government heads]. 2014. East Belitung Regency Government website. Accessed June 12, 2014. http://belitungtimurkab.go.id/Pages/Kepala Daerah.aspx.

'Kontrak Tol Medan-Kualanamu ditandatangani' [Medan-Kualanamu Toll Road contract signed]. 2011. Indonesian Ministry of Public Works website, December 13, 2013. Accessed August 30, 2013. http://www1.pu.go.id/m/main/view/65.

'Law of the Republic of Indonesia Number 32, Year 2004 Concerning Regional Administration'. 2004. Embassy of the Republic of Indonesia, Washington D.C. website. Accessed November 22, 2013. http://www.embassyofindonesia.org/ina-usa/economy/pdf/laws/Law_on_Regional_Administration.pdf.

'Minat Negara Asal PMA s/d Triwulan III – 2012' [Foreign direct investments by country of origin in third quarter of 2012]. 2013. East Java Regional Investment Coordinating Board website. Accessed August 30, 2013. http://bpm.jatimprov.go.id/wp-content/uploads/2012/11/Minat_ngrasl_PMA_tw3.jpg.

Pemilu.Asia. 2012. 'DPD 2004, Sumut' [DPD 2004, North Sumatra]. Pemilu.Asia website. Accessed November 22, 2012. http://www.pemilu.asia/?opt=4&s=7&id=32.

Perhitungan Perolehan Kursi DPRD I [Calculation of seats alloted in provincial legislatures]. 1999. Jakarta: Indonesian Election Committee.

'Primadona PMA' [The prima donnas of foreign investment]. 2013. East Java Regional Investment Coordinating Board website. May 14. Accessed August 30, 2013. http://bpm.jatimprov.go.id/primadona-pma/.

Steer, Liesbet. 2006. 'Business Licensing and One Stop Shops in Indonesia.' The Donor Committee for Enterprise Development (DCED) website. Accessed February 28, 2013. http://www.businessenvironment.org/dyn/be/docs/121/Session2.1Paper2.1.2Steer.pdf.

Surabaya City Government. 2011. 'Data Penduduk' [Population data]. Surabaya City Government website. Accessed March 20, 2011. http://www.surabaya.go.id/rtrw_console/rtrw_sijari/detPenduk.php?nik=3578312802530002.

USAID Office of Democracy and Governance. 2000. *Decentralization and Democratic Local Governance Programming Handbook*. Washington, DC: United States Agency for International Development.

World Bank Group. 2010. 'What is Decentralization?' World Bank Group website. Accessed March 9, 2010. http://www1.worldbank.org/publicsector/decentralization/what.htm#1.

Laws and Regulations

Peraturan Walikota Surabaya No. 56/2010 tentang Perhitungan Nilai Sewa Reklame [Surabaya Mayor Regulation No. 56/2010 on the calculation of advertisement billboard rental rates].

Peraturan Walikota Surabaya No. 57/2010 tentang Perhitungan Nilai Sewa Reklame Terbatas pada Kawasan Khusus di Kota Surabaya [Surabaya Mayor Regulation No. 57/2010 on the calculation of advertisement billboard rental rates in Surabaya City].

Undang-Undang No. 22/1999 tentang Pemerintahan Daerah [Law No. 22/1999 on regional government].

Undang-Undang No. 25/1999 tentang Perimbangan Keuangan antara Pemerintahan Pusat dan Daerah [Law No. 25/1999 on fiscal balance between the central and regional governments].

Undang-Undang No. 32/2004 tentang Pemerintahan Daerah [Law No. 32/2004 on regional government].

Undang-Undang No. 12/2008 tentang Pemerintahan Daerah [Law No. 12/2008 on regional government].

Sources from Newspapers, News Magazines, and Online News Sites

'2 Etnis Tionghoa Akan Duduk Di DPRD Medan' [2 ethnic Chinese are elected to Medan City Council]. 2013. *EKSPOS News*, April 23. Accessed July 28, 2014. http://m.eksposnews.com/view/32/69594/2-Etnis-Tionghoa-Akan-Duduk-di-DPRD-Medan.html.

'10 Cara memilih Anggota DPRD Sumut' [10 ways to elect members to North Sumatra provincial legislature] (advertisement). 2004. *Harian Analisa*, April 1, 5.

'48 Anggota DPRD Medan Maju Lagi di Pileg 2014' [48 city councillors of Medan will contest again in 2014 legislative election]. 2013. *Medan Bisnis*, April 30. Accessed August 26, 2016. http://medanbisnisdaily.com/news/read/2013/04/30/26603/48_anggota_dprd_medan_maju_lagi_di_pileg_2014/#.V8BmYlt95H1.

'50 Calon Anggota DPRD Medan Terpilih Periode 2009–2014, Wajah Baru 39 Orang' [50 candidates elected to Medan City Council for the period 2009–2014, 39 new faces]. 2009. *Harian Sinar Indonesia Baru* (SIB), May 16. Accessed September 30, 2013. http://hariansib.com/?p=75240.

'150 Tokoh Masyarakat Tionghoa Siap Menangkan Ajib-Binsar' [150 Chinese community leaders prepared to help Ajib-Binsar to win]. 2010. *Waspada*, May 7, C7.

'150 Tokoh Masyarakat Tionghoa Siap Menangkan Ajib-Binsar, Perhimpunan INTI Sumut Restui INTI Medan Dukung Ajib-Binsar' [150 Chinese community leaders prepared to help Ajib-Binsar to win, INTI of North Sumatra allowed INTI of Medan to support Ajib-Binsar]. 2010. *Harian Analisa*, May 7, 12.

'2014–2019 Niandu Guohui Yiyuan Huayi Houxuanren (Si)' [Ethnic Chinese national parliamentary candidates for 2014–2019 [4]]. 2014. *Guoji Ribao*, March 14, A5.

'2014–2019 Niandu Guohui Yiyuan Huayi Houxuanren (Wu)' [Ethnic Chinese national parliamentary candidates for 2014–2019 [5]]. 2014. *Guoji Ribao*, March 15, A5.

Abdussalam, Andi. 2010. 'Key Witness in Alleged Police Case Mafia Flees to S'pore.' *ANTARA News*, March 27. Accessed September 3, 2010. http://www.antaranews.com/en/news/1269641303/key-witness-in-alleged-police-case-mafia-flees-to-spore.

Amindoni, Ayomi. 2016. 'Jokowi's New Cabinet Announced.' *The Jakarta Post*, July 27. Accessed August 10, 2016. http://www.thejakartapost.com/news/2016/07/27/jokowis-new-cabinet-announced.html.

Amri, Arfi Bambani, and Muhammad Hasits. 2008. 'Saya Tak Pernah Meminta Jadi Caleg' [I never ask to be a legislative candidate]. *Viva News*, November 18. Accessed January 10, 2014. http://m.news.viva.co.id/news/read/10061-_saya_tak_pernah_meminta_jadi_caleg_.

'Anggota DPRD Sumut Periode 2014–2019 Resmi Dilantik' [East Java provincial legislators officially inaugurated]. 2014. *Berita Sore*, September 15. Accessed January 25, 2015. http://beritasore.com/2014/09/15/anggota-dprd-sumut-periode-2014-2019-resmi-dilantik/.

'Anggota DPRD Surabaya 2009–2014' [Members of Surabaya City Council 2009–2014]. 2009. *Jawa Pos*, May 18, 29, 39.

Arfani, Fiqih. 2010. 'Sholeh Siapkan Rp 2,5 M untuk "Beli" Dukunga[n]' [Sholeh prepares Rp. 2.5 billion to 'buy' support]. *Surabaya Post*, January 18, reproduced in *Viva News*. Accessed January 10, 2014. http://us.nasional.news.viva.co.id/news/read/122262-sholeh_siapkan_rp_2_5_m_untuk__beli__dukunga.

'Bakom PKB Medan Tempatkan Empat Kadernya Sebagai Calon Legislatif, Sudarto: Saat yang Tepat Perjuangkan Hak Kaum Minoritas' [Communicative body for the appreciation of national unity in Medan placed four cadres as legislative candidates, Sudarto: It is the right time to fight for minority rights]. 2004. *Harian Analisa*, February 18, 19.

Bangun, Edward. 2013. 'Ajib Shah Mulus Pimpin Golkar Sumut' [Ajib Shah leads Golkar of North Sumatra with integrity]. *Medan Bisnis*, August 29. Accessed January 12, 2014. http://www.medanbisnisdaily.com/news/read/2013/08/29/47718/ajib_shah_mulus_pimpin_golkar_sumut/#.Ut5c6vsRVH0.

'Basuki Tjahaja Purnama.' 2014. Merdeka.com. Accessed June 12. http://profil.merdeka.com/indonesia/b/basuki-tjahaja-purnama/.

'Batal Maju DPD RI, Simon Dikabarkan Maju Bacaleg Hanura' [After withdrawing plan to run for DPD RI, Simon is alleged to become Hanura legislative candidate]. 2013. *Tribun Surabaya*, April 16. Accessed October 4, 2013. http://surabaya.tribunnews.com/2013/04/16/batal-maju-dpd-ri-simon-dikabarkan-maju-bacaleg-hanura.

'Bekukan Aset Bos PT Indo Palapa, "Tangkap Benny Basri"' [Freezing assets of PT Indo Palapa's boss, 'arrest Benny Basri']. 2010. *Harian Orbit*, October 15, 1–2.

Bhakti, Ikrar Nusa. 2010. 'Lagi, Isu soal Hak Pilih TNI' [Again, the issue of TNI's right to vote]. *Seputar Indonesia*, June 22, 15.

References 203

'Bill Against Racial Discrimination Passed'. 2008. *The Jakarta Post*, October 29. Accessed August 29, 2013. http://www.thejakartapost.com/news/2008/10/29/bill-against-racial-discrimination-passed.html.

'BKM Tuntut Emerald Garden Robohkan Tembok Pembatas' [BKM demands Emerald Garden tear down parapet]. 2014. *Harian Andalas*, May 17. Accessed October 24, 2016. https://issuu.com/media.andalas/docs/epaper_andalas_edisi_sabtu_17_mei_2.

'Buyao Xuan Ceng Yanzhong Qinfan Huaren Jiben Renquan De Yiyuan Houxuanren' [Never vote for candidates who violated human rights of ethnic Chinese in the past]. 2004. *Rela Warta*, March 3, 1.

Budiman, Irfan, and Wenseslaus Manggut. 2003. 'On the Threshold of the Dark Ages'. *Tempo*, March 18–24, 14–16.

'Bupati Lembata Dilantik Kamis' [Chief of Lembata Regency installed on Thursday]. 2011. *Kompas*, August 21. Accessed June 12, 2014. http://regional.kompas.com/read/2011/08/21/1243302/Bupati.Lembata.Dilantik.Kamis.

'Caleg DPRD Sumut dari PPRN Kie Hock Kwen[g]: Masyarakat Harus Gunakan Produk Dalam Negeri' [National People's Concern Party's candidate for North Sumatra provincial parlimentary election Kie Hock Kwen[g]: Local community should use local products]. 2009. *Harian Analisa*, April 4, 30.

'Calon DPD Sumut No. 12 dr Indra Wahidin, Tokoh yang Mengutamakan Kebersamaan' [North Sumatra DPD candidate no. 12 Dr. Indra Wahidin, leader who prioritises unity] (Campaign advertisement). 2004. *Harian Analisa*, April 1, 24.

Chen, Liyu. 2005. 'Yinni Jinfeng Jituan Kanhao Diqu Xiuxian Luyou Qianjing' [Maspion Group is optimistic about the future of regional leisure tourism]. *Jinmen Ribao*, February 24. Accessed August 24, 2017. http://www.kmdn.gov.tw/1117/1271/1272/124988/?cprint=pt.

Chen, Zhiyi. 2010. 'Dongzhaowa Qiyejia Cishan Jijinhui Yu Sishui Huayi Lianyihui Yingsong Dongzhaowa Xinjiu Junqu Siling Jiaqiang Lianxi' [East Java Entrepreneur Charitable Foundation and Surabaya Chinese Association organised welcome and farewell dinner for former and new East Java military chiefs]. *Medan Zao Bao*, October 9, M4.

'Competing Visions.' 2014. *The Economist*, July 5. Accessing April 4, 2015. http://www.economist.com/news/leaders/21606285-political-naif-represents-more-hopeful-future-indonesia-suharto-era.

Cui, Yisheng. 2014. 'Zhishao You Shiwu Wei Huayi Dangxuan 2014–2019 Nianjie Guohui Yiyuan' [At least 15 ethnic Chinese elected as national parliamentarians]. *Guoji Ribao*, May 17, A3.

'Daerah Pemilihan Sumut 1 DPRD Sumut' [North Sumatra 1 provincial constituency]. 2009. *Harian Analisa*, April 28, 12.

'Daftar Cawali Surabaya, Ketua Kesira Jatim dr Benyamin Kristianto MARS Tantang Risma' [Registered as Surabaya's mayoral candidate, East Javanese Kesira head Dr. Benyamin Kristianto MARS challenges Risma]. 2015. *Redaksi*, May 19. Accessed August 26, 2016. http://redaksi.co.id/10516/daftar-cawali-surabaya-ketua-kesira-jatim-dr-benyamin-kristianto-mars-tantang-risma.html.

'Daftarkan Diri ke DPC PDS, DR Indra [Wahidin] Ramaikan Bursa Balon Walikota' [Registered with PDS Medan, Dr. Indra [Wahidin] joins the race for mayor's post]. 2010. *Suara Nasional*, January 26. Accessed December 3, 2012. http://suaranasional.comyr.com/index.php/Medan/3154.html.

204 References

Damanik, Liston. 2014. 'Haryanto: Sekarang Momen Emas PKPI' [Now is the golden moment of PKPI]. *Tribun Medan*, April 3. Accessed August 26, 2016. http://medan.tribunnews.com/2014/04/03/haryanto-sekarang-momen-emas-pkpi.

Dedy. 2009. 'Olo Panggabean Meninggal Dunia' [Olo Panggabean passes away]. *Harian Global*, April 30. Accessed November 6, 2010. http://www.harian-global.com/index.php?option=com_content&view=article&id=6496%3A olo-panggabean-meninggal-dunia&Itemid=99.

Deng, Xiaohua, and Xie Huishan. 2011. 'Sishui 13 Shesuan 14 Ri Juban "Zhonghua Chuantong Jiaoyu" Jiangzuohui, Jingkong Dashi Qinlin Xianchang, Zhong Maosen Boshi Jiangjie Zhonghua Wenhua' [13 organisations in Surabaya held talk show 'The Education of Chinese Tradition' on January 14, Master Chin Kung attended the talk show, Dr. Zhong Mao Sen explained Chinese culture]. *Harian Nusantara*, January 17, 12.

'Dinilai Tidak Dukung Saat Pilkada, Walikota Medan Copot Sejumlah Camat dan Lurah' [Deemed not to give support during local election, Medan mayor removed *camat*s and *lurah*s]. 2010. *Harian Analisa*, August 24, 6.

'dr Sofyan Tan Dianugerahi Marga Ginting' [Dr. Sofyan Tan honoured by Ginting clan]. 2010. *Berita Sore Online*, March 11. Accessed September 4, 2016. http://beritasore.com/2010/03/11/dr-sofyan-tan-dianugerahi-marga-ginting/.

'DPRan PDS Pertanyakan Posisi Simon Lekatompessy' [PDS branch leaders question Simon Lekatompessy's position]. 2013. D-onenews.com, August 14. Accessed October 4, 2013. http://d-onenews.com/blog/dpran-pds-pertanyakan-posisi-simon-lekatompessy/.

'DPRDSU: Pemasok Narkoba Dari Pelabuhan Portklang ke Indonesia Libatkan Mafia Internasional' [North Sumatra provincial legislators: Drug supply from Port Klang to Indonesia involves international mafia]. 2012. *Harian Mandiri*, May 11. Accessed August 3, 2013. http://harianmandiri.com/kriminal/dprdsu-pemasok-narkoba-dari-pelabuhan-portklang-ke-indonesia-libatkan-mafia-inter-nasional.

'Eddy Gunawan Tunggu Pinangan Parpol' [Eddy Gunawan waiting for the approach of political parties]. 2010. Kabardangdut.com, January 14. Accessed January 10, 2014. http://kabardangdut.com/page_detail.php?content=997&category=8.

Edward. 2010. 'Sofyan Tan dan Rahudman Sah Masuk Putaran Kedua' [Sofyan Tan and Rahudman confirmed enter second round]. *Harian Global*, May 18. Accessed May 19, 2010. http://www.harian-global.com/index.php?option=com_cont ent&view=article&id=37208:sofyan-tan-dan-rahudman-sah-masuk-putaran-kedua-&catid=91:pilkada-medan&Itemid=102.

Effendi, Zainal. 2010a. 'Biro Periklanan Minta Walikota Tinjau Ulang Kenaikan Pajak Reklame' [Bureau of Advertising calls upon mayor to review the rise in outdoor advertising tax]. *Detik Surabaya*, November 15. Accessed March 24, 2011. http://surabaya.detik.com/read/2010/11/15/195930/1495021/466/ biro-periklanan-minta-walikota-tinjau-ulang-kenaikan-pajak-reklame.

Effendi, Zainal. 2010b. 'Pajak Reklame Melangit, Dewan Gagas Interpelasi Walikota Surabaya' [Outdoor advertising tax increases, local legislative council plans to file an interpellation on Surabaya's mayor]. *Detik Surabaya*, November 15. Accessed March 24, 2011. http://surabaya.detik.com/read/2010/11/15/185556/1494978 /466/pajak-reklame-melangit-dewan-gagas-interpelasi-walikota-surabaya.

'Ekonomi Perdagangan Jadi Jembatan Persahabatan Tiongkok-RI' [Trade becomes bridge of friendship between China and Indonesia]. 2013. China Radio

International (CRI), January 29. Accessed August 30, 2013. http://indonesian.cri.cn/201/2013/01/29/1s135112.htm.

Elyda, Corry, and Fedina S. Sundaryani. 2014. 'Ahok Becomes Jakarta Governor Today.' *The Jakarta Post*, November 19. Accessed November 19, 2014. http://www.thejakartapost.com/news/2014/11/19/ahok-becomes-jakarta-governor-today.html.

Emont, Jon. 2016. 'A Happy Warrior in a Faltering Battle for Indonesian Gay Rights.' *The New York Times*, August 19. Accessed August 20, 2016. http://www.nytimes.com/2016/08/20/world/asia/indonesia-gay-rights-dede-oetomo.html?_r=0.

'Evaluasi Perda Penghambat Investasi Diperketat Tindaklanjut Keluhan Presiden SBY' [Evaluation of local regulations that hampered investment tightened after the complaint of President SBY]. 2011. JPNN [Jawa Pos National Network], February 23. Accessed November 1, 2012. http://www.jpnn.com/m/news.php?id=85054.

'Gao Jingai De Duzhe Shu' [To all readers]. 2004. *Rela Warta*, April 8, 1.

'Gayus Tambunan Arrested'. 2010. *ANTARA News*, March 31. Accessed September 3, 2010. http://www.antaranews.com/en/news/1270007628/gayus-tambunan-arrested.

'Geng Shenceng Di Renshi Zheng Wenying [Johan Tedja Surya]' [Get to know more about Johan Tedja Surya] (advertisement). 2009. *Harian Nusantara*, April 2, 16.

'Gerindra Usung Hasan Karman' [Gerindra supports Hasan Karman]. 2013. *Tribun Pontianak*, April 28. Accessed December 13, 2013. http://pontianak.tribunnews.com/2013/04/28/gerindra-usung-hasan-karman.

Go, Robert. 2004. 'Chinese wake up to politics'. *The Straits Times*, February 24, 10.

'Golput Bukan Solusi' [Abstention is not a solution]. 2009. *Harian Analisa*, April 2, 11.

'Gunakan Akal Sehat, Pilih Partai PIB' [Use common sense, choose New Indonesia Party of Struggle] (advertisement). 2009. *Harian Analisa*, April 3, 16.

Gunawan, Apriadi. 2004. 'Sofyan Tan, Doctor Who Works for Education.' *The Jakarta Post*, May 21. Accessed August 26, 2013. http://www.thejakartapost.com/news/2004/05/21/sofyan-tan-doctor-who-works-education.html.

Gunawan, Apriadi. 2010. 'Sofyan Tan: Making History in Medan Democracy.' *The Jakarta Post*, August 7. Accessed September 4, 2010. http://www.thejakartapost.com/news/2010/08/07/sofyan-tan-making-history-medan-democracy.html-0.

'H. Anif Shah dan Keluarga Memberi Dukungan Sepenuhnya kepada Pasangan Calon H. Ajib Shah-Binsar Situmorang' [H. Anif Shah and family give full support to H. Ajib Shah-Binsar Situmorang]. 2010. Pancasila Youth of North Sumatra's website, March 23. Accessed August 3, 2013. http://www.ppsumut.com/news/detail/?id=113.

Hakim, Abdul. 2011. 'Perseteruan Pemkot-DPRD Surabaya Sepanjang 2011' [Feud between Surabaya's power-holder and city council in 2011]. *ANTARA Jatim News*, December 20. Accessed October 10, 2013. http://www.antarajatim.com/lihat/berita/78765/perseteruan-pemkot-dprd-surabaya-sepanjang-2011.

Hakim, Abdul. 2013. 'Pencairan Gaji Enam Legislator Surabaya Tunggu Kemendagri' [Disbursement of six Surabaya legislators' salary awaiting approval of Ministry of Home Affairs]. *ANTARA Jatim News*, May 3. Accessed October 4, 2013. http://www.antarajatim.com/lihat/berita/109600/pencairan-gaji-enam-legislator-surabaya-tunggu-kemendagri.

Hakim, Jalil, and Fatkhurrohman Taufiq. 2011. 'Wakil Walikota Surabaya Bantah Terlibat dalam Aksi Pemberhentian Walikota' [Surabaya's deputy mayor denies he's involved in the ousting of mayor]. *Tempo*, January 31. Accessed

October 10, 2013. http://www.tempo.co/read/news/2011/01/31/180310117/
Wakil-Walikota-Surabaya-Bantah-Terlibat-dalam-Aksi-Pemberhentian-Walikota.

'Hakim Tanjung Kembali Pimpin Yasora Medan' [Hakim Tanjung re-elected as president of Yasora Medan]. 2012. *Harian Analisa*, June 22. Accessed December 14, 2012. http://www.analisadaily.com/news/read/2012/06/22/58252/hakim_tanjung_kembali_pimpin_yasora_medan/#.UMrhcVJFan4.

Handoko, Agustinus. 2011. 'Christiandy dan Paryadi Bergabung ke Demokrat' [Christiandy and Paryadi joined Democrat Party]. *Kompas*, September 19. Accessed December 13, 2013. http://regional.kompas.com/read/2011/09/19/15415953/Christiandy.dan.Paryadi.Bergabung.ke.Demokrat.

Hantoro, Juli. 2004. 'Bad News for the Press'. *Tempo*, March 23–29, 42–43.

Harahap, Syafri. 2010. 'Perbedaan Etnis Harusnya Jadi Perekat' [Ethnic differences should serve as adhesion for different ethnic groups]. *Waspada*, May 18. Accessed May 31, 2011. http://waspadamedan.com/index.php?option=com_content&view=article&id=748:perbedaan-etnis-harusnya-jadi-perekat&catid=51:medan&Itemid=206.

'Hari Ini Ratusan Pelaku UKM Unjukrasa Keprihatinan' [Today hundreds of SME owners attending public protest]. 2008. *Waspada*, March 25. Accessed November 16, 2010. http://www.waspada.co.id/index.php/images/plugins/content/highslide/index.php?option=com_content&view=article&id=14447:hari-ini-ratusan-pelaku-ukm-unjukrasa-keprihatinan&catid=14:medan&Itemid=27.

'Hasyim Sosok Ahok Medan, Karena Mau Merakyat Dengan Semua Golongan' [Hasyim is the Ahok of Medan, because you are pro-people]. 2013. *Harian Mandiri*, January 2. Accessed October 1, 2013. http://harianmandiri.com/daerah/hasyim-sosok-ahok-medan-karena-mau-merakyat-dengan-semua-golongan/922.

'Hendi Prayogo, Ketua Komite Tionghoa Indonesia Peduli Pemilu' [Hendi Prayogo, head of Chinese Indonesian Concern Committee for Elections]. 2009. *Jawa Pos*, April 5, 32.

'Huazu Xuanmin Yao Xuan Shui?' [Whom should Chinese voters vote for?]. 2004. *Rela Warta*, June 25–July 1, 2.

Huang, Feng. 2010. 'Huang Yinhua Yisheng Tuichu Jingxuan Mianlan Fushizhang' [Dr. Indra Wahidin pulls out from the race for deputy mayor's post]. *Guoji Ribao*, March 2, B1.

Huda, Larissa. 2017. 'Ahok sent to 2 years in prison for blasphemy.' *Tempo*, May 9. Accessed https://en.tempo.co/read/news/2017/05/09/055873617/Ahok-Sent-to-2-Years-in-Prison-for-Blasphemy.

Hutabarat, Hendrik. 2010. 'PDIP Tuding Ada Pengarahan Masif PNS oleh Pemko Medan' [PDIP claims that there were mass instructions from Medan local government to civil servants]. *Medan Bisnis*, July 18, 2.

'I Have Officially Left Gerindra: Ahok'. 2014. *The Jakarta Post*, September 10. Accessed October 25, 2016. http://www.thejakartapost.com/news/2014/09/10/i-have-officially-left-gerindra-ahok.html.

'Indonesia's Joko Searches for Honest Men'. 2014. *Asia Sentinel*, October 22. Accessed April 4, 2015. http://www.asiasentinel.com/politics/indonesia-jokowi-search-honest-men/.

'Ini Dia 50 Anggota DPRD Kota Surabaya Periode 2014–2019' [Here are 50 city councillors of Surabaya for 2014–2019]. 2014. *Lensa Indonesia*, May 13. Accessed

References

January 25, 2015. http://www.lensaindonesia.com/2014/05/13/ini-dia-50-ang-gota-dprd-kota-surabaya-periode-2014-2019.html.

'Inilah 100 Anggota DPRD Jatim 2014–2019 Terpilih' [Here are 100 elected provincial legislators of East Java 2014–2019]. 2014. *Berita Jatim*, May 12. Accessed July 28, 2014. http://beritajatim.com/menuju_pemilu_2014/206777/inilah_100_anggota_dprd_jatim_2014-2019_terpilih.html#.U9Z4MUDvXIc.

Introductory advertisement of PIB's East Java candidates contesting in the 2004 legislative election. 2004. *Cheng Bao*, April 1, 1.

'Jakarta Election Official Results Almost the Same as Quick Counts'. *The Jakarta Globe*, April 30. Accessed http://jakartaglobe.id/news/jakarta-poll-official-results-almost-quick-counts/.

'Jakarta Governor Ahok Stands Trial for Blasphemy'. Al Jazeera, December 14. Accessed August 26, 2017. http://www.aljazeera.com/news/2016/12/jakarta-governor-ahok-blasphemy-trial-161213035207985.html.

'Jianzu Xingjian Xukezheng Xingpian, INDO PALAPA Gongsi Laoban Bei Yaoqiu Ti Shenpan' [Submitting false information in construction permit application, Indo Palapa's boss was requested to be persecuted]. 2010. *Xun Bao*, November 2, 11.

'Jida Dongnanya Yanjiusuo Cao Jiaoshou Yihang Fangwen Mianlan Jiangxia Gongsuo, Tantao Huaren Canzheng Yizheng Zongjiao Hexie Deng Qieshen Wenti' [Professor Cao and friends from Jinan University's School of Southeast Asian Studies visited Wijaya Social Foundation in Medan, discussed pressing issues on political participation and religious harmony related to ethnic Chinese]. 2009. *Medan Zao Bao*, December 4, B7.

'Jingxuan Zhong De Fengyu' [Troubles in the election]. 2010. *Medan Zao Bao*, April 12, M1.

'Kalla Says "Thug" Needed to Run Indonesia'. 2009. *The Jakarta Post*, February 21. Accessed December 3, 2013. http://www.thejakartapost.com/news/2009/02/21/kalla-says-%E2%80%9Cthug%E2%80%9D-needed-run-indonesia.html.

'Karya Elly, SH: Saya Prihatin Banyak Calon Pemilih Belum Terima Kartu Pemilih' [Karya Elly, SH: I am concerned that many voters have not received their voter ID cards]. 2004. *Harian Analisa*, April 2, 2.

'Kepala dan Sekretaris BPPT Medan Diduga Pungli Rp300 jt Perbulan, "Segera Dipanggil Walikota Medan"' [Head and secretary of BPPT of Medan suspected of collecting Rp300 million of illegal extra money each month, 'should be summoned by the mayor immediately']. 2010. *Harian Orbit*, November 16, 1–2.

'Kepedulian terhadap Masyarakat Harus Ditumbuhkan' [Social concern should be cultivated]. 2009. *Harian Analisa*, April 2, 11.

'Ketua DPP Golkar: Warga Tionghoa Kekuatan Besar' [Head of Golkar's branch: Chinese citizens are powerful]. 2009. *Ini Medan Bung* [Indonesian-Language Online News Site], March 18. Accessed May 31, 2011. http://www.inimedan-bung.com/node/2384.

'Ketua Pimpinan Cabang Partai PIB Kota Medan Sumandi Wijaya: Tidak Ada Keharusan bagi WNI Khususnya Etnis Tionghoa Memiliki SKBRI' [Chairperson of New Indonesia Party of Struggle in Medan: Indonesian citizens especially ethnic Chinese do not need to have SKBRI]. 2004. *Harian Analisa*, February 28, 2.

'Konflik Wali Kota dengan DPRD Surabaya' [Conflict between mayor and city council of Surabaya]. 2011. *GET Networks*, February 1. Accessed October 10, 2013. http://www.indogetnetworks.com/index.php?option=com_content&view=article&id=406:konflik-wali-kota-dengan-dprd-surabaya-&catid=87:jatim&Itemid=445.

'KPU Medan dan Panwas Dituding Berpihak ke Pasangan Rahudman-Eldin, Dua Camat dan PNS Batal Bersaksi di MK' [Medan General Election Commission and General Election Supervisory Committee accused of favouring Rahudman-Eldin, two district heads and civil servant did not testify in court]. 2010. *Harian Analisa*, July 17, 6.

'KPU Sahkan Hasil Pemilu, PDIP Nomor Satu' [General Election Commission validates election results, PDIP is number one]. 2014. BBC Indonesia, May 10. Accessed October 6, 2014. http://www.bbc.co.uk/indonesia/berita_indonesia/2014/05/140509_rekapitulasi_kpu.

Kwok, Yenni. 2014. 'Indonesians Outraged by the Scrapping of Elections for Mayors and Governors.' *Time*, September 26. Accessed October 25, 2016. http://time.com/3431596/indonesia-regional-direct-elections-democracy-prabowo-subianto-joko-jokowi-widodo/.

Kusumadewi, Anggi, and Tudji Martudji. 2012. 'Tri Rismaharini: Sepenuh Hati Menata Surabaya' [Tri Rismaharini: Governing Surabaya wholeheartedly]. *Viva News*, October 25. Accessed January 10, 2014. http://us.sorot.news.viva.co.id/print_detail/printing/362464-tri-rismaharini--sepenuh-hati-menata-surabaya.

Kuwado, Fabian Januarius. 2014. 'Perjalanan Ahok, dari Pulau Timah ke Ibu Kota' [The journey of Ahok, from tin island to capital city]. *Kompas*, February 23. Accessed June 12, 2014. http://megapolitan.kompas.com/read/2014/02/23/0609071/Perjalanan.Ahok.dari.Pulau.Timah.ke.Ibu.Kota.

'Lagi, Al-Washliyah Beri Tamin Keranda Mayat' [Again, Al-Washliyah gives Tamin a coffin]. 2013. *Harian Orbit*, June 25. Accessed July 29, 2013. http://www.harianorbit.com/lagi-al-washliyah-beri-tamin-keranda-mayat/.

Lamb, Kate. 2016. 'Jakarta Governor Ahok's Blasphemy Trial: All You Need to Know'. *The Guardian*, December 12. Accessed May 10, 2017. https://www.theguardian.com/world/2016/dec/12/jakarta-governor-ahoks-blasphemy-trial-all-you-need-to-know.

Lamb, Kate. 2017. 'Jakarta Governor Ahok Sentenced to Two Years in Prison for Blasphemy'. *The Guardian*, May 9. Accessed May 10, 2017. https://www.theguardian.com/world/2017/may/09/jakarta-governor-ahok-found-guilty-of-blasphemy-jailed-for-two-years.

'Law of the Concrete Jungle'. 2003. *Tempo*, March 18–24, 11.

Lin, Youshun. 2010. 'Yinni Huaren Canzheng Kunzu' [The difficulties of Chinese Indonesian participation in politics]. *Yazhou Zhoukan*, August 1, 30.

'Local Elections Are a Violent Business'. 2013. *The Jakarta Post*, September 2. Accessed December 11, 2013. http://www.thejakartapost.com/news/2013/09/02/local-elections-are-a-violent-business.html.

'M. Soka, DRS., SH., MH' (advertisement). 2009. *Harian Nusantara*, March 30, 17.

'Mafia Tanah Hilangkan Nurani' [Land mafia have lost their conscience]. 2011. *Harian Sumut Pos*, November 9. Accessed April 13, 2013. http://www.hariansumutpos.com/2011/11/18567/mafia-tanah-hilangkan-nurani#axzz2QMHXSl77.

'Mafia Tanah Sengsarakan Rakyat' [Land mafia cause suffering to people]. 2011. *Harian Orbit*, December 7. Accessed April 13, 2013. http://www.harianorbit.com/mafia-tanah-sengsarakan-rakyat/.

'Massa Ancam Bakar Hotel Emerald Garden' [Masses threaten to burn down Emerald Garden Hotel]. 2013. *Harian Sumut Pos*, March 23. Accessed July 29, 2013. http://www.hariansumutpos.com/2013/03/54632/massa-ancam-bakar-hotel-emerald-garden#axzz2aQEAafNg.

References

'Menuju Parpol Terbaik di Sumut' [Becoming the best political party in North Sumatra]. 2013. *Harian Sumut Pos*, April 23. Accessed August 3, 2013. http://www.hariansumutpos.com/2013/04/56678/menuju-parpol-terbaik-di-sumut#axzz2arwvU2CP.

Mingyanren. 2010. 'Mianlan Ren Lun Mianlan Shizhang Jingxuan' [Medanese on Medan's mayoral election]. *Guoji Ribao*, June 28, B1.

'Minister Mari Elka Looks Forward to New Creative Economy Task'. 2011. *The Jakarta Post*, October 19. Accessed January 25, 2013. http://www.thejakartapost.com/news/2011/10/19/minister-mari-elka-looks-forward-new-creative-economy-task.html.

'MK Tolak Gugatan Sofyan Tan, Perlantikan Calon Walikota Terpilih Direncanakan Senin' [Constitutional court turns down Sofyan Tan's lawsuit, installation of mayoral candidate scheduled for Monday]. 2010. *Harian Analisa*, July 21, 7.

'Mohon Doa Restu Partai Perhimpunan Indonesia Baru' [Request of prayer for New Indonesia Party of Struggle] (advertisement). 2004. *Harian Analisa*, April 1, 9.

'Mujianto Dituding Mafia Tanah' [Mujianto accused of being land mafia]. 2011. *Harian Orbit*, November 30. Accessed April 13, 2013. http://www.harianorbit.com/mujianto-dituding-mafia-tanah/.

'Murdaya Poo Dipecat dari PDIP dan DPR' [Murdaya Poo dismissed from PDIP and National Parliament]. 2009. *Detik News*, December 2. Accessed August 18, 2017. https://news.detik.com/berita/d-1252970/murdaya-poo-dipecat-dari-pdip-dan-dpr-?nd771104bcj=&nd771104bcj=.

Nirmala, Ronna. 2012. 'What's Worse, a Corrupter or a "Preman" Thug?' *The Jakarta Globe*, February 24. Accessed February 27, 2012. http://www.thejakartaglobe.com/home/whats-worse-a-corrupter-or-a-preman-thug/500191#Scene_1.

'PAC Demokrat Dukung Eddy Gunawan' [Democratic Party's branch leaders support Eddy Gunawan]. 2010. *Jawa Pos*, February 25, 30.

Pamuji, Heru, Luqman Hakim Arifin, and Bernadetta Febriana. 2004. 'Jurus Merapat Lewat Kocek Kandidat' [Approaching candidates through their pockets]. *Gatra*, August 7, 24–27.

Parlina, Ina, and Hasyim Widhiarto. 2014. 'Jokowi's Cabinet Announced, Here Is the Lineup'. *The Jakarta Post*, October 26. Accessed August 10, 2016. http://www.thejakartapost.com/news/2014/10/26/jokowis-cabinet-announced-here-lineup.html.

'Partai Keadilan dan Persatuan Indonesia' [Indonesian Justice and Unity Party] (advertisement). 2009. *Harian Analisa*, April 3, 5.

'Partai Perjuangan Indonesia Baru (10)' [New Indonesia Party of Struggle (10)]. 2008. *Detik News*, December 27. Accessed August 18, 2017. https://news.detik.com/parpol/d-1059858/partai-perjuangan-indonesia-baru-10.

'Partai Pilihan Kami!' [Our choice of party!] (advertisement). 2004. *Harian Analisa*, April 1, 3.

'Pasangan Awang-Abdul Pemenang Pilkada Singkawang' [Awang-Abdul winners of Sikawang's mayoral election]. 2012. *ANTARA News*, September 25. Accessed December 13, 2013. http://antarakalbar.com/berita/306533/pasangan-awang-abdul-pemenang-pilkada-singkawang.

'PDI Perjuangan Serahkan 2,8 Ton Kayu, 280 Lembar Seng, 500 Kg Beras dan Mie Instant' [Indonesian Democratic Party of Struggle passed 2.8 tons of wood, 280 zinc sheets, 500 kg of rice, and instant noodles]. 2008. *Harian Sinar Indonesia Baru*, November 26. Accessed October 12, 2010. http://hariansib.com/?p=50229.

'PDS Gandeng Eddy Gunawan' [PDS supports Eddy Gunawan]. 2010. *Jawa Pos*, January 21, 33, 47.

'Peluang Kursi Caleg DPRD Dapil 1 Medan' [Election results for Medan 1]. 2009. *Harian Analisa*, April 27, 4.

'Peluang Kursi Caleg DPRD Dapil 3 Medan' [Election results for Medan 3]. 2009. *Harian Analisa*, April 27, 4.

'Peluang Kursi Caleg DPRD Dapil 4 Medan' [Election results for Medan 4]. 2009. *Harian Analisa*, April 27, 4.

'Pemilihan Wali Kota Medan Geliat Politik Etnis Tionghoa di Medan' [Medan's mayoral election and political stretching of ethnic Chinese in Medan]. 2010. *VHR Media*, May 15. Accessed July 23, 2010. http://www.vhrmedia.com/Geliat-Politik-Etnis-Tionghoa-di-Medan-opini4185.html.

'Pendukung Pasangan No 10 "Menyemut" di Lapangan Merdeka, Sofyan Tan Nyatakan Komitmen Siap Digantung dan Sediakan Peti Mati Jika Korupsi' [Pair no. 10's supporters crowded at Merdeka Square, Sofyan Tan commits to be hanged and prepare himself a coffin if involved in corruption]. 2010. *Harian Analisa*, June 16, 6.

Peng, Guanyan. 2010. 'Jianzao Huazu Wenhua Gongyuan Sanbuqu' [The trilogy of Chinese Cultural Garden Establishment]. *Guoji Ribao*, December 30, B3.

'Pengobatan Gratis untuk Warga Kurang Mampu' [Free medical aid for people in need]. 2010. *Harian Analisa*, July 5, 6.

'Pengurus Baru Gerindra: 314 Pengurus, Puluhan Jenderal dan Aktivis' [Gerindra's new board members: 314 board members, dozens of generals and activists]. 2012. Beritasatu.com, July 12. Accessed July 19, 2013. http://www.beritasatu.com/nasional/59534-pengurus-baru-gerindra-314-pengurus-puluhan-jenderal-dan-aktivis.html.

'Penyerobotan Tanah Negara di Helvetia Menuai Kemarahan, Tamin Sukardi Resmi Dilapor ke KPK' [Seizure of state land in Helvetia arouses public outrage, Tamin Sukardi has been reported to KPK]. 2013. *Harian Orbit*, June 10. Accessed July 28, 2013. http://www.harianorbit.com/penyerobotan-tanah-negara-di-helvetia-menuai-kemarahan-tamin-sukardi-resmi-dilapor-ke-kpk/.

'Perbandingan Kursi DPRD Jatim Antara Pemilu 1999 dan 2004' [A comparison between number of East Java provincial legislature seats in 1999 and 2004]. 2004. *Jawa Pos*, April 16, 30.

'Perubuhan Masjid Raudhatul Islam, Oknum MUI Cari Keuntungan Materi' [MUI leaders gain material benefits from demolition of Raudhatul Islam Mosque]. 2012. *Harian Orbit*, February 7. Accessed July 29, 2013. http://www.harianorbit.com/perubuhan-masjid-raudhatul-islam-oknum-mui-cari-keuntungan-materi/.

'Pilihlah kami!!!' [Choose us!!!] (advertisement). 2009. *Medan Zao Bao*, April 3, M4.

'Pilkada 2010 Telan Rp14 Triliun Lebih' [*Pilkada* in 2010 consumed more than Rp14 trillion]. 2011. *Jawa Pos*, February 4, 2.

'Pilkada Surabaya: MK Menangkan Risma-Bambang' [*Pilkada* of Surabaya: Constitutional court declares the victory of Risma-Bambang]. 2010. *Politik Indonesia*, August 24. Accessed September 26, 2013. http://www.politikindonesia.com/index.php?k=nusantara&i=8938-Pilkada-Surabaya:-MK-Menangkan-Risma-Bambang.

'PPP, PBB, PBI, PKP Dapat 1 Kursi' [PPP, PBB, PBI, PKP get 1 seat]. 1999. *Jawa Pos*, July 8, 9.

Prakoso, Rangga. 2012. 'KPK detains tycoon Hartati Murdaya over bribery allegation'. *The Jakarta Globe*, September 12. Accessed December 14, 2013. http://

References

211

www.thejakartaglobe.com/archive/kpk-detains-tycoon-hartati-murdaya-over-bribery-allegation/.

Primanita, Arientha, and Pitan Daslani. 2012. 'Basuki's win to pave way for ethnic Chinese in Indonesian politics'. *The Jakarta Globe*, September 25. Accessed January 25, 2013. http://www.thejakartaglobe.com/home/basukis-win-to-pave-way-for-ethnic-chinese-in-indonesian-politics/546345.

'Profile: General Wiranto.' 2004. BBC News, April 22. Accessed January 10, 2014. http://news.bbc.co.uk/2/hi/asia-pacific/3646119.stm.

'Protest Against Mosque Relocation Turns Wild'. 2012. *The Jakarta Post*, January 28. Accessed July 29, 2013. http://www.thejakartapost.com/news/2012/01/28/protest-against-mosque-relocation-turns-wild.html.

'Pungli Berdalih Uang Jasa di BPPT Kota Medan, "Copot Syafruddin"' [BPPT of Medan involved in collecting 'service charge', 'remove Syafruddin']. 2010. *Harian Orbit*, November 15, 1–2.

Purnama, Teja. 2010. 'Ratusan Warga Tionghoa Bersilaturrahmi denga Ajib-Binsar' [Hundreds of Chinese folks interacted with Ajib-Binsar]. *Harian Global*, March 30. Accessed April 10, 2010. http://www.harian-global.com/index.php?option=com_content&view=article&id=33994:ratusan-warga-tionghoa-bersilaturrahmi-dengan-ajib-binsar&catid=91:jelang-pilkada-medan&Itemid=102.

Putri, Ananda, and Angga Kusuma. 2012. 'Pemekaran Daerah Dinilai Hanya Komoditi Politik' [Administrative fragmentation deemed merely a political commodity]. *Tempo*, April 23. Accessed July 6, 2013. http://www.tempo.co/read/news/2012/04/23/078398898/Pemekaran-Daerah-Dinilai-Hanya-Komoditi-Politik.

'Ratusan Produk Hukum di Indonesia Diskriminatif, Etnis Tionghoa Jadi Korban' [Hundreds of laws in Indonesia are discriminative, ethnic Chinese become victims]. 1999. *Suara Indonesia*, September 14, 14.

Ridin. 2012. 'Tol Medan-Kuala Namu Dimulai' [The construction of Medan-Kuala Namu Toll Road commenced]. *Waspada*, November 7. Accessed August 30, 2013. http://www.waspada.co.id/index.php?option=com_content&view=article&id=266925:tol-medan-kuala-namu-dimulai&catid=14:medan&Itemid=27.

'Rusmin Lawin dan Kepedulian terhadap Musik Tradisional' [Rusmin Lawin and his concern for traditional music]. 2009. *Harian Analisa*, April 6, 10.

Sastrawinata. 2012. 'Bubarkan Perkumpulan Tionghoa' [Disband ethnic Chinese organisations]. *Koran Tempo*, May 15, reproduced in Qiao You (Friends of Overseas Chinese) website. Accessed May 15, 2013. http://www.qiao-you.com/index.php/article/detail/uid/8244.html.

'Schools without Boundaries.' 2004. *Tempo*, August 17–23, 67.

Seo, Yohanes. 2014. 'DPRD Berhentikan Bupati Lembata' [The Regency Parliament suspends Lembata Regent]. *Tempo*, February 27. Accessed June 12, 2014. http://www.tempo.co/read/news/2014/02/27/058557951/DPRD-Berhentikan-Bupati-Lembata.

Setianingsih, Dwi As. 2009. 'Junus Jahja dan Semangan Pembauran' [Junus Jahja and the spirit of integration]. *Kompas*, August 20, 16.

Silalahi, Irfan Azmi. 2011. 'Raih Prestasi di Kampus STBA PIA' [Achievements at STBA PIA campus]. *Tribun Medan*, May 20. Accessed December 5, 2013. http://medan.tribunnews.com/2011/05/20/raih-prestasi-di-kampus-stba-pia.

Soed, Bambang. 2002. 'Duel Diantara Anggota, Apel Pemuda Medan Dibatalkan' [Duel between members, Medan Youth Assembly cancelled]. *Tempo*, October 28. Accessed

August 4, 2013. http://www.tempo.co/read/news/2002/10/28/05832595/Duel-Diantara-Anggota-Apel-Pemuda-Medan-Dibatalkan.

'Sofyan Tan dan Hasyim Raih Suara Terbanyak di Medan' [Sofyan Tan and Hasyim gain highest votes in Medan]. 2014. *Harian Analisa*, April 21. Accessed September 4, 2016. http://harian.analisadaily.com/kota/news/sofyan-tan-dan-hasyim-raih-suara-terbanyak-di-medan/23593/2014/04/21.

'Sofyan Tan-Nelly Dapat Dukungan 19 Parpol' [Sofyan Tan-Nelly supported by 19 political parties]. 2010. *Harian Analisa*, June 2, 6.

'Subei Ji Mianlan Yinhua Baijiaxing Xiehui Wei Babuya Hongzai Zaimin Choude 1.1 Yi Dun' [PSMTI's North Sumatra and Medan branches raised Rp110 million for victims of flash floods in Papua]. 2010. *Xun Bao*, October 30, 11.

Sujatmoko, Bambang, Hutasuhut, Affan Bey, Siregar, Irwan E., and Napitupulu, Sarluhut. 1995. 'Si Bergajul Ringan Membunuh' [Rascals who kill people easily]. *Gatra*, March 18, 27.

'Surat Palsu Muluskan Illegal Logging di Tapsel' [Fake letter facilitates illegal logging in South Tapanuli]. 2009. *ANTARA Sumut*, November 11. Accessed December 14, 2012. http://www.antarasumut.com/surat-palsu-muluskan-illegal-logging-di-tapsel.

'Surabaya Deputy Mayor Tenders Resignation'. 2011. *The Jakarta Post*, February 4. Accessed October 10, 2013. http://www.thejakartapost.com/news/2011/02/04/surabaya-deputy-mayor-tenders-resignation.html.

'The Suramadu Bridge'. 2009. *The Jakarta Post*, June 10. Accessed August 30, 2013. http://www.thejakartapost.com/news/2009/06/10/the-suramadu-bridge.html.

Suwandi. 2010. 'Usut Kasus Pajak PT Indo Palapa' [Investigating PT Indo Palapa case]. *Waspada*, October 15. Accessed October 17, 2010. http://www.waspada.co.id/index.php?option=com_content&view=article&id=149939:usut-kasus-pajak-pt-indo-palapa&catid=14:medan&Itemid=27.

'Sweeping di [Em]erald Garden tidak Benar' [Sweeping at [Em]erald Garden is not true]. 2012. *Tribun Medan*, February 4. Accessed July 29, 2013. http://medan.tribunnews.com/2012/02/04/sweeping-di-merald-garden-tidak-benar.

'Tak Mampu Stop Pungli di BPPT Medan, Copot Wirya Alrahman' [Could not stop unauthorised collections, sack Wirya Alrahman]. 2013 *Batak Pos*, December 5. Accessed December 29, 2013. http://batakpos.co.id/read-3274-tak-mampu-stop-pungli-di-bppt-medan-copot-wirya-alrahman.html.

Tambun, L. T. 2012. 'Jakarta Gubernatorial Candidates Praised for Professionalism, Respect'. *The Jakarta Globe*, October 16. Accessed January 25, 2013. http://www.thejakartaglobe.com/home/jakarta-gubernatorial-candidates-praised-for-professionalism-respect/550442.

'Tangkap Tamin, Mujianto & Benny Basri' ['Arrest Tamin, Mujianto and Benny Basri']. 2011. *Harian Orbit*, December 5. Accessed April 13, 2013. http://www.harianorbit.com/%E2%80%98tangkap-tamin-mujianto-benny-basri%E2%80%98/.

'Tangkap Tamin Sukardi' [Arrest Tamin Sukardi]. 2011. *Harian Orbit*, November 17. Accessed January 11, 2014. http://www.harianorbit.com/tangkap-tamin-sukardi/.

Taufik, Ahmad, Bernarda Rurit, and Cahyo Junaedy. 2003a. 'Ada Tomy di "Tenabang"?' [Was Tomy in 'Tenabang'?]. *Tempo*, March 3–9, 30–31.

Taufik, Ahmad, Bernarda Rurit, and Cahyo Junaedy. 2003b. 'Getting Burned'. *Tempo*, March 4–10, 18–19.

References

213

Taufiq, Fatkhurrohman, and Zed Abidien. 2011. 'Walikota Surabaya Diberhentikan DPRD' [Surabaya's mayor suspended by city council]. *Tempo*, January 31. Accessed October 10, 2013. http://www.tempo.co/read/news/2011/01/31/180310080/Walikota-Surabaya-Diberhentikan-DPRD.

Taufiqurrahman, M., and Tertiani ZB Simanjuntak. 2003. '"Tempo" Protested by Tomy Winata Supporters over Fire Report'. *The Jakarta Post*, March 9. Accessed August 3, 2013. http://www.thejakartapost.com/news/2003/03/08/039tempo039-protested-tomy-winata-supporters-over-fire-report.html.

'Terkait Perubuhan Masjid Raudhatul Islam Polresta Medan Mencari Jalan Terbaik' [Medan police seek best way to settle demolition of Raudhatul Islam Mosque]. 2013. *Suara Nasional News*, January 30. Accessed July 29, 2013. http://www.suaranasionalnews.com/?p=18178.

'Terlecut Kawan Jawa' [Javanese friends were motivated]. 2009. *Jawa Pos*, April 5, 32.

'Tidak Beri Uang Keamanan, Preman Pukul Ibu Rumahtangga' [Refused to pay protection money, *preman* beat up housewife]. 2010. *Harian Orbit*, November 12, 4.

'Tionghoa Serukan DPR Buat UU Diskriminasi Etnis' [Ethnic Chinese call upon House of Representatives to devise anti-discrimination law]. 1999. *Surya*, September 15, 10.

'Tokoh Thionghoa Salut Kepada Sofyan Tan' [Chinese celebrities salute Sofyan Tan]. 2010. *Posmetro Medan*, May 5. Accessed August 10, 2010. http://www.posmetro-medan.com/index.php?open=view&newsid=17735&tit=Berita%20Utama%20-%20Tokoh%20Thionghoa%20Salut%20Kepada%20Sofyan%20Tan%20&.

'Tol Medan-Kuala Namu Siap 2014' [Medan-Kuala Namu Toll Road completed in 2014]. 2011. *Medan Magazine*, November 24. Accessed August 30, 2013. http://www.medanmagazine.com/tol-medan-kuala-namu-siap-2014/.

'Tri Rismaharini, Walikota Perempuan Tanpa Kompromi, Meraih Prestasi Adipura 2011 untuk Surabaya' [Tri Rismaharini, an uncompromising woman mayor, regains Adipura Award 2011 for Surabaya]. 2011. *Kompasiana*, June 11. Accessed October 10, 2013. http://green.kompasiana.com/penghijauan/2011/06/11/tri-rismaharini-walikota-perempuan-tanpa-kompromi-meraih-prestasi-adipura-2011-untuk-surabaya-372128.html.

Trihusodo, Putut, and Tuti Herawati. 1998. 'Solidaritas Arek Surabaya' [Surabayan-style solidarity]. *Gatra*, July 18, 72–73.

Wahyudi, Isvan. 2009. 'Hasyim SE Ak, Kepercayaan dan Kejujuran Modal Utama' [Hasyim, *bachelor of* accountancy, trust and honesty are major capital assets]. *Harian Global*, February 2. Accessed August 10, 2010. http://www.harian-global.com/index.php?option=com_content&view=article&id=1646%3Ahasyim-se-ak-kepercayaan-dan-kejujuran-modal-utama&Itemid=91.

'Wali Kota Disidang Pansus Angket' [Mayor questioned by inquiry committee]. 2011. *Kompas*, January 25. Accessed January 10, 2014. http://bisniskeuangan.kompas.com/read/2011/01/25/0424289/Wali.Kota.Disidang.Pansus.Angket.

'Warga Sari Rejo Iri dengan Benny Basri' [Sari Rejo folks envious of Benny Basri]. 2011. *Harian Sumut Pos*, November 8. Accessed April 13, 2013. http://www.hariansumutpos.com/2011/11/18473/warga-sari-rejo-iri-dengan-benny-basri#axzz2QMHXSl77.

'Warga Tionghoa Harus Manfaatkan Peluang yang Dibuka Gubsu' [Ethnic Chinese should make use of opportunities brought by the governor]. 2004. *Harian Analisa*, February 24, 3.

Waristo. 2010. 'Bantu Pengobatan Gratis 200 Warga Kurang Mampu' [Free medical aid for 200 people in need]. *Harian Global*, July 5, 12.

Widianto, Willy. 2010. 'KPUD Belitung Timur Tidak Netral?' [The General Elections Commission of East Belitung is not neutral?]. *Tribun News*, July 29. Accessed June 12, 2014. http://www.tribunnews.com/election/2010/07/29/kpud-belitung-timur-tidak-netral.

Witular, Rendi A. 2009. 'Special Report: "Made in China" Poses as RI's Pride'. *The Jakarta Post*, June 10. Accessed August 30, 2013. http://www.thejakartapost.com/news/2009/06/10/special-report-made-china039-poses-ri039s-pride.html.

'Wong Cung Sen Tak Bayar Sate, Kampanye PKPI di Medan Ricuh' [Wong Chun Sen did not pay for satay, PKPI's campaign in Medan became chaotic]. 2009. *Ini Medan Bung* [Indonesian-language online news site], March 19. Accessed May 31, 2011. http://www.inimedanbung.com/node/2400.

Wu, Yiguang. 2015. 'Fakanci: Women Rulie Le' [Foreword: We have joined the team]. *Zheng Bao Daily*, February 16, 6.

Xiaoxing. 2010. 'Shizhang Houxuanren Chen Jinyang Qingming Jibai, Chengnuo Geiyi Zhongxiaoqiye Daikuan, Rihou Mianlan Ke Pimei Bincheng' [Mayoral candidate Sofyan Tan participates in *qingming* ceremony, promises loans for SMEs, to develop Medan into a city like Penang]. *Medan Zao Bao*, April 8, M1–M2.

'Xuanmin Bushi Huayi Houxuanren Huang Guicai Lizheng Huayi Piaocang' [Chinese voters do not know Chinese candidates, Sumandi Widjaja tries hard to get Chinese votes]. 2009. *Sin Chew Jit Poh*, March 13. Accessed May 31, 2011. http://search.sinchew-i.com/node/298595.

'Xuanmin Yao Jizhu Saba Nian Qian De Jintian, Buyao Zai Xuan Shoujiupai Yiyuan Houxuanren' [Voters must remember the tragedy 34 years ago, never vote for conservative candidates again]. 2004. *Rela Warta*, March 11, 1.

Xunjian. 2010. 'Kaituo Huaren Canzheng De Jiannan Daolu—Fang Xijia Fushengzhang Huang Hanshan Xiansheng' [Paving the way for political participation of ethnic Chinese—Interview with deputy governor of West Kalimantan Christiandy Sanjaya]. *Medan Zao Bao*, August 31, B3.

'Yazhou Guoji Youhao Xueyuan: Zhongguo Laoshi Wei Huozai Zaimin Song Wenxin' [Asian International Friendship Foreign Language College: Chinese lecturers offer aid to fire victims]. 2011. *Guoji Ribao*, November 9, M4.

Yandan. 2011. 'Jingkong Fashi Yu Aitu Zhong Maosen Sishui Juban Tuokouxiu, Jiangjie Zhonghua Chuantong Jiaoyu Cong *Dizigui* Rushou' [Master Chin Kung and follower Zhong Mao Sen attended talk in Surabaya, suggest starting from *Di Zi Gui* to understand Chinese culture]. *Sishui Chenbao*, January 17, S4.

Yaoyin. 2011. 'Dongzhaowa Qiyejia Cishan Jijinhui Yu Zhonghua Zongshanghui Dongzhaowa Fenhui Lianhe Dongzhaowa Gaodeng Jianchayuan Zai Bonuoluoguo Xian Paringan Cun Xingjian Yizuo 80 Pingmi Yiliaosuo' [East Java Entrepreneur Charitable Foundation and Indonesian Chinese Entrepreneur Association's East Java branch work together with East Java High Prosecution Office in setting up a 80m2 clinic]. *Harian Nusantara*, April 18, 16.

'Yao Zhengque Shiyong Women De Xuanjuquan (1)' [We should exercise our voting rights wisely (1)]. 2004. *Rela Warta*, April 2, 1.

'Yao Zhengque Shiyong Women De Xuanjuquan (2)' [We should exercise our voting rights wisely (2)]. 2004. *Rela Warta*, April 3, 1.

'Yinhua Guanxin Puxuan Lishihui Juban Yihui Houxuanren Zuotanhui' [Chinese Indonesian Council for General Election Concerns held candidates seminar]. 2004. *Harian Nusantara*, March 20, 16.

References 215

'Yinni Lijie Zhengfu Neige You Duoshao Huaren Buzhang' [How many ethnic Chinese ministers in every cabinet of Indonesia]. 2016. *Inhua Daily*, July 28, B7.

Youying. 2010. 'Haixiao Wuqing, Renjian Youqing, Subei Hualian Fadong Wei Mingdawei Haixiao Juankuan Chongjian Jiayuan' [MITSU-PSP raised funds for victims of tsunami in Mentawai]. *Subei Ribao*, November 1, 1.

Yu, Gecang. 2012. 'Yinni *Shidai Bao* Kanwen Yaoqiu Jiesan He Jinzhi Huaren Shetuan' [Indonesian-language paper *Koran Tempo* published reader's letter calling for the disbandment of ethnic Chinese organisations]. *Lianhe Zaobao*, May 21, reproduced in *Singapore Literature News* (2012), 60, 1.

Yunianto, Ibnu. 2004a. 'Murdaya Poo, Pengusaha Etnis Tionghoa yang Jadi Caleg PDIP, Didukung Puluhan Pengusaha, Ingin Hapus Diskriminasi' [Murdaya Poo, ethnic Chinese businessman that has become PDIP's candidate, supported by dozens of businesspeople, wants to eliminate discrimination]. *Jawa Pos*, March 26, 30.

Yunianto, Ibnu. 2004b. 'HM Sundoro Sasongko, Satu-satunya Caleg PKS di Jatim dari Etnis Tionghoa, Sibuk Kampanye, Delegasikan Urusan Perusahaan' [HM Sundoro Sasongko, the only electoral candidate of Chinese descent from PKS, busy with campaigning, delegates business to others]. *Jawa Pos*, March 29, 30.

Yunianto, Ibnu. 2004c. 'Ir Arifli Harbianto, Satu-satunya Calon Anggota DPRD Sby, 2004–2009 dari Etnis Tionghoa: Saya Mewakili Partai, Bukan Mewakili Etnis' [Ir Arifli Harbianto, the only Sby city councillor candidate of Chinese descent, 2004–2009: I represent the party, not the ethnic group]. *Jawa Pos*, April 10, 30.

'Zaoshihui Renchao Ruyong, Chen Jinyang Shende Minxin' [Large crowd at campaign rally, Sofyan Tan gains unprecedented public approval]. 2010. *Hao Bao*, June 16, 1.

Zeng, Qingqing. 2011a. 'Zhongguo Jiangxi Nanchang Daxue Daibiaotuan Fangwen Sishui Guoli Daxue, Guoli Daxue Xiaozhang Muchlas Samani Tichu Jianli Sishui Huawen Jiaoyu Jidi' [Representatives of Nan Chang University in Jiangxi, China, visit State University of Surabaya, State University of Surabaya's rector proposes to establish Chinese-language institution in Surabaya]. *Harian Nusantara*, February 28, 4.

Zeng, Qingqing. 2011b. 'Zhongguo Jiangxi Nanchang Daxue Wenhua Xunyan Zai Sishui ITC Longzhong Juxing, Kejiao Shangzheng Ji Huashe Jingying Deng Gejie Renshi Weilin Guankan Geiyu Gaodu Pingjia' [Cultural performance tour by representatives of China's Nan Chang University held in ITC Surabaya, academics, entrepreneurs, and Chinese community elites turn up and are highly impressed]. *Harian Nusantara*, March 1, 16.

Zhao, Jinchuan. 2007. 'Zhongguo Gongshang Yinhang Yinni Youxian Gongsi Zhengshi Kaiye' [Industrial and Commercial Bank of China (ICBC) (Indonesia) officially starts operation]. Xinhuanet.com, November 12. Accessed September 3, 2013. http://news.xinhuanet.com/fortune/2007-11/13/content_7060622.htm.

'Zhongguo Gongshang Yinhang (Yinni) Youxian Gongsi Mianlan Fenhang Zhengshi Kaiye' [Industrial and Commercial Bank of China (ICBC) (Indonesia)'s Medan branch officially starts operation]. 2010. *Xun Bao*, October 22, 6–7.

Books, Articles, Conference Papers, and Occasional Papers

Abdulbaki, Louay. 2008. 'Democratisation in Indonesia: From Transition to Consolidation'. *Asian Journal of Political Science* 16(2): 151–72.

Aizawa, Nobuhiro. 2011. 'Assimilation, Differentiation, and Depoliticization: Chinese Indonesians and the Ministry of Home Affairs in Suharto's Indonesia'. In *Chinese Indonesians and Regime Change*, edited by Marleen Dieleman, Juliette Koning, and Peter Post, 47–64. Leiden: Brill.

Akira, Suehiro. 2008. 'Business Leaders in Contemporary Thailand: Politics, Business Circles, and the Chinese Community'. In *The Rise of Middle Classes in Southeast Asia*, edited by Shiraishi Takashi and Pasuk Phongpaichit, 124–75. Kyoto: Kyoto University Press.

Allen, Pamela. 2003. 'Contemporary Literature from the Chinese "Diaspora" in Indonesia'. *Asian Ethnicity* 4(3): 383–99.

Ananta, Aris, Evi Nurvidya Arifin, and Bakhtiar. 2008. 'Chinese Indonesians in Indonesia and the Province of Riau Archipelago: A Demographic Analysis'. In *Ethnic Chinese in Contemporary Indonesia*, edited by Leo Suryadinata, 17–47. Singapore: Institute of Southeast Asian Studies.

Ananta, Aris, Evi Nurvidya Arifin, and Leo Suryadinata. 2005. *Emerging Democracy in Indonesia*. Singapore: Institute of Southeast Asian Studies.

Ananta, A, Evi Nurvidya Arifin, M. Sairi Hasbullah, Nur Budi Handayani, and Agus Pramono. 2013. 'Changing Ethnic Composition: Indonesia, 2000–2010'. International Union for the Scientific Study of Population (IUSSP) website. Accessed November 21, 2013. http://www.iussp.org/sites/default/files/event_call_for_papers/IUSSP%20Ethnicity%20Indonesia%20Poster%20Section%20G%202708%202013%20revised.pdf.

Anderson, Benedict. 1998. *The Spectre of Comparisons: Nationalism, Southeast Asia, and the World*. London: Verso.

Anderson, Benedict. R. O'G. 1990. *Language and Power: Exploring Political Cultures in Indonesia*. Ithaca, NY: Cornell University Press.

Anto, J. 2009. *Sofyan Tan, Dokter Penakluk Badai* [Sofyan Tan, the storm-conqueror doctor]. Medan: Solidaritas Tionghoa Center.

Asmarani, Devi. 2006. 'Indonesia Passes Landmark Citizenship Law'. *Indonesian Reports – LOG* 23(29): 1.

Aspinall, Edward. 2005. *Opposing Suharto: Compromise, Resistance, and Regime Change in Indonesia*. Stanford: Stanford University Press.

Aspinall, Edward. 2010. 'The Irony of Success'. *Journal of Democracy* 21(2): 20–34.

Aspinall, Edward. 2011. 'Democratization and Ethnic Politics in Indonesia: Nine Theses'. *Journal of East Asian Studies* 11(2): 289–319.

Aspinall, Edward, and Marcus Mietzner. 2014. 'Indonesian Politics in 2014: Democracy's Close Call'. *Bulletin of Indonesian Economic Studies* 50(3): 347–69.

Aspinall, Edward, and Gerry van Klinken. 2011. 'The State and Illegality in Indonesia'. In *The State and Illegality in Indonesia*, edited by Edward Aspinall and Gerry van Klinken, 1–28. Leiden: KITLV Press.

Aspinall, Edward, Sebastian Dettman, and Eve Warburton. 2011. 'When Religion Trumps Ethnicity: A Regional Election Case Study from Indonesia'. *South East Asia Research* 19(1): 27–58.

Azis, Iwan J. 2003. 'Concepts and Practice of Decentralization: Some Notes on the Case of Indonesia'. Paper presented at the Policy Dialogue on 'Empowering Women in Autonomy and Decentralization Processes', New York, United States, May 29.

Backman, Michael. 2001. 'The New Order Conglomerates'. In *Perspectives on the Chinese Indonesians*, edited by Michael R. Godley and Grayson J. Lloyd, 83–99. Adelaide: Crawford House Publishing.

Barth, Fredrik. 1969. 'Introduction'. In *Ethnic Groups and Boundaries: The Social Organization of Culture Difference*, edited by Fredrik Barth, 9–38. Oslo: Universitetsforlaget.

Beittinger-Lee, Verena. 2009. *(Un)Civil Society and Political Change in Indonesia: A Contested Arena*. Abingdon: Routledge.

Bell, Daniel A. 2004. 'Is Democracy the "Least Bad" System for Minority Groups?' In *Democratisation and Identity: Regimes and Ethnicity in East and Southeast Asia*, edited by Susan J. Henders, 25–42. Lanham, MD: Lexington Books.

Bertrand, Jacques. 2004. *Nationalism and Ethnic Conflict in Indonesia*. Cambridge: Cambridge University Press.

Bertrand, Jacques. 2010. 'Ethnic Conflicts in Indonesia: National Models, Critical Junctures, and the Timing of Violence'. In *Collective Violence in Indonesia*, edited Ashutosh Varshney, 77–98. Boulder, CO: Lynne Rienner Publishers.

Bolt, Paul J. 2000. *China and Southeast Asia's Ethnic Chinese: State and Diaspora in Contemporary Asia*. Westport, CT: Praeger Publishers.

Bourdieu, Pierre. 1984. *Distinction: A Social Critique of the Judgement of Taste*. Translated by Richard Nice. London: Routledge.

Bourdieu, Pierre. 1986. 'The Forms of Capital'. Translated by Richard Nice. Marxists Internet Archive. Accessed June 17, 2014. https://www.marxists.org/reference/subject/philosophy/works/fr/bourdieu-forms-capital.htm.

Bourdieu, Pierre. 1990a. *In Other Words: Essays Towards a Reflexive Sociology*. Translated by Matthew Adamson. Stanford: Stanford University Press.

Bourdieu, Pierre. 1990b. *The Logic of Practice*. Translated by Richard Nice. Cambridge: Polity Press.

Bourdieu, Pierre. 1993. *Sociology in Question*. Translated by Richard Nice. London: SAGE Publications.

Bourdieu, Pierre. 1998. *Practical Reason: On the Theory of Action*. Translated by Randal Johnson and others. Stanford: Stanford University Press.

Bourdieu, Pierre. 2005. 'Habitus'. In *Habitus: A Sense of Place*, edited by Jean Hillier and Emma Rooksby, 43–49. Aldershot, Hants: Ashgate.

Brooks, Karen. 2011. 'Is Indonesia Bound for the BRICs?' *Foreign Affairs* 90(6) (retrieved from EBSCOhost).

Budiman, Arief. 2005. 'Portrait of the Chinese in Post-Soeharto Indonesia'. In *Chinese Indonesians: Remembering, Distorting, Forgetting*, edited by Tim Lindsey and Helen Pausacker, 95–104. Singapore: Institute of Southeast Asian Studies.

Buehler, Michael. 2010. 'Decentralisation and Local Democracy in Indonesia: The Marginalisation of the Public Sphere'. In *Problems of Democratisation in Indonesia: Elections, Institutions and Society*, edited by Edward Aspinall and Marcus Mietzner, 267–85. Singapore: Institute of Southeast Asian Studies.

Buiskool, Dirk A. 2004. 'Medan: A Plantation City on the East Coast of Sumatra 1870–1942' [Planters, the Sultan, Chinese and the Indian]. Paper presented at the first International Urban Conference, Surabaya, Indonesia, August 23–25.

Bush, Robin. 2009. *Nahdlatul Ulama and the Struggle for Power within Islam and Politics in Indonesia*. Singapore: Institute of Southeast Asian Studies.

Cao, Yunhua. 2005. 'Malaixiya Yu Taiguo Huaren Canzheng Moshi Bijiao' [A comparison of patterns of Chinese political participation in Malaysia and Thailand]. In *Bainian Huimou: Mahua Shehui Yu Zhengzhi* [100 years of Malaysian Chinese society and politics: Review and prognosis], edited by Hou Kok Chung, 339–54. Kuala Lumpur: Centre for Malaysian Chinese Studies.

Cao, Yunhua. 2010. 'Mianlan Huaren Yinxiang' [An impression of the overseas Chinese in Medan]. *Dongnanya Yanjiu* [Southeast Asian Studies] 1: 70–78.

Carino, Theresa Chong. 2004. 'The Philippines'. In *Chinese Business in Southeast Asia: Contesting Cultural Explanations, Researching Entrepreneurship*, edited by Edmund Terence Gomez and Hsin-Huang Michael Hsiao, 101–23. Abingdon: Routledge.

Chia, Oai Peng. 2010. 'Chinese Education in Southeast Asia'. In *Routledge Handbook of the Chinese Diaspora*, edited by Chee-Beng Tan, 446–58. Abingdon: Routledge.

Choi, N. 2004. 'Local Elections and Party Politics in Post-*Reformasi* Indonesia: A View from Yogyakarta'. *Contemporary Southeast Asia* 26(2): 280–301.

Choi, N. 2005. 'Local Elections and Democracy in Indonesia: The Case of the Riau Archipelago'. IDSS Working Paper 91. Singapore: Institute of Defence and Strategic Studies, Nanyang Technological University.

Choi, N. 2009. *Democracy and Political Parties in Indonesia: A View from Yogyakarta*. Cologne: Lambert Academic Publishing.

Chong, Wu-Ling. 2015. 'Local Politics and Chinese Indonesian Business in Post-Suharto Era'. *Southeast Asian Studies* 4(3): 487–532.

Chong, Wu Ling. 2016. 'Rethinking the Position of Ethnic Chinese Indonesians'. *Sejarah* 25(2): 96–108.

Chua, Amy. 2003a. 'Markets, Democracy, and Ethnicity'. In *Development and Democracy: New Perspectives on an Old Debate*, edited by Sunder Ramaswamy and Jeffrey W. Cason, 145–67. Hanover, NH: University Press of New England.

Chua, Amy. 2003b. *World on Fire: How Exporting Free-Market Democracy Breeds Ethnic Hatred and Global Instability*. London: William Heinemann.

Chua, Christian. 2005. 'Business as Usual: Chinese Conglomerates in Post-Soeharto Indonesia'. In *Democratisation in Indonesia after the Fall of Suharto*, edited by Ingrid Wessel, 67–90. Berlin: Logos Verlag Berlin.

Chua, Christian. 2008. *Chinese Big Business in Indonesia: The State of Capital*. Abingdon: Routledge.

Chua, Christian. 2009. 'Capitalist Consolidation, Consolidated Capitalists: Indonesia's Conglomerates between Authoritarianism and Democracy'. In *Democratization in Post-Suharto Indonesia*, edited by Marco Bünte and Andreas Ufen, 201–25. Abingdon: Routledge.

Clear, Annette. 2005. 'Politics: From Endurance to Evolution'. In *Indonesia: The Great Transition*, edited by John Bresnan, 137–87. Lanham, MD: Rowman & Littlefield.

Comber, Leon. 2009a. *13 May 1969: The Darkest Day in Malaysian History*. Singapore: Marshall Cavendish.

Comber, Leon. 2009b. *The Triads: Chinese Secret Societies in 1950s Malaya & Singapore*. Singapore: Talisman.

Coppel, Charles A. 1976. 'Patterns of Chinese Political Activity in Indonesia'. In *The Chinese in Indonesia: Five Essays*, edited by J. A. C. Mackie, 19–76. Melbourne: Thomas Nelson.

Coppel, Charles A. 1983. *Indonesian Chinese in Crisis*. Kuala Lumpur: Oxford University Press.

Coppel, Charles A. 2002. *Studying Ethnic Chinese in Indonesia*. Singapore: Singapore Society of Asian Studies.

Coppel, Charles A. 2008. 'Anti-Chinese Violence in Indonesia after Soeharto'. In *Ethnic Chinese in Contemporary Indonesia*, edited by Leo Suryadinata, 117–36. Singapore: Institute of Southeast Asian Studies.

Cordell, Karl. 1999. *Ethnicity and Democratisation in the New Europe*. London: Routledge.

Cribb, Robert. 1991. *Gangsters and Revolutionaries: The Jakarta People's Militia and the Indonesian Revolution, 1945–1949*. Sydney: Allen and Unwin.

Cribb, Robert, and Charles A. Coppel. 2009. 'A Genocide that Never Was: Explaining the Myth of Anti-Chinese Massacres in Indonesia, 1965–66'. *Journal of Genocide Research* 11(4): 447–65.

Croissant, Aurel, Paul Chambers, and Philip Völkel. 2011. 'Democracy, the Military and Security Sector Governance in Indonesia, the Philippines and Thailand'. In *The Crisis of Democratic Governance in Southeast Asia*, edited by Aurel Croissant and Marco Bünte, 190–208. Basingstoke, Hampshire: Palgrave Macmillan.

Crouch, Harold. 2010. *Political Reform in Indonesia after Soeharto*. Singapore: Institute of Southeast Asian Studies.

Dahana, A. 2004. 'Pri-and Non-Pri Relations in the Reform Era: A Pribumi Perspective'. In *Ethnic Relations and Nation-Building in Southeast Asia: The Case of the Ethnic Chinese*, edited by Leo Suryadinata, 45–65. Singapore: Institute of Southeast Asian Studies.

Davidson, Jamie S. 2009a. 'Dilemmas of Democratic Consolidation in Indonesia'. *The Pacific Review* 22(3): 293–310.

Davidson, Jamie S. 2009b. *From Rebellion to Riots: Collective Violence on Indonesian Borneo*. Singapore: NUS Press.

Davidson, Jamie S., and David Henley, eds. 2007. *The Revival of Tradition in Indonesian Politics: The Deployment of Adat from Colonialism to Indigenism*. Abingdon: Routledge.

Dawis, Aimee. 2009. *The Chinese of Indonesia and Their Search for Identity: The Relationship between Collective Memory and the Media*. Amherst, NY: Cambria Press.

Dawis, Aimee. 2010. 'Orang Tionghoa Berorganisasi: Yang Kini Lanjutan dari Masa Lalu?' [Chinese getting themselves organised: A continuation of the past?]. In *Setelah Air Mata Kering: Masyarakat Tionghoa Pasca Peristiwa Mei 1998* [After the tears have dried up: Chinese community after May 1998 riots], edited by I. Wibowo and Thung Ju Lan, 49–74. Jakarta: Kompas.

Dhillon, Karminder Singh. 2009. *Malaysian Foreign Policy in the Mahathir Era 1981–2003: Dilemmas of Development*. Singapore: NUS Press.

Diamond, Larry. 1999. *Developing Democracy: Toward Consolidation*. Baltimore: The Johns Hopkins University Press.

Dick, Howard W. 2003. *Surabaya, City of Work: A Socioeconomic History, 1900–2000*. Singapore: Singapore University Press.

Dick, Howard, and Jeremy Mulholland. 2011. 'The State as Marketplace: Slush Funds and Intra-Elite Rivalry'. In *The State and Illegality in Indonesia*, edited by Edward Aspinall and Gerry van Klinken, 65–85. Leiden: KITLV Press.

Dieleman, Marleen, Juliette Koning, and Peter Post, eds. 2011. *Chinese Indonesians and Regime Change*. Leiden: Brill.

Elleman, Bruce A. 2001. *Modern Chinese Warfare, 1795–1989*. London: Routledge.

Erb, Maribeth, and Priyambudi Sulistiyanto, eds. 2009. *Deepening Democracy in Indonesia? Direct Elections for Local Leaders (Pilkada)*. Singapore: Institute of Southeast Asian Studies.

Esherick, Joseph W. 1987. *The Origins of the Boxer Uprising*. Berkeley: University of California Press.

Fasseur, C. 1994. 'Cornerstone and Stumbling Block: Racial Classification and the Late Colonial State in Indonesia'. In *The Late Colonial State in Indonesia: Political and Economic Foundations of the Netherlands Indies 1880–1942*, edited by Robert Cribb, 31–56. Leiden: KITLV Press.

Firman, Tommy. 2009. 'Decentralization Reform and Local-Government Proliferation in Indonesia: Towards a Fragmentation of Regional Development'. *Review of Urban & Regional Development Studies* 21(2/3): 143–57.

Foley, Michael W., and Bob Edwards. 1996. 'The Paradox of Civil Society'. *Journal of Democracy* 7(3): 38–52.

Fossati, Diego. 2016. 'The State of Local Politics in Indonesia: Survey Evidence from Three Cities'. *Trends in Southeast Asia* 5. Singapore: ISEAS – Yusof Ishak Institute.

Freedman, Amy. 2003. 'Political Institutions and Ethnic Chinese Identity in Indonesia'. *Asian Ethnicity* 4(3): 439–52.

Freedman, Amy, and Robert Tiburzi. 2012. 'Progress and Caution: Indonesia's Democracy'. *Asian Affairs: An American Review* 39: 131–56.

Gazali, Effendi, Dedy Nur Hidayat, and Victor Menayang. 2009. 'Political Communication in Indonesia: Media Performance in Three Eras'. In *Political Communication in Asia*, edited by Lars Willnat and Annette Aw, 112–34. New York: Routledge.

Giblin, Susan. 2003. 'Overcoming Stereotypes? Chinese Indonesian Civil Society Groups in Post-Suharto Indonesia'. *Asian Ethnicity* 4(3): 353–68.

Giddens, Anthony. 1984. *The Constitution of Society*. Cambridge: Polity Press.

Giddens, Anthony. 1989. *Sociology*. Cambridge: Polity Press.

Ginsburg, Tom. 2004. 'Book Review: Democracy, Markets and Doomsaying: Is Ethnic Conflict Inevitable?' *Berkeley Journal of International Law* 22(2): 310–35.

Godley, Michael R. 1989. 'The Sojourners: Returned Overseas Chinese in the People's Republic of China'. *Pacific Affairs* 62(3): 330–52.

Goh, Lam Kiong. 2002. 'The Evolution of the Secret Societies in Singapore: The Law Enforcement Perspective'. In *Chinese Triads: Perspectives on Histories, Identities, and Spheres of Impact*, edited by Cheryl-Ann Low, Jaime Koh, and Irene Lim, 49–53. Singapore: Singapore History Museum.

Gomez, Edmund Terence. 2008. 'Introduction: Modernization, Democracy, Equity and Identity'. In *The State, Development and Identity in Multi-Ethnic Societies: Ethnicity, Equity and The Nation*, edited by Nicholas Tarling and Edmund Terence Gomez, 1–17. Abingdon: Routledge.

Govaars, Ming. 2005. *Dutch Colonial Education: The Chinese Experience in Indonesia, 1900–1942*. Singapore: Chinese Heritage Centre.

Hadiluwih, RM. H. Subanindyo. 1994. *Studi Tentang Masalah Tionghoa di Indonesia (Studi Kasus in Medan)* [A study on the Chinese problem in Indonesia (a case study in Medan)]. Medan: Dhian-Doddy Press.

Hadiz, Vedi R. 2000. 'Retrieving the Past for the Future? Indonesia and the New Order Legacy'. *Southeast Asian Journal of Social Science* 28(2): 10–33.

Hadiz, Vedi R. 2003. 'Power and Politics in North Sumatra: The Uncompleted *Reformasi*'. In *Local Power and Politics in Indonesia: Decentralisation and Democratisation*, edited by Edward Aspinall and Greg Fealy, 119–31. Singapore: Institute of Southeast Asian Studies.

Hadiz, Vedi R. 2004. 'Indonesian Local Party Politics: A Site of Resistance to Neoliberal Reform'. *Critical Asian Studies* 36(4): 615–36.

Hadiz, Vedi R. 2005a. 'Reorganizing Political Power in Indonesia: A Reconsideration of So-Called "Democratic Transitions"'. In *Regionalism in Post-Suharto Indonesia*, edited by Maribeth Erb, Priyambudi Sulisttiyanto, and Carole Faucher, 36–53. Abingdon: RoutledgeCurzon.

Hadiz, Vedi R. 2005b. 'Understanding "Democratic Transitions": Some Insights from Gus Dur's Brief Presidency in Indonesia'. In *After the Crisis: Hegemony,*

Technocracy and Governance in Southeast Asia, edited by Takashi Shiraishi and Patricio N. Abinales, 119–33. Kyoto: Kyoto University Press.

Hadiz, Vedi R. 2010. *Localising Power in Post-Authoritarian Indonesia: A Southeast Asia Perspective.* Stanford: Stanford University Press.

Hadiz, Vedi R., and Richard Robison. 2005. 'Neo-liberal Reforms and Illiberal Consolidations: The Indonesian Paradox'. *Journal of Development Studies* 41(2): 220–41.

Harahap, Husnul Isa. 2010. 'Analisis Peningkatan Suara Partai Demokrat di Sumatera Utara' [An analysis of Democratic Party's vote increase in North Sumatra]. *POLITEIA* 2(2): 76–87.

Hau, Caroline S. 2014. *The Chinese Question: Ethnicity, Nation, and Region in and Beyond the Philippines.* Singapore: NUS Press.

Haynes, Jeff. 2001. 'Introduction: The "Third World" and the Third Wave of Democracy'. In *Democracy and Political Change in the 'Third World',* edited by Jeff Haynes, 1–20. London: Routledge.

Heidhues, Mary F. Somers. 1974. *Southeast Asia's Chinese Minorities.* Hawthorn, Victoria: Longman.

Heidhues, Mary Somers. 1993. 'Chinese Organizations in West Borneo and Bangka: Kongsis and *Hui*'. In *"Secret Societies" Reconsidered: Perspectives on the Social History of Modern South China and Southeast Asia,* edited by David Ownby and Mary Somers Heidhues, 68–88. New York: M. E. Sharpe.

Heidhues, Mary Somers. 2006. 'Chinese Voluntary and Involuntary Associations in Indonesia'. In *Voluntary Organizations in the Chinese Diaspora,* edited by Khun Eng Kuah-Pearce and Evelyn Du-Dehart, 77–83. Hong Kong: Hong Kong University Press.

Hellmann, Olli. 2011. *Political Parties and Electoral Strategy: The Development of Party Organization in East Asia.* Basingstoke, Hampshire: Palgrave Macmillan.

Henley, David, and Jamie S. Davidson. 2007. 'Introduction: Radical Conservatism – the Protean Politics of Adat'. In *The Revival of Tradition in Indonesian Politics: The Deployment of Adat from Colonialism to Indigenism,* edited by Jamie S. Davidson and David Henley, 1–49. Abingdon: Routledge.

Heryanto, Ariel. 1999. 'Rape, Race, and Reporting'. In *Reformasi: Crisis and Change in Indonesia,* edited by Arief Budiman, Barbara Hatley, and Damien Kingsbury, 299–334. Clayton, Victoria: Monash Asia Institute, Monash University.

Heryanto, Ariel, and Vedi R. Hadiz. 2005. 'Post-Authoritarian Indonesia: A Comparative Southeast Asian Perspective'. *Critical Asian Studies* 37(2): 251–75.

Hidayat, Syarif. 2009. 'Pilkada, Money Politics and the Dangers of "Informal Governance" Practices'. In *Deepening Democracy in Indonesia? Direct Elections for Local Leaders (Pilkada),* edited by Maribeth Erb and Priyambudi Sulistiyanto, 125–46. Singapore: Institute of Southeast Asian Studies.

Hidayat, Syarif, and Gerry van Klinken. 2009. 'Provincial Business and Politics'. In *State of Authority: The State in Society in Indonesia,* edited by Gerry van Klinken and Joshua Barker, 149–61. Ithaca, NY: Cornell Southeast Asian Program Publications.

Hoadley, Mason C. 1988. 'Javanese, Peranakan, and Chinese Elites in Cirebon: Changing Ethnic Boundaries'. *The Journal of Asian Studies* 47(3): 503–18.

Hofman, Bert, and Kai Kaiser. 2004. 'The Making of the "Big Bang" and Its Aftermath: A Political Economy Perspective'. In *Reforming Intergovernmental Fiscal Relations and the Rebuilding of Indonesia: The 'Big Bang' Program and Its Economic*

Consequences, edited by James Alm, Jorge Martinez-Vazquez, and Sri Mulyani Indrawati, 15–46. Cheltenham: Edward Elgar.

Hofman, Bert, and Kai Kaiser. 2006. 'Decentralization, Democratic Transition, and Local Governance in Indonesia'. In *Decentralization and Local Governance in Developing Countries: A Comparative Perspective*, edited by Pranab Bardhan and Dilip Mookherjee, 81–124. Cambridge, MA: MIT Press.

Honna, Jun. 2011. 'Orchestrating Transnational Crime: Security Sector Politics as a Trojan Horse for Anti-reformists'. In *The State and Illegality in Indonesia*, edited by Edward Aspinall and Gerry van Klinken, 261–79. Leiden: KITLV Press.

Hoon, Chang-Yau. 2006a. '"A Hundred Flowers Bloom": The Re-emergence of the Chinese Press in Post-Suharto Indonesia'. In *Media and the Chinese Diaspora: Community, Communications and Commerce*, edited by Wanning Sun, 91–118. Abingdon: Routledge.

Hoon, Chang-Yau. 2006b. 'Assimilation, Multiculturalism, Hybridity: The Dilemmas of the Ethnic Chinese in Post-Suharto Indonesia'. *Asian Ethnicity* 7(2): 149–66.

Hoon, Chang-Yau. 2008. *Chinese Identity in Post-Suharto Indonesia: Culture, Politics and Media*. Brighton: Sussex Academic Press.

Huang, Kunzhang. 2000. *Fengyu Cangsang Wushi Nian: Dierci Shijie Dazhan Hou Yinni Huaqiao Huaren Shehui De Bianhua* [Fifty years of trials and hardships: Changes of Indonesian Chinese community after the Second World War]. Hong Kong: Danching Publications.

Huang, Kunzhang. 2005. 'Cong *Longyang Ribao* De Tingkan Kan Yinni Huawen Baoye De Cangsang' [Ceasing the publication of *Harian Naga Surya*: The changing phases of Chinese-language dailies in Indonesia]. MediaChina.net, November 28. Accessed March 17, 2011. http://academic.mediachina.net/article.php?id=3200.

Hui, Yew-Foong. 2011. *Strangers at Home: History and Subjectivity among the Chinese Communities of West Kalimantan, Indonesia*. Leiden: Brill.

Human Rights Watch. 2010. *"Unkept Promise": Failure to End Military Business Activity in Indonesia*. New York: Human Rights Watch.

Indrayana, Denny. 2008. *Indonesian Constitutional Reform 1999–2002: An Evaluation of Constitution-Making in Transition*. Jakarta: Kompas Book Publishing.

Jacobsen, Michael. 2007. 'Living in the Shadow of Mainland China: On Delineating Social and Political Constraints among Southeast Asian Chinese Entrepreneurs'. *The Copenhagen Journal of Asian Studies* 25: 28–49.

Jen, Yu-wen. 1973. *The Taiping Revolutionary Movement*. New Haven, CT: Yale University Press.

Jian, Boxiang. 2009. 'Huashe Lingxiu, Mianlan Xianzhe, Subei Gongchen, Hexie Dashi: Zhongguo Laoshi Yanzhong De Huang Yinhua Xiansheng' [Chinese community leader, Medan's celebrity, North Sumatra's hero, ambassador of harmony: Mr. Indra Wahidin in the eye of a Chinese teacher]. In *Jianqiang Fenqi, Bainian Fuxing – Yinni Huaren Wenhua Jiaoyu Shihua Zhisi* [Hundred years of Chinese cultural renaissance: The history of Chinese culture and education in Indonesia, Vol. 4], edited by Li Zhuohui, 187–213. Jakarta: Mandarin Book Store.

Kammen, Douglas. 2012. 'Where Are They Now? The Careers of Army Officers Who Served in East Timor, 1998–99'. *Indonesia* 94: 111–30.

Kammen, Douglas, and Katharine McGregor, eds. 2012. *The Contours of Mass Violence in Indonesia, 1965–68*. Singapore: NUS Press, 2012.

King, Dwight Y. 2000. 'The 1999 Electoral Reforms in Indonesia: Debate, Design and Implementation'. *Southeast Asian Journal of Social Science* 28(2): 89–110.

References

King, Phil. 2003. 'Putting the (Para)Military Back into Politics'. *Inside Indonesia*, January–March. Accessed August 3, 2013. http://www.insideindonesia.org/feature-editions/putting-the-para-military-back-into-politics.

Kua, Kia Soong. 2007. *May 13: Declassified Documents on the Malaysian Riots of 1969.* Kuala Lumpur: Suaram Komunikasi.

Kwee, Tek Hoay. 1969. *The Origins of the Modern Chinese Movement in Indonesia.* Translated and edited by Lea E. Williams. Ithaca, NY: Cornell Modern Indonesia Project.

Lane, Max. 2015. 'Who Will Be Indonesian President in 2014?' In *Watching the Indonesian Elections 2014*, edited by Ulla Fionna and Hui Yew-Foong, 29–37. Singapore: ISEAS–Yusof Ishak Institute.

Lee, John. 2013. 'China's Economic Engagement with Southeast Asia: Indonesia'. *Trends in Southeast Asia* 03. Singapore: Institute of Southeast Asian Studies.

Lee, Kam Hing, and Heng Pek Koon. 2000. 'The Chinese in the Malaysian Political System'. In *The Chinese in Malaysia*, edited by Lee Kam Heng and Tan Chee-Beng, 194–227. Shah Alam, Selangor: Oxford University Press.

Lembong, Eddie. 2008. 'Indonesian Government Policies and the Ethnic Chinese: Some Recent Developments'. In *Ethnic Chinese in Contemporary Indonesia*, edited by Leo Suryadinata, 48–56. Singapore: Institute of Southeast Asian Studies.

Leong, Kai Hin. 2006. 'Malaysian Chinese Businesses in an Era of Globalization'. In *Southeast Asia's Chinese Businesses in an Era of Globalization: Coping with the Rise of China*, edited by Leo Suryadinata, 205–20. Singapore: Institute of Southeast Asian Studies.

Lev, Daniel S. 2011. *No Concessions: The Life of Yap Thiam Hien; Indonesian Human Rights Lawyer.* Seattle: University of Washington Press.

Li, Zhuohui. 2004a. *Minzhu Gaige Shidai Zhengzhi Fengyun – Yinni Cong 1999 Nian Zouxiang 2004 Nian Daxuan Zhenglun Wenji* [The political development of the Democratic *Reformasi* era: Political commentaries on 1999 and 2004 elections in Indonesia]. Jakarta: Mandarin Book Store.

Li, Zhuohui. 2004b. *Zili Gengsheng, Mianxiang Yazhou, Zhenxing Jingji – Yinni Minzhu Gaige Shidai Jingji Pian* [Self-independence, looking towards Asia, economic revitalisation: The economy of Indonesia in Reformasi era]. Jakarta: Mandarin Book Store.

Li, Zhuohui. 2007. *Yinhua Canzheng Yu Guojia Jianshe* [The political participation of Chinese Indonesians and nation building]. Jakarta: Mandarin Book Store.

Li, Zhuohui. 2008. *Nijing Fenjin • Baizhe Bunao* [Struggling against adversity]. Jakarta: Mandarin Book Store.

Li, Zhuohui. 2010. *Gaige Jiliu • Yuhui Maijin* [Keep moving forward for reformation]. Jakarta: Mandarin Book Store.

Liew, Leong H. 2003. 'Ethnicity and class in Malaysia'. In *Ethnicity in Asia*, edited by Colin Mackerras, 88–100. London: RoutledgeCurzon.

Lim, Joo Hock. 1967. 'Chinese female immigration into the Straits Settlements, 1860–1901'. *Journal of the South Seas Society* 22: 58–110.

Lim, Linda Y. C. 1983. 'Chinese economic activity in Southeast Asia: An introductory review'. In *The Chinese in Southeast Asia, Volume 1: Ethnicity and Economic Activity*, edited by Linda Y. C. Lim and L. A. Peter Gosling, 1–29. Singapore: Maruzen Asia.

Lindsay, Jennifer. 2007. 'The Performance Factor in Indonesian Elections'. In *Elections as Popular Culture in Asia*, edited by Chua Beng Huat, 55–71. Abingdon: Routledge.

Lindsey, Tim. 2001. 'The Criminal State: Premanisme and the New Indonesia'. In *Indonesia Today: Challenges of History*, edited by Grayson Lloyd and Shannon L. Smith, 283–97. Singapore: Institute of Southeast Asian Studies.

Lintner, Bertil. 2002. *Blood Brothers: Crime, Business and Politics in Asia*. Crows Nest, NSW: Allen & Unwin.

Lipset, Seymour Martin, and Jason M. Lakin. 2004. *The Democratic Century*. Norman: University of Oklahoma Press.

Liu, Hong. 2011. *China and the Shaping of Indonesia, 1949–1965*. Singapore: NUS Press.

Lohanda, Mona. 1996. *The Kapitan Cina of Batavia 1837–1942*. Jakarta: Penerbit Djambatan.

Lohanda, Mona. 2002. *Growing Pains: The Chinese and the Dutch in Colonial Java, 1890–1942*. Jakarta: Yayasan Cipta Loka Caraka.

Lubis, M. Rajab. 1995. *Pribumi di Mata Orang Cina* [Indigenous people in the eyes of Chinese]. Medan: PT Pustaka Widyasarana.

Lucas, Anton. 1991. *One Soul One Struggle: Region and Revolution in Indonesia*. Sydney: Allen and Unwin.

Mabbett, Hugh, and Ping-ching Mabbett. 1972. 'The Chinese Community in Indonesia'. In *The Chinese in Indonesia, the Philippines and Malaysia*, edited by Charles A. Coppel, Hugh Mabbett, and Ping-ching Mabbett, 3–15. London: Minority Rights Group.

Mackie, Jamie. 1999. 'Tackling "the Chinese Problem"'. In *Post-Soeharto Indonesia: Renewal or Chaos*, edited by Geoff Forrester, 187–97. Singapore: Institute of Southeast Asian Studies.

Mackie, Jamie. 2003. 'Pre-1997 Sino-Indonesian Conglomerates, Compared with Those of Other ASEAN Countries'. In *Ethnic Business: Chinese Capitalism in Southeast Asia*, edited by Jomo K. S. and Brian C. Folks, 105–28. London: RoutledgeCurzon.

Mackie, J. A. C. 1976. 'Anti-Chinese Outbreaks in Indonesia, 1959–68'. In *The Chinese in Indonesia: Five Essays*, edited by J. A. C. Mackie, 77–138. Melbourne: Thomas Nelson.

Mak, Lau Fong. 1981. *The Sociology of Secret Societies: A Study of Chinese Secret Societies in Singapore and Peninsular Malaysia*. Kuala Lumpur: Oxford University Press.

Malley, Michael S. 2003. 'New Rules, Old Structures and the Limits of Democratic Decentralisation'. In *Local Power and Politics in Indonesia: Decentralisation & Democratisation*, edited by Edward Aspinall and Greg Fealy, 102–16. Singapore: Institute of Southeast Asian Studies.

McCargo, Duncan, and Ukrist Pathmanand. 2005. *The Thaksinization of Thailand*. Copenhagen: NIAS Press.

McVey, Ruth. 1968. 'Indonesian Communism and China'. In *China in Crisis, Volume Two: China's Policies in Asia and America's Alternatives*, edited by Tang Tsou, 357–94. Chicago: University of Chicago Press.

McVey, Ruth. 2003. 'Nation versus State in Indonesia'. In *Autonomy and Disintegration in Indonesia*, edited by Damien Kingsbury and Harry Aveling, 11–27. London: RoutledgeCurzon.

Mietzner, Marcus. 2007. 'Party Financing in Post-Soeharto Indonesia: Between State Subsidies and Political Corruption'. *Contemporary Southeast Asia* 29(2): 238–63.

Mietzner, Marcus. 2008. 'Soldiers, Parties and Bureaucrats: Illicit Fund-Raising in Contemporary Indonesia'. *South East Asia Research* 16(2): 225–54.

Mietzner, Marcus. [2009]. 'Indonesia and the Pitfalls of Low-Quality Democracy: A Case Study of the Gubernatorial Elections in North Sulawesi'. In *Democratization in Post-Suharto Indonesia,* edited by Marco Bünte and Andreas Ufen, 124–49. Abingdon: Routledge.

Mietzner, Marcus. 2012. 'Indonesia's Democratic Stagnation: Anti-reformist Elites and Resilient Civil Society'. *Democratization* 19(2): 209–29.

Nagata, Judith. 2003. 'Local and Transnational Initiatives Towards Improving Chinese-Indigenous Relations in Post-Suharto Indonesia: The Role of the Voluntary Sector'. *Asian Ethnicity* 4(3): 369–81.

Oetomo, Dedé. 2001 *Memberi Suara pada yang Bisu* [Giving voice to the voiceless]. Yogyakarta: Pustaka Marwa Yogyakarta.

Ong, Susy. 2008. 'Ethnic Chinese Religions: Some Recent Developments'. In *Ethnic Chinese in Contemporary Indonesia,* edited by Leo Suryadinata, 97–116. Singapore: Institute of Southeast Asian Studies.

Pandiangan, Andreas. 2003. 'Chinese Press after the New Order: Caught Between the Continuity of Idealism and the Logic of the Market'. *Asian Ethnicity* 4(3): 409–13.

Panggabean, Samsu Rizal, and Benjamin Smith. 2011. 'Explaining Anti-Chinese Riots in Late 20th Century Indonesia'. *World Development* 39(2): 231–42.

Pausacker, Helen. 2005. '*Peranakan* Chinese and Wayang in Java'. In *Chinese Indonesians: Remembering, Distorting, Forgetting,* edited by Tim Lindsey and Helen Pausacker, 185–208. Singapore: Institute of Southeast Asian Studies.

Phang, Hooi Eng. 2000. 'The Economic Role of the Chinese in Malaysia'. In *The Chinese in Malaysia,* edited by Lee Kam Hing and Tan Chee-Beng, 94–122. Shah Alam, Selangor: Oxford University Press.

Przeworski, Adam, Michael Alvarez, José Antonio Cheibub, and Fernando Limongi. 1996. 'What Makes Democracies Endure?' *Journal of Democracy* 7(1): 39–55.

Purcell, Victor. 1965. *The Chinese in Southeast Asia.* London: Oxford University Press.

Purdey, Jemma. 2005. 'Anti-Chinese Violence and Transitions in Indonesia: June 1998–October 1999'. In *Chinese Indonesians: Remembering, Distorting, Forgetting,* edited by Tim Lindsey and Helen Pausacker, 14–40. Singapore: Institute of Southeast Asian Studies.

Purdey, Jemma. 2006. *Anti-Chinese Violence in Indonesia, 1996–1999.* Singapore: Singapore University Press.

Purdey, Jemma. 2009. 'Review Essay: *Chinese Big Business in Indonesia: The State of Capital,* by C. Chua (2008). London: Routledge; & *Chinese Identity in Post-Suharto Indonesia: Culture, Politics and Media,* by C. Y. Hoon (2008). Eastbourne: Sussex Academic Press'. *Indonesia* 87: 111–15.

Putnam, Robert D. 1993. *Making Democracy Work: Civic Traditions in Modern Italy.* Princeton: Princeton University Press.

Putnam, Robert D. 1995. 'Bowling Alone: America's Declining Social Capital'. *Journal of Democracy* 6(1): 65–78.

Rajan, Nalini. 2002. *Democracy and the Limits of Minority Rights.* New Delhi: Sage Publications.

Rasyid, M. Ryaas. 2003. 'Regional Autonomy and Local Politics in Indonesia'. In *Local Power and Politics in Indonesia: Decentralisation and Democratisation,* edited by Edward Aspinall and Greg Fealy, 63–71. Singapore: Institute of Southeast Asian Studies.

Reid, Anthony. 1992. 'Economic and Social Change, c. 1400–1800'. In *The Cambridge History of Southeast Asia Volume One: From Early Times to c. 1800,* edited by Nicholas Tarling, 460–507. Cambridge: Cambridge University Press.

Reid, Anthony. 1993. *Southeast Asia in the Age of Commerce 1450–1680, Volume Two: Expansion and Crisis.* New Haven, CT: Yale University Press.

Ricklefs, M. C. 2008. *A History of Modern Indonesia since c. 1200*. Basingstoke, Hampshire: Palgrave Macmillan.

Riggs, Fred W. 1964. *Administration in Developing Countries: The Theory of Prismatic Society*. Boston: Houghton Mifflin Company.

Riggs, Fred W. 1966. *Thailand: The Modernization of a Bureaucratic Polity*. Honolulu: East-West Center Press.

Rinakit, Sukardi. 2005. 'Indonesian Regional Elections in Praxis'. *IDSS Commentaries*, September 27. Singapore: Institute of Defence and Strategic Studies, Nanyang Technological University.

Robison, Richard. 1986. *Indonesia: The Rise of Capital*. North Sydney: Allen & Unwin.

Robison, Richard. 1992. 'Industrialization and the Economic and Political Development of Capital: The Case of Indonesia'. In *Southeast Asian Capitalists*, edited by Ruth McVey, 65–88. Ithaca, NY: Cornell University Southeast Asia Program.

Rush, James R. 2007. *Opium to Java: Revenue Farming and Chinese Enterprise in Colonial Indonesia 1860–1910*. Singapore: Equinox Publishing.

Ryter, Loren. 2000. 'A Tale of Two Cities'. *Inside Indonesia*, July–September, 19.

Ryter, Loren. 2001. 'Pemuda Pancasila: The Last Loyalist Free Men of Suharto's Order?' In *Violence and the State in Suharto's Indonesia*, edited by Benedict R. O'G. Anderson, 124–55. Ithaca, NY: Cornell Southeast Asia Program.

Ryter, Loren. 2005. 'Reformasi Gangsters'. *Inside Indonesia*, April–June, 22–23.

Schulte Nordholt, Henk. 2002. 'A Genealogy of Violence'. In *Roots of Violence in Indonesia: Contemporary Violence in Historical Perspective*, edited by Freek Colombijn and J. Thomas Lindblad, 33–61. Leiden: KITLV Press.

Schulte Nordholt, Henk, and Gerry van Klinken. 2007. 'Introduction'. In *Renegotiating Boundaries: Local Politics in Post-Suharto Indonesia*, edited by Henk Schulte Nordholt and Gerry van Klinken, 1–29. Leiden: KITLV Press.

Sen, Krishna. 2011. 'Introduction: Re-forming Media in Indonesia's Transition to Democracy'. In *Politics and the Media in Twenty-First Century Indonesia: Decade of Democracy*, edited by Krishna Sen and David T. Hill, 1–12. Abingdon: Routledge.

Setijadi, Charlotte. 2017. 'Ahok's Downfall and the Rise of Islamist Populism in Indonesia'. *ISEAS Perspectives* 38, June 8. Singapore: Iseas-Yusof Ishak Institute.

Setiono, Benny G. 2003. *Tionghoa dalam Pusaran Politik* [The Chinese in the political vortex]. Jakarta: Elkasa.

Setyautama, Sam. 2008. *Tokoh-tokoh Etnis Tionghoa Di Indonesia* [Ethnic Chinese celebrities in Indonesia]. Jakarta: Kepustakaan Populer Gramedia (KPG).

Sherlock, Stephen. 2004. *The 2004 Indonesian Elections: How the System Works and What the Parties Stand for*. Canberra: Centre for Democratic Institutions. Accessed November 20, 2012. http://www.cdi.anu.edu.au/_research/2004-05/D_P/Sherlock_Indonesian_Election04.pdf.

Sherlock, Stephen. 2010. 'The Parliament in Indonesia's Decade of Democracy: People's Forum or Chamber of Cronies?' In *Problems of Democratisation in Indonesia: Elections, Institutions and Society*, edited by Edward Aspinall and Marcus Mietzner, 160–78. Singapore: Institute of Southeast Asian Studies.

Shiraishi, Saya, and Shiraishi, Takashi. 1993. 'The Japanese in Colonial Southeast Asia: An Overview'. In *The Japanese in Colonial Southeast Asia*, edited by Takashi Shiraishi and Saya S. Shiraishi, 5–20. Ithaca, NY: Cornell Southeast Asia Program.

Shiraishi, Takashi. 1997. 'Anti-Sinicism in Java's New Order'. In *Essential Outsider: Chinese and Jews in the Modern Transformation of Southeast Asia and Central Europe,* edited by Daniel Chirot and Anthony Reid, 187–207. Seattle: University of Washington Press.

Shiraishi, Takashi. 1994. 'Dukuh: A Golkar Village'. In *Approaching Suharto's Indonesia from the Margins*, edited by Takashi Shiraishi, 75–99. Ithaca, NY: Cornell Southeast Asia Program.

Sidel, John T. 2006. *Riots, Pogroms, Jihad: Religious Violence in Indonesia*. Ithaca, NY: Cornell University Press.

Sidel, John T. 2008. 'Social Origins of Dictatorship and Democracy Revisited: Colonial State and Chinese Immigrant in the Making of Modern Southeast Asia'. *Comparative Politics* 40(2): 127–47.

Simmel, Georg. 1950. 'The Stranger'. In *The Sociology of Georg Simmel*, edited by Kurt H. Wolff, 402–8. New York: The Free Press.

Skinner, G. William. 1957. *Chinese Society in Thailand: An Analytical History*. Ithaca, NY: Cornell University Press.

Skinner, G. William. 1958. 'The Chinese of Java'. In *Colloquium on Overseas Chinese*, edited by Morton H. Fried, 1–10. New York: International Secretariat, Institute of Pacific Relations.

Skinner, G. William. 1996. 'Creolized Chinese Societies in Southeast Asia'. In *Sojourners and Settlers: Histories of Southeast Asia and the Chinese*, edited by Anthony Reid, 51–93. St. Leonards, NSW: Allen & Unwin.

Somers, Mary. F. 1964. *Peranakan Chinese Politics in Indonesia*. Ithaca, NY: Cornell Modern Indonesia Project.

Sukma, Rizal. 2010. 'Indonesia's 2009 Elections: Defective System, Resilient Democracy'. In *Problems of Democratisation in Indonesia: Elections, Institutions and Society*, edited by Edward Aspinall and Marcus Mietzner, 53–74. Singapore: Institute of Southeast Asian Studies.

Sulistiyanto, Priyambudi, and Maribeth Erb. 2009. 'Indonesia and the Quest for "Democracy"'. In *Deepening Democracy in Indonesia? Direct Elections for Local Leaders (Pilkada)*, edited by Maribeth Erb and Priyambudi Sulistiyanto, 1–37. Singapore: Institute of Southeast Asian Studies.

Suryadinata, Leo. 1981. *Peranakan Chinese Politics in Java 1917–1942*. Singapore: Singapore University Press.

Suryadinata, Leo. 1988. 'Chinese Economic Elites in Indonesia: A Preliminary Study'. In *Changing Identities of the Southeast Asian Chinese since World War II*, edited by Jennifer W. Cushman and Wang Gungwu, 261–88. Hong Kong: Hong Kong University Press.

Suryadinata, Leo. 1992. *Pribumi Indonesians, the Chinese Minority and China*. Singapore: Heinemann Asia.

Suryadinata, Leo. 1993a. 'Patterns of Chinese Political Participation in Four ASEAN States'. *Contemporary Southeast Asia* 15(3): 292–308.

Suryadinata, Leo. 1993b. 'The State and Chinese Minority in Indonesia'. In *Chinese Adaptation and Diversity: Essays on Society and Literature in Indonesia, Malaysia & Singapore*, edited by Leo Suryadinata, 77–100. Singapore: NUS Press.

Suryadinata, Leo. 1997. *The Culture of the Chinese Minority in Indonesia*. Singapore: Times Books International.

Suryadinata, Leo. 2001. 'Chinese Politics in Post-Suharto's Indonesia: Beyond the Ethnic Approach?' *Asian Survey* 41(3): 502–24.

Suryadinata, Leo. 2002a. *Elections and Politics in Indonesia*. Singapore: Institute of Southeast Asian Studies.

Suryadinata, Leo. 2002b. *Xian Jieduan De Yinni Huaren Zuqun* [Contemporary Chinese Indonesians]. Singapore: Department of Chinese Studies, National University of Singapore.

Suryadinata, Leo. 2006. 'Introduction'. In *Southeast Asia's Chinese Businesses in an Era of Globalization: Coping with the Rise of China*, edited by Leo Suryadinata, 1–12. Singapore: Institute of Southeast Asian Studies.

Suryadinata, Leo, Evi Nurvidya Arifin, and Aris Ananta. 2003. *Indonesia's Population: Ethnicity and Religion in a Changing Political Landscape*. Singapore: Institute of Southeast Asian Studies.

Tan, Chee-Beng. 2000. 'The Religions of the Chinese in Malaysia'. In *The Chinese in Malaysia*, edited by Lee Kam Hing and Tan Chee-Beng, 282–315. Shah Alam, Selangor: Oxford University Press.

Tan, Mely G. 1991. 'The Social and Cultural Dimensions of the Role of Ethnic Chinese in Indonesian Society'. In *Indonesia: The Role of the Indonesian Chinese in Shaping Modern Indonesian Life*, edited by Audrey Kahin, 113–25. Ithaca, NY: Cornell Southeast Asia Program.

Tan, Sofyan. 2004. *Jalan Menuju Masyarakat Anti Diskriminasi* [Towards an anti-discrimination society]. Medan: KIPPAS.

The, Siauw Giap. 1967. 'Juliuguo Zongjiao Dui Dongnanya Huaqiao Tonghua De Yingxiang' [Religion and overseas Chinese assimilation in Southeast Asian countries]. *Journal of Southeast Asian Researches* 3: 87–94.

Thee, Kian Wie. 2006. 'The Indonesian Government's Economic Policies Towards the Ethnic Chinese: Beyond Economic Nationalism?' In *Southeast Asia's Chinese Businesses in an Era of Globalization: Coping with the Rise of China*, edited by Leo Suryadinata, 76–101. Singapore: Institute of Southeast Asian Studies.

Thock, Ker Pong. 2005. *Ketuanan Politik Melayu: Pandangan Kaum Cina* [The Malay political supremacy: The views of ethnic Chinese]. Kuala Lumpur: University of Malaya Press.

Thompson, Mark R. 2011. 'Moore Meets Gramsci and Burke in Southeast Asia: New Democracies and "Civil" Societies'. In *The Crisis of Democratic Governance in Southeast Asia*, edited by Aurel Croissant and Marco Bünte, 57–74. Basingstoke, Hampshire: Palgrave Macmillan.

Thung, Ju Lan 2009. 'Chinese Indonesians in Local Politics: A Review Essay'. *Kyoto Review of Southeast Asia* 11. Accessed August 15, 2012. http://kyotoreview.org/wp-content/uploads/Thung-Ju-Lan-ENG-.pdf.

Tjiook-Liem, Patricia. 2011. 'The Loa Joe Djin Case: A Trigger to Change'. In *Chinese Indonesians and Regime Change*, edited by Marleen Dieleman, Juliette Koning, and Peter Post, 117–38. Leiden: Brill.

Tomsa, Dirk. 2008. *Party Politics and Democratization in Indonesia: Golkar in the Post-Suharto Era*. Abingdon: Routledge.

Tomsa, Dirk. 2009. 'The Eagle Has Crash-Landed'. *Inside Indonesia*, July–September. Accessed January 10, 2014. http://www.insideindonesia.org/feature-editions/the-eagle-has-crash-landed.

Tomsa, Dirk. 2010. 'The Indonesian Party System after the 2009 Elections: Towards Stability?' In *Problems of Democratisation in Indonesia: Elections, Institutions and Society*, edited by Edward Aspinall and Marcus Mietzner, 141–59. Singapore: Institute of Southeast Asian Studies.

Tomsa, Dirk. 2015. 'Toning Down the "Big Bang": The Politics of Decentralisation during the Yudhoyono Years'. In *The Yudhoyono Presidency: Indonesia's Decade of*

References

Stability and Stagnation, edited by Edward Aspinall, Marcus Mietzner, and Dirk Tomsa, 155–74. Singapore: Institute of Southeast Asian Studies.

Tsai, Yen-ling. 2011. 'Spaces of Exclusion, Walls of Intimacy: Rethinking "Chinese Exclusivity" in Indonesia'. *Indonesia* 92: 125–55.

Tsai, Yen-ling, and Douglas Kammen. 2012. 'Anti-communist Violence and the Ethnic Chinese in Medan, North Sumatra'. In *The Contours of Mass Violence in Indonesia, 1965–68*, edited by Douglas Kammen and Katharine McGregor, 131–55. Singapore: NUS Press.

Turner, Mark. 2005. 'From Centralized Authoritarianism to Decentralized Democracy: Regional Autonomy and the State in Indonesia'. In *Autonomy, Self-Governance and Conflict Resolution: Innovative Approaches to Institutional Design in Divided Societies*, edited by Marc Weller and Stefan Wolff, 213–33. Abingdon: Routledge.

Turner, Sarah. 2003. 'Speaking Out: Chinese Indonesians after Suharto'. *Asian Ethnicity* 4(3): 337–52.

Usman, Syaikhu. 2002. 'Regional Autonomy in Indonesia: Field Experiences and Emerging Challenges'. *SMERU Working Paper*, June. Jakarta: SMERU Research Institute.

Vickers, Adrian. 2005. *A History of Modern Indonesia*. Cambridge: Cambridge University Press.

Wanandi, Jusuf. 2012. *Shades of Grey: A Political Memoir of Modern Indonesia 1965–1998*. Singapore: Equinox Publishing.

Wanandi, Sofyan. 1999. 'The Post-Soeharto Business Environment'. In *Post-Soeharto Indonesia: Renewal or Chaos*, edited by Geoff Forrester, 128–34. Singapore: Institute of Southeast Asian Studies.

Watson, C. W. 2006. *Of Self and Injustice: Autobiography and Repression in Modern Indonesia*. Leiden: KITLV Press.

Weldon, Peter D. 1978. 'Indonesian and Chinese Status and Language Differences in Urban Java'. In *Studies in ASEAN Sociology: Urban Society and Social Change*, edited by Peter S. J. Chen and Hans-Dieter Evers, 256–76. Singapore: Chopmen Enterprises.

Wertheim, W. F. 1965. *East-West Parallels: Sociological Approaches to Modern Asia*. Chicago: Quadrangle Books.

Wessel, Ingrid. 2005. 'The Impact of the State on the Democratisation Process in Indonesia'. In *Democratisation in Indonesia after the Fall of Suharto*, edited by Ingrid Wessel, 5–25. Berlin: Logos Verlag Berlin.

Wibowo, Ignatius. 2001. 'Exit, Voice and Loyalty: Indonesian Chinese after the Fall of Soeharto'. *SOJOURN* 16(1): 238–63.

Widoyoko, J. Danang. 2011. 'The Education Sector: The Fragmentation and Adaptability of Corruption'. In *The State and Illegality in Indonesia*, edited by Edward Aspinall and Gerry van Klinken, 165–87. Leiden: KITLV Press.

Wickberg, Edgar. 1965. *The Chinese in Philippine Life, 1850–1898*. New Haven: Yale University Press.

Williams, Lea E. 1960. *Overseas Chinese Nationalism: The Genesis of the Pan-Chinese Movement in Indonesia, 1900–1916*. Glencoe: The Free Press.

Willmott, Donald E. 1961. *The National Status of the Chinese in Indonesia 1900–1958*. Ithaca, NY: Cornell Modern Indonesia Project.

Wilson, Ian. 2010. 'The Rise and Fall of Political Gangsters in Indonesian Democracy'. In *Problems of Democratisation in Indonesia: Elections, Institutions and Society*, edited by Edward Aspinall and Marcus Mietzner, 199–218. Singapore: Institute of Southeast Asian Studies.

Wilson, Ian. 2011. 'Reconfiguring Rackets: Racket Regimes, Protection and the State in Post-New Order Jakarta'. In *The State and Illegality in Indonesia*, edited by Edward Aspinall and Gerry van Klinken, 239–59. Leiden: KITLV Press.

Wu, Yiguang. 2009. *Yinni Subei Wenren Lu* [Celebrities in North Sumatra, Indonesia]. Medan: Nanfeng wenxueshe.

Yamamoto, Nobuto. 2011. 'The Chinese Connection: Rewriting Journalism and Social Categories in Indonesian History'. In *Chinese Indonesians and Regime Change*, edited by Marleen Dieleman, Juiette Koning, and Peter Post, 93–116. Leiden: Brill.

Yang, Tsung Rong. 2006. 'The Indonesian Chinese and the Ethnic Issue: A Case Study of the Social Riots in the Late New Order (1994–1997)'. In *Demarcating Ethnicity in New Nations: Cases of the Chinese in Singapore, Malaysia, and Indonesia*, edited by Lee Guan Kin, 227–49. Singapore: Konrad-Adenauer-Stiftung.

Yang, Tsung Rong. 2007. 'Xinzhixu Xia De Hunluan: Cong Yinni Baodong Kan Huaren De Zhengzhi Shehui Guanxi' [Chaos under the New Order: The socio-political dimension of the Chinese in Indonesia as seen from the riots of 1994–1998]. Taipei: Taiwan International Studies Association.

Yeoh, Emile Kok-Kheng. 2008. 'Beyond Reductionism: State, Ethnicity and Public Policy in Plural Societies'. In *The State, Development and Identity in Multi-Ethnic Societies: Ethnicity, Equity and the Nation*, edited by Nicholas Tarling and Edmund Terence Gomez, 57–96. Abingdon: Routledge.

Zein, Abdul Baqir. 2000. *Etnis Cina dalam Potret Pembauran di Indonesia* [Ethnic Chinese in the portrait of assimilation in Indonesia]. Jakarta: Prestasi Insan Indonesia.

Zhao, Hong. 2013. 'China-Indonesia Economic Relations: Challenges and Prospects'. *ISEAS Perspectives* 42, July 4. Singapore: Institute of Southeast Asian Studies.

Unpublished Theses and Dissertations

Chong, Peng Hong. 1983/84. 'Chinese Female Immigration to the Straits Settlements from 1901 to 1941'. Undergraduate honours thesis. National University of Singapore, Singapore.

Ryter, Loren. 2002. 'Youth, Gangs, and the State in Indonesia'. PhD dissertation. University of Washington, United States.

Somers, Mary F. 1965. 'Peranakan Chinese Politics in Indonesia'. PhD dissertation. Cornell University, United States.

Tsai, Yen-ling. 2008. 'Strangers Who Are Not Foreign: Intimate Exclusion and Racialized Boundary in Urban Indonesia'. PhD dissertation. University of California, Santa Cruz, United States.

Other Sources

'030406-Yenni Meilina Lie'. 2014. InfoCaleg.org. Accessed August 19, 2014. http://infocaleg.org/caleg/030406-yenni-meilina-lie/.

Ashoka at 30. 2011. Ashoka Deutschland's website. Accessed September 26, 2016. http://germany.ashoka.org/sites/germanysix.ashoka.org/files/Ashoka%20 30%20Anniversary%20Documentation%20Paris.pdf

'BOC & BOD'. 2013. PT Maspion's website. Accessed August 5, 2013. http://www.maspion.com/company/index.php?act=boc.

'Brief History'. 2013. PT Maspion's website. Accessed August 5, 2013. http://www.maspion.com/company/index.php?act=history.

References

231

ChanCT. 2012. 'Re: [GELORA45] Fw: Bubarkan Perkumpulan Tionghoa' [Re: [GELORA45] Fw: Disband ethnic Chinese organisations]. *Budaya Tionghoa* [Chinese culture] online Yahoo discussion group, May 16. Accessed August 12, 2013. http://groups.yahoo.com/neo/groups/budaya_tionghoa/conversations/topics/227.

City Population. 2012. Accessed December 21, 2013. http://www.citypopulation.de/php/indonesia-admin.php.

Encyclopaedia Britannica. 2013. 'fifth column'. *Encyclopaedia Britannica*. Accessed November 11, 2013. http://global.britannica.com/EBchecked/topic/206477/fifth-column.

'*Harian Indonesia (Sin Chew)*'. 2013. Media Chinese International Limited. Accessed December 7, 2013. http://www.mediachinesegroup.com/htm/content.cfm?channel=biz&path=biz_07a&lang=E.

'History of NEC'. 2013. New Era College's website. Accessed November 8, 2013. http://www.newera.edu.my/aboutUs.php?id=113.

North Sumatra's Chinese Community Social and Education Association. n.d. Introductory Booklet on Asian International Friendship Foreign Language College.

'Program Anak Asuh' [The program of fosterage]. 2014. Sultan Iskandar Muda Educational Foundation website, August 15. Accessed September 4, 2016. http://ypsim.sch.id/home/program-anak-asuh/.

'Sejarah Singkat' [A short history]. 2014. Sultan Iskandar Muda Educational Foundation website, August 15. Accessed September 4, 2016. http://ypsim.sch.id/home/profil/sejarah-singkat/.

'Sekilas Tentang PRD' [About PRD]. 2010. People's Democratic Party (PRD) website, July 12. Accessed January 10, 2014. http://www.prd.or.id/organisasi/20100712/sekilas-tentang-prd.html.

Sishui Huichaojia Huiguan Chengli 190 Zhounian Jinian Zhuanji [190th anniversary book of Chinese Indonesian Association]. 2010. Surabaya: Hwie Tiauw Ka Chinese Clan Association in Surabaya.

Stop Rasisme: Konferensi Perjuangan Anti Diskriminasi Etnis dan Ras di Indonesia [Stop racism: The conference on anti-ethnic and racial discrimination struggle in Indonesia]. n.d. Surabaya: Insitute of Ethnic and Racial Unity Studies in Indonesia (INSPIRASI).

The Act of Killing [Motion picture]. Directed by Joshua Oppenheimer. 2012. Denmark: Final Cut for Real.

Index

1955 Bandung Asian-African Conference, 30
A Hie, 184, 196
Aceh, 44n5, 54–55, 77–78, 85
'Act No. 62 of the year 1958 Concerning Republic of Indonesia Citizenship', 30
adat, 53, 54n13, 67, 190
Adi, Soetanto, 187, 196
Agung Cemara Realty, 116
Ahok, 46, 133, 133n13, 134, 197
Aizawa, Nobuhiro, 35
Akademi Akuntansi Surabaya, 138, 190
Al Washliyah, 116
All-Indonesian Association of Islamic Intellectuals. *See* ICMI (Ikatan Cendekiawan Muslim Se-Indonesia)
Amin, 196
anti-Sinicism, 29
Anderson, Benedict, 6, 26. *See also* Anderson, Benedict R. O'G.
Anderson, Benedict R. O'G., 35. *See also* Anderson, Benedict
Ang Ching Peng. *See* Hartono
anti-Chinese violence, May 1998, 13, 56, 73, 88, 126, 142
Anto, J., 86–87
Arabs, in Indonesia, 8, 8n6, 26, 54
Arif, Rudi, 184
Arifin, Syamsul, 52, 150, 161
Armayanti, Nelly, 120, 151, 154–56, 160–61, 171
Armed Forces Sons' and Daughters' Communication Forum. *See* FKPPI (Forum Komunikasi Putra-Putri Purnawirawan Indonesia)

Army Veterans' Youth. *See* PPM (Pemuda Panca Marga)
Arrow Wars, 32n13
Artha Graha Group (GAG), 58, 58n18, 131, 191
Asia Foundation, 100
Asian International Friendship Foreign Language College. *See* STBA-PIA (Sekolah Tinggi Bahasa Asing Persahabatan Internasional Asia)
Aspinall, Edward, 14, 49–50, 53, 123
Asrie, Sigit Pramono, 154
assimilation policies, 7, 34–36, 70
assimilationists, 33, 35
Awey, Vinsensius, 189

Backman, Michael, 98–99
Bagan Siapi-Api, 29–30, 30n10
Bahasa Melajoe Tionghoa, 28, 190
Bali, 29n8
'Bamboo Curtain', 79n13
Banda Aceh, 77
Bandung, 29
Bangka, 34, 69
Bangka Belitung, 133n13
BAPERKI (Badan Permusjawaratan Kewarganegaraan Indonesia), 32–33, 191
Barth, Fredrik, 38, 88
Basri, Benny, 110, 113, 115, 196
Batak, 15, 99, 106n6
Batak Karo, 150, 154
Batavia, 11
Beijing, 11, 27, 92, 93n22, 181
Belitung, 34
Bell, Daniel A., 41
Bertrand, Jacques, 53–57

Besuki, 142

Binjai, 81

BMI (Banteng Muda Indonesia), 58, 190

Bong Sau Fan. *See* Karman, Hasan

Bourdieu, Pierre, vii, 3–6, 66, 90, 106–7, 121, 131, 169; cultural capital, 4; economic capital, 4, 41, 98, 106–8, 169; habitus, vii, 3–6, 66, 90, 106–7, 120–21, 131, 146, 165–66, 169; field, vii, 3–6, 106–7, 121, 131, 169; social capital, 4, 66, 98, 108, 118, 169

Boxer Uprising, 27, 27n4, 32

British Malaya, 7, 69, 69n4; Chinese, 7; divide-and-rule policy, 7; Indians, 7; Malays, 7

Budianto, Fajar, 186

Budiman, Arief, 59, 59n20

Bugis, 29n8

Buiskool, Dirk A., 97, 171

bupati, 25

Cambodia, 77

Cao Yunhua, 74n9, 16

Caritas Switzerland, 86

Central Kalimantan, 54

Chabar Perniagaan / Perniagaan, 28

Chalim MZ. H., Abdul, 187, 196

ChanCT, 94

Chandra, Tansri, 78, 196

Changdao, 81

Chen Yituan, 179, 196

Chengdu, 81

Chin Kung, Master, 75, 196

China, 3, 14–15, 19, 23, 26–27, 27n4, 28, 28n5, 29–32, 32n13, 35, 63, 65–66, 68, 68n2, 69–71, 71n6, 72, 74–75, 77–79, 79n13, 80–83, 90, 92–96, 145, 148, 159, 169. *See also* People's Republic of China (PRC)

China Harbour Engineering Company, 82

China News Agency, 80

China Overseas Exchange Association, 78

China Road and Bridge Corporation, 82

China State Construction Engineering Company, 83

Chinese dual citizenship, 29n7, 30

Chinese Indonesians, vii, 2–3, 5–6, 8, 8n6, 8n7, 8n8, 9–11, 13–14, 17–20, 23, 25, 30, 33, 34, 34n17, 36, 40, 52, 57–58, 58n17, 59–66, 68–69, 69n3, 70–72, 80, 85–86, 89–96, 99, 104, 114–15, 117, 120–21, 132, 134–35, 137–38, 146–47, 158–59, 162–64, 166–70

Chinese Indonesian Association. *See* INTI (Perhimpunan Indonesia Tionghoa)

Chinese Indonesian Social Association. *See* PSMTI (Paguyuban Sosial Marga Tionghoa Indonesia)

Chinese Language and Culture Education Foundation of China, 77

Chinese law of nationality, 1909, 28

Chinese Youth Irregulars. *See* LPT (Laskar Pemuda Tionghoa)

Chong Wu-Ling, viii. *See also* Chong Wu Ling

Chong Wu Ling, viii. *See also* Chong Wu-Ling

Chow Li Ing. *See* Murdaya, Siti Hartati Cakra

Chua, Amy, 41–43, 55

Chua, Christian, 11–13, 37, 53, 131

Cipta Cakra Murdaya (CCM) Group, 131, 131n10, 190

Citizenship Act of 1946, 30

Citizenship Letter. *See* SBKRI (Surat Bukti Kewarganegaraan Republik Indonesia)

Committee for the Monitoring of Regional Autonomy. *See* KPPOD (Komite Pemantau Pelaksanaan Otonomi Daerah)

Committee of Social Concern of Surabaya. *See* Kalimas (Komite Aliansi Kepedulian Masyarakat Surabaya)

Confucius, 28, 76

Confucius Institute Headquarters. *See* Hanban

constructivism, 6, 168

Consultative Body for Indonesian Citizenship. *See* BAPERKI (Badan Permusjawaratan Kewarganegaraan Indonesia)

Coppel, Charles A., 8, 98

Cordell, Karl, 41

Cornell University, 144

Corruption Eradication Commission. *See* KPK (Komisi Pemberantasan Korupsi)
Council of Indonesian Islamic Scholars. *See* MUI (Majelis Ulama Indonesia)
Crouch, Harold, 52
cukong, 36, 190

Davidson, Jamie S., 46, 67
Dawis, Aimee, 70
decentralisation, 17–18, 45–47, 50, 53–55, 99–100
Deli Serdang, 81, 115, 162
Democratic Party. *See* PD (Partai Demokrat)
democratisation, vii, 12–13, 16–21, 23, 40–47, 50, 53–56, 58, 60–61, 98–99, 112, 118, 120, 123, 125, 127, 144, 165–70
DEPDAGRI (Departemen Dalam Negeri), 35, 190
Dewan Harian Daerah 45 Sumatera Utara, 84
Dharmanadi, Joko, 178, 196
Dharmasaputra, Karaniya, 59, 59n19
Di Zi Gui, 76
Diamond, Larry, 40–41, 46, 46n7, 60, 169
Dick, Howard, 47. *See also* Dick, Howard W.
Dick, Howard W., 115. *See also* Dick, Howard
Dieleman, Marleen, 10
Dipojuwono, Budi, 35n19
Diputro, Adhinata Wira, 188
Djawa Tengah, 28
Djuandi, Eddy, 65, 120, 155, 160, 171, 178, 196
D-onenews.com, 140
DPD (Dewan Perwakilan Daerah), 1, 124–25, 148n27, 149–50, 190
DPRD 1 (Dewan Perwakilan Rakyat Daerah 1), 125, 190
DPRD 2 (Dewan Perwakilan Rakyat Daerah 2), 125, 190
DPR (Dewan Perwakilan Rakyat), 109, 124–25, 190
Dutch colonial rule, 6, 9, 26; divide-and-rule policy, 23, 39, 168
Dutch East India Company (VOC), 26, 195

Dutch East Indies, 23, 26, 26n2, 27–29, 38, 69, 192

East Belitung, 133, 133n13
East Java, 14, 29, 75, 80–84, 101, 108–9, 109n8, 113–14, 122, 128, 128n4, 129, 129n5, 135, 142, 145–47, 172–73, 179, 186, 189
East Java Entrepreneur Charitable Foundation, 84, 108
East Java High Prosecution Office, 84
East Java Inter-Religious Harmony Association. *See* Ikatan Kerukunan Umat Beragama Jawa Timur
East Nusa Tenggara, 133
East Timor, 50, 54–55, 126, 141
Edwards, Bob, 48–49
Ek Kiong, 183, 196
Eldin, Dzulmi, 150
electoral democracy, 40–41, 46, 60
Elleman, Bruce A., 32n13
Elly, Karya, 183
Emerald Garden Hotel, 117
ethnic boundary, 38, 88
ethnic minorities, 13, 21, 23, 40–42, 53
Europeans, 11, 11n10, 26–27, 32n13
Export-Import Bank of China, 83

Fauzi, Gamawan, 44n5, 139
'festivals of democracy', 44
'fifth column', 30, 30n11, 35, 93
Firdaus, Sonny, 183–85
First Sino-Japanese War, 27
Fitryus, H. M., 161
FKPPI (Forum Komunikasi Putra-Putri Purnawirawan Indonesia), 52, 101–2, 190
'floating mass', 43
Foley, Michael W., 48–49
FORDA UKM (Forum Daerah Usaha Kecil dan Menengah), 107, 171, 190
Foreign Orientals, 26
FORNAS UKM (Forum Nasional Usaha Kecil dan Menengah), 149–50, 191
Forum Kerukunan Umat Beragama Surabaya, 140, 191
Freedman, Amy, 47
FUI (Forum Umat Islam), 117, 191
Fujian, 15, 32n13, 69, 191
full democracy, 46, 60, 169

Index 235

GANDI (Gerakan Perjuangan Anti Diskriminasi), 89, 191
Gatot, Suherman, 183
Gatra, 16, 103, 131
GAYa Nusantara, 144–45, 191
Gemala Group, 131, 131n7
General Elections Commission. *See* KPU (Komisi Pemilihan Umum)
Gerindra (Partai Gerakan Indonesia Raya), 45, 126–27, 134, 134n16, 141, 164, 183, 185, 188–89, 191
Giblin, Susan, 70
Giddens, Anthony, 3, 5–6; structure-agency theory, vii, 3–4, 10, 66, 98, 118, 121, 169
Ginsburg, Tom, 42
Ginting, Nurlisa, 154
Glodok, 15
Glugur, 76, 78
GMNI (Gerakan Mahasiswa Nasional Indonesia), 137, 137n18, 191
Go, Gunardi, 109n7
Golkar (Golongan Karya), 35n19, 35n20, 36–37, 44, 44n3, 45, 49, 102, 109, 121, 125, 127–28, 129n5, 131, 131n6, 132n12, 134, 143, 146, 150–52, 161, 183–84, 187–89, 191. *See also* Sekber Golkar (Sekretariat Bersama Golongan Karya)
Gomez, Edmund Terence, 42
Govaars, Ming, 27–28
Great Indonesian Movement Party. *See* Gerindra (Partai Gerakan Indonesia Raya)
Guangdong, 32n13, 69, 71n6, 78, 81, 190–91, 194
Guangzhou, 82
Guided Democracy, 31, 51, 52n11
Gumelar, Agum, 131n6
Guoji Ribao, 35n18, 72, 92, 159, 177

Habibie, B. J., 38, 43–45, 72, 124, 141–42
Hadiluwih, RM. H. Subanindyo, 15
Hadiz, Vedi R., 47, 49, 72, 101, 104
Hainanese, 26, 191
Hakka, 26, 46, 71, 75, 133, 191
Hanban, 72, 77, 191
Handoko, Bambang, 186
Hanura (Partai Hati Nurani Rakyat), 45, 126–27, 139–40, 164, 191

Hanurakin, Arifli Harbianto, 187, 196
Hao Bao, 173, 177
Harahap, Rahudman, 100, 150
Harian Analisa, 73n8, 177
Harian Indonesia, 70, 72
Harian Mandiri, 137
Harian Naga Surya, 73n8, 172, 177
Harian Nusantara, 80, 172, 174, 177
Harian Orbit, 62, 100, 113, 116
Harian Promosi Indonesia, 73n8, 173, 177
Hartimin, 178
Hartono, 183
Haryanto, 182, 184–85, 196
Harymurti, Bambang, 59
Hasan, Bob, 35n18, 57
Hasyim, 97, 120, 136–37, 162, 164, 171, 178, 184–85, 196
Haynes, Jeff, 40–41, 46, 60, 169
Haz, Hamzah, 122, 131n6
Heidhues, Mary Somers, 69. *See also* Somers, Mary F.
Hellmann, Olli, 125
Helvetia, 115–16
Henley, David, 67
Heryanto, Ariel, 72
Hidayat, Syarif, 130
Hokkien, 15, 26, 32, 158–59, 190–91, 194
Hong Kong Commercial Daily, 72
Hong Kong Society for Indonesian Studies, 80
Honggandhi, Hakim, 111, 111n9, 196
Honoris, Charles, 187
Hoon Chang-Yau, 9, 30, 35, 67, 70
Hu Jintao, 82, 196
Huashang Bao, 173, 177
Huang Kunzhang, 73n8
Hui Chew, 71, 71n6, 175
Hui Yew-Foong, 10, 38
hukum adat, 67
Husodo, Siswono Yudo, 131n6
Hutasoit, Ruyandi, 126
Hwie Tiauw Ka Chinese Clan Association in Surabaya. *See* PHTKS (Perkumpulan Hwie Tiauw Ka Surabaya)

ICMI (Ikatan Cendekiawan Muslim Se-Indonesia), 38, 191
Ikatan Kerukunan Umat Beragama Jawa Timur, 140, 191

IKIP (Institut Keguruan dan Ilmu Pendidikan), 143, 191
Indar, Kholifah, 132
Indians, in Indonesia, 8, 8n6, 54
indigenous Indonesians, 2, 5, 8–9, 15–16, 18–19, 27, 27n3, 29, 29n8, 34n15, 36, 38, 57–58, 61–62, 65–66, 69, 79, 84–86, 88–89, 91–93, 96–97, 103n3, 114–15, 117, 148–49, 152, 159, 163–64, 166, 168, 170. See also *pribumi*
Indonesia Corruption Watch (ICW), 130, 191
Indonesia Focus, 80
Indonesia Shang Bao, 72
Indonesian Anti-Discrimination Movement. See GANDI (Gerakan Perjuangan Anti Diskriminasi)
Indonesian Buddhists Association. See Walubi (Perwakilan Umat Buddha Indonesia)
Indonesian Chinese Entrepreneur Association. See PERPIT (Perhimpunan Pengusaha Tionghoa Indonesia)
Indonesian Chinese Entrepreneur Community. See PERMIT (Perhimpunan Masyarakat and Pengusaha Indonesia Tionghoa)
Indonesian Communist Party. See *PKI* (Partai Komunis Indonesia)
Indonesian Democracy Devotion Party. See PKDI (Partai Kasih Demokrasi Indonesia)
Indonesian Democratic Party. See PDI (Partai Demokrasi Indonesia)
Indonesian Democratic Party of Struggle. See PDI-P (Partai Demokrasi Indonesia Perjuangan)
Indonesian Justice and Unity Party. See PKPI (Partai Keadilan dan Persatuan Indonesia)
Indonesian National Defense Institute. See LEMHANNAS RI (Lembaga Ketahanan Nasional Republik Indonesia)
Indonesian National Party. See PNI (Partai Nasional Indonesia)

Indonesian National Populist Fortress Party. See PNBK (Partai Nasional Benteng Kemerdekaan)
Indonesian National Students' Movement. See GMNI (Gerakan Mahasiswa Nasional Indonesia)
Indonesian nationalist movement, 9
Indonesian Red Cross, 84
Indonesian Unity in Diversity Party. See PBI (Partai Bhinneka Tunggal Ika)
Indonesian Young Bulls. See BMI (Banteng Muda Indonesia)
Industrial and Commercial Bank of China (ICBC), 82, 191
INSPIRASI (Institut Studi Persatuan Etnis dan Ras di Indonesia), 89, 191
Institute of Ethnic and Racial Unity Studies in Indonesia. See INSPIRASI (Institut Studi Persatuan Etnis dan Ras di Indonesia)
Institute of Teaching and Education. See IKIP (Institut Keguruan dan Ilmu Pendidikan)
integrated school (*sekolah pembauran*), 65, 86, 86n18, 89, 95, 148, 194
INTI (Perhimpunan Indonesia Tionghoa), 1–2, 58, 63–64, 68, 69n3, 71, 75, 77, 81, 84, 111, 112n11, 147, 149, 153, 171–73, 175–76, 178–79, 191
IPK (Ikatan Pemuda Karya), 101–2, 104, 111, 191
Islamic University of North Sumatra, 148
Ismail, Nur Mahmud, 122

Jacobsen, Michael, 68n2
Jahja, Junus, 33, 158, 196
Jakarta, 9, 11–13, 15–16, 18, 29, 34n17, 43, 47, 50, 50n10, 52, 58, 72, 92, 93, 96, 104, 126–28, 133, 133n13, 138, 143, 153, 160, 171–72, 181, 187
Jambon, 84
Janlie, 184–85, 196
Japanese, in the Dutch East Indies, 26–27
Java, 9, 14–16, 25, 26n2
Javanese *wayang* (shadow puppetry), 9
Jawa Pos, 130
Joint Fact-Finding Team (Joint Team), 43
Joint Secretariat of Functional Groups. See Sekber Golkar

Jokowi. *See* Widodo, Joko
Jonan, Ignasius, 133, 196
Justice Party. *See* PK (Partai Keadilan)

Kajang, 76n12
Kalimantan, 25
Kalimas (Komite Aliansi Kepedulian
  Masyarakat Surabaya), 71, 89–90,
  95, 176, 191
Kalla, Jusuf, 53, 131n6, 132n12
Kampung Ilmu (Knowledge Village), 84
Kang Youwei, 28
Kapal Api Group, 110
Kapitan Cina, 26, 192
Karman, Hasan, 133–34, 196
Karo, 81
Kedah, 16
Kie Hock Kweng, 184
King, Phil, 53
KKN, 47, 65, 192
KMP (Koalisi Merah Putih), 134n16, 192
Kompas, 33
Koran Tempo, 92, 181
KPK (Komisi Pemberantasan Korupsi),
  116, 192
KPPOD (Komite Pemantau Pelaksanaan
  Otonomi Daerah), 101, 192
KPU (Komisi Pemilihan Umum), 151,
  192
Kristianto, Benjamin, 188
Kristianto, Benyamin. *See* Kristianto,
  Benjamin
Kuala Namu, 83
Kurnia, Indah, 187–88
Kurniadi, Henky, 172, 182, 187–88, 196
Kwik Kian Gie, 132, 196
Kwik Sam Ho, 183–84, 197
Kwong Wah Yit Poh, 177

Laksono, Antonius Iwan Dwi, 188
Lane, Maxwell, 48–49
Latuperissa, Martius, 102
Lauw Chuan Tho. *See* Jahja, Junus
Law No. 2/1999, 44
Law No. 22/1999, 45
Law No. 25/1999, 45
Law No. 32/2004, 150n31
Law No. 12/2008, 124, 141
Lawin, Rusmin, 183, 185, 197

Lekatompessy, Simon, 136, 138–40,
  163–64, 172, 182, 188
Lembata, 133, 133n14
Lembong, Thomas Trikasih, 133
LEMHANNAS RI (Lembaga Ketahanan
  Nasional Republik Indonesia), 148,
  192
Leo, Ardjan, 63, 76–79, 171, 178, 197
LGBT (lesbian, gay, bisexual, and
  transgender), 142, 144, 145n23,
  191–92
Li In Zhe, 92, 181
Li Peng, 82, 197
Li Po, 28
Li Zhuohui, 35n18
Lianhe Zaobao, 94
liberal democracy, 40–41, 48, 169
Lie Beng Giok. *See* Surjadinata, L. B. G.
Lie Giok Houw. *See* Sudjatmiko, Djoko
Lie Ling Piao, Alvin, 133, 197
Lie, Yenni Meilina, 185
Lie Mo Tie, 36, 197
Lie Po Yoe. *See* Dipojuwono, Budi
Liem Bian Khoen. *See* Wanandi, Sofyan
Liem Bian Kie. *See* Wanandi, Jusuf
Liem Ou Yen, 65, 172, 178, 197
Liem Sioe Liong, 36–37, 52, 68n2, 197
Lim Aho, 184
Lim Ping Tjien, 63, 172, 178–79, 197
Lintner, Bertil, 69
Lippo Group, 68n2, 131, 131n8
Lis, Arsyad, 116
Local Government Working Unit. *See*
  SKPD (Satuan Kerja Perangkat
  Daerah)
Loe Joe Djin, 11
Lohanda, Mona, 9, 26–27
LPT (Laskar Pemuda Tionghoa), 30n9,
  192
Lubis, M. Rajab, 15
Lukita, Enggartiasto, 133, 197

Mackie, J. A. C., 9. *See also* Mackie, James
Mackie, Jamie, 11. *See also* Mackie, J. A.
  C.
Madura Island, 82
Madurese, 29n8, 104
Malari incident, 143, 143n21
Malaysia, 7; ethnic Chinese, 7, 7n3, 7n5;
  May 13, 1969 interethnic riots, 7n2,

238 Index

7n4; New Economic Policy (NEP), 7, 7n2; Peninsular Malaysia, 7; state chief ministers (*ketua menteri negeri*), 7

Maluku, 25, 54–55, 138

Manan, Abdul, 59

Manchu government, 28, 28n5, 32n13

Mandarin, 34, 67, 71–72, 76, 76n12, 77, 138, 145, 192

Markus, Alim, 63, 68n2, 81, 108, 109n7, 110, 132, 172, 178–79, 196

Maspion Group, 68n2, 81, 108, 109n7, 110, 132, 172, 179

Medan, vii, 1–2, 5–6, 13–16, 16n14, 17–20, 29–30, 30n10, 34, 37, 37n21, 53, 59, 63–64, 64n1, 66–68, 71, 71n7, 73, 73n8, 74, 74n9, 75n10, 76–86, 88, 90–91, 95–102, 103n3, 104–8, 110–17, 119–21, 128, 128n4, 129, 134–35, 136, 136n17, 137, 147–162, 164, 168, 170–71, 173, 175, 177–78, 182; 2010 mayoral election, 1–2, 5–6, 56n16, 63–64, 89, 102, 111, 137, 150–62, 166

Medan Angsapura Social Foundation. *See* Yasora Medan (Yayasan Sosial Angsapura Medan)

Medan, Anton, 52, 197

Medan Methodist University of Indonesia. *See* UMI Medan (Universitas Methodist Indonesia Medan)

Medan Zao Bao, 63, 173, 177

Mentawai Islands, 85

Mergonoto, Sudomo, 110, 197

Metro TV, 94

Mietzner, Marcus, 46, 50, 50n10, 130

Ministry of Home Affairs, Indonesia. *See* DEPDAGRI (Departemen Dalam Negeri)

MITSU-PSP (Perhimpunan Masyarakat Indonesia Tionghoa Sumatera Utara – Peduli Sosial dan Pendidikan), 71, 77–79, 85, 171, 175, 178, 192

Moesa, Ali Maschan, 132

Moktar, Brilian, 120, 171, 184–85, 197

MPR (Majelis Mermusyawaratan Rakyat), 124, 192

Mudjiono, 132

Muhammadiyah, 45, 122

MUI (Majelis Ulama Indonesia), 117, 156, 192

Mujianto, 115–16, 197

Mulholland, Jeremy, 47

Mulia Group, 131, 131n9

Murdaya, Siti Hartati Cakra, 131–32, 197

Muslim People's Forum. *See* FUI (Forum Umat Islam)

Muzadi, Hasyim, 131n6

Nadapdap, Budiman P., 160

Nagata, Judith, 15, 86

Nan'an, 81

Nanchang University, 82

Nasution, A. H., 37, 51

National Awakening Party. *See* PKB (Partai Kebangkitan Bangsa)

National Forum of Small and Medium Enterprises. *See* FORNAS UKM (Forum Nasional Usaha Kecil dan Menengah)

National Mandate Party. *See* PAN (Partai Amanat Nasional)

National People's Concern Party. *See* PPRN (Partai Peduli Rakyat Nasional)

Netherlands, 30

New Era College (NEC), 76n12, 192

New Indonesia Alliance Party. *See* Partai Perhimpunan Indonesia Baru

New Indonesia Party of Struggle. *See* PPIB (Partai Perjuangan Indonesia Baru)

New Order, vii, 3, 7–8, 11–14, 23, 34–35, 35n18, 36–38, 38n23, 43, 44n3, 45, 47–50, 52–55, 56n15, 58, 61, 64, 66–67, 70–73, 76, 81, 90, 95, 97, 104, 108–9, 112, 114, 120–23, 125, 127, 132, 136, 138, 145–46, 153, 164–65, 175–76

New York Times, 142

Nias, 77, 85

Njoto, Herlina Harsono, 188–89

North Sulawesi, 29n8,

North Sumatra, 29–30, 52, 62–65, 71, 77–78, 81–83, 83n16, 84–85, 101–3, 107–8, 110–12, 115–16, 128, 128n4, 129, 129n5, 135, 137, 147, 147n25, 148–49, 151, 153, 155, 158–60, 171, 178

Index

North Sumatra Chinese Community
Relief Committee. *See* PTSUPBA
(Panitia Tionghoa Sumatera Utara
Peduli Bencana Alam)
North Sumatra Chinese Community
Social and Education Association.
See MITSU-PSP (Perhimpunan
Masyarakat Indonesia Tionghoa
Sumatera Utara – Peduli Sosial dan
Pendidikan)
North Sumatra Indonesian Chamber of
Commerce and Industry, 63
North Sumatra Local Daily Council
45. *See* Dewan Harian Daerah 45
Sumatera Utara
NU (Nahdlatul Ulama), 38, 45, 122, 192

Oei Kien Lim. *See* Hasyim
Oen Tiong Hauw. *See* Oetomo, Dédé
Oetomo, Dédé, 1, 16, 40, 56n16, 63, 104,
113, 120, 134, 142–46, 163–64, 172,
186, 197
Office of Chinese Language Council
International. *See* Hanban
Olii, Mohammad Irvan, 103
One Stop Shops (OSS), 100, 192
Ong Hok Ham, 33, 197
Onghokham. *See* Ong Hok Ham
Oosthoek, 142
Opium War, 27
Overseas Chinese Affairs Office, 92,
93n22
Overseas Exchange Association of
Guangdong Province, 78

Padang, 85
Palembang, 29
PAN (Partai Amanat Nasional), 45,
121–22, 125, 131n6, 134, 183, 185,
187, 189, 192
Pan Eco Foundation, 86
Pancasila Youth. *See* PP (Pemuda
Pancasila)
Pancasila, 44, 44n4, 67, 121–22, 126, 192
Pan-Chinese Movement, 28, 69–70
Pangestu, Mari Elka, 132, 197
Pangestu, Merta, 188
Pangestu, Prajogo, 131
Panggabean, Olo, 104
Pao An Tui, 29–30, 30n10, 192

Papua, 44n5, 54–55
'pariah business class', 11. *See also*
'pariah class'
'pariah class', 13, 18, 23, 38. *See also*
'pariah business class'
'pariah entrepreneurship', 11
'pariah' ethnic minorities, 61
Partai Perhimpunan Indonesia Baru,
134n15, 189, 194
pass system, 26, 28–29
Pasuruan, 142–43
Pausacker, Helen, 9
'PBBM' (Pontianak, Bangka, Belitung,
and Medan), 34n17
PBI (Partai Bhinneka Tunggal Ika), 138,
186, 189, 192
PD (Partai Demokrat), 45, 50, 110, 115,
125–26, 127, 129, 131n6, 132, 132n12,
134, 141, 150, 182, 184, 188–89, 193
PDI (Partai Demokrasi Indonesia),
35n20, 44, 45n6, 122, 136, 193
PDI-P (Partai Demokrasi Indonesia
Perjuangan), 1, 45, 45n6, 58, 101,
101n2, 121–22, 125, 125n3, 126,
128–29, 129n5, 131, 131n6, 132,
132n12, 134, 137, 149–51, 161, 164,
184–89, 193
PDS (Partai Damai Sejahtera), 1, 64,
125–26, 134, 138–41, 151–52, 152n32,
187–89, 193
Pelly, Usman, 103
Pemalang, 30n9
Pematangsiantar, 137
Penang, 16, 154
People's Conscience Party. *See* Hanura
(Partai Hati Nurani Rakyat)
People's Daily, 72
People's Democratic Party. *See* PRD
(Partai Rakyat Demokratik)
People's Democratic Union. *See* PRD
(Persatuan Rakyat Demokratik)
People's Republic of China (PRC), 70,
83, 109n7
peranakan Chinese, 9, 9n9, 10, 14, 14n13,
28, 142, 193
Perhimpunan Keluarga Besar Wijaya
Medan, 63
PERMIT (Perhimpunan Masyarakat and
Pengusaha Indonesia Tionghoa), 71,
84, 172, 176, 179, 193

240 Index

PERPIT (Perhimpunan Pengusaha Tionghoa Indonesia), 71, 81–82, 84, 172, 176, 179, 193

Persatuan Waria Kota Surabaya (PERWAKOS), 145, 193

Pewarta Soerabaia, 28

Phang Djun Phin. *See* Pangestu, Prajogo

Philippines, 6, 56; Chinese minorities, 6, 6n1, 7; student movements, 123

PHTKS (Perkumpulan Hwie Tiauw Ka Surabaya), 71, 75, 85, 173, 176, 179, 193

pilkada (pemilihan kepala daerah), 124, 124n2, 130, 161, 193. *See also pilkadasung*

pilkada langsung. See *pilkadasung*

pilkadasung, 124n2

PK (Partai Keadilan), 121–22, 125, 193

PKB (Partai Kebangkitan Bangsa), 45, 121–22, 125, 128–29, 129n5, 188, 193

PKDI (Partai Kasih Demokrasi Indonesia), 172, 187–89, 193

PKI (Partai Komunis Indonesia), 9, 33n14, 34n15, 44n3, 48, 123, 193

PKPI (Partai Keadilan dan Persatuan Indonesia), 182, 184–85, 187, 189, 193

PKS (Partai Keadilan Sejahtera), 45, 125–26, 128, 162, 186, 189, 193

PMTS (Paguyuban Masyarakat Tionghoa Surabaya), 71, 81–82, 84–85, 108, 172, 176, 179, 193

PNBK (Partai Nasional Benteng Kemerdekaan), 182, 189, 193

PNI (Partai Nasional Indonesia), 136–37, 137n18, 142, 194

Poh An Tui. See *Pao An Tui*

political marketplace, 47

Polonia International Airport, 83

Pontianak, 10, 29, 34, 163

Poo, Murdaya Widyawimatra, 131, 132, 132n11, 133–34, 136, 186, 197

Poo Tjie Goan. *See* Poo, Murdaya Widyawimatra

Poso, 54

post-Suharto era, 3, 12, 14, 17, 21, 65–66, 73, 83, 93–96, 99, 102, 114, 166. See also *reformasi* era

PP (Pemuda Pancasila), 52, 64, 101, 102–3, 111, 153, 194

PPIB (Partai Perjuangan Indonesia Baru), 134, 134n15, 145, 172, 183–84, 187, 189, 194

PPM (Pemuda Panca Marga), 52, 194

PPP (Partai Persatuan Pembangunan), 35n20, 44, 121–22, 125, 131n6, 194

PPRN (Partai Peduli Rakyat Nasional), 184, 189, 194

Prakasa, Alim, 109n7

Pranowo, Ganjar, 46

Prayogo, Hendi, 63, 197, 71, 89, 120, 145, 172, 178, 182

PRD (Partai Rakyat Demokratik), 122–23, 189, 194

PRD (Persatuan Rakyat Demokratik), 123, 194

preman, 19–20, 51–53, 58–59, 61, 64–65, 98, 101, 101n2, 102–3, 103n3, 104–6, 111, 118, 168–69, 194

'preman state', 53

premanism, 103

Presidential Decree No. 10, in 1959, 31

Presidential Instruction no. 14/1967, 68

pribumi, 2, 6, 8–9, 11, 13, 15, 29, 37–38, 65, 83, 85, 90, 120, 149–50, 156–58, 162, 194. *See also* indigenous Indonesians

Prijatno, Anton, 25, 35n19, 97, 109, 109n8, 110, 120, 146–47, 164, 172, 182, 186, 197

PRN (Partai Republika Nusantara), 184, 187, 189, 194

Prosperous Justice Party. *See* PKS (Partai Keadilan Sejahtera)

Prosperous Peace Party. *See* PDS

PSI (Partai Sosialis Indonesia), 143, 194

PSMTI (Paguyuban Sosial Marga Tionghoa Indonesia), 1, 58, 68, 69n3, 71, 77, 81–82, 84–85, 114, 137, 145, 147, 149, 153, 155, 158–60, 171–72, 175–76, 178–79, 194

PT Adhi Karya, 82

PT Central Business District (CBD), 115, 190

PT Erniputra Terari, 115

PT Hutama Karya Persero, 83

PT Indo Palapa, 113

PT Jatimasindo, 116–17

PT Musi Hutan Persada, 131, 131n9

PT Waskita Karya, 82

PTSUPBA (Panitia Tionghoa Sumatera Utara Peduli Bencana Alam), 77–78, 194
Purdey, Jemma, 9, 12, 38
Pure Land Learning College, 75
Purnama, Basuki Tjahaja, 46, 197, 133. *See also* Ahok
Purnama, Basuri Tjahaja, 133–34
Purnomo, Nurdin, 138, 197
Putnam, Robert D., 48; social capital, 48

Qing dynasty. *See* Manchu government

Rahardja, William, 63, 172, 178–79, 182, 197
Raharja, Bagus, 188, 197
Rais, Amien, 45, 122, 131n6
Rajan, Nalini, 41
Rasyid, Ryaas, 45
Raudhatul Islam Mosque, 117
Raweyai, Yorrys, 52
Red-and-White coalition. *See* KMP (Koalisi Merah Putih)
reformasi era, 19, 56, 58, 60, 64, 93, 102, 118, 130, 132. *See also* post-Suharto era
Regional Forum of Small and Medium Enterprises. *See* FORDA UKM (Forum Daerah Usaha Kecil dan Menengah)
regional representatives council. *See* DPD
Rela Warta, 73n8, 80–81, 113–14, 172, 177
Republic of China (Taiwan), 70
Republic of Indonesia Party. *See* PRN (Partai Republika Nusantara)
revenue farming, 26n2, 27
Riady, James, 68n2, 131, 197
Riady, Mochtar. *See* Lie Mo Tie
Riggs, Fred W., 11
Rinakit, Sukardi, 130
Rismaharini, Tri, 46, 138–39
Robison, Richard, 11, 47, 49
Round Table Agreement on Citizenship, 30
Rush, James R., 26n2
Rwanda, 41–42; Hutus, 42; Tutsis, 41–42
Ryter, Loren, 52

Saiful, Benny, 179, 197

Salim, Sudono. *See* Liem Sioe Liong
Samosir, 81
Sanjaya, Christiandy, 10, 133–34, 163, 197
Santoso, Eddy Gunawan, 120, 140–42, 163, 172, 189, 198
SARA, 67
Sari Rejo, 115
Sasongko, Sundoro, 186
Sastra, Alim Mulia, 109n7
satgas parpol, 53, 194
Satgas PDI-P, 101
Satria, Alim, 109n7
SBKRI (Surat Bukti Kewarganegaraan Republik Indonesia), 35, 194
Schulte Nordholt, Henk, 46
Sekber Golkar (Sekretariat Bersama Golongan Karya), 44n3, 194
Setiono, Benny G., 29
Shah, Ajib, 64, 102, 111, 153, 154n35
Shah, Anuar, 97, 103, 171
Shandong, 82
Shanwei, 81
Sherlock, Stephen, 122
Shiraishi, Takashi, 29
Siang Hwee, 28, 69–70
Sidel, John T., 37–38, 56
Silalahi, Harry Tjan, 35n19
Simmel, Georg, 38–39
Sin Chew Jit Poh, 77
Sin Chew Media Corporation Berhad, 72, 77–78
Sin Po, 28, 28n6
Sindhunatha, K., 33, 197
Singapore, 16, 69, 69n4, 70n5, 94, 106, 109n7
Singkawang, 34, 133–34
singkeh, 32, 194
Sishui Chenbao, 80, 174, 177
Sitepu, Bangkit, 102
Situmorang, Binsar, 111, 154n35
SIUP (*Surat Izin Usaha Perdagangan*), 100, 194
SKPD (Satuan Kerja Perangkat Daerah), 139, 194
SMERU Research Institute, 99
Socialist Party of Indonesia. *See* PSI (Partai Sosialis Indonesia)
Soe Hok Djin. *See* Budiman, Arief
Soe Po Sia, 28, 69–70

Soekarwo, 109, 132
Soenarjo, 132
Soerjadjaja, William. *See* Tjia Kian Liong
Soetomo, Jos, 114, 179, 197
SOGI (sexual orientation and gender identity), 146
Soka, M., 187, 197
Solo, 16, 16n14, 127–28
Somers, Mary F., 10. *See also* Heidhues, Mary Somers
South China Normal University, 78–79
South Korea, 123
Southeast Asia, 6–7, 25, 32n13, 41–42, 68n2, 69, 81, 84
Sri Lanka, 77
State University of Medan. *See* UNIMED (Universitas Negeri Medan)
State University of Surabaya, 82
STBA-PIA (Sekolah Tinggi Bahasa Asing Persahabatan Internasional Asia), 76, 76n12, 77–79, 96, 194
Subei Ribao, 173, 177
Subianto, Prabowo, 43n2, 45, 126, 132n12, 134n16, 141–42
Sudarto, 183
Sudjatmiko, Budiman, 123
Sudjatmiko, Djoko, 35n19
Suhendra, Fajar, 178, 197
Suheri, Indra, 117
Sukardi, Tamin, 115–16
Sukarno, 30–31, 45, 51, 93, 122, 136, 142–43
Sukarnoputri, Megawati, 45, 55, 57, 72, 122, 131n6, 132n12, 149
Sukarnoputri, Rachmawati, 136
Sukarnoputri, Sukmawati, 136
Sukiran, 183, 197
Sulawesi, 25, 55
Sultan Iskandar Muda Educational Foundation. *See* YPSIM (Yayasan Perguruan Sultan Iskandar Muda)
Sumatra, 25
Sun Yat-sen, 28, 197
Sundanese, 29n8
Sunggal, 86–88, 154
Sunur, Eliezer Yance, 133, 133n14, 134
Sunur, Eliezer Yantje. *See* Sunur, Eliezer Yance
Surabaya, vii, 14–20, 56n15, 59, 66–68, 71, 73, 73n8, 74–76, 79–85, 89–91,

95–96, 98–101, 104–5, 108–10, 112–15, 119, 120–21, 128, 128n4, 129, 132, 134–36, 136n17, 138–47, 163–64, 168, 170, 172–79, 182, 186–89
Surabaya Academy of Accounting. *See* Akademi Akuntansi Surabaya
Surabaya Chinese Association. *See* PMTS (Paguyuban Masyarakat Tionghoa Surabaya)
Surabaya Inter-Religious Harmony Forum. *See* Forum Kerukunan Umat Beragama Surabaya
Surabaya-Madura Bridge, 82
Surabaya Post, 141, 145
Surjadinata, L. B. G., 35n19
Surya, Johan Tedja, 187–88, 197
Suryadinata, Leo, 8, 10, 27–28, 32, 43, 68n2, 70, 123
Suryadjaja G., Agoes, 187–88, 197
Syamsudin, Amir, 132

Taiping Rebellion, 32, 32n12, 32n13
Tambunan, Gayus, 106, 106n6
Tambunan, Moses, 102
Tan Hok Liang. *See* Medan, Anton
Tan Kim Yang. *See* Tan, Sofyan
Tan, Lily, 183–85, 197
Tan, Mely G., 97–98, 171, 198
Tan, Sofyan, 1–2, 4–6, 20, 42, 56n16, 58, 63–66, 85–89, 95–97, 107, 111, 120, 137, 147–64, 166, 169–71, 182, 185, 198
Tan Toan Sin. *See* Syamsudin, Amir
Tanah Abang, 58
Tanaka, Kakuei, 143
Tangerang, 29
Tanjung, Hakim, 178, 198
Tanudjaja, Harry, 172, 182, 186–87, 198
Tarigan. *See* Wong Chun Sen
Taufik, Ahmad, 59
tax farming. *See* revenue farming
Team of Ten (Tim Sepuluh), 45
Tempo, 58–59, 86, 88–89
Thailand, 6, 11, 56, 148; Chinese minorities, 6, 6n1, 7
The Act of Killing, 52
The Hague, 11
The International Daily. See *Guoji Ribao*
The Jakarta Globe, 103, 139
The Jakarta Post, 90, 117, 131

The Kian Seng. *See* Hasan, Bob
The Siauw Giap, 26
Thee Kian Wie, 31
Thompson, Mark R., 55–56
Thousand Islands, 133n13
Thung Ju Lan, 9
Tiburzi, Robert, 47
Tjan Kok Hui. *See* Tjandra, Djoko
Tjan Tjoen Hok. *See* Silalahi, Harry Tjan
Tjandra, Djoko, 131
Tjandra, Minarto, 188, 198
Tjia Kian Liong, 36, 197
Tjoeng Wan Hok. *See* Purnama, Basuki Tjahaja
Tjiook-Liem, Patricia, 11
Tiong Hoa Hwe Koan (THHK), 28, 69, 195
Tjongiran, Johan, 97, 106, 171, 183–84, 198
Tomsa, Dirk, 126–27
totok Chinese, 14, 31–32, 194–95
Tribun Medan, 79
Tsai Yen-Ling, 13
Tshai, Frans, 182, 198
Tumbelaka, Rosita, 186
Turner, Sarah, 56

uang keamanan (protection money), 103, 195
UD Logam Jawa, 109n7
UDA (University of Darma Agung), 137, 195
UMI Medan (Universitas Methodist Indonesia Medan), 86, 147–48, 195
UNIMED (Universitas Negeri Medan), 78, 151, 195
United Development Parties. *See* PPP (Partai Persatuan Pembangunan)
United States Agency for International Development (USAID), 99, 195
University of Airlangga, 144
University of North Sumatra. *See* USU (Universitas Sumatera Utara)
University of Surabaya, 146, 172, 186
USU (Universitas Sumatera Utara), 147, 147n26, 148, 195
Utomo, Fandi, 141
Utomo, Imam, 108
Utomo, Uton, 183

van Klinken, Gerry, 49, 130
Vivi A., Susilo, 188
VOC. *See* Dutch East India Company (VOC)

Wahid, Abdurrahman, 45, 57, 59, 72, 122–24
Wahid, Solahuddin, 131n6
Wahidin, Indra, 63–66, 81, 96, 111, 111n10, 112n11, 120, 147–50, 150n30, 152, 152n32, 153, 160, 162–63, 171, 178, 182, 198
Walubi (Perwakilan Umat Buddha Indonesia), 63, 195
Wanandi, Jusuf, 35n19, 36, 131
Wanandi, Sofjan, 131. *See also* Wanandi, Sofyan
Wanandi, Sofyan, 35n19, 98. *See also* Wanandi, Sofjan
Wardono, Tirto, 179
Waria, 145, 193, 195
Wasior, West Papua, 85
Waspada, 107, 113
Watson, C. W., 86
Weldon, Peter D., 15
Wen Wei Bo, 72
West Java, 31
West Kalimantan, 10, 33, 34n15, 69, 133, 163–64; 1999 anti-Madurese violence, 10, 54; 2017 gubernatorial election, 10, 163
West Sumatra, 85
Wibisono, Christianto, 120, 160, 171, 198
Widjaja, Dharwan. *See* Kwik Sam Ho
Widjaja, Samas H., 82, 97, 120, 145, 172, 182, 198
Widjaja, Sumandi, 183, 198
Widodo, Joko, 46, 126–27, 133n13
Widoyoko, J. Danang, 49
Wijaya, Nyoto, 187, 198
Wijaya, Tjia Susanto, 183
Wijaya, Vincent, 111
Williams, Lea E., 28
Wilson, Ian, 51
Winata, Tomy, 58–59, 131, 198
Wiranto, 43n2, 45, 126, 131n6, 132n12, 139–42
Wong Chun Sen, 185
Wongsodihardjo, Aliptojo, 179, 198
Wonohadi, Elisawati, 188, 198

Work Service Youth Association. *See* IPK
(Ikatan Pemuda Karya)
World Bank, 99
World Trade Organisation, 68n2
Wu Nengbin. *See* Purnomo, Nurdin
Wu, Rudy, 184
Wu Yiguang, 149

Xiamen, 82
Xin Bao, 28n6, 70
Xinhua News Agency, 80
Xun Bao, 79–80, 113, 173, 177
Xun Bao Youth, 80

Yamamoto, Nobuto, 9
Yap Juk Lim, 97, 107, 171, 198
Yasora Medan (Yayasan Sosial
Angsapura Medan), 71, 77, 171, 173,
175, 178, 195
Yazhou Zhoukan, 159

Yeoh, Emile Kok-Kheng, 42
YPSIM (Yayasan Perguruan Sultan
Iskandar Muda), 86–89, 170–71, 182,
185, 195
Yu Zhusheng, 94, 198
Yudhoyono, Susilo Bambang, 45, 50, 82,
103, 113–14, 126, 129, 131, 131n6,
132, 132n12, 134n16, 150, 161
Yugoslavia, 41; Croats, 41
Yunnan, 81–82
Yusuf, Saifullah, 132

Zein, Abdul Baqir, 30
Zhao Hong, 81
Zheng Bao Daily, 73n8, 177
Zhong Maosen, 75–76, 198
Zhou Enlai, 30, 198
zoning system, 26–29